DANIEL TO PAUL

JEWS IN CONFLICT WITH GRAECO-ROMAN CIVILIZATION: HISTORICAL & RELIGIOUS BACKGROUND TO THE HASMONEANS, DEAD SEA SCROLLS, THE NEW TESTAMENT WORLD, EARLY CHRISTIANITY, AND THE BAR-KOCHBA WAR.

EDITED BY GAALYAHU CORNFELD, ASSISTED BY BIBLE SCHOLARS, HISTORIANS AND ARCHAEOLOGISTS

1962
THE MACMILLAN COMPANY, NEW YORK
COLLIER-MACMILLAN, LTD., LONDON

Tel Aviv
First Printing

THE MACMILLAN COMPANY, NEW YORK
Collier-Macmillan, Canada, Ltd., Galt, Ontario
Divisions of the Crowell-Collier Publishing Company

PRINTED IN ISRAEL
Layout and Jacket Design by Paul Kor
Peli-P.E.C. Printing Works Ltd, Ramat Gan

ACKNOWLEDGMENTS

For invaluable advice, help, criticism and suggestions, the Chief Editor acknowledges his incalculable indebtedness to

Professor Ch. Rabin, Dr. H. Tadmor and Dr. M. Stern of the Hebrew University of Jerusalem, who read the manuscript and helped to improve its organization and content; to eminent scholars abroad, notably: Professor Stanley B. Frost, Dean of the Faculty of Divinity, McGill University, Montreal; Dr. James Parkes, The Parkes Library, Barley, Royston, Herts, and Professor D. N. Freedman of the Pittsburgh Theological Seminary, Pittsburgh, Pa; all of whose unfailing inspiration and guidance on the intricacies and theological problems of the periods have enabled him to maintain what he hopes is a balanced evaluation of the larger cultural setting of early Christianity; to a much larger number of scholars, historians and archaeologists of the Old and New Testaments throughout the world, some of whose views are quoted in the book, all of whom have contributed in scholarship and judgment to the larger thought of the work; to Dr. F. Cyril James, Principal and Vice-Chancellor of McGill University, Montreal, for his stimulating influence, and to Mr. Clement Alexandre, of the Macmillan Company, for his unflagging interest and help.

Grateful acknowledgment is due to the National Council of Churches of Christ in the U.S.A. for their courtesy and permission to quote the Revised Standard Version of the Bible, and to Professor Ch. Rabin for interpretation of difficult passages of the Qumran Scrolls.

Professors F. M. Cross, Nelson Glueck and J.T. Milik are also thanked for their generosity in supplying photographs. Grateful acknowledgment is made to the museums, institutes and individual scholars who have given permission for the reproduction of the photographs embodied in the book, as listed on its final page.

Finally, the Chief Editor records his appreciation of the work of Valerie Mindlin, whose sharp eye and questioning mind helped to improve the organisation and style of the book.

CONTENTS

C. JEWISH SECTARIES AND CHRISTIAN ORIGINS

D. THE GREAT WAR AND ITS AFTERMATH

AVRIFEX BRATTI R

FOREWORD

DANIEL TO PAUL completes the survey of the Bible and its setting, begun with ADAM TO DANIEL, which dealt with the Old Testament. The present volume covers the period up to and beyond the New Testament, including inter-testamental literature, (the Apocrypha and Apocalypses), the sectarian writings of Qumran, the historical background of the Hasmonean and Graeco-Roman periods in Palestine and the new evidence about the War of Bar-Kosba recently discovered in the Judean Wilderness.

These four centuries, from the end of the Old Testament to the closing scenes of the New, were a time of crucial events and, even more, of deep soul-searching thought. The passionate dialogue between secular forces and religious beliefs, culminating in the conflict between Jewish faith and Roman might, gave rise to both normative Judaism and Christianity. For a time it seemed as though everything must give way to Rome. Yet the spiritual forces working below the surface of the *Pax Romana* were, ultimately, to have the greater effect on history.

The parallel development of these trends is the theme of this book. The course of events and the development of philosophies are viewed in terms of the literature of the period which, with the exception of the New Testament, is practically unknown.

In an attempt to make clear just what forces were at play in these crucial years, historians of the Nineteenth and Twentieth centuries probed all the then existing material. Thousands of books have been written during the last hundred years on the subject of Jesus of Nazareth and almost as many have made evaluations of the New Testament. Yet until recently few made any major contribution to a truer understanding of their subject. There are a number of reasons for this:

Ancient writers, whether Jewish or Christian, were less concerned with history than with theology. The rabbis were occupied with what should be preserved within the canon of the Old Testament and Mishnah. They were careful to select only what they regarded as valuable — which indeed it was — and to exclude material which conflicted with their orthodoxy. In this way some of the great treasures of ancient literature were almost lost, while many important events received only prejudiced or passing mention. In these historical quicksands, Josephus stands out like a beacon. But, although he was writing history, not works with a primarily spiritual purpose, he is only one source. It is not surprising that interpretations made in ancient times from old materials and in old modes of historical writing led to mistaken theories and frustrate rather than enlighten the inquiring historian of today.

The situation has changed radically since the discovery of the Dead Sea Scrolls in 1947 (see Ch. VIII). They dispelled the mists that had shrouded the last couple of centuries B.C.E. and showed the impact of sectarian writings and ways of life on the writers of the New Testament. The newly discovered literature also revealed strong connecting links with the Apocrypha and Pseudepigrapha, important but largely neglected works of this period (Ch. III).

Together these writings provide a bridge across the tremendous cultural gap that had separated Old Testament thought and New Testament times. And it is a bridge which is accessible to everyone. At its beginning is the considerable cultural output of the inter-testamental literature, which is summarized as simply as possible in Ch. III. These writings are essential for an understanding of sectarian thought and as an introduction to the New Testament.

In the first two chapters of the book — the Hasmoneans and the hellenistic period — the editors are indebted to the outstanding work of the late Prof. V. Tcherikover of the Hebrew University, especially his "Hellenistic Civilisation and the Jews". In chapter V on Herod, they have benefitted greatly from Prof. A. Schalit's massive work, "Herod the King" and the original views developed there.

Chapter VII, on the end of the Hasmonean era, the first century B.C.E., puts the spiritual significance of the Pharisee "haburah" and their social ethics into perspective, mainly in line with views expressed verbally by Prof. Ch. Rabin. This marks the new attitude in which the formerly abused Pharisees have come to be regarded.

Chapter VIII on Qumran and sectarian thought will be regarded by many as the pivot of the book. The sectarian deviation from Jewish tradition and theology is currently a subject of warm debate, in which figure such outstanding participants as Professors J. T. Milik, R. de Vaux, F. M. Cross, Y. Yadin, D. Flusser and Ch. Rabin. The editor has attempted to give an up to date and balanced account of the present state of our knowledge and interpretation.

To attempt a presentation of the genesis of Christianity in Chs. IX to XI, based on contemporary Jewish history, the New Testament and sectarian literature, may not be a novel undertaking. These chapters attempt a comprehensive estimate of continuity and differences between Jewish messianism, the beliefs of the Dead Sea Sectaries, and early Christianity; a historical evaluation of John the Baptizer, Jesus of Nazareth, the Jewish-Christians and Paul, and a historical perspective on the attitudes of the Jewish people at the beginning of the Christian era. The editors face both important and obscure points with candour and a historian's balanced judgment on matters on which opinions are bound to differ strongly. The impact of recent discoveries and their significance are faced squarely, exposing a whole area of study on which opinions clash and facts seem to conflict.

The attempt at an objective analysis from the particular angle of studies within Israel, the birthplace of Jesus, represents a useful and unusual contribution.

The closing chapter, (XIII), takes us to the middle of the 2nd century, namely the emergence of the early church in Palestine and the East and, simultaneously, the tragic second Jewish-Roman War, immortalized by the personality and story of Bar-Kosba, called messiah and Prince of Israel. This interlude has been vividly brought to life by the discoveries made by Israel archaeologists in the Judean Wilderness in 1960-61 (illustrated by photographs). The period beyond this saw the survival of Judaism and the expansion of Christianity in the west.

DANIEL TO PAUL incorporates in its text many quotations from the literature of the period. The presentation summarizes the wealth of historical and archaeological data, much of it newly discovered, which bears on the period, illuminated by hundreds of documentary photographs. Together, illustrations and text carry the reader directly into the scenes and emotions of the age. The photographic illustrations, taken from Israel and other sources scattered through the museums and archives of the world, are in themselves a monumental contribution, many of them being hitherto unpublished or known only to a small circle.

The value of the book and its companion volume, ADAM TO DANIEL, is greatly enhanced by the General Index of subjects, names and documentary illustrations covering the Old Testament, the inter-testamental period and the New Testament.

Too often, books intended for the general reader fall short of scientific standards of accuracy and judgment. The professional popularizer cannot control the sources of his information and may be committed to views not based on accepted fact. On the other hand, scholarly works tend to use a specialized jargon and too many technical terms. Between the two extremes, the editors of DANIEL TO PAUL have attempted a work which should be both scholarly and readable.

The hunting group in the elaborate animal frieze in the limestone "painted tombs" of Maresha in southern Palestine, is a vivid example of 3rd century B.C.E. local art. The designs show a mixture of Phoenician (oriental) and hellenistic influences. The town included a colony of Sidonians, who had adopted Greek customs.

A. THE HELLENISTIC AND HASMONEAN PERIOD

I

ON THE EVE OF THE MACCABEAN REVOLT

At the End of Ancient Times, Palestine Meets the West

Between the seventh and second centuries B.C.E., the world saw the rise and then the collapse and disappearance of six great world empires: Assyria, Babylon, Persia, Macedonia, the Seleucid and Ptolemaic kingdoms. With them, died their religions and their culture, leaving behind an indelible imprint on the civilizations that were to come. Throughout all the changes of this time of upheaval, the Jews survived, a distinct cultural and religious entity, indestructible in the face of all vicissitudes.

All through the period covered by the Old Testament, the land of Israel had felt the repeated impact of Near Eastern antiquity. The country had been the battleground for the struggles between the Arameans of Syria, the Emperors of Assyria and Babylon and the Pharaohs of Egypt. With the conquests of Alexander the Great, it was brought for the first time into intimate contact with Hellenistic civilization. This resulted in the greatest single change in all Jewish history, affecting the entire development of Palestine and the Jews as from the early third century B.C.E.

By the end of the Old Testament period, (roughly the late fourth century, B.C.E.), the Jews formed a minor province of the Persian Empire. Living in the inland hills of Judah, they have left the remains of a few mean towns and villages whose only structures of any architectural pretensions are official buildings and tombs. Contact with the civilizations of the Mediterranean was barred by the Phoenician and Philistine settlements that lined the coast and which did maintain trade relations with the adjacent Mediterranean countries. Beyond the coastline, settlements of Greeks and Phoenicians on the island of Cyprus provided the link with the Greek mainland and the islands of the Aegean. It was the Phoenicians, known as the Sidonians, who were the most enterprising mariners in the Mediterranean world and pottery and coins found in Athlit and Dor, Straton's Tower (later Caesarea) and Joppa, bear witness to Phoenician settlement there from 700 to 300 B.C.E. An inscription on the sarcophagus of Eshmunazar II, King of Sidon (Phoenicia, late 4th cent. B.C.E.) boasts: ". . . . furthermore the Lord of Kingdoms had also granted us Dor and Joppa the powerful wheat lands of the plain of Sharon . . . and we annexed them to our borders, that they might be forever under Sidonian dominion." The kingdom of Sidon ruled other coastal towns of Palestine, while the southern coast was held by the heirs of the Philistines and Idumeans. In the 3rd Century B.C.E., the Sidonians penetrated into the interior as far as Maresha, building their first tombs there (see first illustration above). The Phoenicians had provided the navy for the Persian Empire. The destruction of their fleet by the Greeks at the Battle of Salamis in 480 B.C.E., set off the decline of the Persian empire. With its collapse, the whole of the Eastern Mediterranean was opened to direct Hellenic influence. During the century before Alexander the Great's military occupation, Greek tradesmen, mercenaries, even scholars, flooded into Western Asia. Evidence of their penetration in the wake of the Phoenicians is to be found all along the shores of Phoenicia and Palestine, from Acre in the North to Ascalon. In Syria, trading settlements began to appear and their number grew steadily.

Hellenization of the Orient

Whereas during the 7th century, Phoenician culture had influenced Greece and the Eastern Mediterranean coast, now, in the fourth century, Greece became predominant.

Sarcophagus of King Eshmunazar (early 4th century) found in Sidon. Although, like Egyptian and Philistine coffins, it was anthropoid in shape, the body within it was not mummified. The inscription is written in Phoenician characters, resembling archaic Hebrew. The Sidonians dominated the coastline of Palestine and also settled in the south, in Maresha and the Philistine towns.

Numerous marble sarcophagi and steles found in Phoenicia indicate that by this time Greek forms of sculpture had become firmly established in Syria and had spread to Palestine. An extensive market for Greek earthenware pottery developed throughout the Eastern Mediterranean where native pottery was declining. Such contacts paved the way for the inclusion of Western Asia in the Hellenistic empire, under which there was a revival of town life.

Recent archaeological discoveries in the coastal plain of Palestine, combined with the writings of many Greek historians, make it clear that from the fourth century B.C.E. the Phoenician settlements along the coast enjoyed a high degree of prosperity. From these settlements went the ships that traded all over the Mediterranean and, through them, the Greek world reached the Jews. Phoenician traders of Tyre, Sidon, Arvad (Aradus) and Tripoli established markets within Palestine itself and so brought Greek artifacts and pottery into Judah. Although few material remains exist of the history of the Jews in Judah and the rest of Palestine during the last phase of Persian rule over their country, it seems that they were in contact with the Greek mind and the Greek artisan on the eve of the Hellenistic period.

Stamped coinage — a 6th century Greek invention — first made its appearance in Judea in the 4th century B.C.E. The coin shown on the left is a Philisto-Athenian imitation of the tetradrachma with a head of Athena; in the center is a classical coin depicting an apotheosis of Herakles; on the right is a Jewish coin of the 4th century B.C.E. A 6th century Athenian coin was found recently in Jerusalem, indicating contact with the Greeks at this early date.

We need not recapitulate the familiar story of Alexander's campaign and conquests in the Near East and Egypt between 334 and 332 B.C.E. which brought Judah and Samaria under his control. The expansion of the Macedonians began with Alexander's father who had planned to "liberate" Persian-held Greek cities in Asia Minor as part of his defensive strategy. It culminated in the conquest of a vast empire:

> "and he made his way to the ends of the earth and despoiled a multitude ot nations. The whole earth was silent before him, and he became exalted, and his heart was uplifted. He mustered a very mighty army and ruled over the lands and rulers of the heathen, and they paid him tribute. Afterward he fell sick, and knew that he was going to die." (1 Mac. 1: 3–5)

There are very few references to Alexander among Jewish writers except for Flavius Josephus. His "Antiquities of the Jews", although it includes many legendary items which distort the picture, remains the best source for this period of Jewish history.

Briefly, the defeat of the Persians at Issus in Northern Syria in 333 B.C.E. established Greek supermacy. To commemorate the victory, the city of Alexandretta, which still bears its founder's name, was built on the site. (See third colour plate: Victory of Alexander).

Strengthened by this victory, Alexander turned his armies southwards and by capturing the ports of the Eastern Mediterranean, cut off the Persian Fleet from its bases on the Phoenician and Egyptian coasts. The Phoenician towns capitulated and placed their triremes at the disposal of the conqueror. Only Tyre resisted. After a long siege, the town was conquered and completely destroyed. Tyre's opposition to Alexander marked the last upsurge of Phoenician national spirit. With its capture, the Phoenician kingdom of Tyre came to an end. Its commercial leadership of the Eastern Mediterranean passed to the Greeks and the Phoenician settlements of Carthage and other North African coastal towns. On the extreme south of Palestine's coast, Gaza also attempted to stand up to Alexander but was also defeated, laying open the road to Egypt. The Egyptians willingly exchanged masters and welcomed the new invader. The loss of the Egyptian ports completed the neutralization of the Persian Fleet.

Having secured the coastline, Alexander's commander-in-chief, Parmenion, marched into Syria and Palestine, taking a route along the east of the Jordan. From the stories recounted much later in Josephus and the Talmud, which are of doubtful historical value, Alexander is made to appear very unfriendly towards the Samaritans. They, it is told, rebelled against him and killed his deputy, who was immediately avenged by Alexander's general, and a Macedonian colony was established in Samaria. This defeat of their traditional enemies appears to have been to the Jews' political advantage.

The story goes that Alexander's army conquered Jerusalem without a battle and granted religious freedom to the Jews, thereby continuing the tradition which the Persian kings had established long before. It is reported by the contemporary Greek historian Hecateus, quoted by Josephus, that the High Priest ruled as before and the Mosaic Law remained in force among the Jewish population.

In Jewish literature, these events form the basis of the allegory of Daniel's vision of the Ram and the Goat, quoted below. The Book of Daniel was written around 168/6 B.C.E., but some of the material in it is older than that, (see p. 86). It is typical of the apocalyptic literature of the time that Alexander or specific events are only implied — not referred to directly. He is well remembered in ancient Persian folklore. In the Arabic version he is Iskandar (Alexander) "thulkarnayn" — the possessor of horns — to denote his heroic figure. The theme of the horns in Persia seems to have this in common with Daniel's symbols.

Disintegration of Alexander's Empire

Only 11 years separated Alexander's victory over the Persians in 334 and his premature death in 323. During that time his armies conquered the ancient world from the Mediterranean to the Indus River. But at his death there was no single leader powerful enough to take over the greatest empire of ancient times. The account of devastating internal rivalry between his generals makes dreary reading. For two centuries, this lack of consistent leadership was the dominant factor in Western Asia's political development. In the twenty years after his death, Alexander's empire was split four ways — into Macedonia, Asia Minor, Syria and Egypt.

> "As I was considering, behold, a he-goat came from the west across the face of the whole earth, without touching the ground; and the goat had a conspicuous horn between his eyes. He came to the ram with the two horns, which I had seen standing on the bank of the river, and he ran at him in his mighty wrath. I saw him come close to the ram, and he was enraged against him and struck the ram and broke his two horns; and the ram had no power to stand before him, but he cast him down to the ground and trampled upon him; and there was no one who could rescue the ram from his power. Then the he-goat magnified himself exceedingly; but when he was strong, the great horn was broken, and instead of it there came up four conspicuous horns toward the four winds of heaven." (Dan. 8: 5–8)

The third of Daniel's visions also opens with the rise of Alexander's empire. But it predicts that it will collapse and be divided and the different parts be ruled by strangers:

> "Then a mighty king shall arise, who shall rule with great dominion and do according to his will. And when he has arisen, his kingdom shall be broken and divided toward the four winds of heaven, but not to his posterity, nor according to the dominion with which he ruled; for his kingdom shall be plucked up and go to others besides these." (Dan. 11: 3–4)

Palestine under Alexander's Successors

The positions of the kingdoms of the Diadochi — (Alexander's successors) and their frontiers were finally decided by the Battle of Ipsus (301 B.C.E.) in the heart of Asia Minor. By then, Seleucus I had obtained possession of Mesopotamia, the eastern part of Asia Minor and the North of Syria, where he built Antioch as his capital. The era officially known as Seleucid Syria dates from 312 B.C.E. when the term "King of Syria" was used for the first time.

As a result of the battle, the Ptolemies extended the boundaries of Egypt to include Palestine. Ptolemy Lagos, who ruled Egypt, tried to keep the territory he had overrun in 320 when he had annexed Syria south of Aradus, the ancient Phoenician island-port of Arvad. But he was unable to take the chain of seaports on the Phoenician coast, although without these, his new conquests were not very secure. Southern Syria and Palestine apparently formed Egypt's first line of defence, but in fact, Ptolemy had to re-conquer Palestine four times between 320 and 301 before his control of the country was secure. During these years, civil administration as well as religious authority in Judah was taken over by the High Priest.

During the struggles between the two rivals, Jerusalem was conquered several times and following one upheaval, Jewish and Samaritan prisoners were sent captive to Egypt. However, the local populations were not the direct object of the attacks and there seems to have been no serious repression of Jewish habits or faith at the hands of Ptolemies. Under the watchful eye of a garrison and Egyptian officials, Jewish life was allowed to follow its normal course, the only imposition being the demand for prompt payment of the levies imposed from Alexandria.

The Ptolemies Rule Palestine

We learn from the "Antiquities" of Flavius Josephus that in Ptolemaic days, the people were organized into three elements: (a) the people at large; (b) the council of elders (gerousia), on which the leading families were represented; (c) the "leader of the people", who fulfilled the dual functions of chief priest and temporal leader, dealt with all matters of religion, common law and punishment and acted as the head of the nation in everything to do with foreign affairs, mainly the collection and delivery of taxes. From the day of his appointment, this leader had to pay the king a yearly tax in return for royal recognition.

In his "Antiquities", Josephus describes the procedure for obtaining a tax-farming concession under the Ptolemaic regime in Alexandria:

> "All the principal men and rulers went up out of the cities of Syria and Phoenicia to bid for their taxes; for every year the king sold them to the man of the greatest power in every city." (Antiq. Bk XII: Ch. 4: 3)

The one who bid highest became tax farmer for a large area, appointing his own local subordinates. It was said that twenty talents had been the fee paid "out of their own estates" by High Priests of Jerusalem before Onias, to the king of Egypt, probably in return for royal recognition. (The heavy silver talent, approximately 30 kgs. of silver, was worth about two thousand dollars).

It was the policy of the Ptolemies to foster trade and exchanges between their Hellenic and Asiatic subjects. Alexander and his successors settled Macedonian and Greek soldiers to found Greek cities in Palestine. Civilians gradually flocked to these new settlements in the hope of advantage or because they had been driven from their old homes by political or economic developments.

East and West in Palestine — The Hellenistic Towns

For us the main interest of Alexander's conquests lies in this establishment of cities in Syria and Egypt. These settlements formed islands of Greek civilization, complete with all the architectural, social and political forms of the *polis*, and were to prove his most enduring monument.

The *polis* (city) was the central unit of Greek life. In principle, it was a free and independent unit, supplied by the surrounding countryside and villages. Their inhabitants were entitled to come and vote in the elections for the ruling assembly but, in practice, they very rarely did so. Power was in the hands of the urban citizens.

Alexander's conquests carried this Greek institution into the Near East. Of the many cities founded on this model, the most famous was Alexandria, named after him and founded in 332 B.C.E.

Greek and Macedonian settlers soon became an important part of the population. In many cases, life in what had once been Jewish or mixed Palestinian cities, became largely or even mainly Greek in form, e.g. the coastal towns of Acre (Ptolemais), Dor, Jaffa, Ascalon, Gaza, Raphia, Ashdod (Azotus) and Maresha in western Palestine. Similarly many cities east of the Jordan such as Gadara, Philadelphia, Pella, Abil and Gerasa (Jerash), came under Greek influence and became the new political centers for the surrounding countryside. The older towns had been little more than untidy, unplanned huddles of houses, crowded within a walled enclosure. But the new settlements were built on Greek architectural models, well and spaciously planned with wide, straight colonnaded thoroughfares. As a rule, they were named after their founders: Rabbath-Ammon, capital of Ammon in Transjordan was hellenized as Philadelphia after Ptolemy II Philadelphus, but its ancient Hebrew name has survived in Amman, present-day capital of the Arab Kingdom east of Jordan. The port of Acre was renamed Ptolemais; Beth Shean became Scythopolis.

The Ptolemaic and Seleucid kingdoms recognized three different types of self-contained units under their overall control: cities, "peoples" and princes or local rulers. The "peoples", which included the Jews, continued to obey their national leaders who ruled freely up to a point. Relations with the colonial power, whether Egyptian or Syrian, mainly concerned the payment of taxes, recognition of its military supremacy and a few other formalities. The

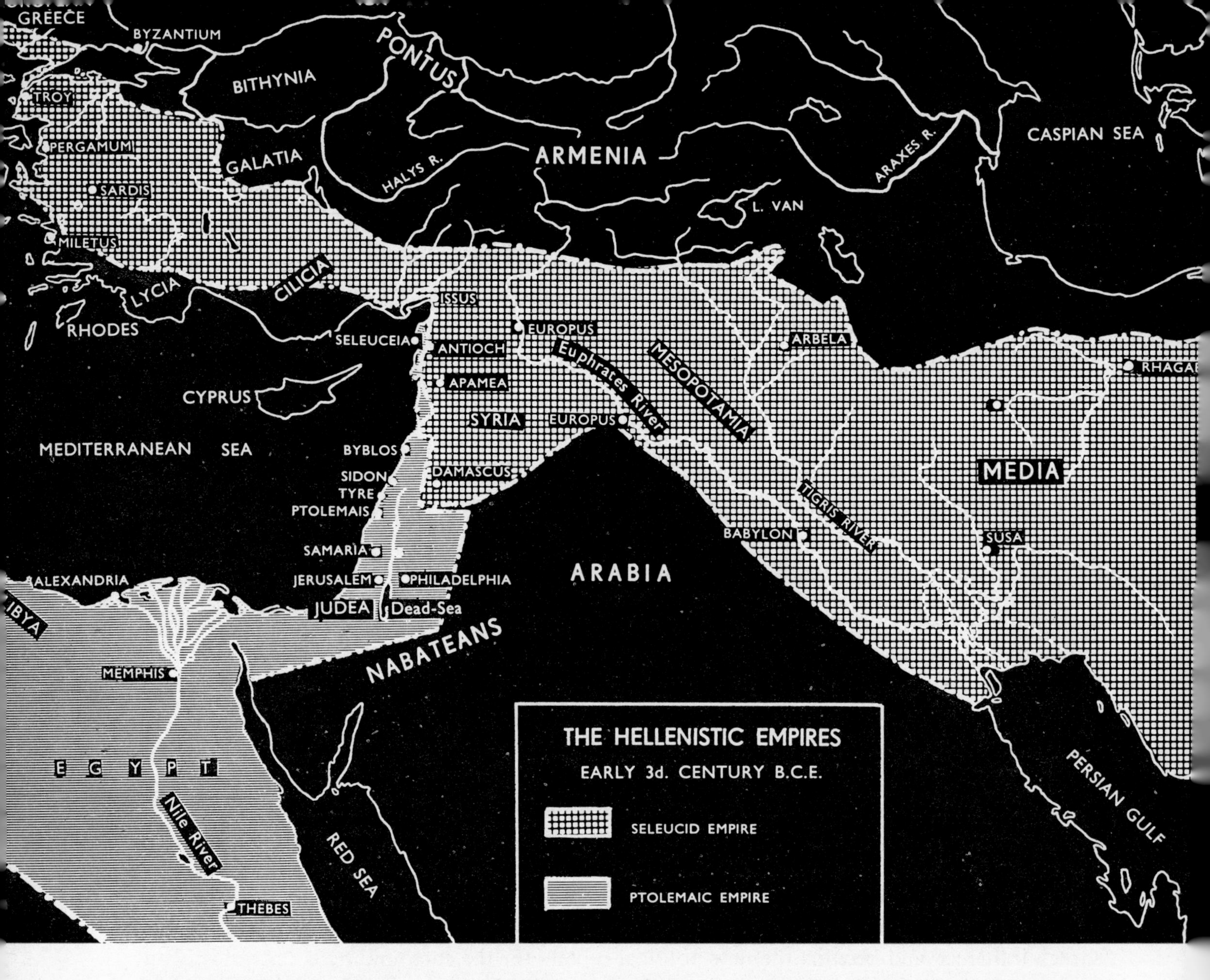

cities had greater privileges. Their wealth, civilization and freedom made a lasting impact on the whole of Jewish life. Not only their architecture, but also their government was modelled on Greek practice. Annually elected representatives of the people formed the *boulé*, the "Council" or governing body, numbering at times several hundred members, which managed the town's own internal affairs on the democratic Greek pattern.

This situation was unaffected by conquest. The Syrian inhabitants of the ancient cities remained as citizens, possessing equal rights with the Greek and Macedonian settlers and, apparently, forming the majority. These cities founded by the Macedonians should not be confused with the Jewish cities of Judah, Galilee or southern Palestine, which had been resettled by Jews in Persian times, following their return from Babylon.

In several of the Syrian-Greek cities, the Jews as a corporation (politema) formed one part of the population and thus belonged to a community larger than their own.

A mutual exchange and penetration between Greek culture and Semitic civilization had begun in Western Asia. This combination, with its oriental affinities, produced the civilization called Hellenism, to distinguish it from the purely Greek or Hellenic. Hellenism triumphed throughout Western Asia and Egypt during the Seleucid and Ptolemaic period and continued under the Roman Empire in the East. It did not, however, upset the purely Semitic political and intellectual life of the area. The population of the cities was presumably bi-lingual but the masses of the people were not Graecized. In Jewish Palestine, as in Aramaic-speaking Syria, the native culture continued, giving more than it received. When speaking, therefore, of the hellenization of these countries, one should not think in clichés borrowed from glamorized classical Greece. It would be more correct to regard the prevailing culture as a mixture resulting from the impact of varied peoples, with ancestral Palestinian, Phoenician and affiliated Semitic civilizations still predominating.

Though Hellenistic decorative art influenced Jewish design, the native oriental element held its own. As in Phoenician times as far back as the 11th century B.C.E., the tremendous and elegant stone sarcophagi, the ossuaries and façades of tombs were distinguished by decorations featuring stylized flower, leaf and tree motifs.

Round towers flanked the western gate of Samaria, one of the new hellenistic cities of western Palestine, built on the ancient Israelite site. The towers were rebuilt by King Herod towards the end of the 1st century B.C.E.

Native dress and types are vividly illustrated by these 4th century vases found in Hebron in southern Judea, which bear a certain resemblance to the frescoes of Maresha. Ceramic making in Palestine was profoundly influenced by the Greeks but these vases, which retain their local oriental character, can hardly be compared with pure hellenic masterpieces, such as the Greek painted amphoras shown in our colour plates.

The monumental tombs of the Kidron valley bear witness to hellenistic-Egyptian influence over Jewish funerary art as early as the 3rd century B.C.E. This monolithic tomb dedicated to the Sons of Hezir dates from the early 2nd century. Beneath the pyramid on the top, the façade is pure Doric.

Joseph Ben Tobiah and the Tobiads

Up to about the second third of the 3rd century, that remained the general situation. During the latter part of the century, however, it appears that a drastic change in the administrative arrangements of the Jewish part of Palestine took place. *The two functions of secular ruler and religious leader of the Jewish people became separated* (see: Priestly Rivalry below).

In the centralized, bureaucratic regime of the Egyptian Ptolemies, the collection of taxes in the provinces of their empire was leased to a local "tax-farmer", who paid a fixed sum to the royal treasury and then levied the payment of Government taxes from the people to himself. Under Ptolemy II, the tax-farmer and agent for Palestine and Coele-Syria was Joseph ben Tobiah. He was a lay member of the Jerusalem Council of Elders who got himself appointed head of the people, in return for an undertaking to increase the tax income. He thus became the chief tax-farmer for the whole province. Apparently, this event was a landmark in the development of Jewish social affairs under the Ptolemies.

This way of raising taxes had, it seems, given rise to a new class of rich men in Jerusalem, who built up their own fortunes out of their operations as tax farmers. Naturally, they were highly unpopular. Their activities were a burden both in the towns and in the countryside, for their incomes came from the workers and peasants, especially those who farmed as tenants or sub-tenants of the king. This meant the majority of all peasants, for, according to Egyptian law, all the land was the king's and he leased it out to be farmed by native tenants, who paid rent to the government officials or the temples. In Palestine, it was not easy to apply this principle, because of the property rights of wealthy landowners and of the many free cities, the "poleis" which controlled the land of the villages around them. However, the greater portion of the country's area was "royal land" and the peasants living there had no option but to pay their taxes to the royal treasury, through the local tax-farmers, or "village lessees."

Evidence for this situation is provided by the so-called Zenon papyri from the Egyptian town of Philadelphia. Zenon was the chief factotum of Apollonius, the Finance Minister of Ptolemy II Philadelphus, and these papyri supply many details of the tax collections and commercial dealings of the minister and his agent, Tobiah. Tobiah, apparently, was in continuous trading relations with merchants supplying the Egyptian court. The papyri contain two letters from him, written in impeccable Greek, featuring the usual invocations of the gods, and bearing a date which corresponds to May, 259 B.C.E. One letter is addressed to Apollonius and the other to King Ptolemy himself.

The king was a fancier of unusual beasts and, to please him, Tobiah sent him a collection of such animals, as well as a gift of eunuchs and a few well-bred slave boys, whose complexion, colour of hair and distinctive features were carefully described. Two of them were circumcized and two were not.

For the history of the Jews from the third century B.C.E., (the early hellenistic period) our main source is the "Antiquities of the Jews" of Flavius Josephus, together with the Zenon Papyri, which provide valuable data on the combination of western with oriental elements in the population which took place during the initial process of hellenization in the towns and the country. For the latter period, i.e. the Maccabean period, abundant material may also be found in the books of Maccabees 1 and 2 and incidental data from other Greek and Roman sources.

Joseph ben Tobiah's family provide a classic example of the hellenization of the upper classes, the principal supporters of a compromise with the hellenistic regime. His son, named Hyrcanus, seems to have been an example of the Greek "dynast".

It appears that he was a capable, ambitious man who was disliked by his brothers. Sent on a mission on behalf of his father to Alexandria, Hyrcanus used the occasion to appropriate his father's twin functions of chief tax-farmer and head of the people and to become chief tax-farmer for Ptolemy III Euergetes.

His action caused a serious split in the Tobiad family. The father and his other sons, still living in Jerusalem, opposed Hyrcanus and in this were supported by the High Priest, Simon II, ("the just", of the house of Onias). On his return Hyrcanus tried to force his way into Jerusalem but he was repulsed. He retired to a "country across the Jordan", a place called "Turos" in "the Land of Tobiah", an independent principality. There with a considerable following, he constructed a "strong fortress" from which he went out on raids against the local Arab tribes. In this stronghold, he waited for an opportunity to take over Jerusalem

The north-eastern corner of the entrance to Qasr-el-Abd, identified with Beit-Tobiah, with its lowest section still hidden by debris and vegetation. The ornamental string course below the frieze of lions can still be seen. The general architecture of Beit-Tobiah is Corinthian in style, but the stone frieze of lions is pure antique Phoenician-Persian and the capitals topping the pillars resemble the Persian capitals of Susa, decorated with bulls' heads.

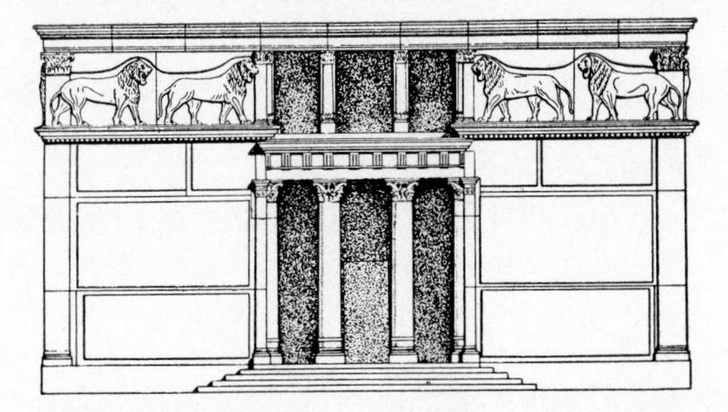

Reconstruction of the front and northern façade of the palace of the Tobiads (after H. C. Butler). This old Judean family had accepted hellenism at an early date. From the 3rd to the middle of the 2nd century it played a leading role in the politics and economy of Judea.

By the side of a door-way leading into ancient caverns the name "TOBIAH", in well formed Hebrew-Aramaic letters, was found, clearly carved on the levelled stone of the mountainside. No other structure in Palestine has so plain an identification mark as this name plate, attributed to various dates from the 6th to the 4th centuries B.C.E.

and rule it for the Ptolemies with the help of the High Priest Onias III, who had succeeded his father Simon, (see Table p. 28).

Priestly Rivalry

Internal intrigues and disputes between the leading families, egged on by the competing rulers of Egypt and Syria, were only one aspect of the tensions inside Palestine. A new crisis arose in Jerusalem's ruling circles over the High Priesthood.

The High Priest had become the central personality in Judea. The Jewish state was a theocracy which formally and actually recognized God as the source of power and the ultimate authority. The exercise of this authority was divided between a civil power (the king) and the High Priest. "In theory, the government had a two-sided character as a theocracy in which the licensed officials (to be anointed) were respectively a king of the house of David and a priest of the house of Zadok. Both functions were clearly regarded as religious. The king as much as the High Priest was a sacred figure, religiously responsible for his actions. The law of the land, whether civil or ecclesiastical, was divine law." (D.N. Freedman). The division of power remained in theory but, in practice before the beginning of hellenistic times, the Persian overlords had been careful to keep the Davidites out of government operations. "They survived only in a genealogical list and in the messianic dreams of the people, with the result that the High Priest exercised both ecclesiastical and civil functions." (D.N. Freedman). Before the end of the second century B.C.E. the High Priesthood would also cease to be the exclusive preserve of the descendants of Zadok. The last legitimate High Priest of this line was Onias III, son of Simon II, "the Just", (see Table p. 28).

Onias III was an orthodox upholder of the ancient way of life and a partisan of the Egyptian Ptolemy. The Egyptians were tolerant rulers and while they controlled Palestine there was no enforced interference in Jewish religious life and social customs. The aim of the Jews remained "to live according to their ancestral laws." The degree of hellenization which took place was a natural response to the increasing influence of the Greek way of life.

On the Eve of the Hellenistic Reform

The manner in which Joseph ben Tobiah ingratiated himself with the Egyptian king and became tax-farmer for Palestine and Syria illustrates the general tendency among rich Jews to welcome the influence of Hellenistic culture, brought by the Ptolemies and their agents. The process seems to have worked smoothly in the former Canaanite, Syrian, Philistine or Ammonite towns. They willingly accepted the social system of the Greek polis, with its settled traditions and organization. Admittedly, by this time, the classic notion of the Greek polis had lost much of its original significance and all citizens no longer had the right to participate in running municipal affairs; but the introduction of the concept into the Semitic Near East nevertheless represented a great innovation.

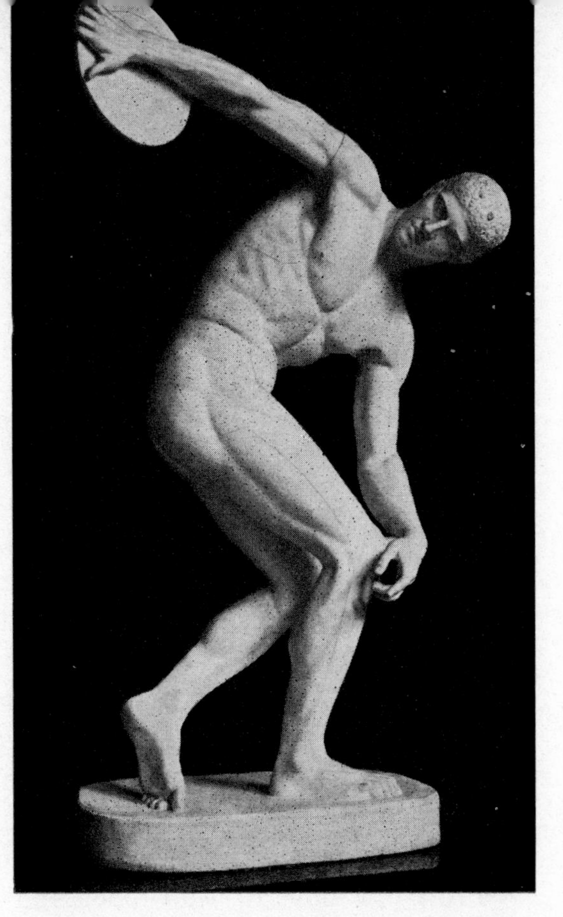

Greek art glorified youth. Ceramic platters and statuettes pictured athletics, games, music-making and dancing. Above is a singing group and a discus thrower. Lower left shows a terracota model of an ephebe with his lyre; lower right — young men at the gymnasium.

Hitherto, life there had been based on the idea of the city-king as absolute owner, lord and master of the common people. The new hellenistic approach gave them the feeling of being part of a living institution. It granted them privileges as well as demanding obligations and, by regarding the king's slaves as citizens, introduced a new, vital urban civilization into the ancient Near East. In this way, the Jews shared in the civilization common to every city ruled by the Greeks.

The Greek Way

The nucleus of the city's organization was the municipal council, one of whose main functions was to supervise the local cults. The Councillors were in charge of the celebrations for the patron god or goddess of the city. Another important activity in local cultural life was the teaching of rhetoric. Every self-respecting Greek city had its school of rhetoric and many of these were centers of literature and art. In this pattern of urban life, the two institutions for the moral and physical training of young men, the *gymnasium* and the *ephebeion*, became established in every city, the gymnasium acting as a potent force in the hellenization of Jewish youth. It also taught the love of beauty and unashamed delight in the body which was essential to the Greek way of life. Besides offering training in physical culture of every kind, the gymnasium acted as the social center and main medium of entertainment for the polis.

From the days of Alexander and his successors, clubs of young men, or "epheboi", attached to the gymnasium, became a regular institution in Greek cities, organized, apparently, under State control. These young men wore a distinctive uniform, a "chlamys" bunched about the shoulders, a broad-brimmed hat and high-laced boots. In state processions, they wore a golden crown. A group of them must have provided a brilliant spectacle.

Jews from many circles must have been attracted to the games and spectacles of the gymnasium. A story is told in 2 Maccabees about the gymnasium built in Jerusalem about 175 B.C.E., by the High Priest Jason, who had usurped his brother, Onias III. Discus and javelin throwing may have been Greek sports, but public games in general were not foreign to Jerusalem in Old Testament days. Nevertheless, the new games offended the traditionalists.

Naturally, the first to endorse this new civilization and adopt the Greek language and Greek customs were circles already in close contact with the authorities and leading personalities in the Greek cities. The Jews were no exception. The social strata most closely involved with the administration, chiefly the priestly aristocracy, the landed gentry and rich merchants, did adopt Greek ways. They had no objection to being labelled "Antiochians". But the Hellenistic pattern of life was foreign to the common people and was bitterly resented by the stricter adherents of the traditional Jewish law.

The story of Joseph ben Tobiah makes it clear that from its very beginnings in Judea, hellenism was closely bound up with the social class made up of the wealthy aristocracy of Jerusalem and Transjordan. The new movement was a useful and effective instrument in their drive for greater wealth and power.

I. Greek art, with its glorification of the human form spread throughout the hellenistic world (see p. 16). A typical example is this 5th century B.C.E. Etruscan bronze statuette of an athlete hurling the javelin.

II. The Greeks decorated their pottery with scenes showing the pleasures of life. Like this 5th century amphora, they form a most important source for the study of Greek painting (see p. 15).

III. Alexander's defeat of the Persians at Issus in 333 B.C.E. opened the East to western domination. This is part of the battle scene from a 1st century Roman mosaic in Pompei, (*see p.* 4).

IV. One of the hellenistic gilded youth, an "ephebe" pouring a libation. This 5th century bronze statuette is a good example of the merging of Attic (*Greek*) *art with Ionian influences from Asia Minor,* (*see p.* 16).

It can be assumed that in Jerusalem (as elsewhere) with a community divided into the "rulers", the "philanthropists", or "great ones" and the poor, there was continual conflict between them, affecting both individuals and whole families.

Palestine Comes into the Seleucid Empire

Internal stress was to be greatly increased when Palestine and Syria became a part of the Seleucid empire. This was one result of the victory of Antiochus III at the Battle of Paneion (site of ancient Dan, one of the sources of the River Jordan) fought between Syria an Egypt in 200 B.C.E.

At first the Seleucids made no particular efforts at hellenization. Several documents have survived from the time of Antiochus III, in particular his edict (quoted by Josephus, Bk. XII, 3 : 3) pledging the Jews permission "to live according to their ancestral Law." This allowed them to organize their life in the way they wished, subject to the higher authority of the king. Antiochus agreed that Judea should continue to be ruled by the High Priest and his council of assistants, the "gerousia", the acknowledged powers "over statutes and judgements."

As advisers, the government and the Jewish Great Assembly turned to the scribes, who combined the necessary intellectual qualifications with a knowledge of the laws and customs and had the task of expounding "judgment and righteousness". Since all Jewish law and the whole of its legal tradition stemmed from the Law of Moses, the scribes became authorities on the Law, as well as its interpreters, qualified to relate it to changing circumstances. They were also experienced in searching out the hidden meaning of ancient parables and wisdom. In the royal charter of Antiochus III given to Jerusalem in 200 B.C.E., the "scribes of the sanctuary" form a special and privileged body of jurists and civil servants, who, perhaps, collaborated with him in drafting his proclamation concerning the ritual arrangements.

He ruled over a vast domain which stretched from India to Palestine. In his battles with the Ptolemies he used elephants brought from Northern India. As a result of twenty years of fighting, he regained some control over the whole of the original Seleucid dominions, which earned him the title "the Great". But in Greece and Asia Minor, he was halted by the new power of Rome which forced an ignominious peace (188 B.C.E.) and a heavy indemnity of 15,000 talents from him, and warned him off his attempted conquest of Egypt. He also had to permit internal autonomy to the oriental kingdoms of Parthia and Bactria, which lay north-east of Iran. He died in battle fighting to keep the Eastern part of his empire intact.

Nevertheless, some ten years after Paneion, a new nationalist spirit awoke in the Jews which, coinciding with a political crisis within the Seleucid empire brought about a changed attitude to the Jews in Palestine. In place of the previous peaceful co-existence, there developed a direct clash between the two cultures and the future of the Jewish nation again hung in the balance.

The family of Joseph ben Tobiah had long since lost control of the post of civil administrator which he had held under Ptolemy. With the change in overlord, however, the Tobiads and their allies saw a chance to take over power again.

Apparently they fulfilled the same function for the Syrian court — where Antiochus III had been succeeded by Seleucus IV — which Joseph had discharged for the Egyptian Ptolemies: acting as tax collectors and financial administrators. The new Syrian king was badly in need of funds to pay reparations to the Romans and Simon, described in 2 Maccabees as "the Overseer of the Temple", which was a judicial and administrative post, offered Seleucus a large subsidy in return for royal support for his candidature for the post of "agoranomos" of Jerusalem. This was a coveted post, for while it represented the head of the civil administration, it also gave control of the Temple treasury and thus represented the key to the city's economic life. Simon was a member of the priestly class, a scion of a leading family but scholars disagree as to his exact relationship to the Tobiads.

Simon and Onias

Simon's claim was opposed by Onias III who suspected him of wanting to use the post as a stepping stone to the higher glory of his own position. In the course of the intrigue that developed, Onias made an alliance with Hyrcanus, still an outcast in his stronghold in the Land of Tobiah. This is probably the explanation for the reference in 2 Maccabees (see below) to the funds which Hyrcanus, although a fugitive, had left in the Temple for safekeeping. The Temple was, of course, not only a religious institution, but the center of government in Judah. Its wealth included both the Temple treasures and money deposited there for safe-keeping.

Simon's reaction to this alliance between Onias and Hyrcanus was to turn to Seleucus' agent and reveal to him the secrets of the Temple treasure:

> "When he failed to carry his point against Onias, he went to Apollonius of Tarsus, who was at that time governor of Coelesyria and Phoenicia, and reported to him that the treasury in Jerusalem was full of such untold quantities of money that the amount of the funds was beyond computation; and that they did not belong to the account of the sacrifices and they might fall under the control of the king. When Apollonius met the king, he informed him of the money that had been pointed out to him. And he appointed Heliodorus, who was his chancellor, and sent him with instructions to effect the removal of this money. Heliodorus immediately set out on his journey, under the guise of visiting the towns of Coelesyria and Phoenicia, but in reality to carry out the king's design.
>
> "When he reached Jerusalem, and had been cordially welcomed by the high priest and the city, he laid before them the disclosure that had been made to him, and explained why he had come, and inquired whether this was really true. The high priest pointed out that some deposits belonged to widows and orphans, and one belonged to Hyrcanus, son of Tobias, a man of very high position—so falsely had the impious Simon spoken; that it all amounted to four hundred talents of silver and two hundred of gold, and that it was absolutely impossible that those who were relying on the sacredness of the place and on the sanctity and inviolability of the temple, which was respected all over the world, should be wronged." (2 Mac. 3: 5–12)

Heliodorus was unmoved by the plight of the widows and orphans and announced the immediate confiscation of the money for the king's treasury.

This aroused "no small distress throughout the whole city" and all the inhabitants joined in the supplication to "him that gave the law concerning the deposits, that he should preserve these treasures safe for those that had deposited them."

Heliodorus went ahead with his plan to seize them but, the book tells us, he was prevented by a miraculous apparition from actually laying hands on the Temple treasures. In fact, it seems that he was defeated by the combined opposition of the high priest and the people.

Nevertheless, the report sent to Seleucus brought the high priest under suspicion of plotting against him with the Ptolemies and with Hyrcanus, well-known to be pro-Egyptian. The king summoned the priest to Antioch. But before any charge could be brought, the king was murdered by Heliodorus and a new king, Antiochus IV "Epiphanes", came to the throne. He kept Onias a prisoner and brought such pressure to bear on Hyrcanus that he was driven to suicide. In Jerusalem, the effect on the Tobiads resulted in fundamental changes in the balance of political power.

THE HELLENISTIC REFORM

Even more than his father, the new king saw himself as a "saviour" and "benefactor" of the ignorant natives of his kingdom, whom he could adapt to Greek civilization. Hoping to profit from this fact, the Tobiads formed a national pro-Hellenistic party. This ensured them the support of the Seleucids, who regarded the pro-Greek elements of their kingdom, including the pro-Hellenistic Jews, as the strongest prop of their rule over a variety of native Orientals. Faced by a common opposition from the troublesome "people" of Jerusalem, the two parties naturally joined forces.

Jason

The new development also brought the Tobiads the support of Jason, the brother of the deposed High Priest, who was eagerly in favour of speeding up the hellenization of Jewry. He offered Antiochus a large sum of money to recognize him as high priest in place of his brother, to build a gymnasium and ephebeion in Jerusalem and "to register the people of Jerusalem as Antiochenes", citizens of Antioch. Many scholars have interpreted this quotation as meaning that Antiochus IV gave Jason permission to convert Jerusalem into a Greek "polis" called Antioch. In any case, the foundations for a comprehensive hellenistic reform were laid, although the proposal offered a compromise on the question of the rule of Jerusalem. Such an arrangement would keep the high priesthood in the Zadok family while giving the civil administration to the Tobiads.

"But when Seleucus departed this life and Antiochus, who was called Epiphanes, succeeded to the kingdom, Onias' brother Jason obtained the high priesthood by corruption, promising the king in his petition three hundred and sixty talents of silver, and eighty talents from other revenues. Besides this he promised to pay a hundred and fifty more, if he was given authority to set up a gymnasium and a training place for youth there and to enrol the people of Jerusalem as citizens of Antioch. When the king had consented, and he had taken office, he immediately brought his countrymen over to the Greek way of living." (2 Mac. 4: 7–10)

"For he willingly established a gymnasium right under the citadel, and he made the finest of the young men wear the Greek hat. And to such a pitch did the cultivation of Greek fashions and the coming-in of foreign customs rise, because of the excessive wickedness of this godless Jason, who was no high priest at all, that the priests were no longer earnest about the services of the altar, but disdaining the sanctuary and neglecting the sacrifices, they hurried to take part in the unlawful exercises in the wrestling school, after the summons to the discusthrowing, regarding as worthless the things their forefathers valued, and thinking Greek standards the finest." (2 Mac. 4: 12–15)

From this, it seems as though the author of 2 Maccabees regarded the establishment of the gymnasium and ephebeion as virtually identical with the reform itself.

From a careful reading it appears that, at this stage, the changes being made in the direction of hellenization were not aimed against the religious faith of the people. True, traditionalist Jews were deeply offended at the sight of young athletes exercising naked, Greek fashion, in the gymnasium, or on learning that Jason had paid for a share in the sacrifice to the orientalized Heracles (— Melkarth) at Tyre. The real purpose of Jason and his allies, however, was to consolidate their power over the civil administration of the city, in the manner of the Greek "polis". They hoped that in this way they would distract attention from Jerusalem as a focus of religious life and would emphasize the attractions and advantages of the way of life of "the nations":

"In those days there arose out of Israel lawless men who persuaded many, saying, 'Let us go and make a treaty with the heathen around us, for ever since the time we became separated from them, many misfortunes have overtaken us.' The plan seemed good in their eyes." (1 Mac. 1: 11–12)

This is how the author of 1 Maccabees saw the hellenizing programme. The slogan of the reformers called for an end to the exclusiveness of the Jews and their tradition of deliberate

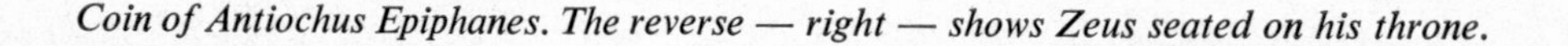

Coin of Antiochus Epiphanes. The reverse — right — shows Zeus seated on his throne.

self-isolation from the gentiles. Instead, the hellenizing programme opened the way to membership of the Commonwealth of Hellenic peoples, with equal enjoyment of the privileges conferred by the status of a Greek "polis". Under the Seleucids, this meant a much better position than the "peoples" or native populations were allowed.

The Policy of Antiochus Epiphanes

This programme had Antiochus' blessing, but it was put forward by the Jewish authorities and scribes in Jerusalem — the official interpreters of the Law of Moses, (the Oral Law). They were not aiming at religious reform, but were acting from political and economic motives, which required the support of Antioch. By granting special privileges to the Jewish towns, Antiochus widened the gulf that existed between their wealthy, sophisticated population and the backward Oriental people of the countryside. He believed that he was thus making sure of support in the event of any threat to his empire developing from the awakening nationalism of the Orient. To this end, he was prepared to grant many privileges to a newly-converted "polis" like Jerusalem.

In other words, Antiochus strengthened an internal class struggle between the powerful hellenizers and the traditionally-minded populace.

His interference broke the tradition that the office of high priest must always be held by a member of the house of Zadok. In the past, their right of succession to the highest religious office had not been challenged even by the Tobiads, although it was not sanctioned by the hellenistic rulers. But Jason, himself a Zadokite, gave Antiochus power to appoint the high priest. In the Greek manner this was now regarded as a municipal office and supreme power in the town belonged to the civil, instead of the religious, body. It was also Greek practice that the position of officiating high priest of the "polis" was not hereditary, but was open to anyone found worthy for civic reasons, or making the highest bid in terms of hard cash.

Accordingly, after Jason had been in office for three years, (174–171 B.C.E.), the Tobiads saw an opportunity to seize power for themselves. They supported the rival candidature of the son of a Temple official, Menelaus, who was not of the priestly Zadok family.

> "After the lapse of three years, Jason sent Menelaus, the brother of this Simon, to take the money to the king and to present papers relating to necessary business. But he, on being presented to the king, extolled him with such apparent authority that he obtained the high priesthood for himself, outbidding Jason by three hundred talents of silver. Upon receiving the royal commission, he came back, possessing nothing that qualified him for the high priesthood, but with the passions of a savage tyrant and the rage of a wild beast. So Jason, who had supplanted his own brother, was supplanted by another, and driven as a fugitive into the country of the Ammonites." (2 Mac. 4: 23–26)

To use the priesthood for political and material ends appeared a degradation of the office to the Jews. Although Menelaus maintained that he had not contravened Jewish religious law (in spite of raiding the Temple treasures to send money to the court in Syria); to the common people, his acts were an offence against the Mosaic traditions and a lowering of the prestige of religious observances. With this apparent decline in Jewish religious life, the way seemed clear for the thorough hellenization of Judea. Jason was now a fugitive in Rabbath-

Ammon, east of Jordan, or the "land of Tobiah" where Hyrcanus was entrenched; the former High Priest, Onias III, who had protested against the depredations of Menelaus, had been murdered in Antioch, and Menelaus, with the full support of Antiochus, seemed free to do as he pleased.

CIVIL WAR PRECEDED THE PERSECUTION

Gradually the situation changed. Religious propaganda aroused the people against Menelaus and his brother, Lysimachus, who had plundered the Temple treasure. With his 3,000 armed men, Lysimachus fought in the streets of Jerusalem and was killed. His brother, Menelaus faced charges in the Court, but bribed his way out.

The conflict between hellenizers and people might have found its own solution, but Antiochus Epiphanes took a hand in the struggle and thus evoked a strong anti-reform movement among the men of the older generation who clung tenaciously to their "ancestral law."

In 168 B.C.E. Antiochus set out on a second campaign against Egypt and rumours soon spread in Jerusalem that he had been killed in battle. Seizing this opportunity, Jason came hotfoot from his exile in Rabbath-Ammon and massacred the followers of Menelaus. Menelaus himself escaped, first taking refuge in the tower of the Akra. This was the new Acropolis of Jerusalem, a self-contained fortified citadel within the city. It stood on a rocky height north of the Temple area.

Symbols of the faith of Israel: Decoration of the stone door to a tomb near Kafr-Yasif in Galilee: upper left — eight branched menorah on a three-legged stand; lower-left — Ark of the Scrolls of the Law. Both symbols are typical of native Jewish art of the 2nd century C.E.

The pagan faith:
A typical Oriental-hellenistic idol of Syria was Jupiter-Heliopolitanus (left), the hellenized form of Baal, the ancient Semitic deity. This stone relief of the god was found near Baalbek in Lebanon (the name was derived from "Baal" of the "Beka" or valley). See p. 25.
The ceramic platter above shows the sacrifice of a pig, another pagan custom introduced into Jewish places of worship, "the abomination that makes desolate".

But Antiochus had not been killed. He had, however, met with a big reverse. In his first campaign against Egypt, he met with almost no resistance and captured the king himself (Ptolemy Philometor). In the second campaign, he laid siege to Alexandria but, because of pressure from Rome — to whom he was still paying instalments on the war indemnity incurred by Antiochus III — he had to raise the siege. The power of Rome was now making itself felt in the eastern Mediterranean and the delegate of the Roman Senate ordered Antiochus to leave Egypt immediately. "Let me think," he said to the Senate's messenger, Popilius Laenas. The Roman drew a circle around the king with his stick, "Think here!" Antiochus had no choice. "I shall do what the Senate wishes", and he had to evacuate Egypt and return home.

The effect of this Roman limitation on his military activity was to make Antiochus more determined than ever that his whole empire must be hellenized. He wanted all his vassal states consolidated on hellenic lines as a defence against the new threat from Rome.

To Antiochus, came Menelaus and his Tobiad supporters with a story that the pro-Ptolemaic Jews of Jerusalem had rebelled against Syria and that civil war was raging. It is difficult to be sure who was actually fighting whom, for Jason was hated by the people as much as Menelaus. The clashes were not mere interfamily feuds, but the opening stages of the people's rebellion against the hellenizing government.

Smarting under the indignity of his Roman encounter, Antiochus believed the accusation of treachery, and made up his mind to punish the High Priest.

> "When news of what had happened reached the king, he thought that Judea was in revolt; so he set out from Egypt like a wild beast and took the city by storm. And he ordered his soldiers to cut down without distinction anyone they met and to slay those who took refuge in their houses. Then there was a massacre of young and old, an annihilation of boys, women and children, a slaughter of girls and babies. In no more than three days eighty thousand people were destroyed, forty thousand of them in hand-to-hand encounters, and as many were sold into slavery as were slain. Not content with this, he dared to go into the most holy temple in all the world, guided by Menelaus who had betrayed both the laws and his country; and took the sacred plate in his polluted hands, and with his profane hands he swept away what had been dedicated by other kings to enchance the glory and honor of the place." (2 Mac. 5: 11–16)

> "And there was great mourning everywhere throughout Israel. Rulers and elders groaned, girls and young men fainted away, and the beauty of the women was altered. Every bridegroom began to lament, and she that sat in the bridal chamber grieved. The very earth was shaken over its inhabitants, and the whole household of Jacob was covered with shame." (1 Mac. 1: 25–28)

2 Maccabees (5, 22, ff.) tells that Antiochus appointed two particularly active "epistates" (governors), one Philip the Phrygian in Jerusalem, the other Andronicas on Mt. Gerizim, with instructions to complete the total hellenization of all Palestine.

This punitive action did not end the opposition. Antiochus stationed a foreign garrison in the Jerusalem fortress and harried the civilians of Jerusalem and the surrounding villages, confiscating their property and reducing them to panic:

> "And they shed innocent blood all around the sanctuary,
> And polluted the sanctuary itself.
> The inhabitants of Jerusalem fled away because of them,
> And she became a place where strangers lived,

And she became strange to her own offspring,
And her children forsook her.
Her sanctuary became desolate like a wilderness,
Her feasts were turned into grief,
Her sabbaths became a reproach,
And her honor became contempt." (1 Mac. 1: 35–39).

True, Menelaus still performed his official functions as high priest of Yahweh but, even before the famous anti-religious laws were decreed against Jewish worship in the following year (167 B.C.E.), the position of the Temple had become totally unacceptable to the Jewish masses.

For the Temple of the Lord had been defiled by the pagan sacrifices made by the foreign mercenaries stationed in the Akra. They had brought their pagan religion with them and sacrificed in the Temple to the Syrian Baal, (hellenized as Zeus and latinized into Jupiter). Syrian cults prevailed on the Temple mount, because the population of the polis of "Antioch-at-Jerusalem" was not entirely Jewish, but included many Syrians. It may be true to say, with V. Tcherikover, that the polluted Temple was abandoned by the natives not after the official persecutions of Antiochus, but before them.

The foreign garrison in the Akra treated Jerusalem as conquered territory, trying the population beyond endurance. Many fled into the villages, others as far as Egypt, to seek shelter among coreligionaries. The refugees found no peace in their rural retreats for the hellenistic officers were instructed to offer sacrifices in every locality, to prevent circumcision and the celebration of the Sabbath, and to destroy the scrolls of the Law. The people resisted everywhere, and everywhere met reprisals:

"and wherever they found the book of the Law, they tore them up and burned them, and if anyone was found to possess a book of the agreement or respected the Law, the king's decree condemned him to death. The Israelites who appeared from month to month in the towns they treated with force. On the twenty-fifth of the month they offered sacrifice upon the altar which was set up on the altar of burnt offering. The women who had circumcized their children they put to death under the decree, hanging the babies around their necks, and destroying their families and the men who circumcized them." (1 Mac. 1: 56–61)

E. Bickermann has drawn attention to the oriental Syrian character of the divine cults practiced at the Temple before and during the persecutions themselves. It was not the Greek gods — Olympian Zeus, Athene or Dionysos (= Bacchus) — who were worshipped, but Syrian deities in hellenistic garb. Baal-Shamin was the chief Syrian deity, reverenced from Phoenicia to Palmyra. He was also identified with Hadad, the god of Baalbek, himself identified with Zeus, as has been demonstrated by Avi-Yonah and N. Glueck. The other gods and goddesses such as Astarte (identified with Venus and Aphrodite) were endowed with Semitic attributes inherited from the Canaanite cults. Zeus (Jupiter) was worshipped in more or less Semitic temples, pictured in traditional dress and flanked by two bulls. An illustration of this is to be found in the Jupiter Heliopolitanus found near Baalbek, also termed Jupiter-Hadad. Associating Baal or Hadad with Helios, the Greeks called Baalbek Heliopolis. A wealth of Greek architecture was lavished on the town.

This, then, was the situation in 168 B.C.E. In December of that year, Antiochus entered the inner sanctuary of the Temple and took away the seven-branched candelabra, the golden altar and the precious instruments of sacrifice. A year later came his order forbidding the observance of the Jewish faith. He further defiled the Temple by erecting a small Greek altar over the great altar of burnt offerings and there sacrificing swine to Zeus Olympus. Some scholars maintain that he encouraged the identification of Zeus with Yahweh.

The gods of the Syrians conferred divinity on the king and this was acknowledged by his loyal subjects. Antiochus IV had proclaimed himself Theos Epiphanes (God manifest). But the religion of the Jews allowed no possibility of worshipping a king as divine.

The visions of the Book of Daniel preserve the spirit of the period for us. He refers to Antiochus' acts of desecration thus:

> "For ships of Kittim shall come against him, and he shall be afraid and withdraw, and shall turn back and be enraged and take action against the holy covenant. He shall turn back and give heed to those who forsake the holy covenant. Forces from him shall appear and profane the temple and fortress, and shall take away the continual burnt offering. And they shall set up the abomination that makes desolate. He shall seduce with flattery those who violate the covenant; but the people who know their God shall stand firm and take action. And those among the people who are wise shall make many understand, though they shall fall by sword and flame, by captivity and plunder, for some days. When they fall, they shall receive a little help. And many shall join themselves unto them with flattery." (Daniel 11: 30–34)

The "abomination that makes desolate" quoted above is the current translation from the Hebrew "hashikutz (abomination) meshomem." J. Morgenstern calls attention to the resemblance of "meshomem" and Shamem, an obvious disdainful "play upon the name Baal-Shamem. . . . with its clear implication that Baal-Shamem was the foreign god whose

A shrine to the Greek woodland god Pan at the Dan headwaters of the Jordan, which gave the name "Paneion" to the locality. This is the largest of the four sources of the river.

worship Antiochus Epiphanes of Syria had adopted, and imposed upon his own people, and which he was now imposing also upon conquered Israel." (Baal-Shamem of the Syrians means the Lord of Heavens).

There begins the story of the struggle between the hellenizers and the pious, with its persecutions, oppression and mutual hatred between the warring sections of the population. Following the political disturbances came the tragic chain of brutality, forced hellenization and religious persecution:

> "Then the king wrote to his whole kingdom that they should all become one people, and everyone should give up his particular practices. And all the heathen assented to the command of the king. And many from Israel agreed to his kind of worship and offered sacrifice to idols and broke the sabbath. And the king sent word by messengers to Jerusalem and the towns of Judah to follow practices foreign to the country and put a stop to whole burnt offerings and sacrifices and drink offerings at the sanctuary, and to break the sabbaths and profane the feasts and pollute sanctuary and sanctified; to build altars and sacred precincts and idol temples and sacrifice hogs and unclean cattle; and to leave their sons uncircumcised and defile themselves with every unclean and profane practice, so that they might forget the Law and change all their religious ordinances; and anyone who did not obey the command of the king should die." (1 Mac. 1: 41–50)

> "On the fifteenth day of Chislev, in the one hundred and forty-fifth year, he erected a dreadful desecration upon the altar, and in the towns of Judah round about they built altars." (1 Mac. 1: 54)

Jewish daily sacrifices were forbidden, while new altars for official worship were erected throughout the towns and villages of Judah and the Jews were bidden to sacrifice pigs as a token of their obedience to the king's decree. Reading of the Law was proscribed and anyone caught with it in his possession was executed. The Sabbath could not be observed nor circumcision practised.

On the evidence of Maccabees, it has generally been accepted that events leading up to the Maccabean revolt developed in the following order:

a) Collisions between parties, priests and personalities among the Jews;
b) Military intervention of Antiochus;
c) Religious persecution by Antiochus;
d) The rebellion of the Hasmoneans.

According to this view, the rebellion was the answer to the persecution. But it has been justly pointed out by V. Tcherikover that from 168 onwards, or the year before the religious persecution was decreed by Antiochus Epiphanes, the people of Jerusalem had been virtually in a state of open war with the hellenizers. "It was not the revolt which came as a response to the persecution, but the persecution which came as a response to the revolt. Only on this assumption can we understand Antiochus' decrees and their political purpose."

On investigating the cause of the unrest in Jerusalem, Antiochus must have come to the conclusion that the root of the trouble lay, not in any individual priest, but in the continued adherence of the people to their Jewish cult and "ancestral laws." So long as these existed, there could be no hope of maintaining order or of integrating Jerusalem and the Jews of Palestine into his hellenistic order.

It is possible that had it not been for the new Roman threat to his empire, Antiochus might have been satisfied with a more gradual — and thorough — hellenization of Palestine, carried out by the extremists among the Tobiads with Menelaus at their head. As it was, his very anxiety to consolidate his possessions produced the opposite result — and changed the face of history. By 167–166, the stage was set for the rise of the Maccabees (so-called from their leader, Judas Maccabee, of the Hasmonean house).

One tradition of the Second Book of Maccabees tells that Judas fled from Jerusalem with nine other men and hid in the 'wilderness'. They were joined by bands of Hassidim warrior-saints and by hundreds of patriots. As the avalanche of persecution rolled on, they filtered into the villages of Judea and gathered some 6000 men under their standard. Historians are inclined to believe this account, *although the narrative of the First Book of Maccabees begins more modestly*, as we shall see.

SYNOPTIC CHRONOLOGICAL TABLE I.

	Seleucid kings	*Ptolemaic kings*	*Judea*
333—323 B.C.E.	Alexander's Conquests		Jaddua, High Priest
305	Seleucus I Nicator (305—280)	Ptolemy I Soter (305—285)	
	Antiochus I (280—261)	Ptolemy II Philadelphus (285—246)	Onias I
	Antiochus II (261—246)	(Translation of Pentateuch into Greek)	
			Simon I (son of Onias I)
	Seleucus II (246—226)	(Ptolemy II Euergetes (246—221)	Eleazar (" " " ")
			Manasseh (uncle of Eleazar)
			Onias II (son of Onias I)
			(Joseph ben Tobiah active)
	Seleucus III (226—223)		
	Antiochus III "the Great"(223—187) (brother of Seleucus III)	Ptolemy IV Philopator (221—205)	Simon II, "the Just" (son of Onias II)
200	(Palestine becomes part of the Seleucid empire)	Ptolemy V Epiphanes (205—181)	
	Seleucus IV Philopater (187—175)		
	Antiochus IV Epiphanes (175—164)		Onias III, (son of Simon II), deposed by Antiochus IV, and replaced by
			USURPING HIGH PRIESTS
			Jason (174—171, brother of Onias)
			Menelaus, who usurped Jason's position and held office after the first Maccabean victories.

War elephants were used in Palestine by the Seleucid armies. Eleazar, one of the Maccabean brothers, met his death beneath such an elephant (Etruscan plate of the 3rd century B.C.E.).

II

THE WAR OF LIBERATION AND THE HASMONEAN PRINCES

"In those days Mattathias, the son of John, the son of Simeon, a priest of the descendants of Joarib, removed from Jerusalem, and settled in Modiin. He had five sons, John, surnamed Gaddi, Simon, called Thassi, Judas, called Maccabeus, Eleazar, called Avaran, and Jonathan, called Apphus." (1 Mac. 2: 1–5)

The Jews had now to choose between apostasy and rebellion. Armed resistance to Antiochus' policy began, according to the story of 1 Maccabees, with the refusal of Mattathias, a humble priest of Modiin (of the family of Bene-Hashmona) either to conform or to acquiesce in the new observances. In answer to the Greek officer who called on him to cooperate in enforcing the new regulations, he declared:

"If all the heathen in the king's dominions listen to him and forsake each of them the religion of his forefathers, and choose to follow his commands instead, yet I and my sons and my brothers will live in accordance with the agreement of our forefathers. God forbid that we should abandon the Law and the ordinances. We will not listen to the message of the king, or depart from our religion to the right hand or to the left." (1 Mac. 2: 19–22)

In addition to this public declaration of his adherence to the traditional faith, he also showed himself prepared to meet force with force. When a renegade Jew came to sacrifice at the altar in Modiin, in accordance with the new edict, Mattathias killed both him and the king's officer sent to enforce the law. This was the spark that set ablaze the smouldering hatred of the whole country.

THE HOLY WAR

Then, calling for supporters to follow him, he took refuge in the hills, and began the organization of guerrilla warfare against the Syrian forces and, in the beginning, the hellenizing upper classes. The holy war against the profaners of Israel was begun, with prayer:

"Let the high praises of God be in their throats and two-edged swords in their hands, to wreak vengeance on the nations and chastisement on the peoples." (Psalm 149: 6–7)

This group of war scenes, taken mainly from Greek art, give a vivid impression of the actual fighting of the Maccabean wars, involving hand-to-hand combat, archery and cavalry (see also colour plate of Alexander at Issus). The main weapons of the infantry were the short sword and lance, shown below right, in a 3rd century terracotta found on an Etruscan urn; or, above left, by a late 5th century Attic gravestone commemorating a soldier dying, with his weapon in his hand. The figure above right is a classic sculpture from the façade of the 6th century Temple of Ergine in Greece. On the left, a warrior binds his enemy, pictured on a 3rd century hellenistic vase, *(see p. 33)**.*

The rebellion found leaders not only among the popular Hasmonean Maccabees but also from the groups of very devout Hassidim. Both the books of Maccabees and also Daniel speak of the important role played by the Hassidim in the insurgent movement. They will by fully described in Ch. III. Briefly, they were ascetics who dedicated themselves to the Law and the observance of the Priestly Codes. They would have refused service in any merely national war, but they became the *corps d'elite* of the Maccabean resistance, which they equated with the holy war of God described in the Old Testament. They had the support of the lower strata of rural priests — such as those of Modiin — and of broad sections of the Jerusalem working class — the craftsmen, labourers and petty tradesmen.

While the aristocratic priesthood stood at the top of the social ladder, the inspiration for spiritual developments did not come from them, nor from their subordinates, the scribes, who formed the intelligentsia of the towns. It was rooted instead in the lower, rural priesthood, like the Hasmonean family of Mattathias. Antiochus had reasoned from what was happening in Judea that the only way to put down the rebellion was to suppress the Mosaic Law entirely. Instead, the Law of Moses became the war cry of the masses.

The local Seleucid forces were sent to crush the revolt. In their first encounter they inflicted a heavy defeat on the rebels. The Greeks opened the battle on a Saturday and, rather than profane the Sabbath by striking a blow in their own defence, the Hassidim and their strictly observant followers offered no resistance and some thousand people were killed. This is one of the early examples of religious martyrdom. Obviously, to meet emergencies, the law had to be changed. Mattathias and the Hassidim declared that, in a holy war, fighting was lawful on the Sabbath, a rule which has been followed in Israel ever since.

The partisans spread through the towns and villages, gathering recruits, destroying the foreign altars, circumcizing male children and taking a heavy toll of the army of occupation. In the following year, Mattathias died and the struggle was carried on by his five sons, Judas acting as the military Commander-in-Chief. He deployed his scanty forces against the army of Apollonius, the Commander of the Samarian province, and defeated him, even taking Apollonius' sword from him:

> "Then Apollonius gathered the heathen together, with a large force from Samaria, to make war on Israel. And Judas learned of it and went out to meet him and he struck him down and killed him. And many fell wounded, and the rest made their escape. And they took their spoils, and Judas took the sword of Apollonius and fought with it all his life." (1 Mac. 3: 10–12)

The great chief's sword in the hands of the rebel leader was a good omen, excellent for the morale of the insurgents. The victory of the rebels called for immediate reprisals. A higher Syrian commander, the governor of Coele-Syria, was sent with a "mighty army." He, too, was beaten at Beth-horon, overlooking the maritime plain. This victory added to Judas' prestige and, consequently, to his forces and he consolidated the nucleus of an organized army.

Judas had beaten a local force, then a provincial army. He had yet to face the king's main force.

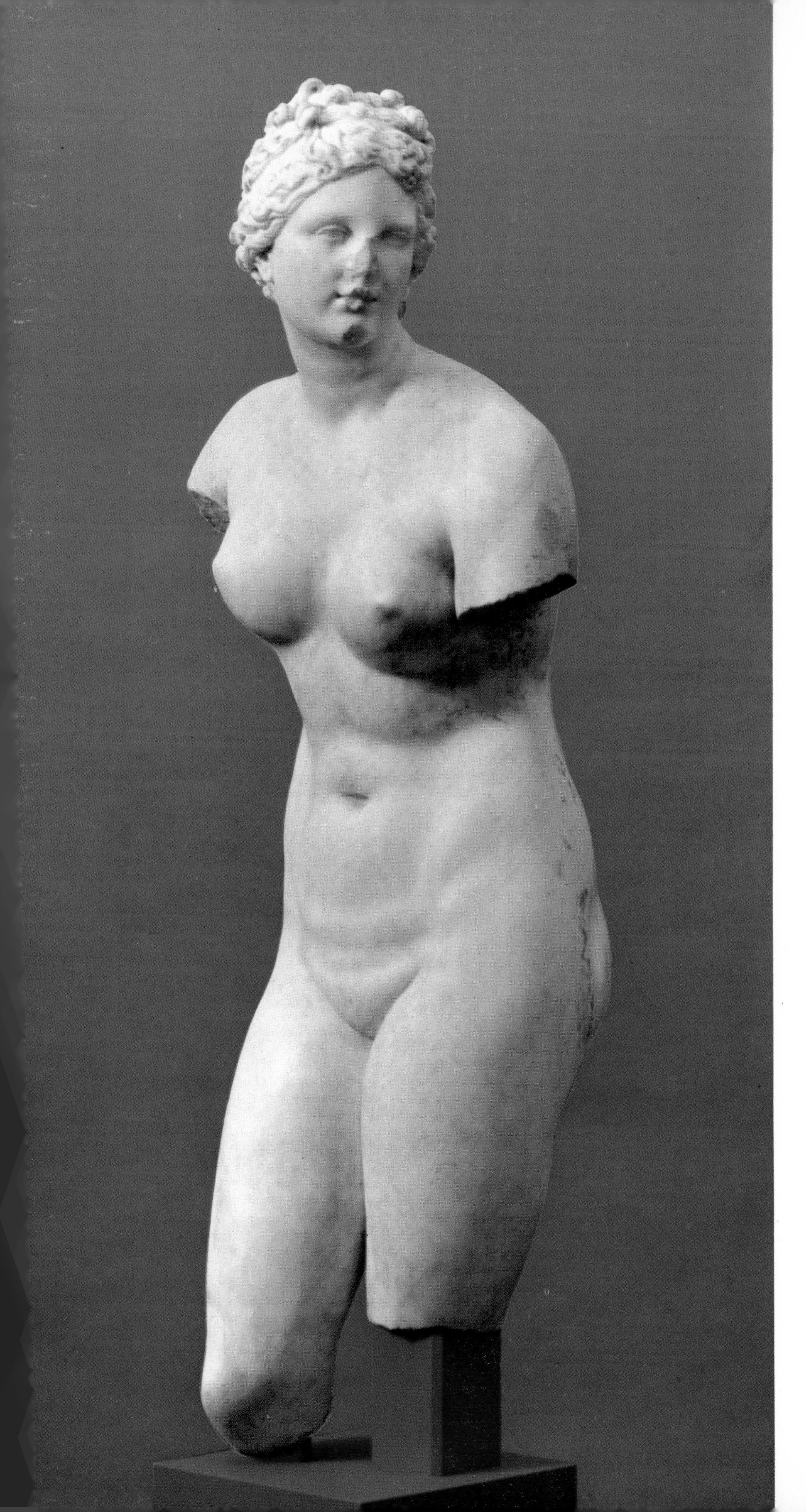

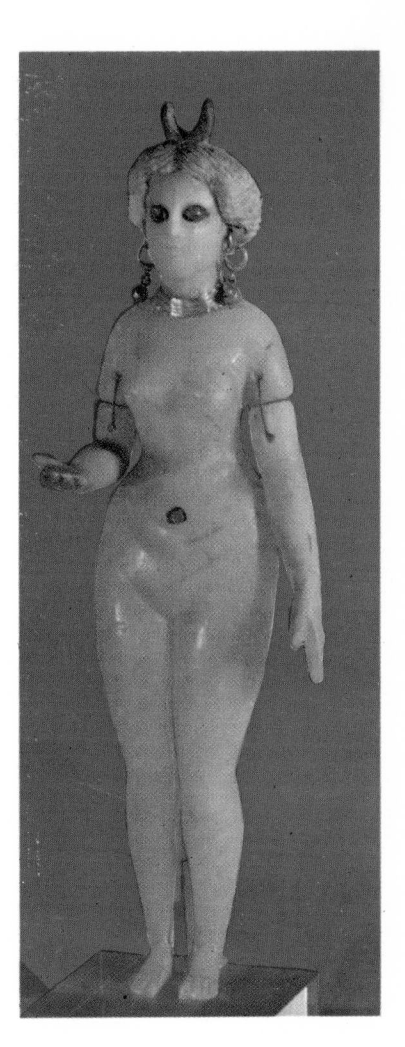

V-VI. Two goddesses, two ideals of womanhood, two styles of workmanship. Left, hellenistic marble Aphrodite of the 4th century B.C.E., peak period for the representation of the female nude. A nude goddess recalls the ritual nudity of prehellenic divinities. The Babylonian statuette, above, is also of the hellenistic period but clearly shows the differences in Asiatic art and physical types.

VII. Egyptian necklace in gold of the hellenistic-Ptolemaic period, still making use of ancient themes, (*see p.* 6).

VIII. Fragment of the oldest known biblical manuscript, found in Cave IV, Qumran. Written towards the end of the 3rd century B.C.E., it is a clearly legible part of I Sam. 23: 9–13 *reading,* 1st *line: "Alav Shaul maharish hara'ah"* (*Saul was plotting evil against him*)*;* 2nd *line: "Yisrael, shamo'a shama' abdekha ki mebakesh Shaul"* (*thy servant has heard definitely that Saul seeks*), (*see p.* 182–4).

Antiochus was away campaigning against the Parthians in his eastern empire. He had left his throne and affairs "from the river Euphrates unto the borders of Egypt" in the charge of his General, Lysias, with instructions to subdue Palestine. Led by Gorgias, the Syrian army came up and established headquarters at Emmaus. Gorgias planned to attack the Jewish forces and wipe them out with one blow, but Judas, apparently, had the better intelligence service. While the Syrian forces were away in the mountains looking for him, Judas launched a surprise attack on the Emmaus camp and destroyed it. This was disastrous for enemy morale and when the two armies met, the result was a smashing defeat for Gorgias and the Syrians.

This defeat brought Lysias himself at the head of a new army but it, too, was defeated by Judas near Beth-zur in 165 B.C.E.

According to Eliezer Galili's military survey, Judas' army consisted of a central mobile body of trained fighters who were joined in several parts of the countryside by local partisans. They were usually peasants who returned to the soil when the fighting was over. The Maccabean guerrilla bands operated in scattered areas which corresponded roughly to the concentrations of Jewish population in Judah, Galilee and elsewhere. We are apt to think of the Gentiles who confronted the Jews at this time as people living outside Palestine. In fact, a considerable proportion of the population of the country were non-Jews, many of them hostile. The Jewish areas of settlement were separated by the large number of hellenistic "poleis" that dotted Samaria, the coastal region, the Valley of Jezreel, the South and Trans-jordan; they served as bases of operation and supply to the Syrian army.

Though small, the Jewish army was fighting a holy war, a national struggle against the well armed and equipped forces of the foreign oppressor. These forces were mainly mercenary troops from hellenized Syria and Mesopotamia and from the Greek provinces of Asia Minor. They had little patriotic attachment compared to the morale of a national army fighting for its homeland. Moreover, Antiochus Epiphanes and his successors were harrassed on their frontiers by Parthian rebellions and had to divide their forces to meet attacks on many fronts. There is reason to believe that the forces sent against Judah were not as large as is reported in the ancient documents, although they were certainly many times larger and better equipped for hand-to-hand fighting, archery and siege warfare than the Jewish army.

Partial Annulment of Antiochus' Decree

It appears from 2 Maccabees that, with the intention of getting Antiochus' decrees annulled, the hellenizers and elders of Jerusalem sent Menelaus on a mission to Antioch, two other emissaries to General Lysias and also a request to Rome to intercede for the Jews with the Government. If they succeeded, Judas, the Maccabees and the Hassidim would lose their most effective rallying cry — defence of religion — and their supporters would return home. A letter was sent to the Jewish people and it ran as follows:

"King Antiochus sends greeting to the Jewish senate and to the rest of the Jews. If you are well, it is what we desjre; we too are well. Menelaus has informed us that you want to go home and look after your own affairs. Therefore those who go home by the thirtieth of Xanthicus will have our assurance that the Jews can fearlessly enjoy their own food and laws, as before; and none of them shall be molested in any way for what he may have ignorantly done. I have sent Menelaus also to cheer you. Goodbye. The hundred and forty-eighth year, Xanthicus fifteenth." (2 Mac. 11: 27–33)

That is to say, after long deliberations in Antioch, a compromise had been reached. The Government was offering the Jews an amnesty and religious freedom. But it had to be put into effect within a fortnight. Either they could leave the rebel camp, disarm and return home immediately, in which case the Government promised — with no guarantee — that it would annul the decrees, or else they could continue the revolt and face a continued persecution. However, this clever piece of diplomacy brought no benefit to the hellenizers. Some six months later, Judas the Maccabee appeared before the walls of Jerusalem and took the city. With this victory a new chapter opened in the progress of the war of liberation.

THE FEAST OF HANUKKAH

Triumphant, Judas occupied Jerusalem, shut up the Greek garrison in the Akra and proceeded to cleanse and purify the desecrated Temple and restore it for worship:

"And he appointed priests that were without blemish and adherents of the Law, and they purified the sanctuary and carried out the stones that had defiled it to an unclean place. And they deliberated as to what they should do about the altar of burnt offering, which had been polluted. And a good idea occurred to them — to take it down, so that it might never be thrown up to them that the heathen had polluted it; so they took down the altar, and deposited the stones in the temple mountain, in a suitable place, until a prophet should come and declare what should be done with them. And they took whole stones, as the Law required, and built a new altar like the former one. And they built the sanctuary and the interior of the temple and consecrated the courts. And they made holy dishes and they brought the lamps and the altar of incense and the table into the temple." (1 Mac. 4: 42–49)

In December 164, three years to the month after its profanation, the Temple was rededicated and the daily sacrifice offered again on the altar. In order to protect the Temple from enemy occupation, Judas had a wall built around Mt. Zion where the Temple stood.

"And there was very great joy among the people, and the reproach the heathen had cast upon them was wiped out. And Judas and his brothers and all the congregation of Israel decreed that the days of the rededication of the altar should be observed at their season, every year, for eight days, beginning with the twenty-fifth of the month of Chislev, with gladness and joy." (1 Mac. 4: 58—60)

According to a folk tale, when the Maccabees regained the Temple, they found nothing undefiled within the sacred precincts except for a small cruse of oil, enough for only one day's lights. Miraculously, however, the lamps filled with this oil continued to burn for eight days. This is the origin of the ancient hymn sung to this day on Hanukkah. There may be fragments of fact buried in this legend but, if so, they have been obscured. Nevertheless, the story has provided the symbol which came to represent the revolt in later generations. It emphasizes the miraculous success of the Maccabean revolt of the brave few against the powerful many. The Jews of the time can hardly have imagined at first that what had started as a movement of civil and religious resistance would culminate in complete independence from foreign rule within the lifetime of the first generation of Hasmoneans. Yet, in fact, the

Ancient versions of the seven-branched candelabrum — the menorah — make it clear that the stand was then conical, with three animal feet. The form is preserved on this 3rd century C.E. coffin from Beth Shearim.

The site of the Temple and its esplanade can be seen to the left of the picture. Between the Temple area and the upper town, to the right, ran the Tyropeon depression which was far deeper in olden days (see p. 61). This view is taken from the north-west.

Feast of Hanukkah (dedication) has been celebrated by the Jews ever since, in commemoration of this event.

Having restored the Temple, the hellenizers were driven out. Judas dispossessed and liquidated many, while others fled to Edom, south of Jerusalem, or took refuge in the Akra. But the Jews living scattered throughout Galilee and Gilead, east of the Jordan, isolated among strange peoples, were in danger of reprisals. Judas set out to help the Jewish settlements east of Jordan, while his brother, Simeon, marched into Galilee. Their purpose was to save their brethren. Until then, Judas had been a rebel general. With the capture of Jerusalem, he became a national leader. His forces were not strong enough to conquer new territory, but they were sufficient to consolidate the frontiers of Judea and many Jews were re-settled for safety within the borders of the country. Hebron was conquered from the Idumeans and burned, then Jabneh, Joppa and Ashdod, peopled by pagan enemies. The towns were destroyed; idolatrous worship suppressed. These assaults on the local Syrian population were justified as part of the holy war for the sanctity of Judaism against pagans. Inspired by the Hassidim, who kept the zeal of the rebels alive, war was conducted to the accompaniment of religious ceremonies and watchwords.

"and he read aloud from the holy book, and gave 'the Help of God' as the watchword, and taking command of the first division himself, he joined battle with Nicanor." (2 Mac. 8: 23)

The watchwords of the Maccabees are paralleled by a great many similar ones in the Dead Sea Scroll of the "War of the Sons of Light against the Sons of Darkness":

"And when they draw near to the battle, they shall write upon their standards: War of God, Vengeance of God, Feud of God, Requital of God; Strength of God; Recompense of God. Annihilation by God of all vain nations." (War Scroll 4: 1—2).

Two years had passed since Lysias had sought to deal with the situation in Judah by a partial annulment of Antiochus' decrees. This interval had given Judas an opportunity of holding Jerusalem and thus demonstrating his strength to the people of Palestine.

During this period, Antiochus Epiphanes had died. His son Antiochus V Eupator, succeeded him, with General Lysias acting as his guardian and wielding supreme power in his name.

Meanwhile, Judas set himself to liquidate the garrison of the Akra and to wipe out the last remnant of the hellenizers. His action brought reprisals and Lysias renewed his campaign in 163–2. Accompanied by the young king, Eupator, he approached Jerusalem from Edom in the south with a very substantial force.

"When the king heard this, he was angry, and he gathered all his Friends, the officers ot his army, and those in charge of the cavalry. And mercenary forces came to him from other kingdoms and from the islands in the sea. And his forces numbered a hundred thousand infantry and twenty thousand cavalry, and thirty-two elephants trained for war. And they passed through Idumea and pitched their camp against Bethsura and fought against it for a long time, and built engines of war. And they sallied out and burned them down, and fought bravely." (1 Mac. 6: 28—31)

Unquestionably the figures of military forces are exaggerated. According to Josephus, each elephant formed a tower for a number of archers and was accompanied by 500 horse and 1,000 foot soldiers. There were so many elephants in this expedition that they had had to march single file. Whatever its size, the army besieged the Maccabean stronghold of Beth-Zur, using war engines against the city walls. Whereas in Lysias' first campaign the town had resisted, this time it succumbed. Thereupon, Lysias turned to Jerusalem, raised the siege of the Akra and destroyed the fortifications around the Temple.

"And he made peace with the men of Bethsura, and they evacuated the town, because they had no food there to support a siege, for it was a sabbatical year. So the king occupied Bethsura and stationed a garrison there to hold it." (1 Mac. 6: 49—50)

In defending the approaches to the south of Jerusalem, Judas was defeated at Beth Zacharias (south of Bethlehem). The narrative of 1 Maccabees gives a spirited account of

List of pagan priests at Bethshean (Scythopolis), a hellenistic city in the Jordan valley, which was not conquered by the Maccabeans. Its inhabitants made retaliatory raids against their Jewish neighbours.

The Maccabean system of walls at Beth-zur, south of Jerusalem. The lower wall held back the slope and protected the base of the large inner wall.

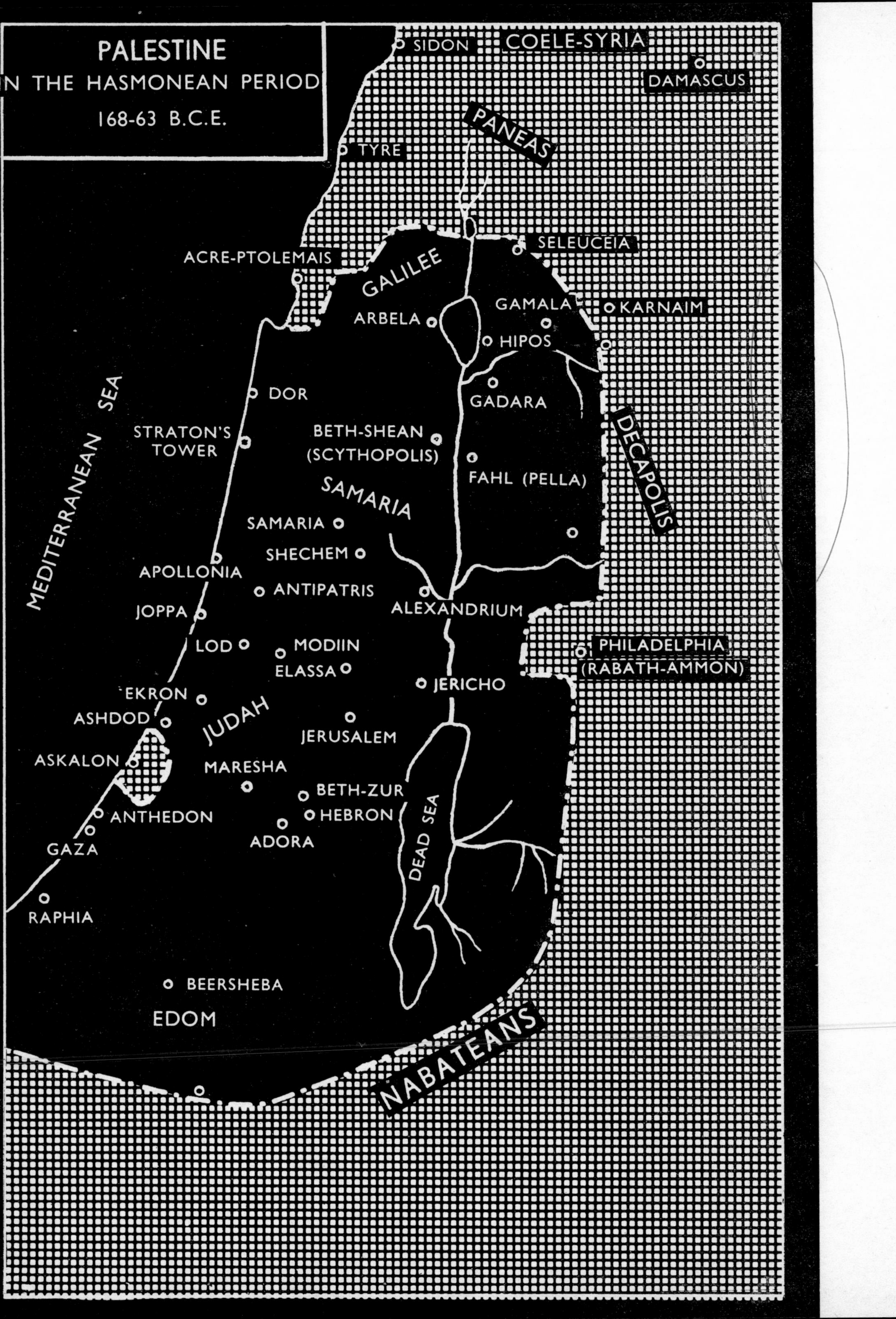

PALESTINE
IN THE HASMONEAN PERIOD
168-63 B.C.E.
SIDON
COELE-SYRIA
DAMASCUS
PANEAS
TYRE
SELEUCEIA
ACRE-PTOLEMAIS
GALILEE
GAMALA
KARNAIM
ARBELA
HIPOS
GADARA
DOR
MEDITERRANEAN SEA
STRATON'S TOWER
BETH-SHEAN (SCYTHOPOLIS)
DECAPOLIS
FAHL (PELLA)
SAMARIA
SAMARIA
SHECHEM
APOLLONIA
ANTIPATRIS
ALEXANDRIUM
JOPPA
LOD
MODIIN
PHILADELPHIA (RABATH-AMMON)
ELASSA
JERICHO
EKRON
ASHDOD
JUDAH
JERUSALEM
ASKALON
MARESHA
BETH-ZUR
HEBRON
DEAD SEA
ANTHEDON
GAZA
ADORA
RAPHIA
BEERSHEBA
EDOM
NABATEANS

the Syrian elephant corps under attack from the Jews, (Ch. 6: 30–47) in which Judas' brother was crushed to death by the fall of an elephant he had himself killed.

Judas retreated behind the walls of Mount Zion, leaving his army fighting at Beth-Zur in bad straits. Then news came to Lysias that his rival, General Philipos was marching on Antioch from eastern Syria. Affairs at home being more urgent, Lysias determined to make peace with Judas and thus be free to return to Syria.

A COMPROMISE PEACE

The first book of Maccabees does not mention it, but we learn from 2 Maccabees, 11, and from the history of Josephus that Lysias and Judas concluded an armistice. Although religious freedom was again assured, and Menelaus was removed from the High Priesthood and executed, Judas still did not control the whole country. Jerusalem remained in the hands of the hellenizers and a Greek garrison occupied the Akra. After three years of fighting, the partisans — peasants who had left their villages — were weary of war and wanted to return home. The Greeks, too, were anxious to avoid further fighting and agreed to grant the Jewish people religious freedom. The terms of the peace were announced in a royal communication from King Antiochus Eupator to his general Lysias in the year 163 B.C.E. The king's letter ran thus:

> "King Antiochus sends greeting to his brother Lysias. Now that our father has departed to the gods, we desire the subjects of the kingdom to be unmolested and to busy themselves with the care of their own affairs, and as we have heard that the Jews will not agree to our father's policy of making them adopt Greek practices, but prefer their own way of living, and ask to be allowed to follow their own customs, we wish this nation also to be undisturbed, and our decision is that their temple be returned to them, and that they follow their ancestral customs." (2. Mac. 11: 22—26)

In effect, his letter was the recognition of the status quo by the Syrian government. Antiochus' decree had, in any case, been annulled by Judas' conquest of Jerusalem and his re-dedication of the Temple. The Syrians confirmed their recognition of the "ancestral laws" of the Jews and thus reverted to the legal situation created by Antiochus III thirteen years previously. Officially, Jerusalem's status as the polis of "Antioch" was abolished. The Temple was restored to its owners and Syrians were forbidden to participate in or establish cults there.

The peace left the Syrian government in command of the situation. However, it still had to decide on which sector of Judean society it should base its authority, the hellenizers having proved a disappointment. Lysias vented his anger at this on Menelaus and had him brutally executed in Syria. As a suitable replacement for the post of High Priest, he selected Alcimus (Greek form of Eliakim), who may have belonged to the Oniad family, and was therefore one of the aristocracy and close to the hellenizers. By these means, Lysias hoped to appease the nationalists and still keep authority in the hands of the wealthy leaders of Jerusalem. But apparently Judas refused to recognize the appointment and forbade Alcimus to officiate.

The summit of the drive for religious freedom had been gained. The hellenistic reform was abolished and the Jews were free to live according to their own laws. What had begun as a religious uprising had developed into a national movement. For the first time in a hundred years, an organized military force had appeared among the Jews. With it, the Maccabees and the nationalists continued the fight for complete political autonomy.

THE HOUSE OF THE HASMONEANS

FROM RELIGIOUS TO POLITICAL AUTONOMY

In the Seleucid kingdom of Syria, struggles for the throne of Antiochus IV Epiphanes produced a new political climate. The rightful heir, Antiochus V Eupator and his guardian general Lysias were both murdered and, in 161 B.C.E., a pretender became Demetrius I Soter (Redeemer).

He confirmed Alcimus' claim to the High Priesthood. This had the support of both the scribes and Hassidim because Alcimus belonged to the priestly house of Zadok. By thus respecting their religion and appointing their traditional leader to be at their head, Demetrius hoped to pacify the people of Judea and win their support. Although the Jews' victory had been won by Judas, he was passed over in the choice of a leader in favour of the priest, Alcimus. But Demetrius still maintained a Greek garrison within the country under his general Bacchides, and he regarded Judah as a subject territory to be governed by him as in the past.

But Judas and the Maccabeans wanted more than the status quo. They aimed at political autonomy and the administration of the land under the ancient laws of the Torah, as expounded by the Hassidim, the traditional authorities for the expounding of the Law. During the struggle between Jason and Menelaus over the high priesthood, the Hassidim had realized that their position was threatened and they had given their allegiance to the Maccabean warrior priests. Now, with the transformation of the holy war for religion into a war of political liberation, many of the Hassidim left the Maccabean camp and offered their allegiance to Alcimus, their traditional leader.

But Alcimus proved a disappointment. Under his rule attempts at hellenizing continued, just as in the previous generation, and these brought about a renewal of the civil war, for Judas continued to oppose the government. The Hassidim soon quarrelled with Alcimus. The High Priest had sixty of them killed and as a result the rest returned to the Maccabean camp. With the resumption of hostilities, the High Priest found he had lost all support in Jerusalem. He appealed to Demetrius Soter for help against Judas and the king sent Nicanor to his aid, at the head of a large army.

> "Then the king sent Nicanor, one of his distinguished officers, who hated Israel bitterly, and ordered him to destroy the people. And Nicanor went to Jerusalem with a strong force, and he deceitfully sent a peaceful message to Judas and his brothers, saying,
> 'Let us have no battle between me and you. I will come with a few men to have a peaceable personal meeting'.
> So he came to Judas, and they greeted one another peaceably. But the enemy were ready to kidnap Judas." (1 Mac. 7: 26–29)

The preliminary battle at Capharsalama resulted in a defeat for Nicanor that sent his army running for cover back to their headquarters in Jerusalem. Nicanor went up to Mount Zion and answered the friendly overtures of a delegation from the priests and hellenizing elders of Jerusalem, who were seeking a compromise to end the civil war:

"And he jeered at them and laughed at them and polluted them, and spoke arrogantly and swore angrily,
'If Judas and his army are not immediately delivered into my hands, it will happen that if I return safely, I will burn this house up'." (1 Mac. 7: 34–35)

The collapse of the negotiations may have been due to Alcimus' influence over Nicanor. In any event, Nicanor prepared for battle again and marched against 3,000 Jewish partisans who were encamped in Adasa, north-east of Beth-horon.

"But Nicanor and his men advanced with trumpets and battle songs. And Judas and his men met the enemy with entreaties and prayers. So fighting with their hands and praying to God with their hearts, they laid low no less than thirty-five thousand, being greatly cheered by God's manifest aid.
When the business was over, and they were joyfully returning, they recognized Nicanor, lying dead, in his armor. And there was shouting and tumult, and they blessed the Sovereign in the language of their forefathers. Then the man who was in body and soul the perfect champion of his fellow-citizens, who maintained the good will of his youth toward his fellow-citizens, ordered them to cut off Nicanor's head and arm and carry them to Jerusalem." (2 Mac. 15: 25–30).

The Jews inaugurated a feast of the "day of Nicanor" in honour of the victory, but, in fact, it was the last time fortune was to favour Judas. Despite their successes, the Maccabeans were in a desperate situation. Turning to diplomacy, Judas applied for help to the Roman Republic, Syria's rival. This established the first contacts between the Jews and the rising Roman power (160 B.C.E.).

"And Judas chose Eupolemus, the son of John, the son of Hakkoz, and Jason, the son of Eleazar, and sent them to Rome, to establish friendly relations and an alliance with them, so that they might relieve them of their yoke, for they saw that the rule of the Greeks was reducing Israel to slavery. And they went to Rome, though the journey was very long, and they went into the senate house and answered and said,
'Judas, who is called Maccabeus, and his brothers and the Jewish people have sent us to you, to make an alliance and firm peace with you, and that we may be enrolled as allies and friends of yours.'
They were pleased with the proposal." (1 Mac. 8: 17–21)

The Roman Senate gave the Jewish delegation an honourable reception and signed a pact of mutual defence with Judea. However, this did nothing to remedy the military weakness of the small Maccabean army, for events showed that the Romans had no intention of intervening in Syria with force. The Senate was only concerned to embarrass its rivals by supporting their enemies.

In 160 B.C.E., five years after the beginning of the revolt, Demetrius sent Alcimus an overwhelming force under Bacchides, the "strategos" or general for the whole division of Coele-Syria, in which Palestine was included. After subduing the stronghold of Arbel, West of the Sea of Galilee, the Syrian army stormed Judah. The defenders were intimidated: And Judas said,

"I will never do this thing, and flee from them; and if our time has come, let us die bravely for our brothers, and not leave a stain upon our honor." (1 Mac. 9: 10).

Judas could muster 3,000 men, of which 800 turned out at Elasa for a last defence. In spite of the odds against them, they fought gallantly but the result was a total defeat. Judas was killed and his army scattered (160 B.C.E). Power was left in the hands of Alcimus and his hellenistic faction.

JONATHAN RULES IN JUDEA

For two years Bacchides and the hellenizers maintained absolute control of the country. They consolidated Greek garrisons in forts throughout the province, although, this time, there was no interference with the practice of the Jewish faith. The adherents of the Maccabeans were terrorized and many were imprisoned as hostages in the Jerusalem Akra fortress, but Judas' supporters did not abandon hope. They appointed his brother Jonathan as their military chief and he went into hiding in the wilderness of Tekoa, near the Dead Sea. Later, pursued by the Greeks, he escaped east of the Jordan. Guerrilla warfare continued. Bacchides fortified many towns in Judea against Jonathan, increasing the garrisons of Beth-Zur, Gezer and the Akra, but he was never able to beat the guerrillas decisively.

The hellenizers had no army of their own and could not crush the rebels without Syrian help. In the end, Bacchides accepted the Maccabeans. He saw that they had the support of the people whereas the hellenizers could not administer the country without permanent outside military help. Apart from the aristocrats and wealthy classes, the Jewish people as a whole were opposed to attempts to impose an alien culture on them. More and more they came to accept the leadership of the Hasmonean family which succeeded Judas.

Without any formal peace treaty being drawn up, the Greeks recognized Jonathan as the de facto ruler of the Jewish community and he felt secure enough over the next five years to establish a rump government in Michmash, a little distance north-east of Jerusalem. At this place, 900 years before, another Jonathan, the son of King Saul, had won his victory over the Philistines. There, the Maccabean Jonathan "judged Israel" as of old. Although the post of High Priest remained unfilled for another seven years, the House of the Hasmoneans had come to stay (157 B.C.E).

DECLINE OF SELEUCID DOMINATION

Not only did the Syrians realize that the hellenizers were powerless in Judea without their support, but Seleucid dynastic squabbles absorbed them more and more. Because the hellenizers could not defeat them alone, the Hasmoneans became firmly established during a long process closely connected with the decline of the Seleucid empire.

The background to the whole Hasmonean struggle had been the essential weakness of the empire. Its disintegration was hastened, according to V. Tcherikover, by the feuds at the royal Syrian court, and the personal inadequacy of the rulers, but these were secondary factors.

Clay figurine from the 1st century B.C.E., excavated at Achsib, an ancient Phoenician and hellenistic settlement on the coast, south of the "Ladder of Tyre". The main approach to northern Palestine from Seleucid Syria was along this coastline.

Already many of its oriental provinces in central Asia: Parthia, Bactria and the Arabian principalities, had thrown off the royal yoke. In the face of this evidence of oriental strength, the Syrian king recognized the independence of parts of his dominions, which developed into a federal state rather than an empire. Into this federal state, Palestine could be accepted by virtue of its own inner strength.

In 152 B.C.E, the Syrian throne was threatened by an alliance formed between an Ephesian pretender, Alexander Balas, and other enemies of the Seleucids. The king Demetrius Soter turned for help to Jonathan as the most powerful person in Palestine, confirmed him in his post in Judea and freed the Jewish hostages taken by Bacchides. Recognition of his status enabled Jonathan to raise an army. With this he took formal possession of Jerusalem and fortified the city, although Syrian garrisons remained in the Akra fortress and at Beth-Zur, offering protection to many fleeing Jewish hellenizers.

The price of Jewish support was obvious. In return for the help of his army, Demetrius promised Jonathan three Samarian districts with the towns of Ramathaim, Lod and Afarim and offered him grants of money for his fortifications in Jerusalem. But Alexander outbid Demetrius by appointing Jonathan High Priest. Although for Alexander this was purely a political move in his own struggle against his rival, his action in sending Jonathan a purple robe and a crown or wreath of gold, set the seal on the victory of the Hasmoneans. From the very beginning, the aristocracy of Jerusalem had dreamed of playing an important role in the Hellenistic world as leaders of a proud Greek "polis", subject to Syria. Now their dream was fulfilled, but in a very different fashion. Judea took its part in the international life of the time as an independent state — not a polis. Jonathan was a high official of the Seleucid empire — strategos and meridarches (military and civil governor) of Judea.

He was also the religious leader and in 152, after the office had lapsed for seven years, Jonathan as High Priest officiated in the Temple of Jerusalem for the sacrificial rites of the Feast of Tabernacles. Thereafter, he ruled Judea as a friendly vassal of Syria without interference and, three years later, Demetrius was finally beaten by Alexander Balas.

The hellenistic Jews were now completely silenced. For the first time since the days of the Israelite kings, a Jewish ruler in Palestine, with an army of his own, played a dominant role in the power politics of both Palestine and the Seleucid empire. The Hasmoneans had become Near Eastern rulers, whose friendship was sought by rival Seleucid monarchs and who became involved in the quarrels between them.

As Alexander's ally, Jonathan drove the Syrian garrison from Joppa (near present-day Tel Aviv) and defeated the Syrian army near Azotus (Ashdod). He burned the Temple of Dagon there and destroyed the last Syrian stronghold in the southern plain. As a reward for this support, Alexander Balas awarded Jonathan Ekron and its surrounding district. Thus by diplomacy and force the Hasmoneans had completed the first stage in their territorial expansion.

Some eight years later, Alexander Balas was murdered and his place taken by his rival's son, Demetrius II. He was only able to maintain himself in Antioch with the support of Jonathan as a loyal vassal. He confirmed his father's promises to the Hasmoneans and added three districts of Samaria to Jonathan's domain, at the same time exempting it from taxation.

General dissatisfaction within the empire culminated in a mob assault on the royal palace in Antioch. In reprisal, the king's mercenaries set fire to the city and, in the resulting panic, started a general massacre. Demetrius himself was saved from death at the hands of the crowd by the Jewish contingent of 3,000 men which Jonathan had sent to the king's aid, and put down the uprising. As further evidence of the increasing weakness of the Seleucids, Jonathan even obtained a promise of permission to take over the Akra, the last Greek garrison and stronghold in Jerusalem.

This promise was not kept. A climax in the Seleucid dynastic conflict was approaching. In the same year as the revolt in Antioch, a movement to make the infant son of Alexander Balas king was begun by a general, Tryphon (Diodotus). Jonathan transferred his allegiance to him, or at least managed to play one party off against the other.

To gain support, Tryphon had made overtures to Simon, Jonathan's brother and commander-in-chief, promising him the position of "strategos" (governor) of the whole coastline of Western Palestine, "from the ladder of Tyre unto the borders of Egypt", with Ptolemais (Acre) as his base. In this early period of Hasmonean rule, the Jewish military leaders appear in the position of high royal officials of the Seleucid state. This however, was a valuable step forward on their path to political independence.

In fact the Hasmonean revolt had produced important changes in the administration of the southern part of the Seleucid empire. The administrative division of "Coele-Syria and Phoenicia" had been abolished after Bacchides' governorship and officials were appointed over each of its various provinces. Two of these, the coastline and Judea, were put under the Hasmonean princes.

Towards Independence

The Jewish star continued to rise. In fighting against the local Syrian forces, Simon captured Beth-Zur, south of Jerusalem and then won further victories on the southern coast at Jaffa and Ascalon. The Hasmonean brothers made full use of these opportunities to consolidate their position, establishing Jewish garrisons in all the places thus won from Demetrius. At the same time Jonathan blockaded the Syrian garrison in the Akra by building a high wall around it. The Syrians, divided amongst themselves, could not face the Jews in a pitched battle.

Military success was again followed by international diplomacy. The Hasmoneans renewed the alliance with Rome, the new mistress of the world, and also sent an embassy to Sparta. In replying to Jonathan's letter to the Spartans, their king, following the custom of the time, claimed descent from Abraham just like the Jews:

> "It has been found in a writing concerning the Spartans and Jews, that they are kinsmen, and that they are descended from Abraham. Now since we have learned this, please write us about your welfare. We for our part write you that your cattle and property are ours and ours are yours. So we command them to report to you to this effect." (1 Mac. 12: 21–23)

However, instead of pleasing his ally, Jonathan's success aroused Tryphon's misgivings. In this alliance against Demetrius, each partner was seeking his own advantage. Having, as he thought, exhausted Jonathan's usefulness, Tryphon decided to get rid of his too-powerful general and ally. He invited Jonathan to occupy Acre (Ptolemais). As soon as he entered the city, its gates were closed, he was made a prisoner and his followers murdered.

Jonathan's vacant place at the head of affairs was immediately taken by his brother, Simon, who, realizing that Tryphon would fight to the end, strengthened the fortifications of Jerusalem and took possession of Joppa on the coast, driving away its inhabitants, settling it with Jews and securing it as a Jewish harbour. The Jews had returned to the shores of the Eastern Mediterranean. A new policy of expansion was adopted, and Jewish settlements were pushed out beyond the boundaries of Judea.

Tryphon tried to invade Judea, bringing Jonathan with him as a prisoner. The royal Treasury was short of money and a substantial ransom would be welcome. Thus, without a battle, he extorted a handsome sum of blood money from Simon. But Jonathan was not released and preparations for an attack on Judea were continued. Advancing to Jerusalem from Joppa, Tryphon found his way blocked by Simon at Hadid and tried to approach Jerusalem from Edom, to the south. His advance was prevented by a heavy snowstorm and, deciding against a frontal attack, he circled Jerusalem and returned to Syria through Gilead, in Transjordan, murdering Jonathan on the way (142 B.C.E). Then Tryphon had the boy-king Antiochus VI assassinated and crowned himself king.

Rock tombs at Modiin, near Lod, where the Maccabeans were buried. The tombs were hewn in the rock and covered with the heavy stones visible in the picture (right). The tomb chambers, (H), which were either single or connected from one to another (F, D) were often shaped as shown in the figure on the left. Burial niches were cut out of the sides of the chambers.

"And Trypho got all his cavalry ready to go, but that night there was a very heavy snow, and he could not go because of the snow, so he set forth and went into Gilead. And when he approached Bascama, he killed Jonathan, and he was buried there. And Trypho went back to his own country again". (1 Mac. 13: 22–24)

Simon buried his brother in the family burial-grounds at Modiin and built a monument over his sepulchre. Had it it not been for his treacherous murder, Jonathan would probably have added the final overthrow of the Seleucid domination to his existing achievements of religious freedom and extended territory for his people and the ascendancy of his party.

THE RULE OF SIMON

Simon turned to Tryphon's rival, Demetrius II. He approved Simon's accession as High Priest and exempted Judea from taxes, thereby acknowledging Judea's future independence from Syria:

"King Demetrius sends greeting to Simon, the high priest and the Friend of kings, and to the Jewish elders and nation. The gold crown and the palm branch which you sent we have received, and we are ready to make a lasting peace with you, and to write to our officials to grant you the immunities you ask. The things we have guaranteed to you stand assured, and the strongholds which you have built shall be yours. Any oversights and deficiencies up to this time we forgive, as well as the crown tax that you owe, and if any other tax was collected in Jerusalem, it shall no longer be collected." (1 Mac. 13: 36–39)

The payment of tribute was always regarded as a sign of subjection. Only if a city were exempt from dues did she regard herself as "free".

"It was in the one hundred and seventieth year that the yoke of the heathen was lifted from Israel. And the people began to write in their contracts and agreements, 'In the first year of Simon, the great high priest and governor and commander of the Jews.' "(1 Mac. 13: 41–42)

Simon continued the fortifications which Jonathan had begun and added further military successes. He conquered Gezer (Gazara) after a desperate resistance and made his son, John Hyrcanus, its governor. The Syrian population was deported and Jews were settled in this strategic stronghold which guarded the western approaches to Judea and commanded the sea route along the coast from Joppa to Egypt.

THE AKRA LIQUIDATED

The following year (May 141) he finally forced the capitulation of the Akra of Jerusalem, which a Syrian garrison had held without a break, since the days of Antiochus Epiphanes. The hellenizers had used the Akra to dominate Jerusalem with foreign help. Its loss meant the end of their party. Political independence for Judea was practically complete. The victory was celebrated every year for two or three centuries.

Simon's rule was now confirmed by the people and a legal framework provided for Judea's new political situation. "Priests and people and leaders of the nation and elders of the country" gathered in the third year of Simon's rule (140 B.C.E) and proclaimed him High Priest and military and civil governor of the Jews, declaring the office hereditary.

Baths in the Maccabean castle of Gezer.

Entrance to Maccabean palace at Gezer.

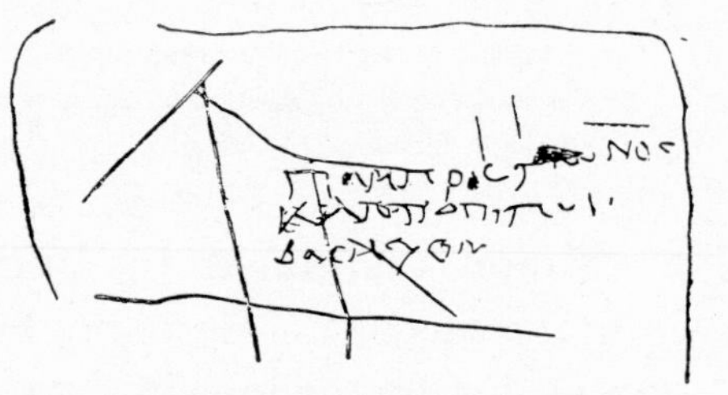

A graffito found in the excavation of the governor's palace at Gezer, formerly occupied by non-Jews, offers a sidelight on the Hasmonean annexation of the town. One of the forced workers, perhaps a dispossessed hellenized native, scratched on a stone he placed in the wall, in careless Greek, the curse: "May fire consume Simon's palace, says Pampras."

"In his days matters prospered in his hands so that the heathen were driven out of their country, as well as those in the City of David, in Jerusalem, who had built themselves a citadel, from which they would go out and pollute the surroundings of the sanctuary, and did great damage to its purity. He settled Jews in it and fortified it to make the land and the city safe, and he made the walls of Jerusalem high. In view of these things, King Demetrius confirmed him in the high priesthood, and made him one of his Friends, and treated him with great honor. For he had heard that the Jews had been addressed by the Romans as friends and allies and kinsmen, and that they had received Simon's envoys with great honor. And the Jews and their priests resolved that Simon should be their leader and high priest forever until a true prophet should appear, and that he should be their general, to appoint them to their duties, and to set them over the country and over the arms and over the fortifications; and that he should take care of the sanctuary, and that all should obey him, and that all contracts in the country should be dated in his reign and that he should be clothed in purple and wear gold." (1 Mac. 14: 36–43)

The powers of the new dynasty came much closer to those of a king than had the Oniad High-Priesthood. Though the Syrian government was still recognized as the central authority, Simon had the position of an independent prince, able to make his own decisions, to build up his state on a firm foundation and to bequeath his authority to his son, on a hereditary basis.

The delegation sent to Rome two years before, now returned with an order from the Senate to the kings of Egypt, Syria, the kingdom of Cappadocia in Asia Minor and several of the Mediterranean islands and independent "poleis" to keep their hands off the land of the Jews and to make extradition agreements with it for the return of fugitives wanted by the Jewish state for enemy acts against it.

Simon's reign lasted for five more years of peace and tranquility. During this time an independent Hasmonean policy began to take shape. Broadly nationalistic, it went further than mere religious fanaticism and had its roots in Jewish history. Opposition to Syrian domination had developed since the first passions of religious zeal and hatred of all things Greek. Now, the Hasmoneans could act in the light of political realities. Those realities had once again to include political developments in Syria.

Demetrius II was overthrown and imprisoned by Mithradates, king of the Parthians, a former vassal. The Parthians had been in revolt against the Seleucids since the middle of the 3rd century. As a result of Demetrius' overthrow, Antiochus Sidetes VII succeeded. He was determined to reestablish the Seleucid state and defeat the pretender, Tryphon. At first, he confirmed the Hasmoneans' privileges — including the right of coining their own money, but he resented Simon's expansion beyond his former frontiers, and the loss of income from the towns that had previously paid him tribute. He sent word to Simon, saying:

"You are holding Joppa and Gazara, and the citadel in Jerusalem, cities of my kingdom. You have laid waste their territories and done great injury to the country, and you have taken possession of many places in my kingdom. So now give up the towns that you have seized, and the tribute of the places you have taken possession of outside the borders of Judea, or else give me five hundred talents of silver for them, and five hundred talents of silver more, for the damage you have done and for the tribute of the towns; or else we will come and make war on you." (1 Mac. 15: 28–31)

In his reply, Simon declared his policy of reuniting the whole of Palestine as in the days of David and the kings of Israel and Judah:

"And Simon said to him in reply,
We have neither taken other men's land, nor are we in possession of other men's property, but of the inheritance of our forefathers; it was wrongfully held by our enemies at one time, but we, grasping our opportunity, hold firmly the inheritance of our forefathers. But as for Joppa and Gazara, which you demand, while they have done great damage to our people and in our country, we will give a hundred talents for them." (1 Mac. 15: 33–35)

The Syrian reacted to this by sending an army into Palestine. This was defeated by Simon's two sons, Judah and John Hyrcanus. Before Antiochus could take up the campaign in person, Simon, already an old man, was murdered at Dokh near Jericho by Ptolemy son of Abubos and commanding officer of Jericho, a Judaized Idumean who had married into the high priestly family.

John Hyrcanus was at Gezer and there he was warned of the plot against all his family. When assassins came for him, he was ready for them, and killed them instead. Then he rushed to Jerusalem, got there before the conspirators and was crowned High Priest and civil ruler.

The site of the fortress of Dokh, on top of a mountain near Jericho, where Simon was murdered. Half-way up the steep rock wall nestles a monastery which commemorates the forty day stay of Jesus in the wilderness.

JOHN HYRCANUS

Hyrcanus now faced Antiochus Sidetes who invaded Judea and besieged Jerusalem. In the Sabbatical year, food was so short that Hyrcanus sent away all those who could not carry arms. The enemy closed their lines to them and they died of hunger. In the end, Hyrcanus had to surrender. The population was disarmed, the fortifications dismantled. He had to agree to pay rent for Joppa and Gezer which his father had taken over, plus a heavy indemnity of 500 talents. He gave Antiochus a number of hostages and also agreed to make him a regular yearly payment. Nevertheless, Antiochus recognized his status as independent prince and High Priest. No longer were the Jewish leaders Syrian officials. Although subject to Syria in a sense, the Jews were recognized as a considerable military power within the Seleucid state. They were even called upon to take part in the Seleucid campaign against Mithradates the Parthian in 129 B.C.E.

Antiochus died in battle later the same year and Judea's dependence upon Syria finally came to an end. The Seleucid state had become a battlefield for warring rival princes and its rapid decline soon made it an easy prey for Rome. Meanwhile, John Hyrcanus ruled Judea with an assembly made up of lay and priestly members who legislated for the whole country.

COLLAPSE OF THE SELEUCID EMPIRE

In fact, an independent Judea was only one example of a general nationalist movement throughout the semitic kingdoms which were breaking away from the Seleucid yoke. As the empire dissolved into a number of small independent principalities, so the Seleucid era was dissipated in numerous petty local dynasties, mainly in the cities of the Phoenician-Palestinian area. Among these were the Ituraeans of the Lebanon, the Ammonites of Transjordan and, in particular, the Arabian Nabateans who, settling in the Negeb, southern Transjordan and Edom, controlled the trade routes from Southern Arabia to Egypt.

All these were ambitious principalities, hungry for adjoining territory. Each of them had a common frontier with Judea and here they met and clashed with the Hasmonean expansionist aims. Henceforth, their histories would intermingle.

Moreover, in the Hasmoneans, the Jewish people had leaders of a broad, worldly outlook who were determined to reap all the advantage they could from the political currents of a rapidly changing world. After the original crisis of the Maccabean revolt, it is they who carved Jewish history and ensured Jewish independence for the next sixty-five years, or until the intervention of the Romans.

This drive to consolidate and expand began with a series of campaigns under John Hyrcanus through Eastern, Northern and Southern Palestine wherever ancient Jewish settlements had come under foreign domination. Among these were the Jewish towns of Transjordan, north and south of Philadelphia (Amman). He captured Madeba and Samaga in Moab, then turned north and conquered Shechem, the principal town of Samaria and destroyed the Samaritan temple on Mount Gerizim.

Then Hyrcanus turned south and attacked the Idumeans of Southern Palestine and the Negeb, from whom there was a danger of raids. He overran the hellenistic towns of Maresha and Adora, and compelled the Idumeans to adopt the Jewish religion and become circumcized. Although there was some opposition at first, it appears that the Idumeans became completely assimilated into the Jewish state within one or two generations. In fact, the last Jewish rulers of Palestine in the days of the Romans were Judaized Idumeans (the Herodians).

THE HASMONEAN STATE AND THE HELLENISTIC WORLD

International status encouraged the Hasmoneans to adopt all the ceremony and magnificence of civil rulers. They appeared before their subjects crowned with Hellenistic splendour, in the same way as their neighbouring monarchs who were setting up their kingdoms in the ruins of the Seleucid empire. In fact, they were secular rulers, with courts whose standards were no higher than those of Antioch or the other capitals of Asia Minor. The Hasmoneans behaved as did the other princes — they feasted, drank, took mistresses and persecuted relatives whom they suspected on political or personal grounds. Prolonged wars necessitated the employment of mercenary troops from Cilicia and Pisidia in Asia Minor and this development created a highly professional standard in the expanding Jewish army. This became a permanent body, drawing pay direct from the ruler and thus acting as his own personal force. This made them at times more dependable than the Jewish people at large, for they were not always willing to accept the increasingly autocratic rule of their new princes.

Having taken over the non-Jewish Semitic settlements and towns, towards the end of his reign, John Hyrcanus set out to complete the conquest of the remaining Greek "poleis" in Western Palestine. These were the prosperous Macedonian colonies of Samaria and Scythopolis (Beth-shean) which still received frequent aid from the kings of Syria.

The siege of Samaria lasted a whole year and was carried out by Hyrcanus' two sons, Antigonus and Aristobulos, who managed to beat off repeated attempts at relief made by king Antiochus Cyzicenus, the ruler of southern Syria. He then appealed for help to Ptolemy Lathyros, eldest and rebellious son of Cleopatra III (who ruled some 50 years before her famous namesake). She maintained good relations with the sons of John Hyrcanus and sent a mercenary army to help them. But it deserted her and went over to Lathyros. What is notable about this about-turn, which was by no means abnormal in itself, is that the expedition included Jewish troops from Egypt and they remained loyal to Cleopatra. The queen had other Jewish commanders in her army, Helkias and Hananiah. The latter, incidentally, was related to the family of Onias, the fourth son of the high priest who had fled from Palestine during the persecutions of Antiochus IV and had settled in the "territory of Onias" in eastern Egypt. He built a Jewish Temple in Leontopolis, situated in the district which had once been known to Moses as the Land of Goshen. A Jewish military colony is known to have lived there for many years.

Once Samaria had fallen, Scythopolis also capitulated, and thus the last foreign-occupied district separating Judean territory from the Jewish towns in Galilee was reintegrated into the Jewish state. The Judaization of the Syrian population was continued as part of a whole political programme. The Hasmonean princes were determined to end the rivalry between the powers in Palestine and to encourage Jewish economic development. If the process was accompanied by brutalities this was an inevitable feature of the wars of the period. The population of the conquered "poleis" were offered the choice between Judaizing or death. Until recent years historians pointed out that even though it was carried out in the name of the one true God, Hasmonean imperialism had its seamy side and that their brutality and oppression were no great improvement on Seleucid brutality and oppression. The Hasmoneans imposed Judaism on the population with the same vigour and ruthlessness with which Antiochus had tried to impose his faith. If, on the whole, the results were less disastrous this was only because the Jewish monarchs were not as powerful and did not operate over so large a territory.

THE HASMONEAN PRINCES' CLASH WITH THE PHARISEES

Modern historians in Israel, however, have moved in a different direction to defend the realism of the Hasmonean leadership. They agree that no one in the ancient world was kind and gentle to opponents. The Jews had to meet the enmity of the hellenists among whom they lived with an equal fierceness and to use against them whatever weapons came to hand. It may be possible to sympathize with the Maccabees and their regal descendants in their desire to make Judea a more successful version of contemporary Near Eastern kingdoms. This overall policy entailed a departure from the traditional policy of priesthood and monarchy as explained (cf. p. 14 ff). It is not likely that the scattered Jews of Palestine would have been knit together into nationhood according to the ideals of the Hassidim, had the Maccabeans not assumed aggressive leadership. The people who followed them both were enabled to deal with most of the dangers that faced them from the enmity of their hellenist neighbours and the designs of the Seleucid monarchs. As the revitalized little nation re-

Coin of John Hyrcanus (135–104 *B.C.E.*).
Left: a wreath of laurel around the inscription: "Jehochanan the High Priest". The obverse (right) records: "The Community of the Jews", with double horns of plenty (cornucopia).

appeared on the historical scene, a new Hebrew renaissance was in progress, (to be described in Ch. VII). It was influenced by Greek culture, but although hellenism continued in Palestine, it had lost all political strength.

The assumption of the prerogatives of priesthood and monarchy on the part of the Hasmoneans must have aroused differences of opinion among the Pharisees as to policy and practice. This became abundantly clear in later years. The pious Hassidim who had made a major contribution towards gaining independence for their country, found their attitude towards the Hasmoneans changing. It is difficult to determine the grounds that slowly led them into this new position, or to define the date at which it became articulate. Their very respect for tradition must have made it difficult for them to accept Hasmonean High Priests. The family, although a priestly one, was not of the line of Zadok. Some scholars think that the breach occurred with the elevation of Jonathan to the High Priesthood and suggest that it was disagreements about who should fill the post that had caused the office to lapse for seven years. Moreover, when Simon became hereditary High Priest, he and his supporters regarded this as a legitimate priestly line, permanently displacing the "House of Zadok". It may be argued that if the hellenizers were worsted in the overall national struggle, in which the central role of the Hasmoneans is unquestioned, the ideals of the Hassidim did not altogether prevail either!

Judging from the evidence of the coins which were minted under John Hyrcanus, public affairs were managed by two institutions: the High Priests and the Great Assembly of the Jews (Cheber-hayehudim). Hyrcanus was not an absolute ruler. He had to respect the constitutional privileges and liberties which, by ancient tradition, belonged to the "rulers of the people and the elders of the land". These elders were, apparently, the Pharisees (Perushim) who, during the reigns of Hyrcanus and, possibly, of Jonathan, became an important sect or political party.

Our knowledge of them comes mainly from sources dealing with the political and religious developments of later days, (Josephus, the Mishnah, Talmud and the Gospels). Each of them described the Pharisees from their own particular point of view so that an objective assessment of them is not easy to make (see Ch. VII, II). Theologically, the sect's growth is bound up with the development of the Mosaic Oral (unwritten) Law from the days of Ezra to the end of the Second Commonwealth. The Pharisees were interpreters of the Mosaic Law and were responsible for the enactment of the laws which governed every aspect of life in the Jewish theocratic state.

At the beginning of his reign, Hyrcanus had good relations with the Pharisees but, from sources concerned specifically with the history of the party during the Hasmonean era, it appears that an opposition trend developed which caused a break between Hyrcanus and his former supporters. This is illustrated by an anecdote found both in Josephus and the Talmud:

"And when he once invited them to a feast and entertained them very kindly, when he saw them in a good humour, he began to say to them, that they knew he was desirous to be a righteous man, and to do all things whereby he might please God which was the profession of the Pharisees also. However, he desired, that if they observed him offending in any point, and going out of the right way, they would call him back and correct him. On which occasion they attested to his being entirely virtuous; with which commendation he was well pleased; but still there was one of his guests there, whose name was Eleazar, a man of an ill temper, and delighting in seditious practices. This man said, 'Since thou desirest to know the truth, if thou wilt be righteous in earnest, lay down the high-priesthood, and content thyself with the civil government of the people.'' (Josephus, Antiquities, Bk. XIII, Ch. 10: 5)

The Talmudic tale, (attributed to the time of Jannai Alexander) also tells of a banquet given by the prince, at which an old man, Judah ben Yedidyah, said to the king Jannai: "Thou hast enough with the royal crown, leave the crown of priesthood to the seed of Aaron" (i.e. the traditional priestly line). (Kidd. 66a).

This implies that Pharisees regarded the Hasmoneans as usurpers who could not qualify for either the High Priesthood or the crown for they lacked the proper genealogy. The Pharisees were willing to allow them to exercise civil authority on an interim basis but only until the historic theocratic pattern could be reestablished with a priest of the Zadokite line and a king of the house of David.

In the opinion of V. Tcherikover, this was no chance quarrel, but a continuation of an ancient feud between the priests and the scribes which reflected the social setting. In earlier times, the scribes had been the backbone of the Hassidim during their struggle against the Hellenizers. The Hellenizers had the backing of the aristocratic priests, whereas the mass of the people of the poorer classes had supported the Hassidim.

In taking as its slogan "leave the priestly diadem to the seed of Aaron", the extreme wing of the Pharisees did not attack Hyrcanus' secular powers. His victories had made him very popular with the common people, as well as with the aristocracy and influential circles. The Pharisees may have reasoned, however, that if the office of high priest could be separated from the secular authority, they would be able to take over the key positions of the Temple with its treasures and revenues and great authority over the people.

Because of this insistence on a separation between the powers of the secular ruler and the high priest, Hyrcanus turned against the Pharisees. He abolished legislation which they had handed down to the people and went over to the Sadducees.

The Hasmonean conquests benefitted the influential classes — the landowners, money-lenders and merchants, for trade between the Jews, their neighbours and the Greek world expanded. However, a policy of territorial expansion, with its accompanying higher taxation brought little comfort to the common people. The gulf between the wealthy and the humble was no narrower than in the days of Ben Sira (see Ch. III).

The influential conservative wing of the Pharisees also maintained that kingship in Israel — the wearing of the "diadem" — was the preserve of the Davidic line and they continued to regard the Hasmoneans as usurpers. To combat the threatened encroachment on their powers, the Hasmoneans again sought the support of those closest to them, the aristocratic priests and wealthy men represented by the Sadducees. Once victory had been won by the Hasmoneans, this class had abandoned their support for hellenizing policies and the hellenistic way of life, now out of tune with the resurgent nationalism of the Jewish

Coin of Alexander Jannai. Left: the solar disc with eight rays and an inscription "Jehonathan the King". Obverse, right: a ship's anchor, possibly an allusion to his sea-power, with his name inscribed around it.

people of Palestine. With the breach with the Pharisees, the Hasmoneans turned to them again.

As relations worsened with the Pharisees, their supporters clashed with Hasmonean adherents and there were riots. However, Hyrcanus quelled these and was able to spend his last years in peace.

THE HASMONEAN KINGDOM

ARISTOBULOS

Before his death in 104 B.C.E., John Hyrcanus appears to have reached some understanding with the extreme Pharisees, for in his will, he provided for the separation of the High Priesthood from the civil administration. He made his wife responsible for secular affairs, while the High-Priesthood was vested in his eldest son, Judah Aristobulos. According to Josephus, he was not content with this. He assumed royal pomp and authority and called himself king, although this title does not appear on the coins attributed to his time, which state only "Judah, High Priest and Community of Jews." Against the evidence of Josephus, Strabo maintains that it was Judah's successor, Jannai (Jannaeus) Alexander, who was the first Hasmonean to add "king" to his traditional title of High Priest. It is possible that to avoid hurting sensitive Jewish feelings Aristobulos may have used the term only in his contacts with the outer world, in the course of negotiations with the Greeks. Aristobulos ruled for one year, but he is remembered for his ruthlessness and his conquests. He had his mother thrown into prison, where she was starved to death. He also imprisoned his brothers with only one exception — Antigonus — and even he was murdered when Aristobulos became suspicious of him.

Aristobulos conquered the land of the Itureans in Coele-Syria and forced its inhabitants to accept Judaism, although it is doubtful whether they remained Jews. They were never heard of again as such. However, their land was an important element in the territory of the expanding Jewish Commonwealth and even Galilee became a part of the Hasmonean realm.

Having secured control of the Palestine sea-coast, Jannai Alexander encouraged an active trade with the eastern Mediterranean. This second-century B.C.E. mosaic from the "Street of the Corporations" in Ostia, Rome's main seaport, shows a sailing boat and a symbolic dolphin.

When Aristobulos died in 103, he was succeeded by Jannai, graecized as Jannaeus Alexander. The Hasmoneans all had a Greek name as well as their Jewish one, such as Aristobulos, Alexander. These names have been the ones by which they are remembered, even among the Jewish people themselves.

Jannai followed the custom of levirate marriage and took Aristobulos' widow, Shlomzion (Alexandra), as his wife, even though she was his senior by many years. He was crowned High Priest and King and his long reign of twenty-seven years (103–76 B.C.E.) proved him to be one of the most successful kingdom builders of the Second Commonweahlt. However, he has been much maligned on the evidence of Josephus, whose source for his record of the times was a Greek historian, by no means friendly towards the king who was mainly responsible for the liquidation of the independent Greek cities of Palestine and the Judaization of their inhabitants. The Hasmonean princes had reached a position, in relation to the hellenistic world about them, where they felt free to attack and absorb the enemy *poleis* and lands piecemeal. Jannai must have based his tactics on the assumption that the Greek kings of Antioch and Damascus, paralyzed by fratricidal struggles, were powerless to help the hellenistic cities on either side of the Jordan.

Although organized into a confederation of ten cities, known as the Decapolis, and well-equipped and armed behind their walls, with mercenary Greek troops in their garrisons, the cities were isolated enclaves. They were surrounded by aggressive Jewish neighbours, led by a brilliant strategist. Their position was in many ways similar to that of the Canaanite city-kings whom David had absorbed into his growing kingdom a thousand years before. Using Roman-style tactics, Jannai hoped to overcome them by a series of long sieges.

However, this master plan was frustrated right at the outset by the complex situation which resulted from the struggle for power in Egypt between Cleopatra III and her son Lathyros. Mother and son had begun as co-rulers of Egypt and Cyprus but a deadly enmity developed between them and Lathyros was deposed. He established himself in Cyprus as a strong military power, in contrast to the stagnating Ptolemies and Seleucids of Egypt and Syria.

At the beginning of his reign, Jannai judged himself strong enough to take over large sections of the coastal districts of Western Samaria in addition to Galilee and Northern Transjordan. He occupied Appolonia and other coastal towns north of the Philistine plain and, in order to gain control of Palestine's commerce with the Eastern Mediterranean, he attacked Ascalon. Joppa (Jaffa) had already been acquired by his predecessors. In 102 he laid siege to Ptolemais-Acre, the most important hellenistic port of Palestine. Its inhabitants fought back with the help of the Phoenician towns and of the people of Gaza, but were defeated. Then they turned for help to Ptolemy Lathyros of Cyprus, who came with a powerful fleet and forced Jannai to lift his siege of Acre and make peace with Lathyros. The latter allowed him to occupy the ports of Dor and Straton's Tower (the future Caesarea).

Jannai's diplomacy did not depend on unilateral alliances. He also established close relations with Cleopatra III. Her army had two Jewish commanders, Hananiah and Helkias, who were highly esteemed and influential (see above: John Hyrcanus).

Lathyros hoped to use Palestine as a stepping-stone to the conquest of Egypt. He went to the help of his ally, Theodorus, tyrant of Philadelphia (Rabbath-Ammon) in Transjordan, defeated Jannai Alexander, and then advanced through Palestine towards the Egyptian border. For a time he seems to have swept aside every obstacle in his path. However, at Rhinocolura (El Arish on the coast of Sinai), Cleopatra rallied her forces and defeated him, forcing him to retire among his partisans in Gaza. Some of her Greek advisers counselled the queen-mother not to be impressed by Jannai Alexander, but to overrun Palestine and annex it, restoring it to its ancient status as a colonial possession of the Ptolemies. At this, Hananiah, knowing that he would be backed by the very numerous Jews of Egypt and the army, demurred:

> "'for (said he) I would not have thee ignorant of this, that what injustice thou dost to him will make all us that are Jews to be thy enemies.' This desire of Ananias (Hananiah), Cleopatra complied with; and did no injury to Alexander, but made a league of mutual assistance with him at Scythopolis (Bethshean), a city of Celesyria." (Antiq., Book XIII, 13:2)

This information also indicates the close ties between the Jews of Palestine and those of the Egyptian Dispersion. They regarded the new Hasmonean kingdom as an established fact and exerted their influence against any attempt to turn back the tide of history. Moreover, no other power in the Near East was in a position to subdue and control this kingdom. Cleopatra gave up her imperial plan.

With Lathyros out of the way, Jannai set out on his cycle of conquests of the Greek "poleis". In 100 B.C.E. he conquered the towns of Gadara and Hamath close to the Lake of Galilee and turned north to take Antiochia (Dan) at the source of the Jordan. He then subdued the wide stretch of land from North to South in Transjordan, including the towns of Gerasa, Pella, Dion and Gamala. Any town that refused to Judaize was destroyed. Eleven towns surrendered and were incorporated in the Hasmonean kingdom.

JUDAIZATION, A POLITICAL NECESSITY

The ruthless treatment meted out to the Hellenistic towns was the climax to the long standing hostility between the Jews and their Syrian enemies. To Judaize the towns' inhabitants at the moment of defeat was part of a political programme rather than a proselytizing religious movement. The defeated towns lost their civic autonomy and if they refused to accept Judaism and allegiance to the Hasmonean state, they were regarded as enemies, doomed to the sword. It was remembered against them that these once independent cities, helped by the Seleucids, had been prepared to suppress the national movement in Judea even before it had begun to gain its religious and political autonomy. The Jews were now the stronger side. They had to dominate the situation or submit to alien rule. They were no more humanitarian than their neighbours who put up a desperate fight to maintain the status quo. Jannai was a fanatical Jew, an oriental and a Sadducee. He had no mercy on the hellenists. Naturally, his harsh treatment of the Greek "poleis" was denounced in the writings of ancient Greek historians. In view of the admiration in which Greek culture is held, their protest found echoes even in recent historical writings. However, an objective historical evaluation must take into consideration both the destructive acts of the Hasmoneans — dictated by necessity — and their undoubted constructive achievements, such as those of Jannai.

CONQUESTS

The first stage of his conquests in the north of Palestine left the eastern and southern borders of Transjordan in the hands of Theodorus, tyrant of Philadelphia and in those of the Nabateans, the Arab power that emerged then as the southern neighbour of Judea, east of the Dead Sea, and in the Negeb. They controlled the rich trade of the caravan routes between Arabia, Syria and Egypt. In fact, the disintegration of the Seleucid power as a result of the fratricidal wars that followed the death of Antiochus VII Sidetes (129 B.C.E.), favoured the rise of the Nabateans just as much as the Hasmoneans. Inevitably, the two nations clashed. Part of the coastal plain remained in the hands of Phoenician and hellenistic cities, like Ascalon, Gaza, Acre, although other ports were incorporated into the Hasmonean kingdom.

Ascalon. Mole and ruins of the ancient port.

Ascalon and other southern coastal towns were pagan cities which continued to practise fertility cults, especially the cult of the goddess Ashtoreth, who became Aphrodite in hellenistic times. This carving of three women probably represents priestesses, called "Kedeshot", or temple prostitutes.

Some time after his defeat by Lathyros in the Jordan Valley, Jannai erected the fort of Alexandrium to guard the central fords of the river and his lines of communication. Later, he erected the fortress of Machaerus on the heights of Moab to protect his conquests on the east of the Dead Sea and keep the Nabateans from the Jewish settlements in southern Transjordan. Both Alexandrium and Machaerus were built on the top of mountains protected by steep earth dykes from the danger of the heavy battering rams which were used in hellenistic times. The Eastern Negeb and Judea near the Dead Sea were protected by another inaccessible stronghold, Masada.

Ambitious to see his country's trade as well as its borders expand, Jannai set out to take over the southern coast. He occupied Raffiah, and Antedon, then turned to Gaza, which was the second most important port on the coast of Palestine and the terminus of the Nabatean caravan route from inland. He laid siege to it for a year, then conquered and utterly destroyed it. It is not certain whether Ascalon, Gaza's trade rival, was occupied by Jannai. The people of Ascalon may well have welcomed the Jews, for they had helped them in the past and they were loyal to Cleopatra, the ally of Jannai. Whether or not he conquered the city, Ascalon later appears as a confederate of Jannai.

Jannai's Character

The life of a bellicose priest-king, who spent much of his life campaigning, had, of course, its Rabelaisian side. Jannai was lusty and direct and, despite his rigid Sadducean philosophy, no better than the people of his generation. As his power increased, the life of his court grew far away from the austerity and stateliness befitting a High Priest, although, of course, the High Priests were also secular rulers. Jannai's Court was modelled on those of the hellenistic monarchies of Antioch or the rich kings of Asia Minor.

The Hasmonean rule easily assimilated the three elements of Jewish life: The traditional theocracy, the people, and the national religion. Moreover, according to priestly tradition, Jannai's person was sacred. He had to avoid any possibility of profanation through impure contact. For instance, when he proceeded from his new palace in Jerusalem, built across

Pavement and drainage ditch uncovered in excavating the Tyropeon vale which separated the Temple mount, right, from the upper town, left. That the Tyropeon depression was once much deeper than it is today can be seen from the height of the debris which later accumulated above the level of the pavement. Stone bridges to connect the Temple area to the upper town were built across the vale. It now forms one of the few underground sites to be excavated – in a city filled with history.

the Tyropeon vale, to the Temple, he crossed a stone bridge built specially for the occasion. Remains of this bridge were found in the excavated Wilson Arch under the debris that had since filled the Tyropeon depression.

THE SADDUCEE KING AND THE PHARISEES

Jannai was a Sadducee. He accepted the ancient traditions without question and revered everything in Jewish ritual connected with them. He had many Sadducee partisans and presided over the "house of judgment" (beth-din in Hebrew; later it became the Sanhedrin) where the Sadducees were in control. Though he was a great builder, he made no attempts to modernize or beautify the modest Temple for, according to Sadducean doctrine, this would have been sacrilege. The task was left for Herod. The "halakhoth" (legal precepts) of the Pharisees, on the other hand, aimed at making observance of the Torah easier for the common man. The first Hasmonean rulers of the generation that preceded Jannai's had seen the emergence of these two leading parties. The Pharisees, as we have seen, had developed from the early Hassidim who had at first supported the Maccabean brothers in their struggle against the Hellenizers and the Syrians. The Sadducees may date back to the Zadokites, from whose ranks the High Priest had traditionally been drawn. When Jonathan, the Hasmonean, first assumed the office of High Priest, the Sadducees joined in the opposition against him, in the hope of regaining their ancient position (see p. 161).

Civil War and the Massacre at the Temple

Though in his early years Jannai had enjoyed the esteem of the Pharisees because of his tremendous influence over the people, as time went on he met with a growing opposition and matters finally came to an open break. Once more the Pharisees raised the issue of the separation of priestly and secular power. With Jannai's defeat in Transjordan, the opposition came into violent collision with the priest-king. Jannai had set out to subdue Gilead and Moab, held by Theodorus of Philadelphia, possibly hoping that an important victory would restore his prestige with the people as a whole. When hard pressed, Theodorus called to his help Obedas (Abdath) the Nabatean king:

> "Moreover he demolished Amathus, while Theodorus durst not fight with him; but as he joined battle with Obedas, king of the Arabians, and fell into an ambush in the places that were rugged and difficult to be travelled over, he was thrown into a deep valley, by the multitude of the camels at a village of Gilead, and barely escaped with his life. From thence he fled to Jerusalem, where besides his other ill-success, the nation insulted him." (Josephus, The Jewish War, Ch. 1: 20)

In the course of the campaign, the Nabateans seized twelve towns in Moab country and in the Negeb, edging ever closer to the Hasmonean dominions and increasing their potential threat to Jewish expansion.

The insult to the king was made on the occasion of the Feast of Tabernacles (Succoth), when Jannai officiated as High Priest:

> "As for Alexander, his own people were seditious against him; for at a festival which was then celebrated, when he stood upon the altar and was going to sacrifice, the nation rose upon him and pelted him with ethrogs (citrons) which they then had in their hands. They also reviled him, as derived from a captive, and so unworthy of his dignity and of sacrificing. At this he was in a rage, and slew of them about six thousand." (Antiq. XIII, 13: 5)

Following Sadducee custom, Jannai had poured out the Water-Libation on the ground instead of the altar. Hence the outcry and Jannai's impulsive order to his Pisidian and Cilician mercenaries (who were attached to him personally) to attack the worshippers, which ended in a wholesale massacre.

The Pharisees fomented a revolt and for six years (93–88) civil war raged between their followers and the followers of Jannai. Insurrections by the Samaritans, in central Palestine, added to the troubles of these years which claimed, according to Josephus, (Antiq. XIII, 14, 5), 50,000 victims, although the figure may be exaggerated as are many in these sources. Jannai proposed to come to terms with his people, but the Pharisees were irreconcilable. They wanted his death. This they hoped to secure through the intervention of his foreign enemies and they even went so far as to invite the Syrian king, Demetrius III Eukairos, to invade the land with a large army which was joined by Jewish soldiers opposed to Jannai. This not only converted an internal struggle into a foreign war (88 B.C.E.) but exposed the country to a renewal of Seleucid rule. Jannai met Demetrius at Shechem and was decisively defeated. He took refuge in the mountains of Ephraim with his entire political fortune, apparently, in ruins.

Whether his plight as a fugitive from a foreign foe produced a reaction amongst the soldiers and people who had turned against him and gone over to the enemy, or whether Demetrius was forced to leave Palestine in order to deal with a new danger threatening in Syria, is not known. In any case, he was not able to follow up his victory and in the face of Jannai's new-found support among the people, he retired. Jannai was able, although with difficulty, to recover his position and to stamp out the rebellion. He besieged and slew the rebels, then drove his remaining opponents into exile. Josephus avers that in the process he crucified captives by the hundred, while enjoying the scene in the company of his concubines, but it is believed that Josephus' source was hostile to the Hasmoneans. Though he remained in undisputed possession of his realm, Jannai's victory was to bring him little profit.

An echo of the strange behaviour of one section of the Jews in appealing for aid to a foreigner, and a hellenistic king at that, is believed to have found its way into a commentary on the prophet Nahum, found among the Dead Sea Scrolls. In one passage, the document reads:

> "This is to be interpreted as referring to Demetrius the Greek king who attempted to enter Jerusalem at the advice of those 'who seek flattery' (dorshei halaqoth)."

Modern scholarship is inclined to place this reference in the context of the events of the time. J. M. Allegro assumes that the same document connects Jannai Alexander with the "Wrathful Lion .... who hangs men alive" (a punishment hitherto unknown in Israel) in reference to Jannai's crucifixion of the rebels who sought an alliance with Demetrius. However, one cannot be dogmatic about such identifications, attractive though they may be.

The sources of the religious friction between the Pharisees, the people and the Hasmoneans, are still in dispute. It seems that the people had never abandoned the magic dream of the eternity of the House of David, "the shoot out of the stock of Jesse". In popular belief, a true prophet would one day arise to say "He who is of the descendants of David is worthy to be king over Israel, as was promised by the prophets." But for this belief, the Pharisees might have adopted a different attitude to John Hyrcanus and Jannai Alexander, and the nation would have accepted them whole-heartedly as venerated conquerors, worthy successors to David, endowed with all the lofty virtues which many prophets had ascribed to him.

THE "JANNAI LINE"

It appears that Jannai had not gained control over the whole of northern Transjordan at the end of the civil war and his campaigns in Samaria. Many towns in Transjordan remained independent or were under Nabatean influence. The situation was aggravated by a struggle for power between the new Seleucid king of Damascus, Antiochus XII and the Nabateans (88 B.C.E.). Antiochus had already led a campaign against them, for the Nabateans were greatly concerned with the Damascus area, being anxious to maintain northern outlets to the Mediterranean, now that Jannai had closed their route to the southern ports of Gaza and Ascalon. In his second campaign, Antiochus resolved to attack the Nabateans and to turn their flank around the southern end of the Dead Sea. This meant going through Palestine, along the easily travelled coastal plain. Fearing that the invader would not respect his neutrality but would encroach upon his possessions, Jannai set out to build a long, fortified trench in the Syrians' path, to stop the army and its train of supplies.

> "So Alexander out of fear of his coming, dug a deep ditch, beginning at Chabarzaba, which is now called Antipatris, to the Sea of Joppa, on which part only his army could be brought out against him. He also raised a wall, and erected wooden towers, and intermediate redoubts, for one hundred and fifty furlongs in length, and there expected the coming of Antiochus; but he soon burnt them all, and made his army pass by that way into Arabia." (Antiq. XIV, 15: 1)

The "Jannai Line" of trench, wooden towers, wall and redoubts, ran south of the River Yarkon as far as the foothills near Antipatris (Rosh-Ha'ayin of today) and traces of it have been found within modern Tel Aviv.

THE NABATEANS AND THE JEWISH STATE

Antiochus was given no chance to settle accounts with Jannai. He was killed in battle and, because of their hatred of the hellenist dynasty, the people of Damascus called upon Obedas's successor, Aretas, to rule over them. By then, Jannai must already have lost some of his possessions in Transjordan and Aretas set out from Damascus to overthrow him completely:

> "He also made thence an expedition against Judea, and beat Alexander in battle, near a place called Adida; yet did he upon certain conditions agreed on between them, retire out of Judea." (Antiq. XIV, 15: 2)

This laconic description of Jannai's defeat in the southern plain, east of Lydda, together with the fact that Aretas came to terms with him, seems to reflect the establishment of a balance of power between the rival states. It may suggest that Aretas wanted to reopen the ports of southern Palestine, held by Jannai, to Nabatean traffic and perhaps this was included in the terms of the treaty.

Although Jannai's power was waning, he was still able to recover. Without encountering Nabatean opposition he managed through a brilliant three-year campaign to regain all the territories he had lost east of the Jordan and in Galilee. Towards the end of his reign, in 76 B.C.E., the climax came. His kingdom stretched almost to the borders of the kingdom of David, controlling the whole of Palestine from the eastern desert to the Mediterranean, from the sources of the Jordan in the north to the Egyptian frontier in the south.

SYNOPTIC CHRONOLOGICAL TABLE II.

B.C.E.	*Judea*	*The Seleucid Kings*	*The Ptolemaic Kings*	*Transjordan; Nabateans*
167	Judas the Maccabee. The War of Liberation	Antiochus IV Epiphanes (175—164)	Ptolemy VI (Philometor) (181—145) Beginning of flourishing period of Jewish history in Egypt	
	Alcimus, *usurping High Priest* under Antiochus V and Demetrius, murdered in 159	Antiochus V Eupator (164—162)		
	The High Priesthood remained vacant until 152	Demetrius I (Soter) (162—150)		
152	Jonathan recognized as High Priest by Alexander Balas	Alexander Balas (150—145) Demetrius II (Nicator) (145—138) Antiochus VI (145—142) and Tryphon, the usurper		
142	Simon (High Priest and Ethnarch) recognized by Antiochus VII	Antiochus VII (Sidetes) (138—129)	Ptolemy VIII (Eurgetes, 145—116)	
	An Independent Jewish State			
134—104	John Hyrcanus, Priest and Conquering Prince, "Chief of the Community of Jews"	Antiochus VIII (Grypos) (125—113) The same and Antiochus IX (Kyzikenos) (113—95)	Cleopatra III (in Egypt) (116—102)	
	Hasmonean Kings			
104	Aristobulos, High Priest and King	Twenty years of internecine dynastic wars. *Disintegration of Seleucid Kingdom*	Ptolemy IX Lathyros (in Cyprus)	Theodorus, Tyrant of Philadelphia, (Amman) in Transjordan
103—76	Jannai Alexander. Jewish state expands its borders	Demetrius III (Eukairos)		Obedas (Abdath). Rising power of Nabateans
88	Syrian invasion defeated at Shechem	Antiochus XII of Damascus Pompey abolishes the Seleucid dynasty (65)		
76	Jannai Alexander's death		Ptolemy X (Alexander II)	Aretas III defeats Jannai

Its commerce and industry prospered and its international contacts reached the far shores of the Mediterranean. Jannai's pride in his maritime trade is indicated by the ship's anchor which he stamped on his coins. The towns expanded and the people's well-being increased. This is reflected in several phases of the early Talmud. That the arts also flourished is indicated by a variety of archaeological evidence.

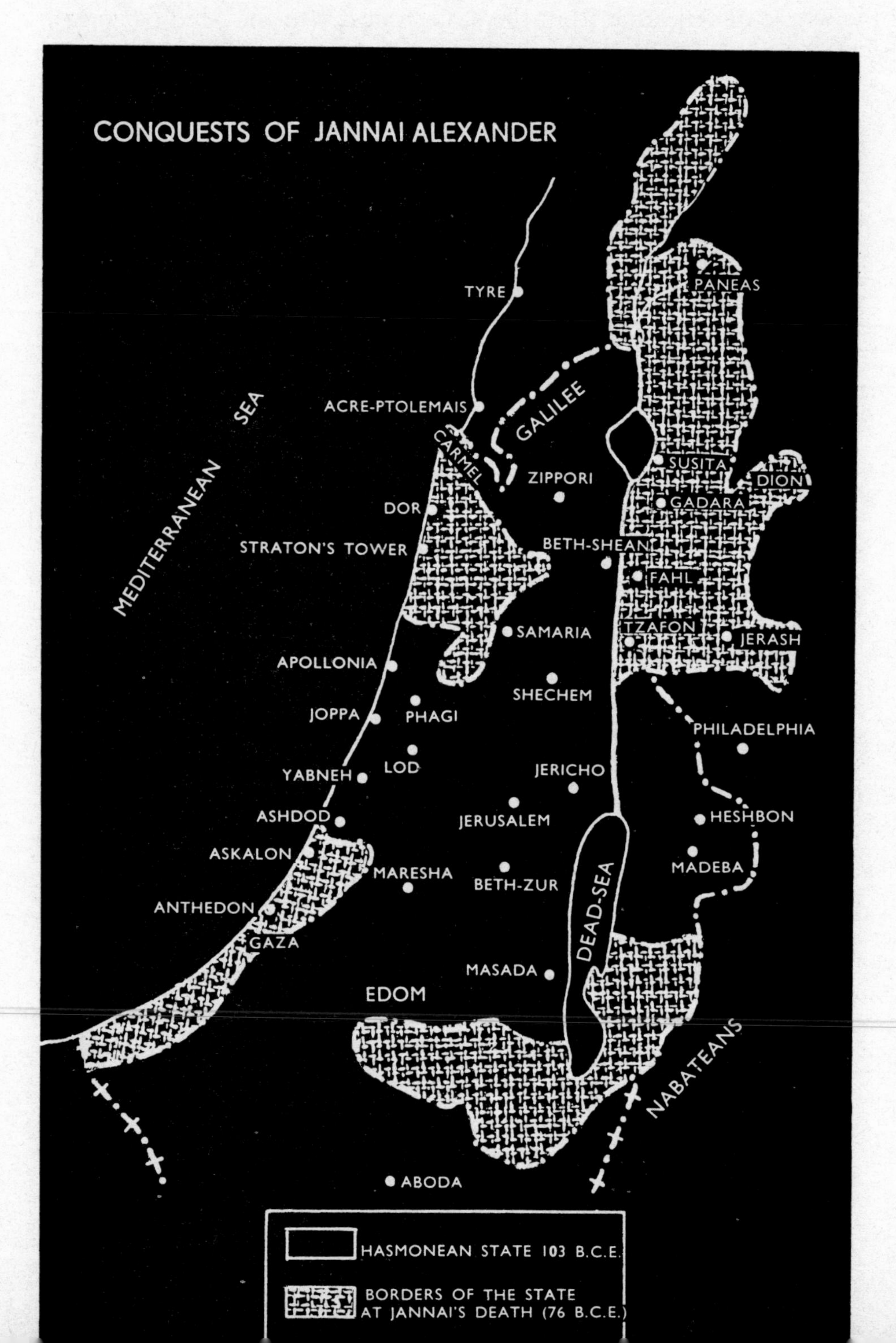

Jannai Alexander's conquests extended his country's borders, as indicated by the shaded areas.

The tale of Susanna and the elders, told in an apocryphal parable (see p. 79 is graphically recalled in this 4th century C.E. plate. The story, which tells of deceit and eventual punishment, was a frequent inspiration for popular art in the early Christian centuries.

III

THE CULTURAL CLIMATE OF THE HASMONEAN PERIOD

THE BRIDGE BETWEEN THE TESTAMENTS — THE APOCRYPHA, APOCALYPTIC TEACHINGS AND LITERARY SURVIVALS OF THE QUMRAN SECT

It can be seen from the events of the Maccabean revolt and the era of the Hasmonean princes that the post-Restoration development of Judaism and its struggle with hellenism cannot be understood in simple black-and-white terms of a direct clash between opposing forces, but rather as the encounter and reaction of two complex civilizations. Obviously the achievements of the Hasmoneans have been enhanced by their success. They had been victorious in a war against an apparently powerful enemy and had saved the Jewish nation in the face of the hellenistic attack. However, that success does not mean that they were concerned solely with a strict religious exclusiveness. The Jewish princes' victory had brought them on to a wider historical stage and they could not escape secular hellenistic influences in their everyday life. Jewish life had become far more cosmopolitan and the princes and their court, like the army and the merchant class, adopted the behaviour and customs of the times. The great progress achieved throughout the whole nation is apparent not only from the architectural remains of the Hasmonean period, but also from the teachings and writings that have come down to us from that time. The profound cultural changes that were affecting every corner and sphere of national life can be seen from excavations from the Palestine of this period. This new spirit fostered an interest in the ancient decorative arts and the ancient language, including the archaic Palestinian pre-Exilic script. In the general ferment of ideas that accompanied and survived the Maccabean revolt, during the period leading up to the New Testament, these changes were intensified.

THE SIGNIFICANCE OF THE APOCRYPHA AND APOCALYPTIC TEACHINGS

Modern historians do not dispute the latest findings on which these conclusions are based. However, one still finds many misconceptions, encouraged mainly for theological reasons, about the relevance of the literature that survives from before this period. The literature is the Apocrypha — i.e. non-canonical Jewish writings — and the Apocalyptic teachings circulating in the four or five centuries from the 4th Century B. C. E. to 100 C. E.

Until recent years, it was almost an accepted tradition that, from a literary point of view, the period between the Old and New Testaments was a barren or dormant age compared to the Old Testament. The classic voice of inspired prophecy was silent. Instead, in the period after the Exile, beginning in the 4th century B.C.E. with Ezra, existing Scriptures were made the subject of intense scholarly study. Over the centuries, a process of selection on religious grounds produced a "Canon" of books which were accepted as authoritative and holy. Certain books were included only after long debate by the rabbinical and scribal councils. Finally, around 100 C.E., the canon was established as distinct from other Hebrew or Aramaic books which had been circulating widely. The ones which did not meet the test of having been inspired by God were regarded as "outside" books and were allowed to fall out of circulation. Some of them were preserved as the Apocrypha and Pseudepigrapha, to be described below (see pp. 70–71). Others were allowed to perish, while some were preserved only by the sectaries of Qumran and were found with the Dead Sea Scrolls.

The Palestinian rabbinical councils were more selective than the Alexandrian Jews. The latter retained several outside books in their canon (the Septuagint, see Ch. VII), mainly in the category of "Writings" (the third and last part of the Old Testament). The early Church, probably influenced by hellenistic circles, may have adopted such extra-canonical books. It was the Christians who preserved the Apocrypha.

It has been suggested that the Synagogue in Judea rejected them because it found them out of tune with the current estimate of Judaism and that the rabbis of the 2nd and 1st centuries B.C.E. and the 1st century C.E. deliberately emphasized the legalistic tradition of the Torah at the expense of the apocalyptic. The teachings of the Torah, with their continuation and supplementation in the Oral Law, were being recast during this time and interpreted in a legalistic and nationalist spirit.

However, this represents only one aspect of the cultural climate in Judea and the Diaspora (see Ch. VII). Although the Jews of Palestine enclosed themselves within the walls of Jewish tradition, they had already been influenced by Persian culture before hellenistic times and hellenization had had a great effect on Jewish intellectual circles, including the Scribes. The hellenizing movement had been resisted in Judea and its influence was not so marked there as among Alexandrian Jewry. Nevertheless, it is now recognized that Hebrew literary survivals of pre-Maccabean times mark a symbiosis of traditional and new tendencies and reflect the contemporary cultural climate (see p. 93). It is impossible to draw sharp lines of demarcation between biblical tradition, incipient change and external influence. Nor can it be suggested that every new tendency was the result of hellenistic influence. Such an evaluation led to the assumption that Pharisaic and rabbinical Judaism (cf. Ch. VII), was synonymous with a spirit of religious exclusiveness and intellectual stagnation in which the details of religious observance were emphasized at the expense of inner content and originality.

It is possible that such estimates still cling to the terms apocryphal and apocalyptic, as applied to this surviving literature. Old Testament scholars and Jewish historians of the last century may have encouraged such a view. They may have given the impression that the selectivity which produced the Canon of Scriptures was a process of rigid exclusion, associated with a decline of the spiritual authority of Judaism. This view has been corrected by modern Christian and Jewish scholars. It is the historian's duty to take account of the entire complex development of the Jewish community which was to provide the spiritual material for both Judaism and Christianity. The first step in this process is to understand the literature that has survived and which must reflect the whole range of interest and opinions within the society which produced it.

With the increased knowledge and understanding of the whole of this period which has come in recent years, especially following the discovery in the caves of Qumran of the "Dead Sea Scrolls", many of which are contemporary with the Apocrypha, there has been a new evaluation of this literature.

The fact that the books of the Apocrypha were excluded from Holy Writ by the Palestinian rabbis does not lessen their importance as a guide to the life and problems of the period — (from the 4th and 3rd centuries B.C.E. to the Fall of Jerusalem in 70 C.E). Indeed, no one is competent to discuss the Old or the New Testament without a thorough grasp of all this literature.

Above all, a study of the writings themselves has finally disposed of outdated theories. It has become clear that not only was there the creation of a valid literature, but also that in these four of five centuries, religion continued to develop and that this was crowned in Palestine and in the Jewish Dispersion (the Diaspora), with a degree of universalism unknown in pre-Exilic days. The Jewish revival of the Hasmoneans changed the subject matter of Jewish writings radically.

Palestinian Thought and Folklore in the Last Four Centuries B.C.E.

Politically and ideologically, Judaism was feeling its way in a hostile world and very little of its literature penetrated to the world outside Israel. The key developments in both literature and religious life were internal. Moreover, it was not in philosophical speculation, but rather in the field of moral living, that the Jewish genius was most at home. It is natural that the Jews should show a particular talent for the moral tale, whether in the form of "embroidered history" or in direct fiction. The literary form they adopted is similar in many respects to the last part of "Writings" in the Hebrew Old Testament (from Psalms to Daniel and Chronicles), and this was continued in the new period.

The absence of prophecy (in the classic form) also gave added impetus to literary trends of a vigorously partisan and sectarian temper. The apocalyptic writings are characterized by prophecy in the form of "revelations", "visions" and "appearances" and are full of obscure imagery and exaggeration. The earliest examples are the books of Jubilees and Enoch. The foremost example of this mystic or apocalyptic literature is Daniel, although, unlike the others, this book found a place in the canon of the Old Testament. In fact, it became the model for a new type of literature that flourished from the 3rd Century B.C.E. to the 2nd Century C. E.

It can now be accepted that these centuries were a very productive period in Jewish literary history.

Many of the Apocryphal books were originally written in Hebrew or Aramaic in Palestine, although they have survived chiefly in Greek or Ethiopic, etc. translations. Others were written in Alexandria and Northern Africa and contain evidence of having been originally composed in Greek.

In addition to the above, a whole library of other books and fragments with some similarity to them, came to light with the discovery of the Dead Sea Scrolls in the caves of Qumran. From these it became clear that the Qumran Covenanters were familiar with the inter-Testamental books, for there is a distinct literary bond between the Apocrypha and the Pseudepigrapha and the writings of the sectaries. These will be dealt with in later chapters (mainly VIII).

WHAT ARE THE APOCRYPHA?

Much of the literature of the three centuries before the Christian era has been familiar for years in the Apocrypha and the apocalypse — books omitted from the Old Testament canon. Quite apart from the Apocrypha, it is now known that the last books of the Old Testament, including the Wisdom Literature and the Psalms, Daniel and Esther, received their final editing during this period.

Furthermore, between the 3rd and 1st centuries, the Jews of Alexandria also translated the Old Testament into Greek (the Septuagint — see Ch. VII). The books of the Apocrypha represent the parts of this Alexandrian canon which were not included in the Hebrew Palestinian canon, and which were again rejected by Luther when he came to translate the Bible into German. However, the texts found in the Septuagint were fully accepted by the Roman Catholic and early Greek churches. They are still regarded as authoritative in the Catholic Church and were not lost in the Protestant tradition until the 19th century when the Bible Societies stopped printing them.

The Greek word "Apokryphos" originally meant "hidden wisdom." It was used of the books which, in many sects, contained the essence of religious belief and were kept hidden from the eyes of the ignorant and reserved for an inner circle of believers. In later centuries, the term has come to mean something doubtful or untrue, and this has also served to keep people away from the writings. The best equivalent of the original term "apocrypha" in Hebrew is "outside books", not Holy Scriptures. It provided a convenient category in which to preserve classic works and to keep rejected works which might be harmful from circulating widely. Some of the books included in the Apocrypha have made a lasting contribution to the history of Judaism and Christianity; others are of only minor significance.

WHAT IS THE APOCALYPSE?

Apocalypse is, in essence, an attempt to explain the nature of history and, in particular, the end to which all history is leading according to God's supreme purpose.

Apocalyptic writings developed directly from classical prophecy. In Martin Buber's opinion, apocalyptic is the extension and metamorphosis of classical prophecy. The central themes are the same in both — the Old Testament doctrine of God's control over history and determination to create a people who will be worthy of Him. The roots of much apocalyptic belief lay in an earlier expectation of a human king belonging to the house of David, who would restore the political fortunes of his people. Apocalyptic writing did not challenge the prophetic doctrines of the history of salvation (see Ch. XXIII ADAM TO DANIEL). Instead, in its attempt to return to this understanding, it created a new theology of history, in which the emphasis was all on "last things" — the theology known as eschatology. In apocalyptic writing, the end of "this" world is final. It is not merely a turning point from which history will continue in a changed manner. It is the ultimate termination of all history.

It is the view of James Parkes that "the flowering of apocalypses was due to the pessimism which doubted whether any Jewish king would be strong enough to overthrow the vast empires which surrounded their little strip of disputed territory." However, this pessimism was combined with their main philosophy of religion and history which looked back, nostalgically, to the triumphs of David and Aaron.

Central Themes

The differences between the prophecy of the Old Testament and the works of the apocalyptists are all the result of this difference in approach. A belief that the end of history was to be the righteous reign of God over his creation already existed in its most spiritual form in the writings of the great prophets. The writers of apocalyptic gave it a more urgent and literal content. In the light of his faith, and by the exercise of free will, man, they believed, might come to control his world. At the same time, he was prepared to face an inescapable pre-determined future with courage. Given this change of mood, apocalyptic need not be despised as a foreign growth in the body of Judaism. Certainly, for peaceful conditions, apocalyptic seems baffling, but in times of religious and social upheaval, its lurid idiom spoke with extraordinary power. Its survival in the New Testament is sufficient proof of this.

Special Features of Apocalyptic

It is the opinion of many scholars that the apocalyptic literature of the Second Commonwealth was intended only for an intellectual elite. The moral teachings and imaginative commentaries that made up the "midrash" were not for the eyes of the ordinary reader, but for the initiated — the chosen vessels. In all these writings we find the assumption that it is God who has decided that his "purpose" shall be hidden from the mass of mankind and be revealed only in parables and symbols.

Apocalyptic has been described as prophecy in a new idiom specially suited to the distress of the time. It has three notable features.

The first is best exemplified by the Book of Enoch where the authors turned for relief from present-day worries to eschatological visions — mystical revelations of things to be expected in the "last days" which they confidently anticipated. The overthrow of history is usually communicated to the anonymous authors in a turgid, obscure and complex imagery in which visions of the future and portraits of legendary figures are mixed with prophetic rebukes for sinful behaviour; all in the language and idiom of "wisdom" as it was understood at the time.

Secondly, in many of the very muddled and confusing visions of the overthrow of history, a supernatural figure appears in the role of divine agent of the cataclysm.

Finally, the writers of these works remained anonymous, choosing another name, usually that of one of the patriarchs, hence the term for all these works, "Pseudepigrapha" — writings under an assumed name. All the books are similar in form to Daniel, the only one of them to be included in the Old Testament.

We list these books below, grouped according to their general type. In this chapter we shall describe some of the most representative and try to give an idea of the historical, religious or cultural reasons for which they were written. The groups are:

I. Short stories and homilies such as Judith and Tobit.

II. Recensions (rewritings) and additions to Old Testament books, such as Jubilees, Susanna, Bel and the Dragon, I Esdras and the Genesis Apocryphon from the Dead Sea Scrolls.

III. Wisdom literature, e.g. Ben-Sira (Ecclesiasticus) and the Alexandrian Jewish "Wisdom of Solomon".

IV. Apocalyptic (and Pseudepigraphic) literature. The best known of these are Enoch and the older Testaments of the Twelve Patriarchs. Much later, but of the same type, are the sectarian Qumran (Dead Sea) Scrolls such as the "War of the Children of Light against the Children of Darkness", the "Rule of the Community" (the Discipline Scroll), or the "Psalms of Thanksgiving" (see Ch. VIII).

V. Works of history, such as the books of Maccabees I and II, already quoted; the Zadokite Fragments (Damascus Document) and allusions to historical situations in the Dead Sea Scrolls.

Dates of Origin

Modern scholars have made a further classification of the books on the basis of their date and place of origin. In this connection, we follow the most recent evaluations and group them under pre-Maccabean (4th century to 175 B. C. E.) and post-Maccabean Apocrypha.

The book of Daniel was composed in Maccabean times. Although it is so similar to apocalyptic eschatology, it was included within the Hebrew Canon of Scriptures — the only one of its type (see p. 86: Relevance of the Apocalyptic).

Their Place in Jewish Life

The Apocrypha and the Apocalypses provide one of the main links between the Bible and Talmudic-Midrashic literature in its broad sense.

The messianic hopes of the apocalyptists provided an outlet for the national talent for poetry and story telling and for the craving for marvels among the common people. These attitudes were overlooked by the Scribes, Pharisees and early Tannaim of the Mishnah — who were mainly concerned with "Halakhah" (rules of doctrine) and literal interpretation of the Hebrew Scriptures, restricting themselves to close scrutiny and commentary upon separate verses or single words, rather than allowing the free flowering of their imagination in "Aggadah" (see p. 79).

The development in religion during this period was not an orderly process, and the literature that was produced covers a wide variety of themes and subjects. The origins and background of the books, too, are not identical. For an understanding of the spirit of the Jewish nation, the apocryphal and apocalyptic books written in Hebrew in Palestine are, of course, much more

This terracotta statuette of a young woman gives a good idea of elegance in hellenistic times, (4th and 3rd centuries B.C.E.). Over her pleated dress, or "chiton", she wears the "himation", a mantle which covered the back of the head. The fashion was general throughout the Near East. This statuette comes from the Tanagra workshop in Greece, which was inspired by the art of the great sculptor, Praxiteles.

valuable than those which were originally composed in Greek or in Alexandria, and accordingly subject to foreign influences. We shall consider mainly the books written in Palestine in Hebrew and Aramaic, including some of which the original Hebrew has been lost, and also some of Palestinian origin discovered in Greek translation.

To avoid complications, many modern scholars have suggested that all the non-canonical books, including the Pseudepigrapha, be called apocryphal and, in the main, we shall follow this terminology.

Sandal

Golden necklace, bracelet and buttons.

Neckband and ear rings.

I. STORIES AND HOMILIES

(*Pre-Maccabean*)

THE BOOK OF JUDITH

Probably the best known of the stories of the period is the historical tale of Judith and Holofernes. Powerfully written, the story opens with an introduction (Chs. 1—7) setting the military and political scene and then (Chs. 8—16) gives a vivid account of Judith's exploits.

During Nebuchadrezzar's campaign against the Medes, the story goes, he called for aid from his western vassals, including Palestine. As he received no response, he sent an army of 120,000 foot soldiers plus 12,000 of his mounted archers, under the command of Holofernes. Once they had conquered Syria and Phoenicia, an expanded army turned to punish the "hill people" of Palestine and laid siege to Bethulia in Galilee. Shortage of food and of water had brought the people to the edge of despair when Judith appeared as a deliverer.

She was a widow of outstanding piety, carefully observing all the dietary laws and fasting regularly. But she was also beautiful and daring. With the blessing of the elders of Bethulia, she set out for the Assyrian camp with only her maid:

"And she took sandals for her feet, and put on her anklets and bracelets and rings and earrings, and all her ornaments, and made herself very beautiful to attract the eyes of any men who might see her." (Judith 10: 4).

She claimed to have an important message about the prevailing situation for the Commander, but it was also her beauty that persuaded the Assyrian soldiers who met her to take her to Holofernes.

To him she delivered the message but, again, other arguments prevailed on him to give her a special status in the camp, allowing her to come and go with her maid, and to invite her to a banquet. She attended, but not to eat. Her own food she had brought with her, but she sat by whilst Holofernes became exceedingly drunk and then collapsed on his bed while his officers withdrew. Seeing Holofernes helpless and unguarded, Judith, with a prayer to God for strength, drew his own scimitar and, with two strokes, cut off his head. Hiding it in the bag that had carried her provisions, she and her maid left the camp unchallenged and returned to Bethulia.

"Then she took the head out of the bag and showed it, and she said to them. 'Here is the head of Holofernes, the commander of the army of Assyria, and here is the canopy under which he lay in his drunkenness. For the Lord has struck him down by a woman's hand'." (Judith 13: 15)

Holofernes' head was hung upon the battlements of the city and Judith proclaimed the deliverer. Israel was saved from its enemy and enjoyed peace for many years, Judith herself living to the ripe old age of 105.

For a long time it was assumed that the book was originally written during the Hasmonean period (second century B. C. E.) and that the characters represented Hasmonean heroes. However, it is now believed that it contains a historic kernel and an early literary origin which has nothing to do with that period but belongs either to the end of the Persian Empire, when Artaxerxes III was fighting rebellions in Sidon (Phoenicia) and Egypt in 352 B. C. E., or to the time of the rebellion against his predecessor, Artaxerxes II which spread through Western Asia and, apparently, included Syria and Palestine.

THE TALE OF TOBIT

(*Tobiah*)

This is a moralistic novelette about a Jewish family in Persia written in the idiom of the 3rd century B. C. E., with an important erotic element.

Tobi (or Tobiah) was a native of Galilee, carried off to Nineveh at the time of the dissolution of the northern state of Israel. He had been a scrupulous follower of the Temple ritual in Jerusalem and, while in exile in Nineveh had refrained from breaking the dietary laws. In Nineveh he married Hanna who belonged to his father's family and, through her, had a son, Tobiah.

Tobi, the father, was kindly to the living and respectful to the dead. The latter point was specially relevant because foreign customs sometimes prevented exiled Jews from being buried as tradition decreed. As an example of his attitude, an occasion is cited when Tobi, travelling through a distant land, found the dead body of a defaulting debtor (who did not rate honourable burial according to the prevailing code) and gave it a decent burial.

Tobi was blinded by getting a bird's dropping in his eye when he was sleeping under a tree. At first he was cared for by his cousin, Achikar, but then Achikar went away and Tobi's wife took over the task of providing for him. The injection of this name is significant as we shall realize in dealing with the form and origin of this tale. Tobi's wife taunted him with the reward which his righteousness had earned and, sadly, he prayed to his God:

"Then I was grieved and wept, and I prayed sorrowfully, and said,
'Lord, you are upright, and all your doings and all your ways are mercy and truth, and you always judge truly and justly. Remember me and look upon me; do not take vengeance on me for my sins and my ignorant acts, and for those of my forefathers, which they committed in your sight, for they disobeyed your commands. You have given us up to pillage and captivity and death, and made us a proverb and a reproach among all the nations among whom we have been scattered. And now your judgments which are many are right, in exacting from me for my sins and those of my forefathers, because we did not keep your commandments, for we have not walked uprightly before you. So now deal with me according to your pleasure; command my spirit to be taken from me, so that I may be released and return to dust, for I had rather die than live.'" (Tobit 3: 1–6).

"On the same day", as the story has it, the same prayer was uttered by Sara, daughter of Raguel at Ahmata (Ecbatana) in far off Media (once the summer capital of the kings of Persia).

She had been given seven husbands in succession and not one had survived the wedding long enough to consummate the marriage. This extreme misfortune was blamed on Asmodaeus, the evil demon.

Both the prayers were heard by God and the good angel Raphael was detailed to put matters right for both of them and, at the same time to effect a meeting between the characters.

Much earlier Tobi had deposited ten talents of silver in Raga (today Teheran, capital of Iran) with a kinsman. Now that he had prayed for death, he called Tobiah and sent him to collect the money. In bidding his son farewell, he conformed to dramatic custom throughout the ages and provided him, also, with some beautifully phrased fatherly advice. Many of the precepts which are listed here come from a 7th century B. C. E. Babylonian book of wisdom — the book of the sage Achikar which had a wide popularity among the exiled Jews who adapted it to their own needs and beliefs. For example:

"Scatter your bread on the graves of the upright but do not give to sinners." (Tobit 4: 17)

This may refer to the custom of offering sacrifice on the graves of saintly men and is almost a quotation from Achikar.
Here comes the first written mention in Hebrew of one of the famous aphorisms of the age; the golden rule which became part of the teachings of Christ: "And what thou thyself hatest, do to no man." (Tobit 4: 15)

Tobiah, as every other dutiful son, promises to "do all that you have commanded me" and sets off to find a guide for his journey. The guide, of course, is the angel Raphael in the guise of a kinsman, Azarias. On their journey, the pair camp for the night by the River Tigris and Tobiah catches a fish. The fish is served for their supper but, on the angel's advice, Tobiah preserved the heart, liver and gall-bladder.

When they approached Ecbatana, Raphael told Tobiah the story of Sara, who was his sole surviving cousin, and advised him to marry her, thus obeying his father and following the practice of cousin marriage. By marrying her, Tobiah, according to the ancient biblical law of "geulah" (redemption), would inherit the whole of the family's property. Accordingly the match is proposed. Sara's father, Raguel, is enthusiastic and writes out the marriage instrument, the "Ketubah"; this is another first literary reference, this time to a custom which has been law in Jewish life since the days of the Second Commonwealth. At the same time, Raguel cautiously prepares a secret grave, just in case. . . . .

But Tobiah follows the angel's instructions. On entering the bridal chamber, he performed the ceremony of exorcism, using the heart and liver of the fish to frighten away Sara's guardian devil, and before consummating the marriage he prayed to God. With the money safe and the wedding properly celebrated, Tobiah parted from his relations and with his bride and his heavenly companion returned to his anxiously waiting parents in Nineveh. When he met his father, the angel had provided him with further directions and by putting the gall from the fish into his eyes, Tobi was cured of his blindness.

The inscription on the bowl is a magical incantation in the style of a "get" (divorce) or exorcism of Lilith and the devils who plague a woman, Newanduch, and her family. Written incantations and exorcisms were considered potent charms to direct the course of destiny or ward off evil.

This folk tale was of Palestinian authorship, the Alexandrian Jewish Greek version coming later. The story shows the influence of the philosophy and folklore of Persia and Mesopotamia, and it is possible that it contains a kernel of an older Mesopotamian folktale. But its religious concepts are similar to those of the books of Esther and Judith. Apparently, it was written during the third century B. C. E.

II. RECENSIONS AND ADDITIONS TO THE OLD TESTAMENT
(*Pre-Maccabean*)

One of the outstanding features of Second Commonwealth literature was the writing and discussion of new versions (recensions) of Old Testament stories — a discipline known as Midrash in Hebrew.

Some of the shorter examples of this form are the parables of Susanna and Bel and the Dragon, while the Book of Jubilees and the other Apocalyptic works are more elaborate examples.

THE PARABLE OF SUSANNA

This is found at the end of the Book of Daniel in the Greek versions. Like the Book of Bel and the Dragon, it is an early example of the detective story. The parable of Susanna (see illustration on p. 67) concerns the need for more careful cross-examination of witnesses and demonstrates Daniel's wisdom and foresight. It is similar to the story of Joseph and Potiphar's wife, with the roles reversed. Two respectable men (elders of the city) lusted after the virtuous Susanna, were repulsed and charged her with adultery. At the trial, Susanna was found guilty on the basis of their testimonies, but, when she was at the point of execution, Daniel intervened. He adroitly convicted her accusers of perjury and the men met the fate that she had faced. They were thrown into a ravine and there consumed by a fire from heaven.

BEL AND THE DRAGON

This is another example of expansions of the legend of Daniel. There must have been many others, but only these two found their way into the Greek version. The many symbolic and miraculous elements in this story made it very popular with the Jews. Bel was a heathen idol whom Daniel refused to worship. Its priests claimed that the idol ate enormous quantities of food but Daniel, by using ashes to obtain the footprints of the men who secretly carried away the food, proved them liars. Again Daniel's wisdom triumphed over his enemies, for the king ordered the priests of Bel to be slain and the idol destroyed.

Daniel and the Dragon has a similar theme but in this case, not Daniel's human mother-wit, but divine intervention provides the happy ending. Daniel had killed another object of heathen worship, a "dragon" or "serpent" and thus aroused the anger of the people. They had Daniel thrown to the lions but, miraculously, he was protected from harm, the prophet Habakkuk even being transported from far-away Palestine to bring him food (this seems to have been put in later). Finally, after seven days, Daniel was liberated and his accusers were thrown to the lions in his stead — where, of course, they were immediately devoured.

THE BOOK OF JUBILEES

(*Early Pre-Maccabean*)

A typical example of "midrash" (recasting and interpreting the Old Testament) is the book of Jubilees — apparently the most ancient "midrash" we have.

Its authors set out to re-write the Book of Genesis and part of Exodus from their own theological point of view, emphasizing moral values, and points of doctrine (known as Halakhah in Hebrew). Their main interest was in the legends which formed the basis of their laws and they drew widely on the whole fund of folk tales, legends and sayings which were still popular. Together, all this folk lore is called Aggadah and, with the Midrash and Halakhah it was to provide the main elements of later Talmudic literature. However, the forms were a familiar part of the Jewish literary scene at a much earlier date.

The Book of Jubilees was originally written in Hebrew in the 4th or 3rd century B.C.E. It was entirely preserved in an Ethiopic translation, and also partly in Latin. Fragments have been found at Qumran.

A Jubilee, according to the book, is a period of 49 years and it uses this measurement to set a date for each of the memorable events mentioned in Genesis and Exodus — so many Jubilees after the twenty-two acts of the days of creation.

The acts of creation are connected with the 22 Patriarchs — the fathers of mankind — from Adam to Jacob, which is a typical Midrashic approach, as is the interpretation of Abraham's life as a cycle of tests.

The book begins with the story of the revelation on Mount Sinai (Exodus 24) where an archangel tells Moses of the creation of the world. This is a much enlarged story in which the six days of creation known to Genesis are expanded to twenty-two separate creative acts, with particular importance being given to the Sabbath.

The book then gives stories of the Patriarchs rewritten or reinterpreted so as to present them in a more favourable light. Some of the less flattering stories of Genesis are omitted altogether.

The book's emphasis on the sanctity of the priesthood and the rules controlling ritual show it to be older than the later Pharisees or the literature they produced. The book is also older than the Sadducees as a sect. It is possible that the material in it may have been taken from a common archaic source which influenced both early Pharisees and Sadducees.

The book of Jubilees and the earlier cycles of Enoch (see p. 87) are especially valuable for an understanding of the main religious developments of the post-Exilic period and of the beliefs and practices of the time. These concern particularly the calendaric teachings (i.e. the arguments that were used in the current dispute about the proper calendar to use), halakhah doctrines and laws and the warnings issued to the common people against leaving the faith in the face of religious persecution.

Jubilees and the Dead Sea Writings — One Line of Tradition

In 1955 the Dead Sea Scrolls were found to include a few fragments of a Hebrew text similar to the Book of Jubilees but with certain variations.

Because of its extreme views on religious questions, it is believed to have come from the Hassidim, one of the early forerunners of the Qumran sectaries, (as explained below) who accentuated the extreme views of the original book of Jubilees. The main difference between this and the writings of these sectaries (identified with the Essenes, in the opinion of many scholars) is that the author of Jubilees still shows some feeling for the community of Israel, whereas his spiritual descendants disavow any such loyalty. The sectaries aimed at achieving moral perfection and, to do this, they cut themselves off from all contact with the corruption of the world.

In Qumran, a solar calendar was used, which differed in some respects from the Jerusalem lunar calendar and which closely follows the calendar system of Jubilees and Enoch. The many similarities between the theological views of the latter books and the writings of Qumran are also evident, especially from the book of the Wars of the Sons of Light and the Sons of Darkness.

F. M. Cross believes that "the concrete contacts in theology, terminology, calendrical peculiarities and priestly interests, between the editions of Enoch, Jubilees and the Testaments of Levi and Naphtali found at Qumran on the one hand and the demonstrably sectarian works of Qumran on the other are so systematic and detailed that we must place the composition of these works within a single line of tradition. . . much of the Apocalyptic literature found at Qumran originates in Essene or proto-Essene (presumably Hassidic) communities. . . . ."

CONGREGATION OF THE HASSIDIM

THE PROTO-ESSENE MOVEMENT

This raises the question of the historic background of the proto-Essene trends during the Hasmonean period. One of the more obvious links is with the Congregation of the Hassidim from which came, eventually, both the Pharisee and the Essene "haburah" (see Ch. VIII,1).

The Hassidim originally dedicated themselves totally to the Law and to the observance of similar forms of abstemiousness and Levitical purifications as the ancient Nazirites. According to rabbinical tradition, the early Hassidim were all Nazirites (in Hebrew: one dedicated; a person specially consecrated to God by virtue of a vow). Their "congregation" was not a party, in the sense of the Maccabean or Hellenistic parties and we cannot be sure whether they were even a single organized group. Certainly, their "congregation" did not survive in any communal or political sense but their ideas triumphed in the exclusive puritanism of the later "haburoth" of the Pharisees and the separatism of the Essenes. In general, their movement appealed to the poorer provincial priests, in contrast to the worldly Zadokite aristocrats of the Jerusalem priesthood.

The first reference to the congregation of the Hassidim occurs in the early days of the Maccabean revolt — shortly before the death of Mattathias (166 B. C. E.), but they did not suddenly emerge then as a completely new movement. Although in their first encounter with the Seleucid forces their refusal to fight on the Sabbath led to disaster, they learned their lesson and, adjusting to the realities of the situation, they became warriors in a holy war for the Law:

> "Then they were joined by a company of the Hasideans, war-like Israelites, every one a volunteer for the Law. And all who had fled to escape harsh treatment joined them and reinforced them." (1 Mac. 2: 42–43)

Probably these Hassidic "congregations" and similar communities of the Maccabean and late pre-Maccabean era, provide the first sources of apocalyptic works. In the nationalist revival that accompanied and followed the Maccabean rebellion, many literary forms appeared which were codified a few centuries later. The beliefs and philosophy of the Hassidim (proto-Essenes) may have followed an even more pietistic pattern. The spirit of profound trust in God's mercy in the Psalms and in the prophets, is especially attributed to them. However, later Essene editions of some of the Apocalyptic works which were found among the library of Qumran, are apparently based on such sources. Moreover the Essenes and their forerunners prove to be the bearers and, to a certain extent, the creators of the apocalyptic tradition of Judaism. F.M. Cross maintains that "Probably among the congregations of the Hassidim, devoted to the ancient Law and, no doubt, to the Zadokite priesthood, uneasy allies of the Maccabean warrior priests, we find ancestors of the Essene sectaries who appeared in the desert of Qumran in the next generation."

III. WISDOM LITERATURE
(*Pre-Maccabean*)

THE WISDOM OF BEN-SIRAH (ECCLESIASTICUS)

> "All wisdom comes from the Lord, And remains with him for ever," (Ecclesiasticus 1: 1)

Ecclesiasticus — the Wisdom of Jesus ben Sira — was written early in the second century B. C. E., before the days of the Maccabees and during the time that a vigorous new house of reigning priests was replacing the Zadok line.

It is possible to fix an approximate date for the book with some certainty at around 200 B. C. E. Ben Sira was a contemporary of Simon II, the last of the great Zadokite high priests of the Oniad family, who died at that time. There is also a literary history of the book by Ben Sira's grandson who translated it into Greek. He went to Egypt in 132 B.C.E., which confirms the suggested date for his grandfather.

In his book, Ben Sirah tried to emulate the Book of Proverbs and the two books are partly similar. The best of his sayings are quoted in Talmudic literature. However Ben Sirah was aware that he represented a comparatively late development in the tradition of wisdom:

Picture of an Oriental School

"Take your stand in the throng of elders;
Which of them is wise? Attach yourself to him.
Be willing to listen to every godly discourse,
And do not let any wise proverbs escape you.
If you see a man of understanding, go to him early,
And let your feet wear out his doorstep." (Ecc. 6: 34–36)

"Let thy house be a meeting house for the wise; sit amidst the dust of their feet and drink their words with thirst."

Boys crushing grapes. Greek metal work of the 4th century.

"I was the last to wake up,
Like one who gleans after the grape-gatherers;
By the blessing of the Lord I got ahead,
And like a grape-gatherer I filled my winepress.
Observe that I have not labored for myself only,
But for all who seek instruction.
Hear me, you leaders of the people,
And you rulers of the assembly, listen to me." (Ecc. 33: 16–18).

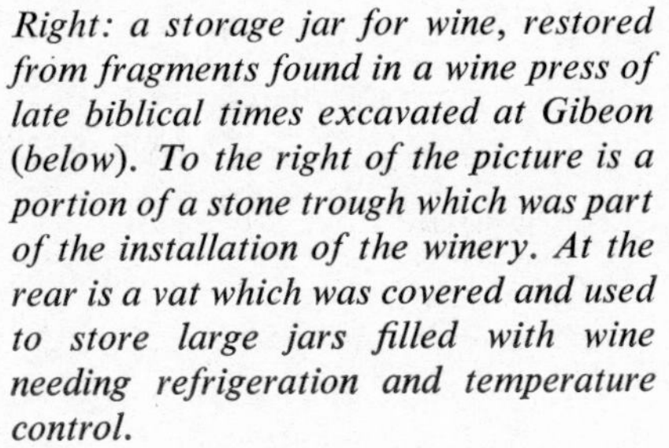

Right: a storage jar for wine, restored from fragments found in a wine press of late biblical times excavated at Gibeon (below). To the right of the picture is a portion of a stone trough which was part of the installation of the winery. At the rear is a vat which was covered and used to store large jars filled with wine needing refrigeration and temperature control.

His whole purpose was similar to that of the more humble anonymous teachers and scribes who were slowly penetrating into every town and village. Like them, he takes passages from Scripture, expands and expounds them and uses them as a basis for practical rules of life.

While Proverbs is part of universal "wisdom" literature, Ecclesiasticus shows a new, specifically Israelite spirit together with some independent thinking. Speaking in praise of "wisdom", he identifies it with preaching the doctrine and morality of the Law of Israel, with special emphasis on keeping the commandments. His book offers a guide to the observance of that Law, giving precepts for good behaviour in social and religious affairs, in conduct towards women, the aged, parents and children, stressing the need for self-control and moderation in order to enjoy the pleasures of life in this world, "for in sheol there is not delight." He teaches the correct use of wealth and the right attitude to poverty and warns against falsehood, pride and the company of the wicked. Ben-Sira was conservative and conciliatory throughout, putting forward a cautious middle-of-the-road philosophy of life. To Ben Sira, wisdom is that quality of common sense that enables a man to distinguish between what is to his advantage and what is harmful. He also draws the distinction between reality and the world of dreams:

"Vain and delusive are the hopes of a man of no understanding,
And dreams give wings to fools.
Like a man who catches at a shadow, and chases the wind,
Is the man who is absorbed in dreams.
A vision of dreams is this against that,
The likeness of one face before another." (Ecc. 34: 1–3)

He saw no remedy for the state of permanent hostility between rich and poor, expressing the view of his time that differences in economic and social position were the will of God. He therefore seeks the way of peaceful conciliation between the rich and the humble who are morally "righteous and religiously devout".

"Good and evil, life and death,
Poverty and wealth, are from the Lord." (Ecc. 11: 14)

He taught that it was useless to attempt to remedy the situation by popular revolts and conspiracies in Jerusalem and, in this, he carried on, in a direct line, the traditional teaching of the Old Testament.

A Mirror of the Times

The concepts of freedom of thought and of philosophy for its own sake were Hellenistic. Ben Sira, intent on promoting traditional Judaism, rejected Greek culture. Greek wisdom and free enquiry, cut off from the fear of God, were a threat to Judaism and he warned his followers from treading this path:

"Do not seek for what is too hard for you,
And do not investigate what is beyond your strength;
Think of the commands that have been given you,
For you have no need of the things that are hidden.

Do not waste your labour on what is superfluous to your work,
For things beyond man's understanding have been shown you.
For many have been led astray by their imagination,
And a wicked fancy has made their minds slip." (Ecc. 3: 21–24)

He campaigns against the early hellenizers who had adopted the way of life of the West and had begun to be ashamed of traditional ways. Freethinkers, in his eyes, are a "despicable race".

> "What is an honourable posterity? A human posterity!
> What is an honourable posterity? Men who fear the Lord.
> What is a base posterity? A human posterity!
> What is a base posterity? Men who break the commandments." (Ecc. 10: 19)

The real value of the book for us lies in the mass of information it contains on the thought, life and customs of the Jews of the time. Because of its wide scope, it is one of our most important sources for the social and economic conditions of the period.

The atmosphere of the book suggests that tranquil conditions had been normal for a considerable time and that there were plenty of opportunities for amassing wealth. Wealth is good if pride, licentiousness and transgressions of the fundamental Commandments of Judaism do not accompany it, but the sage knows that such cases are rare.

The Cosmic Status of Wisdom

The book is mainly preoccupied with "wisdom". For the first time, the cosmic significance of wisdom and its identification with the Law of God is proclaimed. Wisdom was created before all things, says Ben-Sira, and then poured out upon all that God made. The beginning of wisdom is fear of the Lord and observance of the Commandments. Wisdom is personified as something external and primal, like breath from the mouth of God:

> "I issued from the mouth of the Most High,
> And covered the earth like a mist.
> I lived on the heights,
> And my throne was on the pillar of cloud." (Ecc. 24: 3–4)

Two men conversing; painted in red on a Greek vase. Philosophy and ethics were accepted as subjects for intelligent conversation to a much greater extent than today.

But while in Old Testament wisdom writings the sage is a "wise man", irrespective of nationality, and Scripture is hardly mentioned, in the later wisdom literature, the sage is a Jew. Writers in the later phase of wisdom constantly draw on the biblical record for illustrations of divine grace and mercy accorded to Israel, the people of God. By identifying "wisdom" with the Torah, Ben Sira brought wisdom literature into the central stream of the Mosaic tradition. It became part of God's historical efforts for the redemption of mankind. The note of religion is sounded more frequently here than in Proverbs. "In short we have a synthesis of the old teaching with new adaptations in Ben Sira. The book has been justly valued in the Catholic Christian tradition, including the Anglican." (D.N. Freedman).

RELEVANCE OF THE APOCALYPTIC

(*Pre — and Post Maccabean Writings*)

NEW EVALUATIONS

Apocalyptic literature (see pp. 70–72) used to be interpreted by relating what had survived to events of contemporary history. In recent years increased knowledge has provided a much clearer picture of this little known period and its cultural environment. The relevance of Apocalyptic is no longer a matter of speculation. With the discoveries of the writings of the Dead Sea sectaries at Qumran, the understanding of apocalyptic can be firmly based on points of contact between the two.

First of all, there are many parallel patterns of teachings and attitudes. Secondly, it is clear that these are not the productions of a sectarian group who had withdrawn from the life around them. References and allusions to historic events are mingled inextricably with the "midrash" (imaginative interpretation) and the reflections of the pious, retired from the world.

The Book of Daniel written in the 2nd century B. C. E. is an excellent example of the form. The first part, Chs. 1—6 portrays Daniel's career as an honoured scribe or wise man among the heathen and is obviously the older part of the book. The second section contains a series of visions which clearly refer to the distress and religious persecution of the days of Antiochus Epiphanes. It is probably true that the historical allusions in apocalyptic works were subsequently so much worked over as to become practically unrecognizable, but their analysis will bear out the distinction between allusions to historic events and mystical meditations or pietist elements.

This seems sufficient evidence for the belief that apocalyptic teachings were the concern of both layman and priest, relating even to points of history, tradition and law. The movement rested on broad, popular foundations.

These books were apparently much closer to the spirit of the time than the Apocrypha. They reflect the popular view of history and philosophy from the time of the Hasmoneans to the Destruction of the Temple, and thereby give us a clearer understanding of ways of thought which were later to influence early Christianity, which, in turn, preserved them for posterity to a far greater extent than the Jews.

M. Friedlander and J. Klausner were later to dub them "popular prophets". The best of the books — Enoch, Jubilees, the Testaments of the Twelve Patriarchs and some of the sibylline Oracles — date from the Hasmonean period. The later Pseudepigrapha such as the Assumption of Moses, the Apocalypse of Baruch and the Book of Esdras IV, belong to the period of tribulations which began with the rule of the Herods and continued to the calamity of the Destruction of the Temple.

ENOCH, AN EARLY MESSIANIC BOOK

(*Early Pre-Maccabean*)

The Book of Enoch or, more correctly, the Books of Enoch, since the one title covers a number of writings which differ in time and in authorship, is the largest of the apocalypses, containing 108 chapters. Different sections date from the third (possibly the fourth) century B. C. E. to 68 C. E., (i.e. from pre-Maccabean days to the destruction of the Temple). Modern scholarship, from I. Charles to J. Klausner, divides the Book as we now know it into anything from three to five separate sections, according to their origin and teachings:

a) The oldest part of the earlier section of the book is the "Apocalypse of Noah" (Chs. 6—11), which is the central part of the whole section of Chs. 1—36 and dates far before Maccabean days, to the third and, some believe, the 4th century B.C.E.

The story concerns the fallen angels, or nephilim, of Genesis, who brought evil into the world. In a vision, Enoch hears God's judgment on the nephilim: They shall die and their souls shall become evil spirits intent on the destruction of mankind and shall thus continue until the Day of Judgment.

With Azazel (a figure of Satan), they went among men and taught them arts and crafts. But everything they taught was put to an evil purpose. Metal casting was learned only to make arms, wage war and spill blood. The art of writing resulted in the "making of books without end" (a warning to authors and publishers for all time, which has gone unheeded). Knowledge of the cosmetic art led to the self-adornment of women.

In the earlier sections of the Book of Enoch, the vision of the Messianic age is firmly placed on earth. It is not transplanted to the heavens until the later section of the visions of history (see 'd').

The following section, comprising Chs. 37—71, known as the "Similitudes of Enoch" was written in the first part of the 1st century B.C.E.

b) The wicked in the heavens and the social struggle on earth are the subjects of Chs. 72—108. As an accompaniment to the destruction foretold for the wicked, many evils are also predicted for sinners. Even the moon and the stars will change their courses to confuse men who study them and make gods of them. Such men will also be destroyed. One section, chapters 84—95, reveals a concern for social conditions. Here, Enoch speaks with fury of the wealthy, who build up their fortunes without concern for righteous behaviour, oppressing the poor and persecuting the rich — a picture of acute class hatred emerges.

c) The section termed the "Book of the Heavens" Chs. 72—81) is a semi-apocalyptic work, belonging to the third or second century B.C.E. It contains minute descriptions of the heavens, the movements of the sun, the moon, the stars, the winds, the divisions of the year and the succession of the seasons. It represents an attempt to find in mystic speculation answers to the ultimate questions of God's purpose for man and the destiny of the world. The writers clearly drew heavily on the mythology of Israel's neighbours, especially on Babylonian and Persian sources. However, the Jewish prejudice against hellenism cut them off from the discoveries of Greek science. Accordingly, "the astronomical sections of the book of Enoch are obsolete notions of the ancient Orient, a medley of popular legends harnessed to a lunar calendar which the author upheld as being most orthodox. ... yet at that time Erathostenes had founded a scientific geography and Hipparcus had discovered the precision of equinoxes and measured to a fair degree of accuracy the distance between the earth and the moon." (Lagrange). Nevertheless, however misguided, the attempt of the apocalyptists is evidence of the deeply questioning spirit of the Jewish thinkers of the time, and their concern with the ultimate problems of God and man.

d) Chapters 83—95 relate a series of dream visions of history. Like the Book of Daniel, this historical section offers an allegory for the whole history of the world, man and Israel down to its own time — which it sees as the prelude to the Days of the Messiah. As in Daniel 7 and 8, different nations are represented by animals and birds. This form of literary allegory was also common in Persian literature, for example the description of Alexander the Great as "he of the two horns" ("thul-qarnayn") which is still found in an Arabized classical tradition (see p. 5).

"And I saw that a white bull was born, with large horns and all the beasts of the field and all the birds of the air feared him and made petition to him all the time. And I saw till all their generations were transformed, and they all became white bulls. The first among them became a lamb, and that lamb became a great animal and had great black horns on its head. And the Lord of the sheep rejoiced over it and over all the oxen." (Enoch 90: 37—38)

The climax of the drama, the birth of the Messianic child, appears as a fulfillment of all the visions, with their allusions to historical situations implied in the vision of the End of Days. Though it bears no direct relation to the birth of Christianity, it adds to the background for the study of the New Testament.

e) The last book dealing with the coming of the Temporary Kingdom (Chs. 91—108) and the resurrection of the righteous is similar in teaching to the Book of Heavens. These sections unquestionably provide the richest source of background material for the study of the New Testament and are an additional illustration of the search for the hidden mysteries of nature which had so large a part to play in Jewish literature in the post-Exilic period. It has been suggested that certain parts may be post-Christian.

The mystic speculations and imaginings about nature (which are also represented in the art of the time) together with the high ethical level of this series of books are a clear denial of the charge, accepted in many circles, that the Judaism of pre-Hasmonean days was a matter of formal religious observance combined later with a rabid nationalism. Instead, contemporary literature reveals a spirit of religious exaltation and a striving for better understanding and greater beauty.

The Book of Enoch used to be known as the "Ethiopic Enoch" because it was known for a long time only in this version. This was based in turn upon a Greek version, much of which was known. This, again, was assumed to have been based upon a Hebrew original which had been lost. Some fragments have now been recovered in Qumran.

An ancient tablet from Gezer. The ancient art of astrology retained its hold on the popular imagination right through post-Exilic days.

(*Post-Maccabean*)

This Book is similar in some ways to the Book of Jubilees. Its older sections, the Testaments of Levi and Naphtali, were apparently written in the last quarter of the 2nd century B.C.E. and it is commonly thought that its background was the prosperous days of John Hyrcanus' reign. In spirit it echoes the orthodoxy of the Hassidim, while its literary form follows an old, standardized, three-part pattern:

> The first section gives an historical survey and a legendary system of laws (Aggadah) for each of the twelve sons of Jacob (the patriarchs of the tribes).
> This leads up to the second section which consists of a summary of the lessons to be drawn from the virtues or sins of the patriarchs. Good conduct is praised while warnings are issued against bad conduct. For instance, Reuben's sin with Bilhah, whom he saw in her nakedness, led to the breaking of a sex taboo and the loss of his birthright as the eldest son. This serves as a warning against the lure of feminine beauty. Simon's story is of envy. Levi's concerns the advantages of priesthood and the pitfalls laid for pride, thereby showing the importance of having civil power in the hands of the High Priest, as in the Hasmonean days, although the story speaks of a Messiah whose functions go far beyond the achievements even of the Hasmoneans. Judah's story warns against the temptations of riches and, through the tale of Judah and Tamar, against promiscuity. Issachar extols innocence and brotherly love. Zebulon's story preaches mercy; Dan's — the danger of anger and lies showing that hatred will be punished by dire consequences.

The Testaments of the Twelve Patriarchs offer remarkable anticipations of the moral teaching of the New Testament. For example, the Testaments' plea for forgiveness:

> "Love ye one another from the heart; and if a man sin against thee, speak peaceably unto him, and in thy soul hold not guile; and if he repent and confess, forgive him. But if he deny it, do not get into a passion with him, lest catching the poison from thee he take to swearing and so thou sin doubly. And though he deny it and yet have a sense of shame when reproved, give over reproving him. For he who denieth may repent so as not again to wrong thee; yea he may also honour thee, and be at peace with thee. And if he be shameless and persist in his wrongdoing, even so forgive him from the heart, and leave to God the avenging." (Test. Gad 6: 3—7)

It becomes clear that the concept of Torah, as the already revealed divine will, did not have the limiting effect on the Jewish spirit that early and later Christian writers have claimed. Instead, this spirit was still developing. All these works, just as much as the New Testament, were written by Jews. It is clear that there was considerable difference of opinion within Judaism about the value of the tradition of the classical prophets. The Testaments of the Twelve Patriarchs written during the rule of the Hasmoneans as well as other inter-Testamental and later works, provide a useful analysis of social behaviour with more illuminating examples than the older writings.

The Testaments of the Twelve Patriarchs proclaim that salvation is to come through a Messiah stemming from Judah and Levi — not Judah alone as in the tradition of the Old Testament. They may have been providing for the possibility of two Messiahs — one priestly and one Davidic. According to most authorities, the sectaries of Qumran also expected two Messiahs (see Ch. VIII, I). The authors of the Zadokite Fragments (Damascus Document) and the Book of Jubilees, had a similar view.

Further fragments of Jubilees and of a Testament of Levi, believed to be a source for the Testaments of the Twelve Patriarchs and the Book of Enoch, together with fragments of Enoch, have been found in Qumran. Everything, according to H. H. Rowley, O. Eissfeldt and F. M. Cross points to a close association between these works and the Scrolls. This is more easily understood if they had a common background in the events of the second and third quarters of the second century B. C. E.

V. HISTORICAL WRITINGS

(*Post-Maccabean*)

FIRST BOOK OF MACCABEES

On the whole, Judean literature kept to its traditional forms. First Maccabees was written on the inspiration of the Hasmoneans, yet its form is the same as the biblical books

This head of a philosopher is a potent reminder of an age of deep thinking, whether by Greek or Hebrew sages.

of Joshua and Judges. It has a simple, almost naive style, but it is a reliable account and without it, it would have been almost impossible to learn Palestinian history during the Seleucid period. It is concerned mainly, as quoted in the previous chapters, with the Maccabean rebellion (167 B.C.E.). It opens with the events which led up to the exploits of Judas Maccabeus and offers a straightforward historical narrative of events until the death of Simon. It was written in Palestine in about 100 B. C. E. and is the most trustworthy record we have for essential information about the period of hellenization in Jerusalem.

SECOND BOOK OF MACCABEES

This is a second and independent account of the events leading up to the rebellion, as illustrated by several quotations in the previous chapters.

It is not a sequel to the First Book of Maccabees. It was written at the same time, as an abridgement of a five-volume work in Greek composed by a Jew of one of the Diaspora communities — Jason of Cyrene (North Africa).

It covers the short period from 175—161 B.C.E — the period of the hellenizers' rule in Jerusalem and the persecutions of Antiochus Epiphanes which led up to the revolt of Judas the Maccabee. The original was apparently a full scale historical work, written by an educated man in the international language of the period for the Greek-reading Jews of the Diaspora.

The book is notable for its exaggerated religious tone. In later centuries it gained great popularity among the literature of the martyrs on account of its sensational descriptions of atrocities, acts of heroism and nobility of character, and stories of miracles and wonders.

One of the last stories in the book is the inspiring account of how, after repeated attempts, Razis, an elder of Jerusalem, committed suicide rather than be captured by Nicanor, archenemy of Judas the Maccabee.

The book was immortalized by the story of the martyrdom of Hanna and her seven sons who died nobly at the hands of the persecutors, "rather than transgress the laws of their fathers" and eat pork:

"But their mother was surpassingly wonderful, and deserves a blessed memory, for though she saw her seven sons perish within a single day, she bore it with good courage, because of her hope in the Lord. And she encouraged each of them in the language of their forefathers, for she was filled with a noble spirit and stirred her woman's heart with manly courage. . . ." (2 Mac. 7: 20—21).

In both books of the Maccabees, God is regarded as the supreme being who need no longer intervene directly in worldly affairs. In 2 Maccabees it is angels who fight for Israel; the divine name is not mentioned. The Jews' victory over Lysias, for example, is described as having been achieved with the aid of a rider who "appeared at their head in white apparel, brandishing weapons of gold." But in 1 Maccabees, it is the good generalship of Judas that gains the victory.

IMMORTALITY AND THE MACCABEANS

Belief in the immortality of the spirit, which was essentially Greek, appealed very strongly to many Jewish thinkers in the post-Exilic period. This represents a development beyond pre-Exile thinking. The Hebrew mind of the Old Testament which had accepted Sheol (the underworld) as the ultimate resting place, slowly came to a belief in some form of conscious life continuing after death. By the second century B. C. E. the ideas both of immortality of the soul and a resurrection of the body were known to Israel's neighbours, whether Persian or Greek, and must have had an effect on the Jews of the time. There are traces of such an influence in many of the contemporary writings including Daniel, Jubilees and Enoch.

During the Maccabean revolt, the Jewish soldiers fighting for the cause of religion naturally turned to the idea of a happier existence in the world to come as something more than merely wishful compensation. The certainty of a future existence for their people as a whole was no longer sufficient inspiration. The traditional Hebrew idea was that after death the individual continued to exist either in the grave or as a shade in Sheol.

As late as 200 B.C.E. Ben Sira could refer to the "rest" of the departed after death. But some years later, the author of the Book of Daniel could reflect an advance on the older idea. He put forward a clearly defined concept of resurrection in which the dead would be raised from the grave, reclothed in bodily life and rewarded or punished according to their desert.

"And many of them that sleep in the dust of the earth shall awake, some to the everlasting life, and some to the reproaches of everlasting abhorrence." (Dan: 12: 2)

ANGELOLOGY, DEMONOLOGY, AND THE TRANSCENDANCE OF GOD

The Jews in Palestine in the post-Exilic era had been subjected to a variety of foreign influences: Chaldean star-worship; Zoroastrian dualism; Persian worship of angels and the Hellenistic mystery cults. The world was filled with angels and spirits of good and evil. The Jews believed, in the words of the book of Jubilees, that the universe was crowded with "the angels of the presence. . . ."

The ruling demon — known elsewhere as Satan, Beliar, Asmodeus, Devil and Prince of Darkness — is called Mastema — the spirit that draws men to evil ways. The book is a useful guide to the state of Jewish religion at the time and the development of the Mishnah and the Talmud. According to it, Adam and Eve were taught how to till the soil by angels who were also responsible for the sacrificial covenant with Abraham and his testing at the sacrifice of Isaac. Angels had also rescued the Jews from Egypt.

The author of the Testament of Levi put into the mouth of Levi (son of Jacob), a deathbed exhortation to his children:

"And now, my children, ye have heard all; choose, therefore, for yourselves either the light or the darkness, either the hand of the Lord or the works of Beliar." (T. Levi 19: 1).

Beliar was the embodiment of evil — a mutation of the Old Testament Belial. In the Dead Sea Scrolls, he is the Lord of Darkness, and he stands over against God, the Lord of Light.

In one important respect, post-Exilic Judaism differs considerably from earlier periods. This is in its attitude to God. The doctrine of one supreme, all-powerful God had long protected Jewish monotheism from being corrupted by contemporary polytheistic (many gods) religions. Now, there was a further development in this process of emphasizing the unique nature of God. Instead of using the familiar anthropomorphic terms, He was regarded as being above the paltry concerns of men and His contact with human affairs was seen as being carried out through superhuman intermediaries, the angels. As we have seen, belief in angels goes back to Mesopotamian and Persian influences, but a popular angelology and demonology developed among the Jews of this later period. An elaborate hierarchy of angels was worked out, as we have seen in Daniel. Four archangels, Michael, Gabriel, Raphael and Uriel appear frequently in the pre-Maccabean sections of Enoch and in Tobit (approximately contemporary with Ben Sira). It has been pointed out that the link with Mesopotamia and Persia covers too long a period. D.N. Freedman believes that "the rich development of angelology in the inter-Testamental period probably reflects popular religion of great antiquity rather than a sudden new emergence."

By the third century B.C.E. another result of this exaltation of God had become evident. This was the prejudice against using the divine name. Instead, He is called Lord (Adonai), the King of Heaven, or, simply, as in 1 Maccabees, Heaven. He is also Head of Days, the Great Glory and, most frequently, the Most High God (in Daniel, Jubilees, Ben-Sira and elsewhere). Alternatively, one particular aspect of God could be substituted for His Name — the Divine Wisdom, the Divine Word.

On balance, it seems that Jewish literature and culture in this long period maintained their oriental individuality. At the same time foreign influences had had their effect. It is probably true to say that Jewish literature was the product of individual and indigenous inspiration combined with a certain amount of borrowing and adaptation.

Fragment of a scroll of Ecclesiastes

A Roman bireme. The fact that her ships could sail freely through the Mediterranean also explains Rome's prolonged impact on Judea.

B. THE ROMAN PERIOD

IV

THE HASMONEANS IN DECLINE

QUEEN ALEXANDRA SALOME

Alexander Jannai died in 76 B. C. E. He left his kingdom not to either of his two sons, but to his widow, Alexandra Salome (Shlomzion) although at 62 she was already an old woman. Before he died, he had made her realize how important it was to reach a compromise with the Pharisees. One of the prominent Pharisees of the time, Simon ben-Shetah, appears to have been closely related to her (some sources call him her brother), and through his influence she avoided opposing the popular party. Indeed, she went so far as to alter her husband's policy to meet their wishes. The effect of their joint measures was to revolutionize Jewish internal government and alter the history of the Hasmonean state. The party struggles between Pharisees and Sadducees which are an essential part of this situation are summed up briefly in Ch. VII, I.

For 25 years the Pharisees had been excluded from membership of the Sanhedrin — the supreme court for the administration of justice and religious matters, whose members had been recruited exclusively from the aristocratic Sadducees. Now the Pharisees took control. In reprisal for past slights, they in their turn scorned the Sadducees. Party differences became ever more marked, bringing the country eventually to the brink of civil war. However, the immediate result of the change was that during the nine years of the queen's rule the country enjoyed a peaceful lull in the political storms that threatened on the horizon. The internal conflict between the ruling families and parties remained the greatest threat to continued Hasmonean rule, more dangerous, for the moment, than any external hazards.

Hyrcanus and Aristobulos

In this situation, the queen chose her elder son, Hyrcanus II for the post of High Priest, mainly on the grounds of seniority. As he enjoyed the support of the Pharisees, his appointment may have helped them gain supremacy in face of the growing opposition of Sadducee circles. The Sadducees were led by the High Priest's brother, Aristobulos II. As the queen's life drew to its close (67 B.C.E.) the scene was set for a bitter struggle between the two brothers and parties. The High Priest claimed that, by tradition established by their father, the throne should come to him. Aristobulos, a more passionate and belligerent character, replied that Hyrcanus had displayed none of the qualities needed to make a good king.

Hyrcanus was obstinate, short-sighted, arrogant and none too tactful. But he had the backing of the Pharisees. To clear the way for him, they appealed to the queen to take action to destroy the growing opposition. Before she could intervene, she died. Aristobulos who was already in control of most of the country's fortresses, took advantage of the situation to rebel openly against his brother.

Whatever the limitations of her internal administration, Alexandra had been more successful in her foreign policy. By payment of a heavy tribute she had, at least during her lifetime, warded off a threatened invasion by Tigranes, King of Armenia. He had been invited by the hellenistic cities of Syria to put an end to the civil wars raging in the dilapidated Seleucid kingdom. Now he occupied Ptolemais (Acre) and threatened Palestine with an army reputed to be a quarter of a million strong.

ROME ENTERS THE PICTURE

The situation in the Near East became further complicated by the arrival of Rome on the scene. A Roman army, commanded by General Lucullus, sent to Armenia to attack Tigranes finally succeeded in defeating him and expelling him from Syria. The Romans then re-established the Seleucid throne under an Antiochian prince, who ruled as a vassal. Syrian independence was at an end (69 B. C. E.). Four years later Pompey completed the conquest of Asia Minor and Syria and divided the area into the Roman provinces of Pontus,

Bithynia and Syria. Thereafter, Syria was one of the territories of the Roman Empire, ruled by a Roman proconsul who had power to levy troops and engage in war. The new province, with Antioch as its capital, was considered of the greatest strategic importance for all Rome's Asiatic possessions (see map of the Roman Empire in Ch. VI).

Hyrcanus and Antipater

While Roman intervention had saved Palestine from Tigranes, the threatened civil war had materialized. Hyrcanus, the legal ruler, had been defeated by Aristobulos and had to resign to him his twin positions of king and High Priest.

It was hardly likely that Hyrcanus would accept this situation for long. His dissatisfaction offered an opportunity to a new personality, Antipater. He was a son of Alexander Jannai's governor of Edom. The Idumeans had been forcibly converted to Judaism by the Hasmonean conqueror and Antipater was known in Jewish circles as a "half-Jew". Nevertheless he was accepted as a member of Jewish high society and in the prevailing confusion found a climate that perfectly suited his talents.

He won Hyrcanus' confidence and began to urge him to make an attempt to recover his throne. He would have the help, Antipater promised, of the neighbouring king of the Nabateans, Aretas III, who lived in Petra, and was eager to recover lost territory in Transjordan. Hyrcanus made the journey to the south to meet Aretas and the king led his army against Aristobulos and defeated him. He sought refuge in the stronghold of the Temple in Jerusalem, where Aretas and Hyrcanus besieged his depleted forces. The people of Jerusalem, especially the Pharisees, sided with Hyrcanus and the question might have been finally decided in his favour, but for the fact that Judea once again became the center of wider affairs.

THE IMPACT OF ROME

To besieged and besiegers came the startling news that Pompey's army under General Scaurus, having secured Syria, had appeared on the borders of Palestine. Rome's preoccupation with Armenia, Parthia and Syria which had so far protected the Hasmonean state, would no longer be of any help. The future of their country depended upon the Jews and their leaders and the course of their relationship with the expanding Roman power. As Rome took a hand more frequently in oriental affairs, it became clear that her intentions were potentially less friendly than they had once appeared.

Pompey and the Jews

With the conquest of Syria, the Romans had achieved complete control of the Eastern Mediterranean. Palestine they had always regarded as the southern extension of Seleucid Syria and quite likely it seemed to them high time to put an end to the ambitious and

IX–XI. Jewellery belonging to a prominent Syrian and his wife in the 2nd century B.C.E. Above: Gold bracelet ornamented with carved gems, vine design, filigree work and granulation. Right: The armbands would go six times round their wearer's arms. Their workmanship is Oriental-hellenistic rather than Greek, (see p. 9). Left: Finger rings with large carved gems in a setting of wide-flaring shoulders. The right to wear a gold ring sometimes went with distinctions of rank conferred by the king on his "first friends."

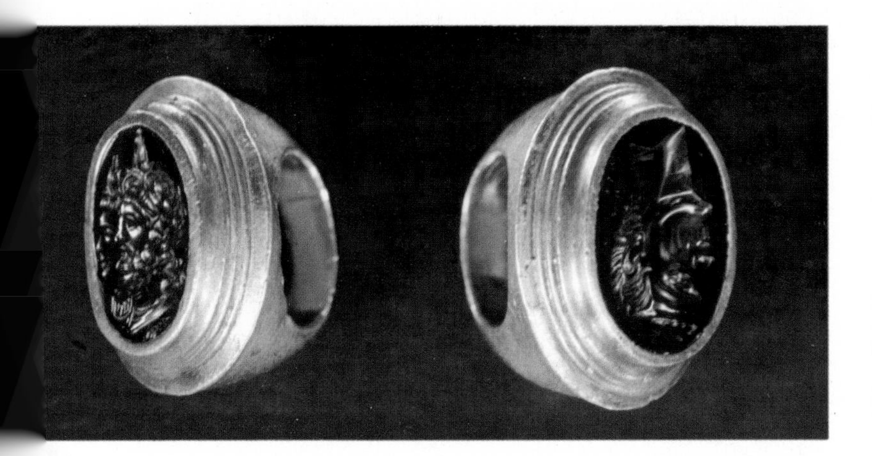

XII. Cleopatra, pictured crowned with elephant tusks, holding a horn of plenty in her hand and with the snake on her breast (see p. 112). *The symbols surrounding her represent the hellenistic-Egyptian pantheon. The lion on the left, for instance, was the sign of Cybele. This silver cup, buried under the ashes of Vesuvius in* 79 *C.E., was discovered in the Villa Boscoreale near Pompei.*

XIII. The beautiful decoration of the ceilings and walls of this 1*st century patrician home in Pompei was also copied in Palestine by architects who worked for princely and high-priestly families. The hellenistic architecture was modified by introducing Oriental patterns into the detail of the ornamentation, (see p.* 157).

dynamic Hasmonean house. They had no particular interest in maintaining native oriental dynasties. Existing rulers were respected only if they co-operated with Roman Imperial rule and with its loyal allies, the hellenistic cities and other dependencies of Western Asia.

Josephus, in his "War of the Jews" (Bk. III Ch. V) has left a striking testimony to the awe which the might of Rome's unconquerable legions evoked wherever they went. He lists their virtues "not so much with the intention of commending the Romans, as . . . for deterring others from attempting innovations under their government."

At this juncture, they were given an immediate opportunity to assess Hasmonean political judgment. The rival leaders in Judea appealed to Pompey as arbiter in their dispute, even before he made a move. Both sides sent envoys to Damascus to his governor, General Scaurus. The envoys came with their arguments well prepared and substantial gifts in support — four hundred talents apiece, approximately half a million dollars.

Scaurus listened to them and then declared for Aristobulos, ordering Aretas to raise his siege of the Temple and to stay within his own borders. As he complied, Aristobulos took his revenge, inflicting heavy damage on the retreating army. However, he was not immediately allowed to enjoy his military and diplomatic victories.

On Antipater's advice, Hyrcanus determined to appeal against the decision to General Pompey in person. When the Roman arrived in Syria, in the winter of 64-63, both Jewish contenders appeared before him, Aristobulos supporting his arguments with the gift of a vine made of silver weighing five hundred talents.

After listening to the accusations and counter-accusations Pompey refused to commit himself before settling his score with the Nabateans, merely bidding the two parties appear before him again in the spring. By that time, a third delegation had arrived to represent the "Jews" at large, or the common people. They begged Pompey to rid the country of both the Hasmonean brothers who had for too long abused their powers and brought havoc to the land. The people, claimed their delegation, would prefer to be ruled by a High Priest as of old. As evidence of the general lack of confidence in any possible peace under the existing regime, it is significant that according to Josephus a certain holy man, who had been seized by one of the armies in the current civil war, cried:

> "O God, the King of the Whole World! since those that stand now with me are thy people, and those that are besieged are also thy priests, I beseech thee, that thou will neither hearken to the prayers of those against these, nor bring to effect what these pray against those." (Josephus, Antiq. Book XIV, 2: 1)

JERUSALEM CONQUERED BY POMPEY

Finally Pompey decided in favour of Hyrcanus, as being the one most likely to prove tractable to Rome. Meanwhile both Jewish princes accompanied him on his expedition against the Nabateans. Before the decision was made known, Aristobulos, suspecting the worst, abandoned Syria for Judea. Ordered to surrender the fortresses he held, he gave in, but retreated with all his forces into the fortified Temple area of Jerusalem

On opposite page: Roman legionnaire and centurion, figures which have remained the symbols of Rome's majesty.

Above: two Roman marble busts. Left: How the Jews pictured Rome and Romans, harsh and unrelenting. Right: Pompey the first Roman to ride roughshod over Jewish susceptibilities.

among his old allies, the Sadducees, destroying the bridge that connected the lower city to the Temple hill. Pompey followed him in person and prepared to lay siege to Jerusalem. The people opened the gates of the city to him and Aristobulos retreated into the Temple stronghold. On a Sabbath, when the Jews refused to conduct military activities unless attacked, the Romans threw up earthworks to reach the Temple, placed their battering rams in position and surrounded Aristobulos and his band. They held out for three months but at last the Temple was breached, officiating priests cut down at their posts and Aristobulos imprisoned. Pompey entered the sanctuary to the indignation of the people, but he did not seize the Treasury. He even had the Temple cleared of debris after his victory.

THE END OF THE HASMONEAN STATE

Then Pompey announced his terms: Aristobulos and his family were taken prisoners to Rome. They appeared in the triumphal procession of Pompey through the city. The kingdom of the Hasmoneans was abolished. Hyrcanus was recognized as High Priest — but no more. Pompey further proposed to take from the Jews all the territories east of the Jordan and the western sea ports peopled by hellenistic gentiles — practically all the hellenistic cities conquered by Hyrcanus I and Alexander Jannai. Judea remained a subject

Temple of the Sun at Jerash (Gerasa) a Transjordan city of the Decapolis, and one of the most imposing monuments to the spacious way of life which hellenization brought. The original hellenistic buildings were later replaced by a Graeco-Roman city, famous for its many pagan temples, its hippodrome, three theatres and two public baths.

state within the province of Syria, while the cities regained the status they had originally enjoyed under the Ptolemies and Seleucids and were granted internal freedom under the Roman provincial governor. The same privileges were given to other hellenistic colonies in Syria and Palestine. Judea as a country was limited to the small rural core of Judea, Samaria, Galilee, Perea (the Jewish part of Transjordan), and Edom, while its capital, Jerusalem, was reduced to the status of a small provincial center paying tribute to the Roman overlords. The coastline, from Gaza to the Carmel range, became part of the newly organized Roman province of Syria. The remainder of the country was split up into independent districts that paid their tribute to Rome, like every other territory in the Empire. Ten of the hellenistic cities (nine of them lying east of the Jordan) joined together to form a defensive league known as the Decapolis.

This confederation was to endure for centuries. The hellenistic 'poleis' (cities) enjoyed an easier and probably pleasanter life than in the Hebrew towns and villages. They had achieved a harmonious synthesis of the west and the Orient, in terms of policy, language

(Greek) and culture. This is the epitaph Meleager, a native of Gadara (Gader in Transjordan), one of these cities, composed for himself:

"Art thou a Syrian? Shalom (peace) to thee. Art thou Phoenician? Long live Audoni (my Lord); art thou Greek? Khaire (greetings). And do thou the same to me."

A still better picture of the Graeco-Syrian synthesis may be gained from his epigram:

"The island of Tyre has nursed me, but my motherland is the Attica of the Syrians at Gadara. An offspring of Eucrates and a companion of the Muses, I have followed diligently the Monippian Graces..... Is there anything untoward in my being Syrian? Though strangers we all live in the same fatherland — the world. We were all engendered as mortals from the same chaos. Heavy with years, I have traced these lines on tablets before going down to the tomb, old age being so close to Hades." (Palatine Anthol. VII, 417)

Thus 63 B. C. E. saw the first steps towards the reduction of Palestine to the status of a conquered province. Her independence was lost. The pride and respect which the Hasmoneans had earned in the days of Judas Maccabeus had turned to disgust and hatred. Now the pious in Judea were prepared even to forfeit independence if that would spell the end of the Hasmonean house. On religious grounds, the Pharisees had always opposed the Hasmonean policy of conquest, fearing that the conquered peoples would contaminate the purity of Israel, especially in Jerusalem. Palestine had become a battleground of cultural worlds. The visible challenge to Jewish faith and customs is well illustrated by an anonymous Pharisee poet in the apocryphal "Psalms of Solomon" dating from the last days of the Hasmonean dynasty.

They express an elevated but straight-forward Pharisaism, deploring Aristobulos, the Maccabean prince who favoured the Sadducees, and exulting over the death of Pompey which occurred fifteen years later. These imitations of the Old Testament Psalms form part of the apocalyptic writings of the period and are strikingly different, in mood and theology from their biblical model.

Yet it is difficult to think of a more noble and exalted expression of the Messianic view than is to be found in Psalms 17 and 18, which contain all the popular longing for a Davidic Messiah:

"Behold, O Lord, and raise up unto them their king, the son of David,
At the time in which thou seest, O God, that he may reign over Israel Thy servant.
Gird him with strength to shatter unrighteous rulers. And to purge Jerusalem from the nations that trample her down to Destruction." (Psalms of Solomon, 17:21–22)

This is the style in which the "Magnificat" and other messianic songs in Luke 1–2 were composed.

WHY THE HASMONEANS WERE DEFEATED

Traditionally, among the pious Jews, especially the Pharisees and the circles they influenced, it was felt that religious considerations had to be put first, before all else in the country. Nevertheless, political and sociological factors applied in Judea just as elsewhere. Politically speaking, the Pharisees and their supporters had made a major blunder. Weary of internal struggles and civil war though they were, it was folly to suppose that alien Rome – former treaties of friendship and expressions of goodwill towards the Hasmoneans notwithstanding — would prove more considerate of religious traditions than a native Jewish prince.

Added to this miscalculation was the fact that the civil war between the two princes had clearly played into Pompey's hands. Aristobulos was in the best position to save the Hasmonean state, had he realized as many of the Pharisees did, that it was wiser to compromise with the Romans rather than make a hopeless attempt to maintain the integrity of the Hasmonean state, which he had inherited. He could have negotiated with Pompey as a "socius et amicus populi Romani," (an ally and friend of the Roman people). However, from the very beginning Pompey saw that Aristobulos and his people did not belong to this category. They showed themselves at the outset to be a self-willed and rebellious community for whom stern measures would be needed, even military action. It was an ominous beginning in the relations between the might of Rome and a weak subject people.

Moreover, overnight, the prosperous and dynamic state of Alexander Jannai had lost its most important cities and seaports. Its inland and international trade had been destroyed and it had been forced to restore to the hellenistic cities everything that had been gained during the previous century. These cities now made up a dangerous and vengeful force against the Jews. As in the early days of the Maccabean victories over the Greeks and their hellenistic allies, they would naturally side with the Romans in any issue and would play their part in crystallizing Rome's anti-Jewish policies.

Looking back, we can realize the full significance of the events of the time with all their consequences for the future of western civilization. Josephus, whose writings are the most important and reliable record of contemporary events, throws the full blame for Roman intervention on internal Jewish dissension and intrigue, but this ignores the fact that Rome would obviously have annexed Palestine sooner or later. Nor should Aristobulos' uncompromising patriotism be painted quite so black as many historians have tended to do. The proud bearer of the glorious Hasmonean tradition was a fine figure of a man who impressed Pompey very favourably at first. His fault was that he did not want to acknowledge Roman hegemony.

The inclusion of Palestine in the Roman empire was probably inevitable but the process might have gone differently had he and his brother played their cards more skilfully. By patient negotiation, they might have been able to preserve the political unity of Palestine as a semi-sovereign state within the Imperium Romanus, with its own Hasmonean kings and religious hierarchy. Instead, the whole state was torn apart and an antagonism against Rome created that led inevitably to the final Jewish catastrophe a century later. A. Schalit believes that a more realistic diplomacy on the part of the Jews in Palestine could have avoided the war of 66–70 C.E. Had that been possible, and the Jewish state been maintained until Rome's own decline, it would have affected not only Judaism, but the history of Christianity.

JEWRY UNDER THE PROCONSULS

A very brief experience of Roman domination and extortion under the proconsul Gabinius was enough to make the Jews regret their invitation to the conqueror. The people were particularly bitter against Gabinius' attempts to rebuild the Greek cities and resettle them with foreigners. Alexander, the son of the exiled Aristobulos, had reappeared in Palestine to lead another desperate rebellion in 57 B. C. E. He could count on the strongholds of Hyrcania, Machaerus and Alexandrium, but he faced the whole power of Rome. Defeated, his strongholds were surrendered to the enemy and destroyed and, in an attempt to weaken local autonomy, the country was divided into five administrative districts, while the High Priest was stripped of all political powers and became exclusively a religious functionary. During the following two years, new rebellions were led by Aristobulos who escaped from Rome, and by Alexander, but they were suppressed.

The exactions of the proconsuls continued, particularly under Crassus who pillaged the Temple treasury. A new revolt was led by the Jew Pitholeous. But it was hopeless. The result was disaster with some 30,000 Jews of Galilee sold into slavery and a heavy repression by the Romans.

JULIUS CAESAR, ANTIPATER AND HEROD

In the last years of the Roman Republic, the whole realm was shaken by the internal wars that developed between rival generals. Palestine, like the other states in the Near East, was inevitably involved. In 49 B. C. E. civil war broke out between Pompey and Caesar.

After military successes in Egypt, where he had been helped by Antipater, Julius Caesar moved on to Greece. Aristobulos, freed from prison, took Caesar's side although many rulers in the east sided with Pompey. Aristobulos was given a couple of legions and a command in Syria but, before he could reach there from Rome, he died from poisoning. At the same time, as Caesar's star rose, so Antipater hastened to ingratiate himself with the new ruler of Egypt and the Orient. Finally Caesar granted him Roman citizenship and made him procurator of Judea, while his patron, Hyrcanus, was confirmed as High Priest and Ethnarch, ruler of the nation.

According to their agreement, the Jews had to pay in tribute to Rome one-eighth of the total wheat they sowed, delivery every two years being made at Sidon. On the other hand, Caesar proved the most benevolent Roman ruler to the Jews. He restored the port of Jaffa, abolished the hated system of tax-farming and exempted the Jews from military service.

Hyrcanus was excluded from politics and Antipater had a clear field. Conscious of his new power, he appointed his sons as "strategoi", (district governors), notably his son Herod to the governorship of Galilee. In this post Herod, an energetic, charming and worldly hellenizer, served his apprenticeship and his activities there gave a good guide to his character and later proceedings. He suppressed an uprising of Zealots, termed "brigands", without legal sanction, for which the Sanhedrin, fired by the oratory of old Rabbi Shemayah, summoned him to stand trial. He appeared before them surrounded by a guard of armed lieutenants. A terrorized Sanhedrin had then to withstand the urgings of the Roman governor of Syria for his release. The trial continued, but Hyrcanus won a postponement of the final sitting. In this way Herod escaped punishment, but he nursed a grudge against the men who had dared to call him to account.

After the murder of Julius Caesar on the Ides of March, (44 B. C. E.) with civil war raging in Rome, Cassius, one of the Republican leaders, came to Syria. He did all he could to reverse Caesar's generous policy and imposed the heavy burden of maintaining his large army on the local population of Syria and Palestine. Judea was ordered to contribute 700 talents, (close to a million dollars). Some towns, Gufna, Emmaus, Lod, Timnah, refused to pay; they were razed to the ground and their inhabitants sold into slavery to cover the bill. Antipater and his sons were most diligent in collecting the money and Herod showed particular efficiency in his desire to please Cassius.

As a result, Herod was recognized as the strategos of Coele-Syria. There were even rumours that Cassius would have him crowned king as soon as he had finally defeated the successors of Julius Caesar. Meanwhile, Antipater remained as virtual dictator, although there was continuous rebellion against him and his sons. The supporters of Hyrcanus were even afraid that an opportunity would be found to dispose of the High Priest. As a preventive measure, a follower of Hyrcanus poisoned Antipater at a dinner.

MARC ANTONY AND THE SONS OF ANTIPATER

The two Idumean princes in Palestine had pinned their hopes on Cassius. Then, in 42, came the shattering news of Philippi. Marc Antony and Octavius had routed the Republican forces. Their leaders, Cassius and Brutus were dead. Herod made haste to meet Rome's new dictator and to ingratiate himself by means of a heavy bribe. Such arguments easily persuaded Antony of the Idumean's loyalty to his cause and he agreed to disregard a Judean delegation who had arrived to present a complaint about the exactions of Herod and his brother, Phasael. Moreover, the High Priest Hyrcanus obtained Antony's consent to release the Jews who had been sold into slavery because of non-payment of levies imposed during Cassius' time, also to respect the religious rights of the Jews in the Diaspora, including their right to send contributions in bullion to the Temple in Jerusalem.

Accordingly, when a second delegation from Judea met Antony at Antioch with a specific demand for the removal of the Idumeans, Antony's reaction was to appoint them Tetrarchs, (a rank representing the civil administration of a district): Herod over Galilee and Phasael over Jerusalem. Above them, the High Priest as Ethnarch (ruler of the nation) had authority over the whole country. In reality, the two Idumeans were in control of all civil and military affairs.

When a third delegation attempted to approach Antony at Tyre, they were forcibly repelled, every one of them being wounded or killed, while the earlier delegation to Antioch, which had since been imprisoned, was put to death.

Antony and Cleopatra

From Palestine, Antony's attention was turned to Egypt. He demanded an account of its attitude during the Civil War. To render it, the Roman governor sent Cleopatra VII Thea, herself, the same beautiful temptress who had been crowned Queen of Egypt by Julius Caesar in his heyday. She sailed majestically up the river Cydnos to Tarsus to meet the new ruler of Asia Minor. Her barge was fitted with vermillion sails and silver oars dipped rhythmically to the music of flutes and zythers. There, under a golden awning and fanned by surrounding cupids, the Egyptian Queen lay, dressed as Aphrodite. "She is calling on the god Dionysus," said the people, according to Plutarch, the biographer (see illustration on p. 94).

Instead of a god, she met the mortal, if almost super-human, Antony. He was not slow to remark that at 28, the queen had lost none of the fascination she had exercised fourteen years previously on the General of Cavalry Gabinius. After assuring him of her loyalty to the Caesarian party, Cleopatra set sail again, leaving the new Dionysus to settle affairs in Syria before hastening to join her in her palace in Alexandria.

Marc Antony was ridiculed in Judea for his association with Cleopatra. He was, nevertheless, Herod's patron and staunch friend.

In Palestine, Herod was still faced with enemies at home and from outside. He had Marc Antony behind him but his family had still not finally defeated their Hasmonean rivals. Moreover, the international situation was developing dangerously for both sides. The peoples of the Orient, tired of Roman soldiers and tax-gatherers, were eagerly seeking a new liberation. They found hope in the rising strength of Parthia, which was carving a great kingdom out of the ruins of the Seleucid possessions in Persia and Mesopotamia.

Taking advantage of Marc Antony's preoccupation with Cleopatra, the Parthians crossed the Euphrates in 40 B. C. E. and seized control of Syria. They were led by a Roman general, Quintus Labienus, the son of a former lieutenant of Julius Ceasar's who had turned against him in the Civil War. Labienus had been sent by the republican opponents of Caesar to reach a settlement with Parthia. When the news of Philippi reached him he realized that his side had been utterly defeated by Marc Antony and Octavius (42 B. C. E.). Instead of peace, he urged the Parthians to seize their opportunity to take over all Rome's possessions in Western Asia. They heard him with willing ears and, dividing their army into two, sent one arm under Labienus to conquer Asia Minor while the other turned westwards across the Euphrates to occupy Syria.

The days of Roman rule in Judea seemed numbered. The imminent Parthian invasion, moreover, seemed to many people to offer a golden opportunity to rid themselves of their hated Idumean rulers.

Antigonus Gains the upper Hand

This situation brought Antigonus, the son of Aristobulos, back from his exile in Lebanon. He gathered a host of partisans around him in Galilee and appealed to the Parthian commander, Pacoros, to invade Palestine. As an inducement, he offered to crown the Parthian king and promised a thank offering of a thousand talents of silver and five hundred women— to be chosen, needless to say, from among their joint political enemies. The fact that an alliance with Parthia made him an enemy of Rome and put any possibility of compromise right out of court, did not deter Antigonus. He was his father's son and he was bent upon the same headlong course of impulsive nationalism. A side effect of his action, naturally enough, was to create a close alliance between the Idumean pretenders and the supporters of the High Priest Hyrcanus, who was afraid that the people would rally to Antigonus. Indeed a variety of Hasmonean supporters had joined him on Mount Carmel. Together, they hastened to Jerusalem. Antigonus, they thought, should be re-established on the throne as the rightful heir of the Hasmonean dynasty. Once in the capital, the people turned out on his side. Herod and his brother, Phasael, barricaded themselves into the Hasmonean Palace but things were going very badly for them when the time for the Pentecost pilgrimage brought an influx of country people into Jerusalem from all over Judea. Until then, the Parthians had planned to let Antigonus and Herod fight it out and to intervene only if it became necessary to ensure the victory of their ally, Antigonus. As it was, the invading side proposed negotiations.

These were conducted on behalf of Antigonus by the Parthian commander. He invited Hyrcanus and Phasael to meet him for talks, then seized and imprisoned them. The two prisoners were handed over to Antigonus, who had Hyrcanus' ears cut off so as to disqualify him for the position of High Priest which he intended henceforth to fill himself. Old Hyrcanus had been High Priest for 36 years, ever since the death of his father, Alexander Jannai. Herod tried unsuccessfully to buy his brother's liberty and, rather than face continued imprisonment or some worse fate, Phasael committed suicide. Herod managed to get his family away secretly to the fortress of Masada and then escaped himself and sought the help of the Nabateans.

HEROD CROWNED IN THE ROMAN SENATE

For the next three years, while war raged without ceasing in and around Palestine, Herod's fate hung in the balance. For many generations, the land of Galilee which, technically he still ruled, had been honey-combed with enemies of Rome. Herod had to undertake a campaign against the Jewish rebels who were in hiding in the caves of Arbel. Meanwhile, Antigonus stayed on in Jerusalem with little thought for the troubles of his patriotic allies in Galilee. He escaped the punishment inflicted on disloyal enemies of Rome by means of a skilful distribution of gifts.

It seemed to Herod that while he remained in Galilee, his future would remain undecided. He was utterly alone, for none would come to his aid, not even the Nabateans. Accordingly, he put his affairs into what order he could and taking a roundabout route through Egypt and Rhodes, he set off for the heart of the Empire. When he reached Rome, he was able to win the support of Antony and Octavius. Josephus relates that —

> "Antony was moved with compassion at his reverse of fortune; and influenced by the recollection of Antipater's hospitality but above all by the heroic qualities of the man before him, determined there and then to make him King of the Jews, whom he had previously appointed Tetrarch." (Wars Bk. 1, 15:4)

This time Herod aimed at the crown of Judea (which meant all of Palestine). The two Roman leaders saw in him a useful pawn in their struggle against Parthia.

Accordingly, the Senate came together in solemn session and heard two of Rome's great orators present the case for Herod. The Senate listened, approved and formally appointed Herod King of Judea as "amicus et socius populi Romani". Antigonus was pronounced an enemy of Rome. At the end of the meeting, the Senate made a solemn procession to the Capitol, led by the consuls and Magistrates of Rome. With the "triumvirs" Marc Antony and Octavius on either side, Herod moved through the streets of the capital

The Forum of Rome, setting for so many great historical events. It was in the Capitol that Rome's leaders crowned Herod King of the Jews.

in triumph. In the Capitol, a sacrifice was made to Jupiter Capitolinus and Herod's appointment was confirmed by the registering of the formal decision.

The ceremonial of Herod's coronation seemed, according to A. Schalit "to symbolize the character of his kingship. This kingship, Janus-like, possessed two faces: One faced Rome and the hellenistic world; the second — the Jewish people and its specific civilization. The purpose, as will be seen, was to erect a bridge between these two worlds and to find for the Jewish nation a place and function in the framework of the Roman Empire." The rest of Herod's story is an account of the tragic failure of this futile attempt.

Herod conquers his kingdom

Herod could now claim to be king but Antigonus, in spite of his rival's better legal position, had the advantage of complete freedom of action. He retreated to Jerusalem, to await the return of his allies, the Parthians. In a series of campaigns against him, Herod established his control over parts of the country. Galilee proved the biggest stumbling block; moreover, many Roman generals still favoured the generous Antigonus.

Marc Antony had given orders to his provincial general in Syria to provide Herod with a contingent of soldiers. However, while the Romans were still mainly concerned with the Parthian attacks, this order had been ignored. With the final routing of the Parthians in 38, Herod renewed his appeal for help to Antony in person, at Antioch. This time two Roman legions were put at Herod's disposal.

THE LAST HASMONEAN KING

His struggle with Antigonus, however, continued. While still in Antioch, Herod learned that his brother Joseph had been defeated by Antigonus' forces near Jericho and that this reverse had triggered off rebellions in Galilee and other parts of the country. Herod first dealt with this rising, then advanced to meet Antigonus' main forces, centered in Jericho. At first there were merely skirmishes. Then Antigonus split his army, sending a strong force to Samaria to cut Herod's lines of communication. Instead the force came face to face with Herod's army in the narrow defile at Yeshana north of Bethel and was destroyed. At that moment Herod was assured of the final successful outcome of his struggle for possession of the country.

As soon as the spring of 37 made it possible, Herod laid siege to Jerusalem. Starting alone, he was joined by one of Antony's Generals, Sosius. Together they then mustered sixteen legions, a tremendous force. Inside Jerusalem, the Pharisees advised reaching a compromise that would save the city, but Antigonus and the city's defenders refused.

The attackers began their assault by building great siege engines and hurling battering rams against the northern walls of the city. After forty days, the walls were breached. The besiegers stormed the city, slaughtering anyone who fell into their hands, plundering and destroying the town. Antigonus himself surrendered to Sosius, who sent him in chains to Antioch. There, after horrible tortures, he was put to death, with Herod's compliance and on the orders of Marc Antony. Thus ended the last prince of the Hasmonean dynasty and, with him, all prospects of power. Hasmonean descendants lived on and people might dream of their restoration, but these dreams would be drowned in blood.

Roman battering ram, the great "siege engine".

View of Jerusalem from the air: (1) *the Citadel now called 'Tower of David', site of Herod's palace;* (2) *cupola of the Holy Sepulchre;* (3) *mount Zion and the Cenacle;* (4) *the lower end of the Tyropeon Vale which was originally much deeper;* (5) *the Garden of Gethsemane in the Valley of Jehosaphat beneath the eastern wall;* (6) *the Temple esplanade;* (7) *Dominus Flevit church on the slope of the Mount of Olives.*

V

HEROD KING OF THE JEWS

THE KING AND THE HASMONEANS

Just at the time of the siege of Jerusalem, Herod had married the beautiful Hasmonean princess, Mariamme, granddaughter of Hyrcanus and niece of Antigonus. He loved her dearly all his life and was to pay dearly for his passionate love. It was no mere dynastic marriage, as assumed by many, aimed at reinforcing his claim to the throne. He saw no need to intrigue for influence by trying to establish family connections with the Hasmoneans. Nevertheless, he made good use of the fact of his alliance to establish relations with the extreme Pharisees.

They were the circles from which stemmed the "Psalms of Solomon", quoted above. It was their view that the Hasmoneans had usurped a throne which belonged, according to ancient tradition, exclusively to the house of David. Herod's overtures to them were of a piece with his desire to eradicate even the memory of the Hasmoneans.

Herod entered Jerusalem and was crowned king of the Jews. By means of rich presents he induced Sosius to withdraw his marauding troops from the capital. Herod then applied himself to securing the foundations of his new kingdom.

One by one all those who had sided with the Hasmoneans were eliminated. Opposition leaders of Jerusalem were murdered, while those who had been Herod's partisans were honoured and given high positions. Even among the Pharisees, the two leaders, Shemayah and Abtalyon, who had counselled moderation and advised the citizens to open the city to Herod, were spared. Wherever he could, he aimed at establishing a favourable background. To this end, the aged Hyrcanus was made welcome from his exile.

The thorniest problem in the internal organization of Jewish life was the nature of their commonwealth. It was a theocracy — government by the direct rule of God, through the priests. Their short experience of secular kingship under the Hasmoneans had not changed this basic feature which marked the Jews as different from other nations, then and forever. Their destiny, they believed, was not only of this world, but of the next (see Ch. III). The Pharisees were insistent that such a destiny could never be embodied in a secular monarch, except one of the Davidic line. That, Herod could never be nor could he ever win the High Priest's exclusive right to enter the Holy of Holies of the Temple. The Jerusalem theocracy was an impossible foundation for a hellenistic state such as Herod wanted. In order to establish such a state, it seemed politic to separate the monarchy from the priesthood and this operation Herod carried out, although it meant that this Herodian state did not rest on a foundation of national traditions.

His subjects could not easily forget that this new king had none of the blood of their own princes. The Hasmoneans regarded him, of course, as a usurper. To the aristocracy he was, in addition, a brigand who, when short of money himself, had no compunction in seizing their wealth, sometimes to pay his bribes to Marc Antony.

Herod's whole past career demonstrated his unbalanced character. Physical courage and good generalship he had displayed on many occasions. However, indifference to bloodshed inspired terror, not confidence, when it meant the massacre of most of the members of the Sanhedrin, the destruction of influential men of Jerusalem, or the wanton slaughter of the rebellious peasants of Galilee. From the very beginning of his reign, he faced internal and external problems: under-ground opposition of the defeated Hasmoneans and their numerous supporters; domestic rivalries and intrigues at his court; the deep hatred of Cleopatra, her intrigues against him and her dynastic designs on Palestine; and the perennial menace of complications within the Roman empire.

Herod overcame them all with cold cruelty or matchless diplomatic skill. In order to thwart any repetition of Hasmonean claims, he decided the tenure of the High Priesthood in his own way. The rightful holder of the post was another Aristobulos — grandson of King Aristobulos II, and younger brother of Mariamme. In his place, Herod appointed as High Priest a certain Hananael (or Hanamael), scion of an obscure priestly family of Babylon or Egypt. By doing so, Herod incurred the enmity of his mother-in-law, Alexandra, who deeply resented the slight to her son. She found an ally in Cleopatra, who bore Herod a mortal hatred and also hoped to wrest some territory from Judea. With her help, the mother prevailed upon Marc Antony to make Herod appoint Aristobulos to the post of High Priest.

Herod complied, but the young man proved disastrously popular with the High Holiday Jerusalem crowds of 36, or 35, when he appeared before them in the robe of the high priesthood. In their clamorous acclaim of the High Priest, Herod heard undertones of revolt against himself. His reaction was to have the youth "accidentally" drowned during a party at his estate in Jericho, by a friend who held the High Priest's head under water until he expired. At the funeral Herod so overdid the paroxysms of his mourning that no one, least of all the mother, was deceived.

The Hasmoneans, claimed Herod, had flouted tradition by assuming the double crown of king and high priest. After suppressing them, he tried to prove that he wanted to restore the traditional position and would leave the high priesthood to the rightful priest in accordance with the wishes of the people. However, he kept the office subservient to his own royal power. The high priesthood was not a hereditary position, nor did Herod believe it should be held for life. Instead, he made it a temporary post, subject to his choice. We know of eight high priests in Herod's lifetime.

HEROD AND CLEOPATRA

Violence did not end there. Alexandra, again through Cleopatra's intervention, persuaded Marc Antony to call Herod to account. Ordered to appear before the Roman to answer charges of responsibility for his crime, Herod left instructions that if he were to be condemned, Mariamme should be murdered by his brother-in-law Joseph. While Herod was away, Joseph told the queen of her husband's orders. Yet again Antony proved a friend to Herod and acquitted him of the charge. Whereupon Herod returned home to learn of the betrayed secret. Mariamme escaped for the moment, but Herod ordered Joseph's immediate execution.

Cleopatra dreamed of expanding the Egyptian realm by "recovering" its lost Asiatic provinces. In the year 36 she persuaded her lover to give her possession of the territories from Phoenicia and the Lebanon (Chalcis) to Damascus and Baalbek (Heliopolis). But Herod's expanding kingdom stood in the way of her territorial dreams. There was no love lost between the two because of this, but Herod had a powerful friend in Antony, who found him a very useful ruler of a difficult area and was prepared to support him, even though it meant denying Cleopatra. Eventually, however, she won. Antony granted her not only the rich coastal plain of Palestine, but also the beautiful plantation lands of Jericho, the city of palms, (see map, p. 116). Herod had no alternative but to submit with what good grace he could muster. Much as it must have irked him to have to receive Cleopatra as the ruler of some of his most valuable territory, he made up for it by paying her a substantial yearly rental for it and "farming" this out to his advantage. In addition Herod guaranteed

XIV. Section of the great aqueduct on the shore of Caesarea (*see p.* 123–4).

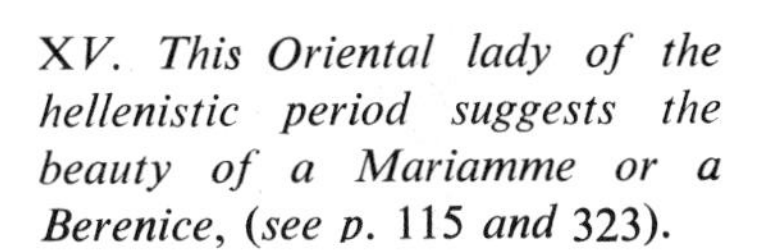

XV. *This Oriental lady of the hellenistic period suggests the beauty of a Mariamme or a Berenice*, (*see p.* 115 *and* 323).

XVI. The "Wailing Wall" of Jerusalem is part of the western enclosure of the Temple terrace (p. 131–2) *from which all gentiles were excluded. It is twelve metres high and has preserved several layers of large Herodian blocks. Others are buried to a depth of* 21 *metres in the accumulated debris below the level of the pavement.*

XVII. This hellenistic marble known as the "head of Hercules", shows a subtle blending of strength and noble thought. Although dating from the 4*th century B.C.E. it is a good representation of Middle Eastern manhood in the later Graeco-Roman centuries.*

Cleopatra the tribute from Melichos, the Nabatean king, and this concession was to serve him well.

In the crucial days of the struggle betwen Antony and Octavius (32 B. C. E.), Cleopatra saw another chance to get the better of Herod. Acting on her advice, Antony sent him to subdue Melichos, who had refused to pay his tribute. She still nursed the territorial dreams of the Ptolemies of old and hoped that an exhausting war between the two powers would give her a chance to take over their kingdoms. Supported by Cleopatra's army, the Nabateans administered a crushing defeat on Herod. Almost immediately another disaster followed. A severe earthquake in Palestine killed tens of thousands of men, and destroyed great quantities of cattle and property throughout the land. Herod tried to negotiate a truce with the Nabateans but they murdered his envoys and prepared to invade Judea. But disastrous though they seemed, the wars with the Nabatean Arabs had the beneficial effect of preventing Herod from joining Antony in his last struggle against his rivals in Rome.

Throughout his career Herod proved himself a masterly general and, once again, despite the weariness of his troops, when he drew them up for battle against Melichos near Philadelphia (Amman), he was victorious. The Jewish forces suffered 5,000 casualties but they routed the Arabs and drove them panic-stricken into the desert where they perished of thirst.

Had Antony needed proof that Herod could indeed be relied upon to maintain peace in this section of the borders of the Roman Empire, this success in the face of overwhelming odds would have provided it. But Antony was beyond caring. Defeated by Octavius at Actium, he and Cleopatra had committed suicide, thus setting the seal of tragedy on a romance that was to echo down the ages.

HEROD AND AUGUSTUS

Herod's enemies saw the fall of his patron as an omen of his own downfall. Surely Octavian, now Emperor Augustus, would punish Herod's unfailing loyalty to Antony. But Herod himself was undeterred. While Augustus was visiting nearby Rhodes, Herod presented himself to the new ruler of the world and set about winning his favour. Leaving aside the robes of a reigning monarch, he appeared before Augustus simply as a private citizen. The services he had rendered Antony were listed in detail, but Herod laid particular stress on the enmity that had existed between him and Cleopatra and on his endeavours to weaken her influence over Antony. He made much of his essential loyalty to Rome and called on Augustus to form an objective judgment, not based on personalities. Such frankness appealed to Augustus and, in any case, Herod seemed likely to be a useful ally. After listening cordially, he replaced Herod's crown upon his head, urging him to serve his future patron as faithfully as he had Antony.

As an immediate token of his favour, he approved Herod's recapture of Jericho and Gaza and gave him in addition the coastal towns of Anthedon, Jaffa and Straton's Tower, (later Caesarea), as well as Gadara and Susita east of the Lake of Galilee, which had been taken from the Hasmonean state by Pompey. Samaria was his too. Thus he could unite

Marble bust of Augustus (c. 20 B.C.E.), now in the Vatican.

Judea and Galilee in one territorial unit. Augustus promised other favours later and Herod must have felt that the 800 talents (close to a million dollars) he paid over to the Emperor had been well spent. Once again, spectacular success had been wrested from seeming defeat. Herod made a triumphant return to Jerusalem and could smile at the surprise and chagrin felt by the people there.

At about this time, Herod added to his court a colourful personality, Nicolaus of Damascus who taught him history and rhetoric. Nicolaus had been the tutor of Cleopatra's children and he planned to write a history of the whole world. To him we are indebted for a detailed history of Herod's time as part of his universal history. In spite of its flattering, respectful tone, this supplied Josephus with a source for his first book on the Jewish war and the "Antiquities of the Jews". The later historian made his own estimate of Herod's character and times, but Nicolaus supplied him with a contemporary account of events.

MURDER OF MARIAMME

As so often in Herod's varied career, triumph snatched from the edge of despair was marred by his wilful drive towards violence and cruelty — even towards himself.

Before he left Jerusalem for Rhodes, he had ordered the aged Hyrcanus, Mariamme's grandfather, to be strangled, thus eliminating any possibility that a scion of the Hasmonean house should be used as the rallying point for a revolt during the king's absence.

However, this was not all. Mariamme, his wife, he dearly and passionately loved. But both she and her mother Alexandra loathed him and berated him for the murder of Mariamme's grandfather and brother. Though she had borne Herod three sons and two daughters, Mariamme now refused to share his bed or even to speak civilly to him. This only served to inflame his jealous love. His pathological jealousy made him an easy prey to allegations impugning her chastity. Salome, Herod's sister, saw to it that there were many of these. He could not bear the thought that anyone else might ever win her favours if he were to disappear. Accordingly, just as he had done before, on his departure to visit Augustus he had left orders that Mariamme should be murdered if he failed to return. On this occasion too, all the machinery of intrigue within the court with Salome as chief instigator, was given free rein. When Herod did return, the rumours, accusations of attempted poisoning and other slanders reached such a pitch that, in a fit of rage at what he thought was evidence of his wife's infidelity, he ordered her sent to the executioner, together with her mother, Alexandra. Mariamme bore her fate with great dignity and courage, so that even her mother when she hurled bitter accusations at her, was shamed into silence.

Herod bitterly regretted his action, but he was a slave to his own suspicions and fears, from which only his death would bring release. Mariamme was always present in his fevered mind:

> "for his love to her was not of a calm nature, nor such as we usually meet with among husbands."

These are some of the more sensational of the murders during the early period of Herod's reign. By themselves, they give little idea of his elaborate system of espionage throughout the land or of the staggering number of ordinary people put to the sword. He completed the destruction of the Hasmonean house, slaying other distant blood relations. Nor was the Idumean, Costobar, who had plotted with Cleopatra against him, spared. With the death of this man, Herod could comfort himself with the thought that he had at last eliminated all his enemies.

HEROD'S STATE

Herod was now forty-four. The brilliant levantine charmer and extrovert who had captivated men and women had sunk deeper into vindictive, suspicious moods, subject to sudden excesses of passion. Nevertheless, in the 25 more years he had to live, he could give his whole attention to ruling Judea. In this sphere and in his building program his career showed a brighter side.

Augustus' recognition of Herod in 30 B. C. E. carried with it confirmation of the decision of the Senate ten years earlier which had named him "amicus et socius populi Romani." Thus established as an ally of Rome, Herod was endowed with powers and prerogatives which can be divided under several headings:

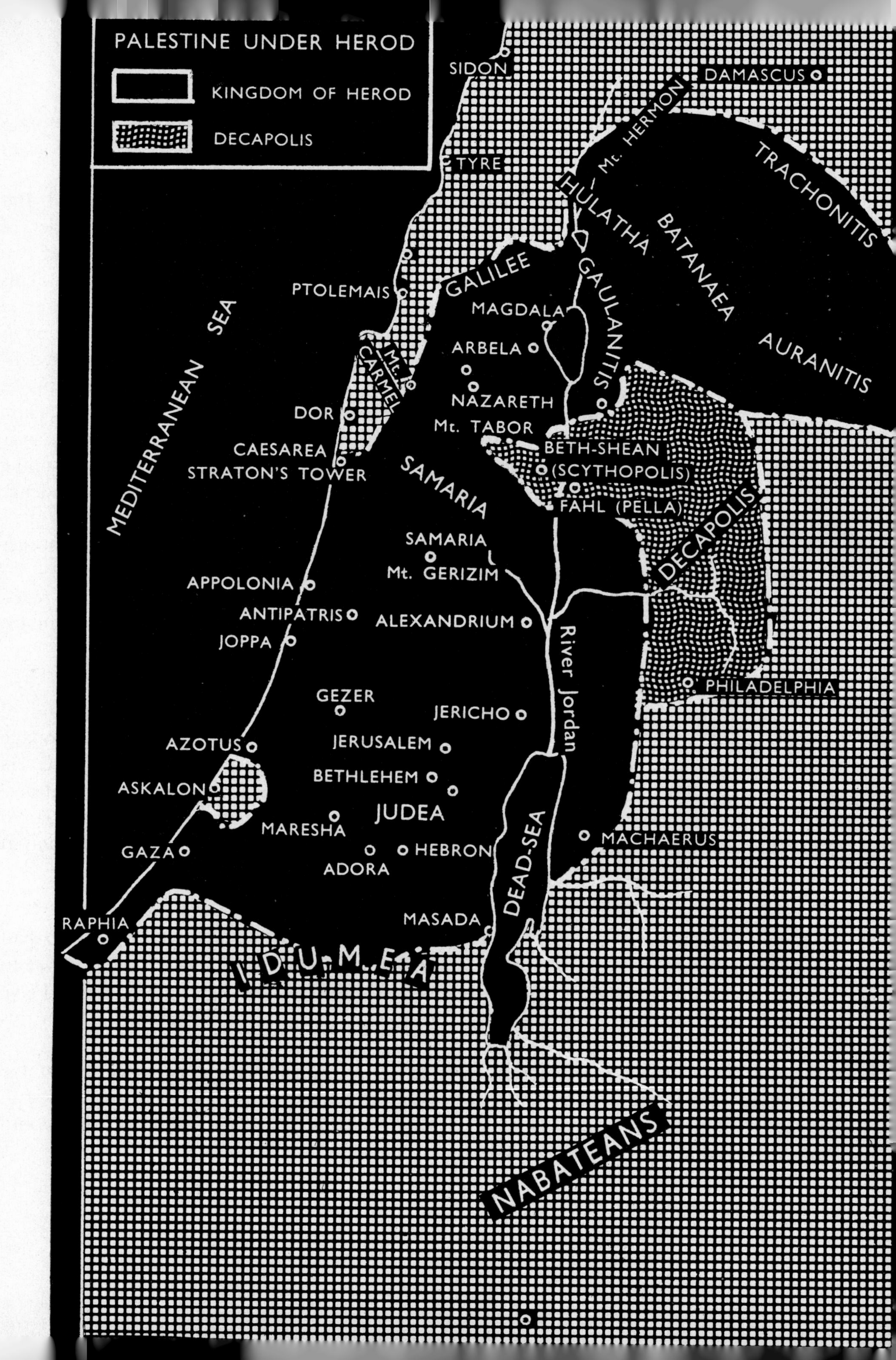

PALESTINE UNDER HEROD
KINGDOM OF HEROD
DECAPOLIS
SIDON
DAMASCUS
Mt. HERMON
TYRE
TRACHONITIS
HULATHA
BATANAEA
GAULANITIS
GALILEE
PTOLEMAIS
MAGDALA
AURANITIS
MEDITERRANEAN SEA
Mt. CARMEL
ARBELA
NAZARETH
DOR
Mt. TABOR
BETH-SHEAN
(SCYTHOPOLIS)
CAESAREA
STRATON'S TOWER
SAMARIA
FAHL (PELLA)
DECAPOLIS
SAMARIA
Mt. GERIZIM
APPOLONIA
ANTIPATRIS
ALEXANDRIUM
JOPPA
River Jordan
PHILADELPHIA
GEZER
JERICHO
AZOTUS
JERUSALEM
BETHLEHEM
ASKALON
JUDEA
MARESHA
DEAD-SEA
MACHAERUS
GAZA
HEBRON
ADORA
RAPHIA
MASADA
IDUMEA
NABATEANS

The army: This was recruited with Rome's assent, but its organization was more hellenistic than Roman. Its backbone consisted — even more than in the time of Alexander Jannai — of foreign levies and hired mercenaries. Apparently this was a deliberate policy to ensure that his army owed him a direct personal loyalty to balance the possible disaffection of locally recruited soldiers. At the end of their term of service, these foreign mercenaries were employed in the internal administration of the country. They were concentrated mainly in the hellenistic towns which had been restored to Herod's kingdom where they strengthened the oriental-hellenistic elements of the country.

Expansion and organization: Thanks to the Emperor's favours, Herod managed in 23 to expand the borders of his realm beyond the districts formally granted to him in Rome, particularly in north eastern Transjordan: the Trachonitis, Batanaea and Auranitis. In 23, he acquired Iturea to the north of Palestine (see map). His kingdom covered in fact most of the traditional ancient kingdom of David, including Edom, his native land, but without the hellenistic enclaves and territories in southern Transjordan held by the Nabateans.

The population of the country in those days was probably between one million-and-a-half and two million of whom by far the larger part were Jews (a similar number of Jews lived in the Dispersion). This number is indicative of the dense settlement of the country.

The country was divided into "toparchies" or districts: eleven in Judea, five in Galilee and three in Transjordan, each one having its administrative center in an important town. They were ruled by district governors directly responsible to the king. The independent hellenistic cities and adjoining territories were administered by governors who were also answerable to Herod. Above him there was no foreign governor. He was the absolute ruler of his kingdom.

An Absolute Monarchy: As ruler of the land and its army, the final arbiter in all legal questions and in control of a treasury that represented the major portion of the national income, he was able to transform his royal authority into that of an absolute monarch. All other public and social institutions had been divested of political potential. The Sanhedrin was reduced from the supreme legal and civil court, to the status of an exclusively religious tribunal. All the political authority the High Priest had once exercised had been shorn from him. Herod had gradually cancelled any other elements of independence that remained in Jewish society or its institutions which might have threatened his absolute authority.

As an appointee of the Roman Senate, Herod had the right to apply its laws. By virtue of this right he sentenced Jews convicted of theft to be sold as slaves abroad. This was contrary to the rules laid down in the Torah, but it was in line with the Roman policy of condemning people of the lower classes to perpetual hard labour in the mines. It is believed that the "brigands" and "underground thiefs" of Herod's time were not ordinary thieves but the remnants of the nationalist Hasmonean party who opposed Herod's rule. In order to rid himself of them he declared them common thieves, caught disturbing the peace. He may have made use of them in the copper mines which he hired from Augustus. Apart from this case, we have no evidence of Herod disregarding Jewish Law. Where there was no threat of opposition to his rule, he was content to abide by the traditional precepts.

The Administration: By virtue of the power vested in him Herod was able to organize a sound internal administration, maintain a strong army and pay his tribute to Rome. This was lighter than it might have been. As a result of the Emperor's generosity, Herod was an immensely rich man. His own possessions included the family estates in Edom and lands confiscated from the murdered Hasmoneans and their supporters. He lent money to the Nabateans on which they paid interest. His great income came first from the high taxes imposed on his people — the head-tax, the land tax, (about a quarter of the proceeds of each harvest); the tribute tax to Rome, the house taxes, and the crown taxes. These were paid in coin or in kind. He imposed import duties on all goods coming into the country — a large proportion through his port of Caesarea. In addition, he imposed tolls for the use of roads, bridges, wharves, docks and so forth. He did not allow any possible means of raising income which hellenist or Roman traditions offered, to be overlooked. Together, these made up the equivalent of a modern state's national budget. P. F. Abel estimates that the total annual revenues of Herod amounted to 2,115 talents (21,150,000 silver drachmas), a tremendous amount of money considered in terms of contemporary purchasing power, far more than its modern equivalent of $2.5 to 3 million. In addition he had a large income from the caravan trade and commercial transactions, linking Arabia and the Mediterranean. The positive side to his heavy exactions will be seen from his many programs for development covering all aspects of national life.

His Secret Police: To prevent the formation of any serious internal opposition, Herod established a rigorous police force with an elaborate system of espionage. He forbade all public assemblies and, in general, the oppressive atmosphere of a huge prison prevailed throughout the country.

Herod was not even above disguising himself in order to mix with the crowds and try to overhear what might be plotted against him. Exactly what his subjects thought of him was made perfectly clear, after his death, to Augustus. The Jewish deputies told the Emperor:

". .he was not a king, but the most barbarous of all tyrants, and that they had found [him] to be such by the sufferings they underwent from him: that when a very great number had been slain by him, those that were left had endured such miseries, that they called those that were dead happy men; that he had not only tortured the bodies of his subjects, but entire cities, and had done much harm to the cities of his own country, while he adorned those that belonged to foreigners; and he shed the blood of Jews, in order to do kindness to those people who were out of their bounds; that he had filled the nation full of poverty, and of the greatest iniquity, instead of that happiness and those laws which they had anciently enjoyed; that, in short, the Jews had borne more calamities from Herod, in a few years, than had their forefathers during all that interval of time that had passed since they had come out of Babylon, and returned home, in the reign of Xerxes." (War. Bk. 11, 6:2)

It was Shemayah who said, "do not court the ruling power,"(Abot 1:10). This gives the key to the whole of Herod's reign. From the day of his first entry into the royal palace until his dying breath, fear ruled in the land and terror was made the instrument of policy.

"for when we have respect to his magnificence, and the benefits which he bestowed on all mankind, there is no possibility for even those that had the least respect for him to deny, or not openly to confess, that he had a nature vastly beneficent: but when anyone looks upon the punishments he inflicted, and the injuries he did, not only to his subjects, but to his nearest

Bronze coin of Herod (37–4 B.C.E.). On the left, inscribed in Greek "of King Herodes". In the centre is a tripod with basin. The reverse, on the right, shows a censer between two palm branches.

relations, and takes notice of his severe and unrelenting disposition there, he will be forced to allow that he was brutish, and a stranger to all humanity; insomuch that these men suppose his nature different, and sometimes at contradiction with itself." (Antiquities of the Jews Bk.XVI, 5:4)

THE LOVER OF THE ROMAN PEOPLE

It is debatable whether, as some historians have claimed, Herod was really no worse than his predecessors. He was far more ruthless and unprincipled than they. He ruled entirely according to the accepted hellenist-oriental precepts of an enforced tyranny. Above all, nothing in his reign corrected the shortcomings of his predecessors, the Hasmonean princes. They had put party before national interest and had to that extent departed from the abiding values and concepts of their people. Nevertheless, they had felt themselves akin to that people and in their common blood had an overwhelming claim to the loyalty of their subjects. Herod on the other hand, despised Pharisees and Sadducees equally. He did not rule his country with its vital interests foremost in his mind. For party loyalty, he had substituted the interests of Rome and it was the Roman method of government which he tried to enforce.

He was not a real Jewish king. He was king of the Jews, subject to Augustus, and his relationship with him reflected his status vis-a-vis Rome. In 27 Augustus had been crowned sublime emperor and thus formally established the Roman Empire. Within this new organization, Syria was regarded as an imperial province of the Empire, whereas Judea was recognized as an allied kingdom, ready to act in the defence of the Empire.

Nevertheless, regardless of the distinction and prestige his foreign policy may have achieved, to his subjects his title of "rex amicus et socius populi Romani" was intolerably appropriate. Like other similarly dependent rulers, Herod called himself a "lover of Caesar" and a "lover of the Roman people". In his case this was more than an empty formality. His rule was founded on Roman power and his political outlook accepted wholesale the principles and social attitudes of Rome. The Roman rulers were his models, down to the last excesses.

Herod had surrounded himself with heathen advisers and was known to be particularly interested in pagan culture. No wonder therefore that, in spite of his territorial successes — and he extended the country's boundaries only with Rome's permission — his people felt themselves oppressed, and found their true representatives, not in the royal palace, but in the Pharisaic academies.

POLICY OF A GREAT BUILDER

Thirty four years — from 37 to 4 B. C. E. — are a long reign and Herod was never idle. His policy was clear cut in respect of three main purposes he was bent on achieving: to suppress nationalism, which he considered a suicidal folly; to promote the welfare and honour of Judaism according to his own lights — both in Palestine and in the Diaspora; finally to foster westernization (hellenization) which meant pleasing Augustus and Rome while imitating the hellenistic way of life. This he did by a series of political measures, and a great building program. This was spread over a number of years, but all items formed instalments of a single policy. It may be noted also that some of the building programs carried out so diligently were partly a means of alleviating adverse economic conditions, but above all, were for his own glorification and the pursuit of his own policy for the country. *His outstanding achievement was the rebuilding of the Temple.*

FORTRESSES AND DUNGEONS

The first objects of his building plans were the extensive fortifications, barracks and small forts which he constructed as a protection against enemies of his regime beyond his borders — and inside them. The internal security of the kingdom was reinforced by a remarkable chain of fortresses and castles in Jerusalem and Judea — forming a closely knit system. Among these was the imposing fortress of Hyrcania (Khirbet Mird), an old Hasmonean stronghold, actually a fortress-prison to which he committed all his enemies

Sanctuary of Obodas II, (30–9 B.C.E.) at Petra, the capital of the Nabateans, who deified their kings. As the Seleucid empire weakened, large areas of its territory were annexed by the Nabateans whose prosperity reached its peak during Roman times. They maintained the great caravan route from Syria to Egypt and Arabia which skirted the borders of Herod's kingdom and carried the international trade in spices, furs, etc.

Interior of a Nabatean dwelling cut out of the soft limestone of the Negeb, (above left). The oriental-hellenic façades of the rock city of Petra (above right) belong to the 1st century B.C.E. Four connecting high columns break up the uniformity of the façade of this tomb; arches and ruins of the town can be seen below. Petra, situated in a deep valley south of the Dead Sea, was a center for the variety of goods imported from inland Asia. The town charged heavy duties on all goods crossing its territory and provided large warehouses cut out of the rock and also comfortable relay houses for merchants and their caravans. Below right, is the inside of a Nabatean well.

Herod's palace of Masada. This view is taken from the northern slope of the mountain. In the background are the mountains of Moab, on the other side of the Dead Sea.

and which was the place of their execution. Alexandrium was rebuilt by his brother during the wars with Antigonus. It was here that his wife and her mother were held prisoner before Herod set off for his meeting with Octavius after Actium. To protect his eastern borders against the Nabateans, he built Machaerus, overlooking the Dead Sea and the Southern Transjordan of the Nabateans. Probably this also provided dungeons for Herod's enemies, as it did in the days of his successor Herod Antipas, who imprisoned and killed John the Baptist there (see Ch. IX).

The furthest south of these fortresses was Masada in the mountains bordering the Dead Sea. This had been a Hasmonean stronghold and was a truly impregnable fortress. Herod rebuilt and enlarged it, adding a palace and equipping it with a water works and means of communication to its defenders. In addition, he built the fortified palace of Herodium in the wilderness near Bethlehem, where he was finally buried as he directed in his will.

These forts were all built on top of hills or mountains and were protected by a steep glacis which prevented anyone from climbing up to them. This gave them the conical appearance visible to this day. Vast cisterns for the storage of rainwater surrounded the base of the forts, lined with hydraulic cement. Wherever possible, an aqueduct would bring additional supplies of water, generally rain-catchments from adjacent hills or gullies, or occasional springs. Below some of them, faubourgs (suburbs) of which traces remain, were attached to the forts, which were dwelling places as well as citadels.

For such a system of defence, good communications were essential. New roads kept pace with the expansion of Herod's kingdom and with the growth of Palestine's trade, both inside the country and with the neighbouring lands. Herod was also careful to maintain the road to the east through Trachonitis, east of the Jordan, and the "road of the spice caravans" which connected Gaza, on Palestine's southern sea coast, to Damascus and inland Syria.

THE HERODIAN CITIES

Herod's redeeming quality was the fact that his great dynamic energy and flair for organization were also directed to the constructive development of his country. In spite of the toll of the wars he fought and the political oppression of his regime, under his guidance the country's economic life flourished. Moreover, the western vision which he brought to the country's affairs and the effect of the new cities he built was to transform Palestine. It was Herod who made out of the provincial Jerusalem of hellenistic and Hasmonean days, the great and glorious city we know from the descriptions of Josephus and the New Testament. Above all, he is remembered as the monarch who built Caesarea — named in honour of his patron Augustus — which became the greatest of Palestine's ports and second only to Alexandria in the wealth of its commerce and the brilliance of its cosmopolitan population of Oriental-hellenists and Jews.

Especially during the years 25—13 B. C. E. he was occupied with an extensive construction program. He built new cities; gymnasia and theatres throughout the country including in Jerusalem; amphitheatres in the capital and in Caesarea and Sebaste (Samaria); fortresses, seamen's dwellings, ports and palaces, every kind of lasting monument to his greatness and care for his country.

CAESAREA

Although Julius Caesar and Augustus did not follow the Seleucid policy of settling immigrants and other Roman citizens in Judea, Herod made up for this through his construction of Caesarea and by rebuilding Sebaste. They were to become bastions of the oriental type of Roman-hellenistic culture of the period. They deserve special mention

Ruins of Caesarea's ancient harbour. The port was begun by Herod in 22 B.C.E. Enormous blocks of limestone were used to build breakwaters to provide a safe anchorage for seagoing vessels. When completed, the port was larger than Piraeus, the port of Athens. Over the years, it was occupied by Romans, Byzantines, Crusaders and Arabs.

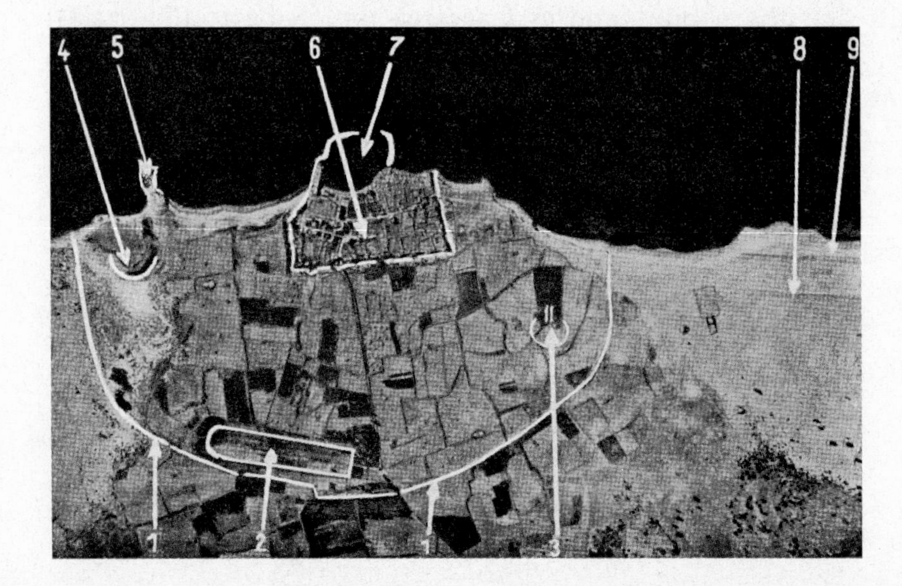

Aerial view of Caesarea showing: (1) *ancient Roman wall;* (2) *ancient hippodrome;* (3) *amphitheatre;* (4) *theatre;* (5) *ruins of a pier;* (6) *the Crusaders' town;* (7) *the ancient circular harbour and breakwaters;* (8) *the low Roman aqueduct;* (9) *the high aqueduct.*

Beautiful capitals and countless numbers of columns can be found for miles around, a mute testimony to Caesarea's grandeur.

Caesarea's theatre, excavated in 1960 *with the aid of modern equipment. The whole structure, including the columns of the orchestra, has been revealed. The public buildings, says Josephus, were all in a style worthy of the city's renown. Herod also instituted quinquennial games, dedicated to Caesar.*

among the Herodians' many great achievements in promoting art, because we can still see several imposing remnants.

The transformation of the little anchorage of Straton's Tower into the great harbour and metropolis of Caesarea was Herod's greatest achievement, with the exception of the Temple, to be described below. To build a breakwater and quay for an artificial harbour on a sandy beach, enormous stone blocks 50 × 10 × 9 ft, or larger, were lowered into 20 fathoms of water. This seawall protected the harbour, the wharf buildings, warehouses and the towers of the port. A Greek temple to Zeus dominated the scene and a vast town covered the sand with a well-laid market-place, a forum, a theatre and amphitheatre, a hippodrome and a great palace. The town was inaugurated in 9. B. C. E. with great Olympic Games. On this occasion Augustus and Livia joyfully contributed 500 talents (over half a million dollars). Caesarea took twelve years to build.

SEBASTE IN SAMARIA

Over the ruins of the Israelite town of Ahab, Herod rebuilt a substantial Greek hill town, with an Acropolis topped by a glistening temple built in the Corinthian style. He

Flight of steps from the temple to Augustus on the hellenistic acropolis of Samaria (Sebaste), all that remains of the magnificent Corinthian-style building. The temple was erected over the debris of the ivory-plated halls of Omri and Ahab, which were uncovered by deep excavations, (left).

Caesarea's chariot races and athletic games were a normal part of the hellenistic way of life. This stone relief shows the more sophisticated Circus Maximus in Rome. The wild excitement of the race, among the contestants and their supporters in the galleries has been vividly captured.

erected an Augusteum in honour of Augustus, with a huge statue of the emperor, and named the town Sebaste — the Greek for Augustus.

The city was largely a military colony and the home of foreign veterans. In hellenistic style, the city was provided with a stadium, amphitheatre, forum, temples and the facilities demanded by the contemporary mode of life.

Herod's widespread undertakings provided employment for many, expanded the country's facilities and added to the beauty of many places. Men were happy to earn. In fact, Herod's determination to shine as a great builder and to outdo all other hellenistic rulers in this respect, did produce many tangible lasting benefits. However, what seemed more important at the time was that the cost of the projects was met by exorbitant taxes on the people. Funds were needed not only to pay for construction works but also to meet the tribute that had to be paid to Rome and to support the royal household, a luxurious court and the strong armies, all of which formed totally non-productive drains on the wealth of the country.

FESTIVALS AND THEATRES IN JERUSALEM AND CAESAREA

Moreover, since a large number of the projects concerned pagan, not Jewish activities, they antagonized many people. For instance, Caesarea was anything but a Jewish city and the many theatres were an abomination to the pious, no less than the pagan temples.

Shortly after his entry into Jerusalem as a conqueror, Herod instituted the "Actian Games", a periodic festival on the lines of the Olympic games which included chariot-races, musical and athletic contests and gladiatorial shows. As a setting he provided Jerusalem with a hippodrome, a theatre and an amphitheatre. Chariot-races were popular with the Jews. The hippodrome lay near the South wall of the Temple Area, shaped like a very narrow U.

A little distance from the city Herod built a theatre on a high hill and further away still, an amphitheatre. This was a circular area in which lions or other powerful or rare beasts were to fight with each other and where wrestling contests and bouts took place between naked competitors. Exposure of the human body was regarded as impious by Jews, but the foreign spectators were charmed. Lavish prizes had attracted the first athletes and artists of the day. The amphitheatre was decorated with inscriptions praising Augustus' victories and between them were erected gold and silver trophies, shields, breastplates, helmets, swords and lances arranged in artistic groups. But these aroused the indignation of the godly and in 27, ten men plotted to assassinate the king there. They, the ringleaders and their entire families were executed.

Herod regarded himself as a sophisticated hellenist, i.e. as belonging to the leading culture of his day. He was determined that the ostentation and splendour of his court, the visible strength of his armies and the magnificence of his tribute to the divinities of Greece and Rome should all be unequalled. It may seem strange and tactless that a king of the Jews should thus ape Roman manners and devote himself zealously to pagan installations. However, Herod pretended that he had to humour the wishes of his great Roman "patron".

This hellenistic trend in Herod's policy, which was so abhorrent to tradition-loving Jews explains why a number of his measures, sincerely intended to benefit his people, were still not able to win their approval. One example is his swift and efficacious action in dealing with the drought of 25. He used all the resources of his treasury, even melting down works of art, and the gold and silver fittings and plate of his palace into ingots, so as to purchase wheat from the Roman prefect of Egypt to feed the hungry masses during the famine. He distributed 1,200,000 bushels to his own people and 152,000 to Syrian farmers to replenish their granaries. Another example is his remission of a percentage of all taxes in 20. But all was to no avail. He had defied sacred laws. His people would not be won over by a little bread or a handful of copper.

PALACES

As the upper town of Jerusalem prospered, so its northern and western quarters grew. As merchants, landowners and private citizens vied with each other in keeping up with the times, so the houses and streets, many with colonnades and shop-arcades, began to look more hellenistic. The different quarters of the city were arranged with intersecting streets as on a chess-board. Whole new quarters were built looking like all other new towns of the Eastern Mediterranean.

The capital was the greatest of his achievements. He pulled down the ruinous Akra, the fortress on the acropolis that dominated the Temple area (cf. p. 25) and rebuilt nearby the

XVIII. A Roman lady at her toilette, a cupid on the left, is a good example of Roman painting of the beginning of the 1st century C.E. (Villa dei Misteri in Pompei).

XIX. A beautiful fresco of garlanded "ephebes" (see plate IV) decorated the house of the patrician Celio in Rome.

XX. Julius Caesar. Marble (*p.* 103).

XXI. The emperor Augustus. Marble (*p.* 119—126).

XXII. Sword in hand, gladiators fought to the death in the arena (*p.* 127).

Antonia Tower named in honour of Marc Antony. It served as a palace for a dozen years as well as a fortress and prison. It was also the High Priest's dwelling and the place where his sacred garments were kept under the government's watchful eye. Underground passages (of which traces still remain) as well as two great stairways connected it with the Holy Places.

Herod decided to build a more sumptuous palace on the hill where Jerusalem had expanded westwards. On the north side of this new acropolis, he built three imposing towers, the Hippicus, named after an old friend; the Phasael, in memory of his dead brother, and the third, called Mariamme, either to commemorate his first Mariamme, or to flatter the new beautiful Mariamme he had married as his third wife. The towers were 128, 138 and 72 feet high respectively. Recent excavations show that the tower Phasael was located where the Citadel, also called the Tower of David, now stands. The other two must have stood slightly southwest and east of Phasael. Within this area, Herod built a theatre and, finally, a new palace to the south of the towers.

THE TEMPLE REBUILT

This done, Herod announced that he would build a new sanctuary to replace the modest battle-scarred Temple. This was to be his crowning triumph and in Jewish annals he has been given full credit for its achievement. When the idea was put forward, there were many who were appalled, fearing that Herod intended to erect a pagan shrine in place of the most sacred building in Judea. However, Herod gave a solemn undertaking to respect the traditions and sanctity of the place and, finally, the objections were overcome.

> ". . and the whole structure, as also the structure of the royal cloister, was on each side much lower, but the middle was much higher, till they were visible to those that dwelt in the country for a great many furlongs, but chiefly to such as lived over-against them and those that approached them." (Antiq. Bk. XV, 11:3)

The project was begun in the 17th or 18th year of Herod's reign, (20 B.C.E.). A new Temple was in fact constructed over and around the modest 5th century building. Herod planned it as the ultimate expression of the magnificence of his reign.

A thousand chariots were needed to cart the great stones; 10,000 skilled workmen were drafted to the site and, to ensure that the inner sanctuary and the Holy of Holies should not be defiled by profane hands, a thousand priests were trained in masonry, carpentry, decoration and so on, and attended to the construction of those two most precious portions, dressed in their ceremonial priestly garments.

The major part of the work was accomplished in ten years. Additional work was done in later years and, in fact, the Temple was only completed after many years. Then it appeared in its full splendour. Built on a high esplanade, surrounded by columns and beautiful gates, its shining white stone could be seen for miles in every direction.

Herod spared neither money nor effort to achieve his dream of unparalleled magnificence. He did not alter the size of Solomon's inner Temple, nor its general pattern (see Ch. XIII

The Tower of Antonia stood at the northwest corner of the Temple area. Nothing now remains of the fortress except traces of foundations in the rock at the right of the minaret and the subterranean cisterns nearby.From where it stood, the tower dominated the Temple area.

ADAM TO DANIEL), but in the overall plan he achieved much greater splendour and vastness, rivalling many contemporary structures. First of all, he doubled the area of the outer courts of the Temple by smoothing the rock surface and especially by filling in the steep south-western and south-eastern corners. In certain places the substructure ran 90—125 feet deep before resting on the virgin rock below. The remains of the south-eastern supporting walls are still visible today. Above them and still below the wide esplanade on the Temple Area was a vast arched crypt, now known as "Solomon's Stables". Herod's masons certainly knew their job. One can still admire their craftsmanship in the hewn stone and masonry of the Wailing Wall which stood at the western end of the esplanade, (see colour illustration).

"And as he came out of the temple, one of his disciples said to him, 'Look, Teacher, what wonderful stones and what wonderful buildings!" (Mark, 13:1)

The esplanade was built in the form of a double trapezium (two parallel sides, of unequal length), one superimposed over the other. Walls, porticoes and rows of columns divided its area into different sections and eight gates gave access from all sides. The area finally produced was 35 acres in extent. In the north and south the enclosures ran 351 and 309 yards. On the east and west they were 518 and 536 yards. It has been immortalized by the many documents written during and close to the period—the Mishnah, Josephus and the New Testament.

"They feasted and celebrated this rebuilding of the Temple; and for the King, he sacrificed three hundred oxen to God; as did the rest, every one according to his ability: the number of which sacrifices is not possible to set down; for it cannot be that we should truly relate it; for at the same time with this celebration for the work about the temple, fell also the day of the king's inauguration, which he kept of an old custom as a festival, and it now coincided with the other; which coincidence of them both made the festival most illustrious." (Antiq. Bk. 2:6)

The Temple itself, and its inner courts, were protected by the first outer "wall of the Gentiles", beyond which no pagan might penetrate. A Greek inscription warned strangers off (see illustration).

In spite of the pride many Jews must have felt in their new architectural adornments, these had done nothing to change Herod's unpopularity. Even the fact that the building, carried out on a very lavish scale, had come as a welcome relief at a time of severe stress and unemployment, was not allowed to affect the people's opinion of him. Even while it became a popular proverb that "he who has not seen Herod's Temple, has never seen stately structure" (Sukkah 51b), the prevailing bitterness continued unabated.

Tablet from Herod's Temple, with an inscription forbidding entrance to strangers. It reads: "No stranger may enter within the balustrade round the temple and enclosure. Anyone caught doing so will bear the responsibility for his death which will surely follow."

Aerial view of the Temple area from the south east, since covered by the Moslem Haram-al-sharif, and the Dome of the Rock which stands in the center where the Temple once stood. Other landmarks of Herod's time are ancient remains of the Double Gate (foreground) and the Golden Gate along the east wall (right), overlooking the Valley of Jehosaphat. Remnants of the western "Wailing Wall" (not visible here) stand near the cypresses west of the esplanade (left-hand corner). Two thirds of the height of this wall, 21 *metres, are buried under debris below ground. Below is a reconstruction of the Temple, suggested a century ago by De Vogue and still regarded as the most likely.*

At least one object commemorates the façade of the lost Temple — the shekel struck by Bar Kochba in 135 C.E. Beyond the façade with its four fluted columns and architrave is a "torah" shrine with shelves and two scrolls of the Law. The star above the architrave is inscribed "Shimon" (see Ch. XIII).

The south-eastern corner of the wall of the Temple mount overlooking the Kidron valley and Ophel. Only 25 metres of the original 47 metres high wall are visible. One stone at this corner facing south and east is 7 metres long by 1.85 and weighs over 100 tons. In the western wall there is a stone 12 metres in length.

This elegant sculptured column in hellenistic style made a corner in one of the walls of Herod's Temple.

Even if Herod had deliberately planned the Temple as a means of capturing his people's good-will, he would have wrecked his own scheme when he placed a Roman eagle on the Temple gates. In the last year of his life, two young rabbis sparked off an unsuccessful revolt by tearing down the hated object, for which Herod killed them, to the great distress of the people.

HEROD'S FOREIGN POLICY IN THE DIASPORA

Herod took a keen interest in the welfare of Jews living outside Palestine. He used all his tact and gave generous gifts to Syrian and Greek cities to conciliate those that were hosts to his co-religionaries, and to secure from his Roman patrons unequivocal ratification of their privileges. One instance of this is his intervention on behalf of the Jews of Ionia, whose civic rights were being ignored by the Greeks. This policy can be explained not only by his desire to protect possible commercial ties with them but also his ambition to appear as the champion of Jews everywhere. An additional potent incentive was the substantial contributions these Jews made to the maintenance and construction costs of the Temple. No doubt he dipped into this fund when necessary and he naturally sought to ensure their continued good-will and — donations. To the Herodian family during the closing years of Herod's life a comment of Hillel's may well apply. Noticing a man's skull floating on a river, he exclaimed:

> "because thou didst drown others, wast thou drowned, and the end of them that drowned thee will also be drowning." (Aboth 2:6)

Incompatibility

Herod always boasted that he had expanded the borders of the Jewish state almost to those of David's empire, and had built up its wealth and prosperity until they rivalled Solomon's. After centuries of miserable and, as he saw it, useless struggle by the Hasmoneans, he was rescuing the lost glory of the house of David. For ten centuries the Jews and their prophets cherished dreams of this ancient glory. It was he, Herod, who had made them reality. All credit and honour should therefore be due to him.

On the basis of recent research, A. Schalit finds that Herod tried to establish his status as "redeeming king" by claiming kinship to the House of David and, moreover, to compare his kingdom to the Messianic Kingdom (see pp. 211—12). However, M. Stern and other scholars believe that this theme has been overworked in the evaluation of Herod.

In any case, no Jew and certainly no Pharisee or Essene, would accept the idea that the redemption of Israel could come through Rome. Whether or not he aspired to it, Herod would never suit the role of such a Messiah. No wonder the people and their spiritual leaders the Pharisees, the Essenes and the sectaries of Qumran utterly rejected his version of a Roman-Herodian redemption. Israel might be physically part of the Roman Empire. Its people never regarded themselves as in any way committed to Roman philosophy in either politics or ethics.

Accordingly, in addition to all the other reasons which Herod's people had found to hate him, they now saw that his ambitions were in direct conflict with all the teachings and traditions of the Torah. The very essence of the unique national and religious identity of the Jews was challenged. Herod's concept would deny it outright.

Naturally enough, Herod's attempts to pacify the Pharisees and win them over to his policy of harmonizing pro-hellenistic and pro-Roman ways with Jewish contemporary life, met with a cold reception. In the words of P.F. Abel: "From this, Judaism, after its awakening by the Maccabean upheaval, had become a force with which to contend. The time is past when a High Priest constructed a gymnasium near the Temple and exercised there, throwing the discus. After the successes of Antiochus Epiphanes, religion had become a political and spiritual right. This return to the Torah as into a fortress manifests one of the most characteristic reactions of the oriental spirit against western ways. Great teachers and promoters of Jewish faith and custom had lived in Herod's century. The latter was obliged in the end to recognize the incompatibility between these external forces and Judaism and to govern accordingly." But Herod was too arrogant to admit even this.

THE PRETENDER; ANTIPATER AND HEROD'S PSYCHOSIS

In handling the question of the succession to his throne, Herod had at first chosen his two sons by the beloved Mariamme, Alexander and Aristobulos. With this in mind, he sent them to Rome to be educated. But they grew up into spoilt, vain, arrogant young men, frankly at odds with their father. Nevertheless, they were popular with the masses, who saw in them the last remnant of the Hasmoneans. Inevitably they became the target for all the intriguers of Herod's court so that the latter years of Herod's life were filled with plot and counterplot.

These came to a head in 14 B.C.E. when Herod was already 60 years old. His sister, Salome, plotted with Antipater, one of his sons by his first wife, Doris, who had recently been permitted to return from exile. As the elder, Antipater considered himself the rightful heir and he and his aunt so poisoned Herod's mind against Alexander and Aristobulos, that he demanded their trial. His fury directed itself mainly against his son Alexander, who described his father's state as "furorem et insaniam" (madness and complete irrationality):

> "And what more can be said, but that those who before were the most intimate friends, were become wild beasts to one another, as if a certain madness had fallen upon them, while there was no room for defence or refutation, in order to the discovery of the truth, but all were at random doomed to destruction! so that some lamented those that were in prison, some those that were put to death, and others lamented that they were in expectation of the same miseries; and a melancholy solitude rendered the kingdom deformed, and quite the reverse to that happy state it was formerly in. Herod's own life was also entirely disturbed; and, because he could trust nobody, he was sorely punished by the expectation of further misery; for he often fancied in his imagination, that his son had fallen upon him, or stood by him with a sword in his hand; and thus was his mind night and day intent upon this thing, and revolved it over and over, and no otherwise than if he were under a distraction. And this was the sad condition Herod was now in." (Antiq. Book. XVI, 8:5.)

The king brought his sons before Augustus and there accused them of plotting against him. Alexander's defence emphasized the ludicrous side of the pathological suspicions of the aging king. Augustus declared the princes innocent and brought about a reconciliation with their father. Whereupon, Herod ruled that the succession should go by age, first Antipater, then the two sons of Mariamme. Meanwhile, he declared himself absolute ruler.

But the plotting did not end. The arrest of Alexander was followed by a second reconciliation, but in the end, the web of intrigue woven against the princes proved too much for them. In 8 B.C.E. they were taken under arrest to be tried at Berytus (Beirut) by the Governor of Syria. According to imperial law, no Jewish prince could try such a serious case without Imperial consent. On the Emperor's advice, a high court, similar to the Sanhedrin was set up in Berytus. There Herod poured out a torrent of accusations while the prisoners were kept away from the proceedings. Found guilty, they were taken to Sebaste (Samaria) and there strangled. This did not bring peace to the king's household. Thereafter the beast in him was unchained.

True, the death of the two brothers left Antipater as the effective ruler. However, impatience defeated his ambition. Although Herod's sick body seemed on the point of death — it is possible that he suffered from cirrhosis of the liver, diabetes, or, perhaps, cancer — he would not die. First by litter, then by boat across the Dead Sea, he journeyed to the hot springs of Calirrhoe in search of a remedy. They could not stop the progress of the disease, but Antipater would not wait. He organized yet another conspiracy aimed at his immediate accession to the throne. By so doing, he brought about his own downfall. Betrayed, charged and condemned, he was executed only five days before his father died (4 B.C.E.) in his beloved palace at Jericho.

Before his death, however, Herod had again changed his will and had named as his successor his son by a Samaritan wife, Archelaus. His brother, Antipas, was appointed Tetrarch of Galilee and Perea (Jewish Trans-jordan); while a third son, Philip, child of a

Entrance to a tomb west of the walled town of ancient Jerusalem, believed to be of the Herodian family. It illustrates the way in which a large stone was rolled over the entrance to close it, (as in the tomb of Jesus of Nazareth).

Jerusalemite Cleopatra, was appointed tetrarch of Gaulanitis, the Trachonitis, Bashan and Banias (see map. p. 116).

What caused the dying king most distress was his certainty that the news of his death would be greeted by rejoicing throughout the country. To avoid this, he ordered that as soon as he died, the most distinguished of the popular leaders should be seized and slaughtered in the hippodrome of Jericho. Mourning for them would replace jubilation at his own end and would also give the impression to Rome that his devoted subjects lamented their king's passing.

The order was never obeyed. Neither did the people ever forget that Herod had been their enemy to the last.

> "Accordingly he (his son) brought out all his ornaments to adorn the pomp of the funeral. The body was carried upon a golden bier, embroidered with very precious stones of great variety, and it was covered over with purple, as well as the body itself; he had a diadem upon his head, and above it a crown of gold; he also had a sceptre in his right hand. About the bier were his sons and numerous relations; next to these were the soldiery distinguished according to their several countries and denominations; and they were put into the following order; — First of all went his guards; then the band of Thracians; and after them the Germans; and next the band of Galatians, every one in their habiliments of war; and behind these marched the whole army in the same manner as they used to go out to war, and as they used to be put in array by their muster-masters and centurions; these were followed by five hundred of his domestics, carrying spices. So they went eight furlongs to Herodium; for there, by his own command, he was to be buried; — and thus did Herod end his life." (Antiq. Bk XVII, 8: 3)

Herod's bequests were as follows: to Augustus, 1,000 talents, (10,000,000 silver drachmas) or about $1,200,000; to the Empress, 500 talents, or $600,000; his sister Salome, 50 talents, or $60,000, plus several towns and their territories. Josephus was amazed at this enormous wealth in such uncertain times.

HEROD'S CHARACTER

The structure of Herod's achievements collapsed with his death. His political policy and despotism had been rejected by his people who had cordially hated him. They announced their verdict on him by epithets such as "the cruel Herod" or "the Idumean slave". Jewish tradition was to wipe out any favourable memory of him. The genuine benefits his people had gained from his policies and especially his program of construction, were forgotten. He was to be remembered only as a cruel, cunning and despotic tyrant.

The modern historian can acknowledge the many occasions when Herod acted from admirable motives and with the best intentions. Although his achievements were to be disregarded at the time and so quickly destroyed, they are evidence of his greatness. He wished to secure for the Jews of Palestine and the Diaspora a secure existence in the secular world. It may be said in his favour that he had kept the Romans at a distance for several decades before Judea became the Roman province of tortured memory. It is arguable that by the standards of royal behaviour of his time, even his murderous excesses might be excused as legitimate protection of his position and person. But coupled with the Mariamme episode and his treatment of his sons, the annihilation of the Hasmoneans can be seen as one more facet of his complicated, ambivalent and psychopathic nature.

The "Gemma Augustea", onyx cameo by Dioscourides, one of the authentic graphic representations of the Roman Way, showing Augustus Caesar as the King of the World, with his family. The scene at the bottom shows the erection of a victory trophy. The cameo dates from the end of the 1st century C. E.

VI

ROMANS AND JEWS

THE KINGDOM DIVIDED

With Herod's death, his son Archelaus, 18 years of age and fresh from his studies in Rome, took over the powers of the king. The title would be his only after Augustus had given his approval to Herod's political and personal will, which had aimed at preserving the unity of the kingdom under Archelaus, with his brothers as vassal rulers of the two northern districts, (see pp. 136–7).

The people welcomed their new ruler with high hopes. They laid before him a petition calling on him to abolish the poll tax and sales tax; to free political prisoners; to discharge the High Priest appointed by Herod and other hellenized or Greek officials, and to punish the advisers of Herod who had supported the burning alive of the two eminent scholars, Judas and Mattathias who had incited a mob to tear down the Roman eagles from the gate of the Temple. The repercussions of their execution were still felt years afterwards.

The extreme Pharisees had used the occasion of Herod's funeral to stage a demonstration of their own true feelings. At the time of the Passover, when masses of pilgrims were crowded into the town and Temple area, they arranged a spectacular mourning for the two executed scholars. When Archelaus tried to remonstrate with them, they demanded immediate punishment for those responsible for the execution. Soldiers, sent to restore order, were halted by the crowd. Whereupon the whole army was mobilized and in the ensuing action 3,000 people were killed, the rest of the demonstrators fleeing into the hills. These riots demonstrated the increasing opposition of the people to the Idumean dynasty and the harm that had been done by the uncertainty about the succession.

To obtain Augustus' confirmation of his appointment, Archelaus set off for Rome (4 B.C.E.), leaving his brother Philip, who was loyal to him, as his regent with full powers. Augustus proved in no hurry to settle the matter. Already he had been importuned by two other delegations, one led by Archelaus' rival, his second brother, Antipas, and the other made up of fifty leaders of the people. Both begged for the deposition of Archelaus and total abolition of the monarchy. Instead, they asked that the whole of Judea might be placed under the direct government of Rome, although retaining its national autonomy.

HEROD'S KINGDOM DIVIDED

Augustus' decision when it was finally announced replaced the single monarchy by three independent ethnarchies, each with its own ruler, Archelaus being the Ethnarch of Judea, Samaria and Edom, including Caesarea and Joppa; Antipas ruling Galilee and Perea, and Philip taking charge of Auranitis and the district of Paneas in the north (see map). Some Greek towns were declared independent and Salome, Herod's sister, was left in possession of the towns and territories willed to her by her brother. The Ethnarchs were allotted generous incomes, although Archelaus got twice the share of his brothers.

Thus, although Herod's proposals for the administration of the country had been adopted, his main purpose had been thwarted and the unity of his kingdom destroyed. Augustus hoped that the change would have a calming effect and would lessen the dangers of upheaval in the country.

The War of Varus

During the long interval while Augustus was pondering what action to take, confusion had been spreading in Palestine. Augustus had appointed a certain Sabinus to guard Herod's treasury and administer the country temporarily. He set about his task with the utmost stupidity, using soldiers in an attempt to seize the Temple treasure by force. With the coming of the Passover, the thousands of pilgrims gathered in Jerusalem first resisted, then attacked, the Roman force. Sabinus was obliged to seek protection in Herod's palace, where he was besieged. At this, sedition flared up over the whole country.

In Galilee, a man named Judas, the son of Hezekiah who had been a rebel in Herod's time, stirred up rebellion in the neighbourhood of Zippori; in Transjordan, an upstart, Simeon, had himself declared king, while another pretender, a former shepherd, roamed over the whole country claiming to be its ruler. To establish order, the Roman legate (governor) of Syria, Varus, came down to Palestine with two legions plus auxiliary foreign forces. Killing, burning and pillaging, the Romans went through the land. In Jerusalem, Varus raised the siege of Sabinus, crucified two thousand Jews and then departed, leaving a garrison to maintain order and, incidentally, to back up Archelaus, who was unpopular.

THE ETHNARCH ARCHELAUS

Having obtained Rome's backing, Archelaus returned to Jerusalem as Ethnarch and set about imitating his father in splendour and cruelty. He disposed of his enemies and terrorized the opposition. He also undertook big building schemes. The family estate in Jericho had been burned during the insurrection and, to replace it, he built himself a town of palms in the plain nearby, which he named after himself, Archelais.

However, he lacked his father's outstanding abilities. By violent and oppressive treatment of all his subjects he united traditional enemies against him. Thus, in the year 6 C.E., the Jews and the Samaritans sent a joint delegation to Rome with a request that Herodian rule be ended and the country be made part of the Roman province of Syria, to be ruled by a Roman governor like many other parts of the Empire. As Archelaus had no standing in Rome, Augustus agreed. He exiled the young king to Vinelobane (Vienne) in Gaul, north of the Alps (6. C.E) and annexed Judea to Syria.

Coins of Archelaus and Antipas. Upper left: high helmet and cheek band, inscribed "Ethnarch" (Archelaus). Lower left: reverse: a bunch of grapes on a twig, and a leaf. Right: coin of Herod Antipas, contemporary of John and Jesus, decorated with a palm branch and laurel; dated 32/33–36 C.E.

Thus began a new era in the political affairs of Palestine. Ten years earlier, the leaders of the people and the Pharisees had pleaded for this status, disdaining the appearance of autonomy which the Herodians had maintained and preferring outright Roman provincial governance to the tyranny of hellenized despots. They were not conscious of any loss of prestige in this. They recognized no true native prince since the destruction of the Hasmoneans and even they were regarded by extreme Pharisees as usurpers of the throne of David.

Although part of the Syrian province, Judea was a separate administrative area with its own governor or "procurator" (supervisor) appointed by the Emperor. Procurators were generally the Emperor's financial managers and had the rank of "knights", coming third in order of precedence, after other provincial governors. In addition to his responsibility for collecting taxes and tribute, the procurator also had the "ius gladii" (the right of the sword), which gave him the right of decision in cases involving the death sentence, (although a Roman citizen could appeal against such decisions at the emperor's assizes) and, in addition, command of auxiliary troops, though not of legions, which were not permanently stationed in Palestine before 70 C.E. As mentioned (p. 103), Jews were not usually recruited for the Imperial army.

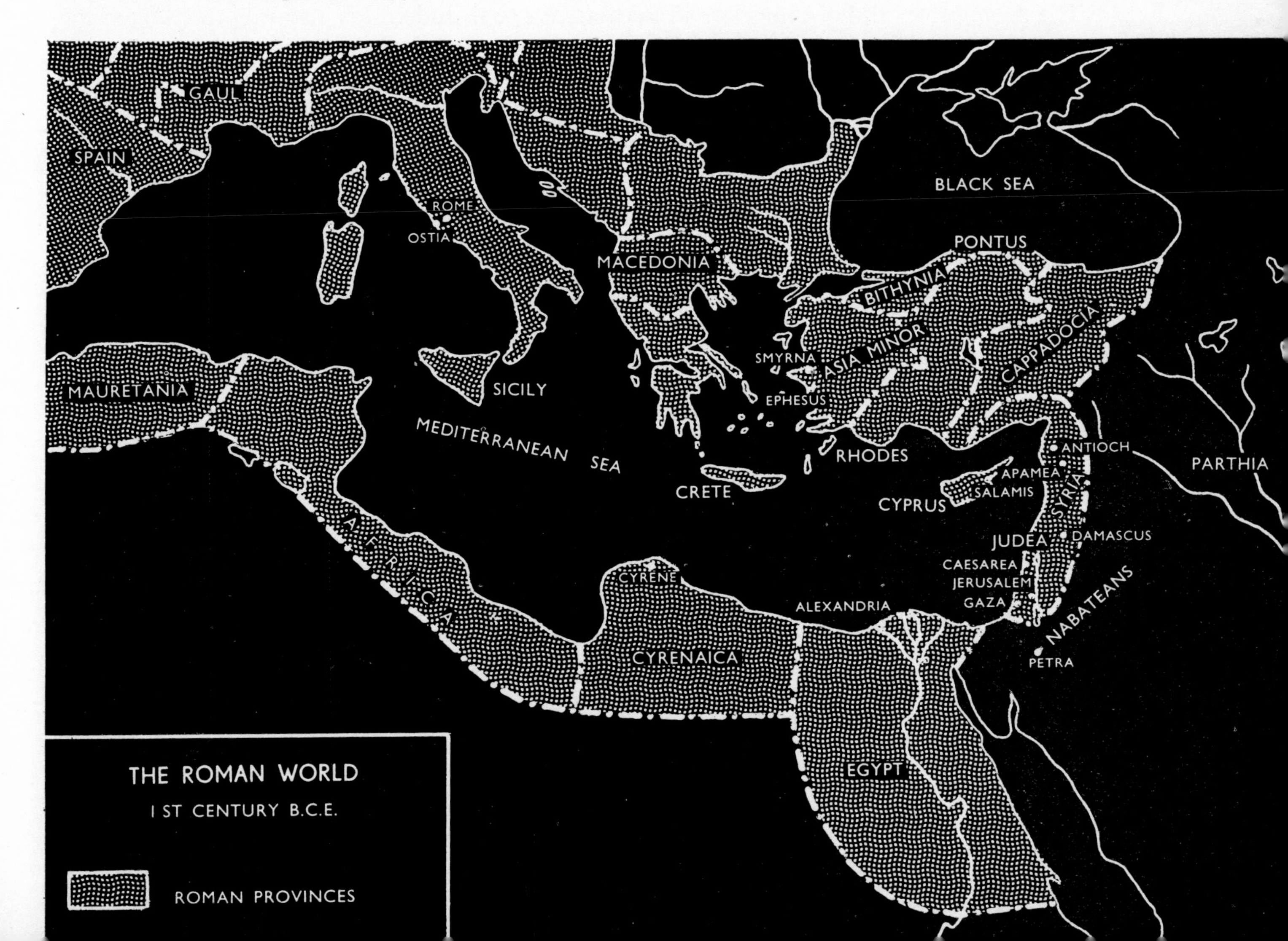

The Pharisees were to be disappointed. Roman rule administered by the procurators proved very different from their hopes. Indeed, conditions in Judea brought out all the weaknesses of the system.

The Romans regarded the Mediterranean countries they had conquered as an "estate of the Roman people", that is, they governed their provinces with the sole aim of raising the greatest possible treasure from them for Rome. The more developed a province, the more oppressive became the hand of Rome. In Judea, this general situation was further aggravated by the absence of solid cultural links between most Jews and Romans

However much he may have been hated, Herod had at least paid lip service to Jewish traditions. The Roman procurators however, appointed principally as financial administrators, had no understanding of the ways of the people they governed, nor much sympathy with the intricacies of their local problems. The fact that the procurators chose to live in Caesarea — in Herod's palace there — rather than in Jerusalem was an outward token of their desire to keep aloof from their subjects, although, of course, this place of residence allowed them to enjoy all the amenities of Roman civilization without restraint.

The Jews raised no objection to this slight of their holy city, for in a sense it enhanced Jerusalem's prestige as the center of religious life and ensured its unsullied purity.

The procurators did not interfere in matters of ritual. Judea was also exempted from the tax which elsewhere accompanied the worship of the Caesars. Instead, it became customary to offer a daily sacrifice in the Temple "for Caesar and the Roman people" and special sacrifices were made in the emperor's honour on ceremonial occasions, thus reviving a practice which dated from the time of the Persian empire.

The procurators appeared in Jerusalem only at the time of the great holidays, a fact which repeatedly resulted in increased friction. However, in theory, the people were granted the autonomy they had desired "to live according to the tradition of their fathers".

THE PRIESTLY OLIGARCHY

The abolition of the monarchy helped to restore its ancient prestige to the office of High Priest. During Herod's reign a number of priestly families had emerged and they now formed an oligarchy within the highest strata of society. Josephus applied the term "aristocratic oligarchy" to the period following Archelaus, during which the High Priests acted as the people's representatives. The Pharisees were careful to maintain the prestige of the highest religious office and to insist on its representative character. Before his most solemn function on the Day of Atonement, the High Priest was addressed by representatives of the Sanhedrin:

> "You are our deputy and the deputy of our court; we adjure you by Him who made his name dwell in this house, that you change nothing of what we have told you." (M. Yoma 1:5)

Thus the High Priesthood, the Temple and the sacrifices there remained the central pillar of Jewish ritualistic life in Palestine. The High Priests were not elected by the Jews but were appointed by the Roman authorities who, with an eye to public opinion, made their choice from among the ruling priestly families. The High Priests did not distinguish themselves particularly by their piety or scholarship and they lasted for only short periods at their posts. They were closely allied to the leading families of both urban and rural Judea. The Sanhedrin, the national high court, which was headed by the High Priest, was recruited from among this aristocracy together with the leaders of the Pharisees. It is known that between 37 B.C.E. and 66 C.E., 28 High Priests succeeded one another, coming from four distinguished families. Later Rabbis have rightly characterized this oligarchy:

"Woe is me because of the house of Boethus; woe is me of their stick; woe is me of the house of Hanan .... They are high priests, their sons are financiers, their sons-in-law trustees, and their servants beat the people." (Talmud, Pesahim, 57a)

THE CENSUS OF QUIRINIUS AND THE ZEALOTS

The first procurator of Judea was Coponius. Two events of his regime give a good indication of the manner and limitations of provincial rule. The first was the census of the population, its goods and real estate. The second concerned serious incidents between Jews and Samaritans who were accused of trying to defile the Temple.

Censuses were taken at regular intervals and formed the basis for the imposition of poll (head) taxes and property and land taxes. There is evidence which suggests that the practice for censuses began during the reign of Augustus, 27 B.C.E. to 14 C.E. Judea was attached to the Roman province of Syria, which was governed by Quirinius. He was

Funerary inscription of A. Aemilius Secundus, referring to a census carried out in Apamea (Syria) by order of P. Sulpicius Quirinius, governor of Syria. The date is not specified. Found in Venice.

entrusted with the taking of a census of the whole province and Coponius would probably follow a similar procedure in Judea.

There is an Egyptian Papyrus in the British Museum (approx. 103 — 104 C.E.) which contains a proclamation calling upon all who reside elsewhere to return to their homes for the census which took place in Egypt every 14 years. A similar requirement may lie in the background of the story of Jesus' birth in the gospel of Luke.

The demand for the census and the manner in which it was taken aroused the widest public indignation and resentment. This general opposition also provided a setting for the creation of a new, revolutionary sect, the Zealots, possibly a splinter group from the left wing of the Pharisees.

The leaders and majority of the members of this new sect were young people who rebelled against the double tyranny, Roman or Herodian. To them, God alone could claim to be king of Israel. No earthly monarch — not even Caesar — could do more than usurp the throne. Like the recluses who withdrew from the world to prepare themselves for a Kingdom of God, the Zealots believed that the Kingdom would come when the Messiah appeared. But this day, they maintained, could be hastened by action. They urged armed opposition to Roman rule, for surely God would come to the help of the people of Israel, as soon as they were ready. This "new, fourth philosophy" as Josephus called it, (the others were the Sadducees, Pharisees and Essenes) found ready ears among the mass of the people, the town labourer, the impoverished peasant of the countryside. A number of different religious and political forces all joined together to produce a movement of great explosive potential.

That potential was realized first in armed opposition to the census takers. Led by Judas the Galilean and a Pharisee, Zadok, the new party attempted to rouse the whole people to rebellion. Only with the help of the priests and the moderate Pharisees, did Quirinius calm the people and, finally, manage to conduct his census.

Prelude to Disaster

The salient fact in the history of Palestine during the six decades that followed the census of Quirinius (6 C.E.) is the continuation of its administration under the procurators. This particular brand of rule as a "province" of the Roman Empire resulted in increasing restiveness among the Jews and, for this reason, these sixty years are regarded as a prelude to the destruction of Jerusalem and the Jewish Commonwealth.

The vexations and oppression of their rulers gave rise on the one hand to the growth of the Zealots as a militant political party and, on the other, to the development of Messianic sectarian activity among the Essenes. (It is now generally agreed to relate the sectaries of Qumran near the Dead Sea with the Essenes; see Ch. VIII). Moreover, these years saw the emergence of two Jewish personalities, whose lives, while they seemed of minor importance to their times, were ultimately to influence the whole course of Western Civilization: John the Baptizer and Jesus of Nazareth.

XXIII. Wall painting on a black ground, from Pompei (see plate XIII). A fine example of Graeco-Roman art, used for luxurious homes in Italy and Palestine.

XXIV. Conversation between a man and a woman. This Roman wall fresco illustrates the realism with which people, characteristics and costume were recorded, in contrast to the Greek tradition of idealized types.

XXV. Street in the old City of Jerusalem. This bears little resemblance to the biblical city which lies buried in debris below, but it gives some idea of the old architecture and atmosphere. Houses in New Testament times were apparently flat-roofed, the use of vaulted ceilings coming later.

XXVI. Threshing floor and olive groves in a Galilean Arab village, little changed in 2,000 years.

Augustus died in 14 C.E. and was succeeded by Tiberius. The new Emperor left everything concerned with Palestine to his officials there. Complaints from the natives had no chance of affecting the activities of the procurator, provided he continued a satisfactory watch-dog and tax collector for the Empire. Procurators followed each other almost as rapidly as the High Priests of Jerusalem, until the appointment of Pontius Pilate as the fifth procurator of Judea. His conduct and policy are dealt with in connection with the story of Jesus of Nazareth (Ch. X).

During this period, Philip ruled as tetrarch of Transjordan for 28 years. When he died in 33 or 34 C.E. the territory was joined to the province of Syria. In the same way, Galilee and Perea remained the tetrarchy of Antipas for 33 years until 39 C.E. when he was exiled to Gaul. The history of both these petty princes forms a part of the gospels and the Acts of the Apostles and their careers will be considered in Chs. IX, X, XI.

However, to understand fully the social, religious and historical background of those documents and of the lives of John and Jesus, the relations between Palestine and Rome are not the only things that must be considered. In addition, it is necessary to grasp the facts concerning the sectarian Essenes and the Covenanters of Qumran as these are revealed by the Dead Sea Scrolls.

Bust of Tiberius.

Marble statuette of an unidentified man of the hellenistic period — a time of close contacts between the Jewish and hellenistic civilizations in thought, art and everyday life. Whether gentile or Jewish, he evokes his age and environment.

VII

THE CULTURAL AND SOCIAL CLIMATE IN PALESTINE AND THE DISPERSION

PART I

By the first century B.C.E., Palestine's Jewry had successfully absorbed hellenistic culture into the fundamental pattern of Jewish life. The various stages of this transformation were considered in Ch. III in terms of the development of literature from folklore to the sectarian apocalyptic writings which flourished before and after the Hasmoneans. Under the impact of a foreign cosmopolitan culture, Judaism had evolved from the simpler biblical pattern to a more complex civilization. Generations of hellenists living close to the Jews in Palestine had left behind them unmistakable traces in literature, language, daily customs, law and the more material aspects of Jewish civilization. In the dispersion, of course, these influences had made a much deeper impression on Jewish life (see Part II).

Contacts with Graeco-Roman civilization involved centuries of stress but, through them all, the Jews found the strength to meet the new influences on their own ground. The Jews — of whatever party — remained the only people of antiquity who were able to come to terms with Greek culture without losing their own. After the threat of aggressive hellenism had been repelled, national life under the Hasmoneans followed its traditional course. Herod's attempts at hellenization were mainly superficial and affected only secular fields. The future of Judaism as a religion remained a matter for the Jews themselves, whether Pharisee, Sadducee or Essene.

HISTORICAL BACKGROUND TO PHARISEE-SADDUCEE STRIFE

One of the main features of the period is the conflict between the Pharisees and the Sadducees — the two leading parties — which covered the widest areas of religious, civil and political life. Beginning with questions of "halakhah" (guidance in civil and ritual matters, including customs, decrees and ordinances), it spread to the whole range of social-economic problems. Strife between the two parties continued for more than two centuries, taking different forms at different periods. With the passage of time, the mass of the people came to support the Pharisees, who were the party of the middle class of merchants and artisans as well as of the scholars and interpreters of the Law. The tension between the parties gives a comprehensive picture of the whole social, religious and political life of the time.

The Pharisees and Rome

During Herod's long reign, Palestine became more than ever before the battleground of cultural forces. Moreover, as we have seen (Ch. V), Herod put an end to the inner political life of the Jewish Commonwealth. While he reigned, anyone wishing to voice political opinions did so in fear, or was forced underground. Both Herod and the Romans were continually on the look-out for independent movements which might contain a threat to their rule. Any such indications were ruthlessly quelled. When Herod's long reign of terror came to an end, there were many, particularly among the younger, more reckless idealists, who thought the time had come to strike a blow for freedom.

Among them, a "left-wing" movement developed among the progressive Pharisees that finally split off to form a new, independent section of the Zealots. More fanatical than the main body of Pharisees, they were bent on reviving the dynamic revolutionary spirit of early Hasmonean days. The motivation for many of these Jewish patriots was their conviction that Roman rule, supporting hellenistic ways, would destroy not only national liberty but the whole Jewish way of life. Like their forbears, the Hassidim of Maccabean days, the moderate Pharisees were concerned more with religious freedom than political power. They aimed at avoiding open conflict with their rulers — either Rome or Herod. Nevertheless, they were fundamentally opposed to Herod and his policies.

In contrast, the Sadducees and priests who depended on the existing political set-up had no quarrel with Herod or with Roman rule. In this they were out of step with public opinion, for among the middle class few loved Herod. Even though many grew rich during his busy and prosperous reign, there were others who were impoverished by excessive taxation. Their difficulties may be one reason for the Pharisees' deadly hatred of Herod, apart from moderates like Shemayah and Abtalyon who supported Herod in his war with Antigonus.

Still, these sages and all good Pharisees refused to swear the oath of allegiance to Rome. To do so would have been a negation of their doctrine of a theocratic state (ruled by God) which rejected kingship. The Pharisees also insisted on a distinction between secular power and religious life.

SOCIAL AND RELIGIOUS BACKGROUND

Any consideration of the two parties and the conflicts between them faces a number of problems because of the inadequate sources available. There are two sources of information on the cultural and religious issues of the age dealing particularly with Pharisee doctrine and practice. These are (a) the works of Josephus and (b) the sayings of the Tannaitic teachers which have been preserved in the Talmud. The Tannaitic rabbis were the successors of the Pharisees and continued their doctrine. The accounts given in these two sources frequently contradict themselves and each other.

Josephus was writing for a pagan, educated readership. In one work, the "War of the Jews", he shows two political parties struggling for power. In another, the "Antiquities of the Jews", he deals with the conflict of parties in terms of abstract philosophical questions of religion and ethics.

The Talmud's View

The Talmudic writers were unable or unwilling to judge the social and political factors involved and concentrated instead on the civil and religious law being disputed. Their account of historic facts tends to be superficial and to leave out the dynamic forces of real life which were the aspects of most interest to the Pharisees. As a result, "the Talmud tends to see everything as controversies on halakhah and therefore simply makes the Sadducees into poor halakhists." (Ch. Rabin). One might add that the Talmud fell into the error of the Sadducees because, in its literary form, it echoes their own yearning for tradition.

In fact, taken together, it becomes clear that the accounts of Josephus and the Talmud do not really conflict. They deal with the same topics from different angles and reflect trends during the first century of the Christian era which took different forms at different times. Another primary source for information about the Pharisees is the New Testament which, although biased against them, does reflect contemporary knowledge and experience of Judaism in the period before the destruction of the Temple.

Drawing on greater knowledge and sources other than either Josephus or the Talmud, modern scholars have been able to produce a fuller picture of the organization and activities of both parties, particularly those of the Pharisees.

The figure of 6,000 Pharisees quoted by Josephus probably refers to the number of the initiated who, as "haberim" (associates) took vows of purity and holiness and belonged to the organization, the "heber". Before being admitted, each candidate had to undergo a two-stage probation to test his suitability. As S. Lieberman and Ch. Rabin have pointed out, they felt the same concern for ritual purity and observed ritual practices similar in many respects to those of the sectaries of Qumran (see Ch. VIII on the Dead Sea Scrolls). The initiation of the Pharisee "haberim" was accompanied by a ritual bath (tebilah) and followed by participation in the ritually pure meal of the "heber". Other scholars believe that the sectaries were much stricter in their application of the principles of initiation and purification and that the Pharisee rank and file were content to wash their hands and did not insist on complete immersion.

The pious Pharisee devoted himself to a "life under the Law" in every respect, even shouldering the heavy burden of eating all food under the conditions of levitical ritual purity which the scriptures imposed only on priests eating offerings. A "haber" had to be sure that everything he touched was perfectly pure.

To fulfill the minute details essential for such purity, it was easier for men of this way of thinking to live together in small separate villages, or to be organized into a close community within the towns. Such a group could wield considerable influence and this was most felt in Jerusalem.

Vessels, Uncleanness and Ritual

Some of the regulations concerning ritual purity of food appear meaningless considered by themselves. To understand their place in Pharisaism, it is essential to remember that such physical ritual observances went quite naturally side by side with the ethics of the Pharisees which also demanded much higher standards of love and forgiveness than were required of society in general. They were both parts of a total concept of personal purity and holiness before God.

For instance, they were enjoined (Numbers 18 : 26) to pay to God a tithe of all the food they bought or ate. Urban Pharisees bought rather than grew their own food and they could not control the paying of the tithe themselves. Rather than rely on the farmer's or seller's assurance that tithe had been paid, and risk being a party to disobedience to the Torah if it had not, they paid the levite's "tithe of a tithe" on all food and drink which they bought, and refused to eat in any houses where they feared there was no guarantee that the tithe had been paid, i.e. in the homes of the "amme-haaretz", the ordinary people. This situation is reflected by the gospels, although negatively. Jesus might be invited to eat in the house of a Pharisee. But they were shocked when he ate with the "publicans and sinners" of the "amme-haaretz". The "reliable" Jew, even if he was of lower degree than a "haber", kept the law of tithing most punctiliously, trusting only himself to be sure that it was done, "even if it involved tithing things which may have already been tithed, and avoiding the shadow of doubt involved in eating at the house of an am-haaretz, though he could tithe as he eats." (Ch. Rabin). He would actually deduct the tithe from each course of food or drink that he ate.

RITUALLY PURE FOOD "TOHOROTH"

The ritually pure food of the Pharisee "haberim" became impure through contact with an impure person. To allow it to be contaminated was in itself sinful.

> "A haber shall not minister at the banquet or dinner of an am-haaretz unless everything has been properly dealt with and tithed by him personally, including the wine in the carafe. If a haber ministers at such a banquet, people will assume that tithe has been given." (P.T. Demai 2:23)

To take part in the common meals of the Pharisee "haburah" it was also necessary, of course, to observe levitical purity of clothing.

The problem of the food itself may explain one of the big controversies of the time, concerning the susceptibility of metal and glass vessels to ritual uncleanness. The Pharisees insisted that not only wooden, stone or pottery vessels — the materials in common use since biblical days — were subject to the laws governing ritual contamination. The more luxurious vessels made of glass or metal which had been imported into Palestine by wealthy Jews since hellenistic times must also, they declared, comply to the regulations laid down in Scripture. Otherwise they would be unfit for use by their owners.

Another subject that raised passionate feelings was the question of who might be permitted to pay for the burnt offering sacrificed daily in the Temple. The Sadducees, with a string of hair-splitting interpretations of scriptural text, held that the lambs for the sacrifice might be purchased from contributions made by wealthy individuals. The more

Pottery and vases found in Judea, resembling Roman models.

Examples of pottery of old and new times found in Judea, reflecting import or imitation from the whole of the Eastern Mediterranean. The Cypro-Phoenician jar (above) is of the 8th century B.C.E., reminiscent of early biblical days. The deep Cypriote bowl with curved handles (below) is from the 6th century; but the iridescent Roman glass bottle (left) of the 1st century B.C.E. — 1st century C.E., found on Mount Carmel, was a modern importation.

Greek terracotta model of a woman kneading dough in front of the portable oven in which she would bake it. Such homely figures were common to the whole Mediterranean.

democratic Pharisees, afraid that this would restrict the share of ordinary people in the Temple worship, insisted that, instead, the sacrifices should continue to be paid for out of the half-shekels contributed to the Temple each year by every worshipper.

Many non-Jewish scholars have found it hard to realize that the apparently academic disputes about the interpretation of a biblical verse, as recorded in the Talmud, were in fact closely related to social conditions. What may appear to be trivial differences of opinion on "halakhah", reflect the fundamentally opposed attitudes of the two parties to religious, social and economic questions.

Vestiges of ancient ritual

A few of these ancient rituals have survived as important elements in modern orthodox Judaism. For instance, a Jew of the priestly class (e.g. one named Cohen, "priest", or a levite, one belonging to the tribe of Levi), must take care to avoid being defiled by contact with a corpse; the laws of "niddah" which relate to women's menstruation and pregnancy; the careful immersion of any food vessels bought from gentiles; or the special "mikveh" (ritual bath house) where orthodox Jews purify themselves by complete immersion. Washing the hands before and after meals is a mild remnant of the ancient elaborate levitical purifications. Nevertheless, these and the dietary laws (on kasher foods, etc.), still sway orthodox Judaism to an important degree.

But there was more to these rituals than the mere details of their performance. Judaism laid great stress upon the intention (kavannah) behind each action and it was recognized that all good deeds just as much as religious observances should be governed by the Torah (Mosaic Law) which thus became the center of Jewish life. Fulfilling the commandments of God was one way to worship Him. There was no attempt at rational explanations. To eat pork, for example, was wrong simply because God said so. Moral law was as important as ritual and man glorified God in his everyday behaviour as much as with prayers and sacrifices. At the same time, the commandments which God had given man sanctified God's people.

The conception of living by the Torah exalted every sphere of life. Acceptance of this joyful burden of "mitzvoth" (performance of commandments) covering the whole of life within the family and the community is a far cry from the withdrawal from the rest of the world practised by ascetic sects like the Essenes (see Ch. VIII), but it was regarded by religious leaders as offering equal opportunity for holiness and the service of God:

> "The possessor of Torah is one who recognises his place, who rejoices in his portion, who makes a fence of his words, who claims no credit for himself, is loved, loves all present, loves his fellow creatures, loves righteous ways, welcomes reproof of himself, loves uprightness, keeps himself far from honours... shares in the bearing of a burden with his colleagues." (Sayings of the Fathers, "Pirke Aboth" 6:6)

There is nothing in this to suggest the mistaken picture of the Pharisees as thinking about nothing but how to fill ordinary life with burdensome and meaningless rules, without caring about their effect on religious or spiritual values.

Rather, their pledge on initiation was first, "to build a fence about the Torah" by a strict application of its precepts to every detail of daily life, i.e., in relation to dietary laws, dress, the Sabbath; secondly the reiterated obligation to pay the tithes on agricultural produce prescribed in Scriptures; thirdly the preservation of personal ritual purity, independently of temple worship. This brought about as an unintentional side-effect, the separateness which appeared as such unjustified arrogance to the gentiles and which was the cause of so many of the controversies to be met in the gospels.

THE PHARISEES WERE NOT "HYPOCRITES"

Over the years, the terms Pharisee, pharisaical or pharisaism, when used without direct historical reference, have come to acquire unfortunate overtones, making them synonymous with pedantic legalism and hypocrisy. Paradoxically, the process can be traced in part to the New Testament, the earliest Christian source for the Pharisees. Yet the New Testament itself shares many of the doctrines of the Pharisees who were the most important group within Judaism, and Jesus spoke approvingly of their teachings. However, it seems that Jesus and his followers were engaged in a fierce conflict with the Pharisees for the allegiance of the masses, (see Ch. X). No wonder the authors of the gospels were biased against them. This provided the Church with material for an unwarranted attack upon them and their successors, the Rabbis. The New Testament seems to give a very one sided picture of the Jewish religion of the time but its attitude was accepted and continued by gentile scholars, less familiar with the fields of rabbinic Judaism. It is proper to correct that picture now.

The New Testament is only one of the ancient documents that deal with this very complex period. It must be supplemented by the Talmud and other documents produced during the years following the Roman destruction of the Jewish state. These can be evaluated by writers who, living within the cultural tradition of Judaism, are in a better position to understand them. The fact is that there are negative criticisms of the Pharisees in the Talmud and Josephus, alongside positive comments. These should be sufficient indication that we are dealing with a human phenomenon. Like every movement, the Pharisees were a mixture of good and bad, better in principle and theory than in every detail of practice. Jesus' critique of the Pharisees was, in a sense, based upon the teachings of the prophets, who similarly attacked the religious leaders of their day, not for their professions, but for their practice. In short, there were good and bad Pharisees.

The task of the scholar is not to take sides, but to sift the material and arrive at the most balanced judgment possible. It has been pointed out that some Jewish scholars steeped in the Jewish tradition tend to be biased favourably towards the Pharisees, making them immune to criticism, just as gentile scholars have distorted the picture in the other direction. The truth lies somewhere between them.

Any study of the period, with its common interest for Christianity and Judaism must include the results of modern research into the Pharisees. One of the greatest achievements of modern theological scholarship lies in the work of Christian and Jewish scholars who, using all the findings of historians and on the basis of the whole range of available sources, have established the group as worthy of the respect and admiration of all men. After centuries of prejudice, these scholars are prepared to defend the Pharisees against the age-old charge of hypocrisy.

DEVELOPMENT OF THE PHARISEES' ORAL LAW

The distinguishing feature of the philosophy of the Pharisaic groups was the fact that they recognized that Scripture alone was not the whole of Judaism. In the old days it had been customary to declare that the old Mosaic Law, the original Torah, or "Written Law" was a complete legal code needing no further interpretation. However, with a changing and more complicated society, the application of Mosaic Law to actual conditions became more difficult. The Pharisees believed that this Law was a continuous revelation and they developed the extensive oral tradition that provided for the new needs. They understood that unless the content of Scripture was continuously re-interpreted to meet altering conditions, the Bible would become a dead letter. Accordingly, they put interpretation right into the center of their teachings. From this dynamic standpoint they were able, for instance, to declare that the "lex talionis", the eye for an eye of Scripture, was not intended literally, but was a convenient shorthand way of saying that a victim should be compensated for physical damage suffered. It was innovations such as this, introduced by them into the Oral Law, which determined the later development of Judaism.

According to Josephus they professed to be more religious than the rest of the people and to be able to explain the laws more precisely:

"They delivered to the people a great many observances by succession from their fathers, which are not written in the Law of Moses." (Josephus, Antiq. 13, 10:6)

They even went so far as to claim that their interpretations of the Law should be binding upon the nation as a whole, the Sadducees included. One reason for the popularity of the Pharisees among the people was the intelligent social consciousness expressed in their teachings. Moderate, pious and learned, they deplored excesses of any kind and strongly disapproved of too much severity in punishment. It may be said that the essence of Judaism is the struggle between the spirit and the flesh. The Pharisees dealt realistically with the conflict and adopted a moderate position. They did not seek to mortify the flesh as a means of increasing spirituality. Evidence for this is repeated in a late Talmudic teaching:

"the Holy One, blessed be he, does not lay burdensome laws upon Israel." (Pesikta de'Rab Kahana)

Their Social Ideals

One of the grounds on which the Sadducees taunted the Pharisees was their simple, unostentatious manner of living.

"It is a tradition among the Pharisees to afflict themselves in this world; yet, in the world to come, they shall have nothing."

There was a double meaning in the mockery. It ridiculed at the same time a doctrine of the Pharisees that "in the world to come" each soul would be judged. Without denying the old biblical belief that a man's actions were dependent upon God's will, they insisted that each individual is a free moral agent. The biblical doctrine of reward and punishment rests on the assumption that a man is free to make his own choice between good and evil behaviour. A man could not be called to account for "doing evil in the sight of God" if he had not thereby deliberately rejected doing "good". The Pharisees emphasized the idea of reward and punishment, holding that freedom of moral choice was a matter of either rejecting or co-operating with God's will. As Rabbi Akiba was to put it much later, despite the fact that "everything is foreseen, yet freedom of the will is given", meaning that a man can choose his way in life. ("Sayings of the Fathers" — Pirke Aboth 3 : 15). The oriental fatalism inherent in hellenism, holding that every step in a man's life had been determined from birth and that he must suffer for offences of which he was not guilty, never penetrated Judaism. "The Greeks who inherited most of their culture from the

Near East, returned it, transformed by their own genius, but still retaining many elements from its origins. This may explain why hellenism was both attractive to and compatible with the culture of the Near East." (D.N. Freedman).

As regards the hopes for the coming of the Messiah, which grew out of popular frustrations and longing for freedom, the Pharisees maintained that the Law of Moses must come before everything else. "With all their love for freedom and their belief in the Messiah, their devotion to Torah superseded their desire for political freedom." (J. Klausner). Thus they did not advocate rebellion against Herod or Rome as a means of hastening the coming of the Messiah. The Messiah would come, they taught, "when God shall will it", without any prompting from an impatient mankind.

Religion in the Home

Their effect on religious observance was enormous. They built up the synagogue. They brought religion into the homes of the people. The Passover celebration, for instance, held within the family in the homes of the people, became a solemn service, the head of the household acting as priest. The Pharisees always championed the cause of popular ethnic traditions and religious customs against the rigid conservatism of the Sadducean priesthood. There are countless instances of this. One example is their support for the great popular festival "simhat beit hashoevah", a water procession with torches during the Feast of Tabernacles, in which water was brought from the Pool of Siloam and poured out at the base of the Temple altar.

On the occasion of a technical discussion of this libation, later rabbis came to this pronouncement:

> "... deeds of loving kindness are greater than charity ... Charity can be done only with one's money, but deeds of loving kindness can be done with one's person and one's money ... he who executes charity and justice is regarded as though he had filled all the world with kindness." [Sukkah (Tabernacles), 49b]

Most notably, however, the Pharisees boldly transferred the power of atonement for sins, connected with the Day of Atonement, from the High Priest and his ritual in the Temple, to the actual day itself.

In general, the Pharisees paid more attention to world Jewry than the Sadducees whose horizons were necessarily limited to the borders of Palestine.

Ablution vase from the temple of Amathonte, Cyprus.

Decoration of the lintel of the façade to a rock-cut tomb in the valley of Jehosaphat, Jerusalem.

THE PEOPLE — THE "AMME-HAARETZ"

The organized Pharisee groups (haburoth) were devoted to enforcing "life under the Law". Upon whom did they enforce it, having as they did no means of coercion? The bulk of the population probably did not belong to any party, but were the "amme-haaretz" of rabbinic literature. R. Marcus terms them an "unclassified center group". Among initiated haberim, party-members and sectaries, the phrase meant all Jews who did not conform to their high standards.

During the time of Herod, when the Pharisees sought to separate religious from secular life, they began a movement to put the life of the people on a solid nationalist foundation of Hebrew tradition. Abandoning any attempt at interference in affairs of state, they limited themselves to teaching the people. They insisted on the necessity for educating the boys of every village. At the same time they established in each village a "beth-midrash", or house of learning for adults which served for both adult education and prayer. It was not used exclusively for worship in the early days. People could come to it at the end of their day's work and could read, or listen to the teaching.

> "When a man comes from his field in the evening, he shall enter the synagogue; if he is trained to read (Scripture) let him read; if he is trained to study the oral law, let him study." (P.T. Beraitha 4, b)

Judaism was the only one of the religions of the ancient world which set out to teach the laity, thereby setting an example which Christianity was to follow.

A JEWISH RENAISSANCE

Synagogues devoted to worship alone were built only after the destruction of the Temple, mainly from the second century C.E. (see end Ch. XIII). The architecture and the mosaics that enriched them, belonging to the second and third centuries C.E., provide evidence that the fusion of hellenistic with native artistic traditions in the preceding centuries, had produced an intrinsically Jewish decorative style which yet reflected Alexandrine patterns. The first evidence of this was in the excavations of the Tobiad palace of pre-Hasmonean times (see p. 13). Excavations of later periods show that Jewish places of worship and funerary objects were decorated with representations of earthly figures. The most popular motifs were borrowed from the plant world, using flowers, fruit, roses and bunches of grapes.

Jewish sarcophagus found at "Dominus Flevit" on the Mount of Olives, decorated in a style specific to Judea. Jewish tradition forbade the use of human images in decoration but allowed patterns of leaves, folioles and pairs of rosettes. Hellenistic funerary decoration featured human and mythical figures. The rule about human images was relaxed in the 3rd—5th centuries C.E. when the image was separated from the essence of the thing portrayed. The old fear of images returned in the 6th century C.E.

Dancing girls, neo-Attic style, a rhythm common to all the Eastern Mediterranean.

Flutes and Pan pipes, used in group song and dance.

There is plenty of evidence for the adaptation of Roman art to Jewish purposes in the detail of monumental and funerary architecture, tombs and their contents.

Out of the varied trends within Jewish life came a great upsurge in intellectual activity. The text of Scriptures was searched and studied, giving rise to the keen interpretations, judgments and commentaries on social laws which were to develop into the Mishnah and Talmud.

J. Klausner considers this sudden expansion of intellectual activity among the early Pharisees to be another result of their political isolation under Herod. Some of the varied midrashim, aggadahs and halakhahs that were subsequently to enrich the Talmud have their origin in the teachings of two rabbis who lived during the reign of Herod: Hillel and Shammai. Their teachings and spirit colour Judaism to this day and they provide a good insight into the cultural background of their time and the moral state of Jewry during the century that preceded the destruction of Jerusalem.

THE ACADEMIES AND THEIR GREAT TEACHERS

The rabbis worked in the same way whether teaching the people, giving rules for behaviour or passing judgment on misdeeds. Their method of interpretation, called "midrash" or investigation, was to quote relevant verses of Scripture, then to elaborate on them in a commentary; for instance:

> "And the officers shall speak unto the people, saying, What man is there that hath built a new house and hath not dedicated it? Let him go and return to his house." (Deut. 20:5)
> *Commentary:* 'It is all one whether he builds a barn for straw, a stable for cattle, a shed for wood, or a storehouse; it is all one whether he built, purchased or inherited it, or somebody had given it to him as a present."

The academic principles taught by the schools, in fact, covered much more than scholarship. The academies were no isolated havens for purely intellectual exercise. Law was developed there, and the laws affected the society's every citizen, learned or otherwise. The kind of law, the kind of culture that was to become a national possession very often depended on the agenda of the discussions that went on inside the schools and academies.

THE SCHOOL OF HILLEL

Hillel was a native of Babylonia. In search of learning, he migrated to Palestine, where the most important Jewish schools were to be found. He was a poor man and he had to support himself during his studies and pay his admission fees by doing whatever work he could get — including the heaviest labour.

The two "great expositors" at the time of his arrival were Shemayah and Abtalyon. In their Academies he found the store of traditions without which no one could hope to become a distinguished scholar. This was not all however. From them, he learned a discipline, and principles of research and interpretation which, when perfected, were to make possible the whole development of the Talmud. Hillel recognized the possibilities of his teachers' methods and applied them to his seven principles which were to become known to later generations as "Hillel's formulae". They also clearly reflect the extent to which contemporary Jewish learning was affected by Graeco-Roman principles of rhetoric.

To the debates in the academy, Hillel brought a vision that went far beyond the traditional lines of interpretation. He did not reject what had been passed down from earlier ages, but he insisted that in each generation scholars were entitled to search the Torah thoroughly and to derive new meanings and, from them, new laws to meet new conditions. As a jurist, Hillel had none to equal him in his generation. He welcomed everyone to his school, rich and poor, prominent and humble, pious and negligent. His followers disapproved of the exclusiveness of the academy run by his contemporary, Shammai. Further, also contrary to Shammai, Hillel attempted to express the larger intent of Scripture, not merely its literal, limited implications.

HILLEL'S GOLDEN RULE

Hillel's tact and patience were proverbial. Men might bet that they could make him lose his temper but only to their own loss. Persistent questioners who were rebuffed by the more arrogant Shammai never annoyed Hillel. Once, when a heathen who had been discouraged by Shammai, appeared before Hillel and asked, "What, in a nutshell, does Judaism teach?" Hillel understood that such a man was principally concerned with the essential message of Judaism, not with details of its ritual. He replied:

> "What is hateful to thee, never do to thy fellow-man. This is the whole Torah; all else is commentary. Now go and study it." (Talmud, Sabbath, 31a)

To quote other sayings of his at random:

> "Judge not your neighbour till you have been in his place."
> "If I am not for myself, who is for me? And if I am only for myself, what am I?" (Mishnah, Aboth 2:4)

He was not a remote pedant, concerned only with the books of the Law. He associated with the common people — with the farmer, artisan, labourer or merchant, made himself familiar with their problems, and in his reforms translated social-mindedness into action. He originated a current that was not to be resisted. The Pharisaic movement was quite fluid and democratic during this early period. The more liberal views of Hillel were adopted as binding by the Council of Jabneh (see p. 164).

THE SCHOOL OF SHAMMAI

The second of the outstanding pair of sages who headed the schools during this generation before Christianity was Shammai. He was an admirable counterpart to Hillel, for he represented the more conservative element and temperament in the country. Himself a man of means, he was perhaps inclined to voice the interests of the well-to-do and to look at problems from their point of view. Unlike Hillel, who thanked God if he had food sufficient unto the day, Shammai, for instance, found nothing strange in recommending the sort of marketing that is only possible to a rich man.

What discouraged strangers in meeting him was his short temper or, rather, his lack of a sense of humour. Nevertheless, it would be unfair to Shammai to picture him as a harsh, uncivil fanatic. In fact, he was famous for his saying, "Greet all men with a cheerful countenance," and significantly, it is from his school that the more "courtly" rules in regard to women were derived. However, it seems that the man seldom rose above the limitations of respectability.

So deep was the impact of both Shammai and Hillel on their age, that the academies over which they presided came to be known henceforth as Beth-Shammai and Beth-Hillel, the Shammaite school and the Hillelite school. Like scholars everywhere, the members of these two schools engaged in all kinds of intellectual controversy. The range, no less than the number of their interests is amazing. Eventually, such debates added to the content of Jewish tradition. Moreover, the Shammaites and the Hillelites exemplified the meaning of scholarship for future students. Lively debate, exciting sessions, were to mark the school system ever after. Much of these discussions was theoretical and scholastic, particularly after Rome appropriated more and more of law-making to herself. But much, too, was the expression of issues then stirring society. In these, the Hillelite school would reflect the needs of the masses, the Shammaites representing the interests of the propertied groups. Both, however, were dedicated to the native civilization. Both schools were Pharisaic and the discussions between them, however heated they might become, were still inside the family. While the ruling power removed itself from the experience of the population, the sages came to be regarded as the people's guides, "the fathers of the universe."

THE SADDUCEES

The Sadducees were, essentially, the priestly party. Their life centered around the Temple ministry. As the party of the leisured and wealthy class, they drew support mainly from the rich priests of Jerusalem who had taken over the position earlier held by the Hasmonean aristocracy. Having been closely associated with many Hasmonean princes, they had enjoyed periods of very great power. Among the mass of the people, their following was limited because of their wealth, haughty bearing and reputation for religious severity which alienated many. Inflexible and conservative, they spurned popular beliefs rejected by their educated neighbours.

Better educated generally, and more strict than the average Pharisee, the Sadducees accepted the Written Law as binding under all circumstances. New laws and new institutions had, to them, no true authority. Thus they rejected legislation enacted to deal with the existing

Sacrifice of a heifer reproduced on a 1st Century votive stela at Carthage. It has external affinities to ancient Jewish custom.

situations of a changed world. Every action, statement or belief must have the direct authority of the Scriptures or they would have none of it. They rejected the doctrine of determinism outright. In their opinion, man was entirely free to do as he pleased. There was no path "destined" for him from the beginning. He himself must make his own choice between good and evil.

They denied divine intervention in human affairs. God, they believed, was concerned only with spiritual matters. The mundane considerations of everyday life were beneath His notice. (And, it must be remembered, the Sadducees and their wealthy supporters were likely to be more vitally interested in material aspects of life than their opponents). They also rejected the ideas of resurrection and a life after death, and the popular eschatological views held by the masses and the Pharisees.

An early source in the Talmud relates that at the time of the break between Alexander Jannai and the Pharisees (see Ch. IV), the Sadducee, Eleazar ben Po'erah advised the king to trample his opponents under foot. The king, fearful of the civil and ritual effects of any interference with the traditional interpreters of the law, asked:

> "And what will happen to the Torah?" Answer: "It will be wrapped up and laid in a corner and all who wish to come and study it, let them come and study." (Kidd., 66a)

In other words, everyone would make his own interpretations, or so claimed the Pharisees as they recounted the event, mocking the Sadducees. The Pharisees were sure that the Sadducee seizure of power would result in anarchy and civil and religious strife. The Sadducees, of course, had a similar pessimism in regard to possible Pharisee domination.

THE TEMPLE TREASURY

The Sadducees' economic position owed its origin to their control of the Temple treasury. In addition to its permanent treasures, this was also the depository for a substantial public fund. Every year each Jew throughout the world was taxed one half-shekel to meet the Temple costs. These included the lamb — known as the "Tamid" — sacrificed as a burnt offering every morning and evening; the display of Shewbread; the preparation of incense; the wages of the women who wove the Temple curtains; the rich garments of the High Priest; and the red heifer and the scapegoat sacrificed each year. The fund also supported the Temple librarians and scribes and provided for the maintenance of the buildings.

In addition to the millions of half-shekels which flowed into the Treasury each year, immense voluntary donations were made to the Temple by Jews from all over the Diaspora. It is not difficult to understand the power — religious and political — wielded by the guardians of the Temple sanctuary.

DIFFERENCES BETWEEN PHARISEES AND SADDUCEES

Whilst the Sadducees placed so much emphasis on maintaining their authority as representatives of the Temple, the Pharisees achieved a much greater influence throughout the country because of their more lenient interpretations of the law, and their organization of groups living among the people. They "demanded study of the Law from everyone, in contrast to the Sadducees, where Law was dispensed by priests only. Their advanced methods of interpretation, derived partly from hellenistic rhetorical theory, enabled them to mitigate the Law in matters where changed circumstances had turned formerly useful provisions into harsh restrictions." (Ch. Rabin)

Of course the written Law did not provide for all cases, nor was it always clear. The Sadducees only accepted *traditional* interpretations (case law), while the Pharisees claimed a right to independent interpretation, holding that this was contained in the Law itself (halakhah le-Moshe mi-Sinai): When God gave Moses the written Law on Mount Sinai — so they claimed — he also transmitted to him oral laws which commented upon those written. Rabbi Akibah and other rabbis endeavoured to derive these "halakhot" from the Pentateuch (the written Law).

We are told by Josephus that in matters of supplementary law, and the traditions on which this was based, the Saducees tended to follow the lead of the Pharisees, in order to avoid popular discontent. However, on some points the Sadducees clung rigidly to the letter of the law, rejecting innovations which the Pharisees introduced. The Sadducees, for instance, denied popular beliefs in angels or resurrection and they despised and ridiculed any ritual which suggested, in however symbolic a fashion, the astral mysticism of the time. "Come and watch the Pharisees purify the moonlight," they jeered on one occasion, observing their Pharisee colleagues at the Temple subjecting the seven-branched candelabrum to a ritual washing. The Pharisees, on the other hand, accepted such importations from Babylon as a valid part of living popular tradition. Although they stopped short of the wilder extravagances of apocalyptic literature, particularly the references to angels and demons, (see Ch. III), they were prepared to find a place for it as one facet of a many-sided vital Judaism. But they restricted it to a corner of the Aggadah (parables and commentary used to illustrate the Scriptures).

CONCLUSION: THE PERIOD OF THE EARLY TANNAIM

What has been said may help to explain how it came about that following the fall of Jerusalem, the future of Judaism as a religion rested on the Pharisees as the most vital Jewish party, and on the Tannaitic rabbis as their successors. Their tradition was to live on in rabbinic, Talmudic and orthodox Judaism. Thus what became known as "normative Judaism" represented the continuing traditions of the Pharisees, among the Tannaitic and later rabbis. A third stream within Judaism, that of the separatist Essenes, will be dealt with in Ch. VIII.

The "rabbinic period" of Judaism can be said to have begun by 30 C.E. with the successors of Hillel and Shammai. It was with these upholders of Pharisee traditions that Jesus studied and argued.

During this time, the interpretation of Scripture became more a matter for theory. Controversies flourished in all spheres right up to the end of the 1st century C.E., when the Council of Jabneh made the more liberal Hillelite interpretations binding upon all teachers or Tannaitic rabbis (see Ch. XII).

Although the political history of Jewry comes to a temporary standstill in 70 C.E., there is no parallel break in the growth of the rabbinic-Tannaitic tradition. Rabbi Gamaliel who is quoted in Acts was a grandson of Hillel. Even though differences emerged between the Pharisees of one period and the rabbis of another, due to the latter's adaptation to changing circumstances, it would be true to say that the rabbis were the Pharisees of a later age. The rabbinic period of the Tannaim lasted until the codification of the Mishnah about 200 C.E.

It would be incorrect to call the early Tannaitic period that of the Pharisees, and then to try to distinguish them somehow from the "rabbis", although many Christians do this. This imposes an artificial separation between the Pharisees and rabbinic Judaism, which merely confuses the significance of the continuous trends of development in Judaism during the first two Christian centuries.

A bilingual stela, inscribed in both Greek and archaic Hebrew characters, typical of the cultural environment of Diaspora Jewry after the 4th century B.C.E. The decoration has a certain resemblance to that of funerary objects in Judea, shown above.

PART II

IN THE JEWISH DISPERSION (DIASPORA)

Second in importance to the growth of Judea and the development of the Hasmonean Commonwealth, was the widespread expansion of Jewry in the Diaspora during this period. Beginning in the 6th century B.C.E. this continued unabated until their numbers exceeded those living in Palestine on both sides of the Jordan Valley. The homeland was a mere narrow strip of country and the Jews were a fertile people. Emigration was a natural consequence. Actually, however, the main cause of the growth in numbers in the diaspora was not emigration, but natural increase over a long period of time.

The general areas of distribution included all the hellenistic states and beyond: from Parthia, Persia and the Caucasus to Egypt, as far as Elephantine; from Syria and Cyprus to the northern shores of Asia Minor and the Crimea on the Black Sea, as well as the Mediterranean shores of North Africa (Cyrene) and southern Europe — in fact, the whole civilized world outside India and China (see map). The greatest concentrations were in the Eastern half of the Mediterranean, particularly in Cyrene, Cyprus, Babylonia and Egypt. Alexandria, whose population numbered over 300,000 at its height, boasted a large percentage of Jews. At the head of the Jewish community stood an Ethnarch, like the ruler of an independent state. Later, it was ruled by a Council of Elders numbering seventy-one.

Jews and gentiles met at every turn: in the cities as well as in the small provincial towns and the countryside; in the ranks of the armed forces and in every other field. As early as 140 B.C.E. the author of the Sibylline Oracles testified that "the Jews were for all mortal men the guides to the way of life ..... the whole land and sea are full of Jews." They had a considerable influence on the indigenous peoples.

Their actual number is debatable. In the face of widely divergent estimates, varying from one million to three millions or more, it would be unwise to attempt a hard and fast figure. The question of their number was most important at times of crisis; for instance, the widespread rebellion of the Diaspora Jews against Trajan in 115 C.E. when they actually threatened Roman domination in the eastern Mediterranean (see Ch. XIII).

Some writers regard the surprising increase of Jews as due to their natural growth, whereas others believe that the great increase was also due to proselytes swelling their numbers.

JEWISH PROSELYTES AND GODFEARERS

Direct and indirect evidence suggests a Judaizing movement among the gentiles. The most famous converts were the kings of Adiabene, across the River Tigris in upper Mesopotamia, in the first century C.E., but it is not known whether many of their people followed their example.

Indirect evidence is provided by numerous references in the Talmud and the New Testament to the proselytes, their initiation, circumcision, baptism, and those who did not persevere.

> "If a proselyte and a gentile inherit jointly from their father who was a gentile, the proselyte may say to the other, 'Do thou take what pertains to idolatry and I will take the money' or 'Do thou take the wine (of libation) and I will take the produce'; but after the property has come into the possession of the proselyte it is forbidden to him to make any such proposal." (Mishnah, Demai 6:10)

> "Woe to you scribes and Pharisees, hypocrites! for you traverse sea and land to make a single proselyte, and when he becomes a proselyte, you make him twice as much a child of hell as yourselves." (Matthew 23 : 15)

Left: Sarcophagus of Queen Saddan of Adiabene, inscribed "Saddan Malkata". She converted with her family to Judaism and came to Jerusalem. Right: Interior of the royal tombs of Adiabene, (called the Tombs of the Kings).

We must distinguish between the real proselytes, those whose conversion was complete and who accepted the legal status of Jews, and the larger number of half-proselytes — "Godfearers", "Sabbatarians", and the like, who remained officially outside the organized Jewish communities. During the period of the Second Temple, Greek, Roman and Syrian "Godfearers" attracted by Judaism, accepted its teachings, forsook paganism and became half-proselytes, Their respect for Jewish monotheism and way of life was sincere, as was their admiration for the beautiful Jewish Sabbath customs, the Sabbath rest, their hygienic food laws and abstention from marriage with sisters (as in Greece). They visited the synagogues, read the Scriptures in Greek and observed many of the less difficult customs or rites (but not circumcision). This undefined status, involving knowledge and acceptance of Jewish ethics and theology, existed among a wide circle of gentiles. They provided the human material on which Christianity was to draw (see Chs. XI, XII).

THE DIASPORA IN HELLENISTIC TIMES

Though the Jews possessed many civic rights and privileges in the Greek cities, they did not enjoy full citizen rights of the Greek city ('polis') nor did they occupy a leading position in Greek society. In any case these rights were not uniform and the organized Jewish community, which was generally self-governing, with elected lay chief officers, stood juridically outside the Greek 'polis'. As a result the focus of Jewish life in the Diaspora became the privileges of the Jewish Communities and the right to live according to their ancestral laws. This involved the right to worship, observe the Sabbath, and send money to Jerusalem. The Jews were organized into special Communities, most of which had Councils to supervise the affairs of the group, their synagogue and other institutions. They had the fundamentals of cultural autonomy. They kept the Sabbath and Feasts, practised circumcision, and most of them guarded themselves carefully against forbidden foods. The extent of their privileges often aroused the hatred, born of envy, of the Greeks. The existence of the community with its own authority, side by side with the Greek 'polis' and its institutions, frequently caused the two forces to collide. A common life confronted both peoples with a number of questions whose solution was often difficult. This had no small effect in fostering anti-Semitism among the Greeks, Romans and other non-Jews, as will be explained below. The "Jewish Question" faced the Greeks, and later the Romans, with the same intensity that it to-day faces the Western world.

Economic and Social Conditions

The Jews in the Diaspora lived under the ordinary economic conditions of the natives. No single class existed there which was not part of the people's social structure in Palestine, apart from the priests. There were agricultural labourers, slaves, craftsmen, estate owners, tax-farmers, policemen, moneylenders, soldiers, generals, physicians, scribes and the like. Jewish activity and personnel were not restricted to a single field.

Membership in the Jewish Community held great economic advantages both for local residents and itinerant merchants.

In the course of events the ethnic factor triumphed. Ancestral customs had struck deep roots in the Jewish soul and could not be erased or influenced by peoples whose spirit was so alien. A most potent reason for the persistence of a Jewish culture was the vital strength of their communities. While the Greek 'polis' preserved hellenism outside Greece, by the same token the tight organizations of Jews, scattered though they were, but living as semi-autonomous groups, safeguarded their traditions.

Left: merchant weighing grain. While two seated boys steady the scales, a bearded man adds enough grain to balance the weight. Painting on a jar of 540–530 *B.C.E. that had held either oil or wine. Right: metalworkers forging knives, Roman bas-relief of the* 1*st century B.C.E.*

Diaspora Jewry was much weaker and was exposed to immeasurably greater threats to its identity. It would not usually struggle against them by a "one-time mobilization of national forces, but by a ceaseless, stubborn, day-by-day and hour-by-hour defence of its national heritage. . . . To exist in the alien environment, the Jew is forced to develop his spiritual powers and to exert his uttermost endeavours, for he is assisted neither by local tradition, personal contacts, language, nor national customs. . . " (V. Tcherikover). There were those who sought to assimilate out of a desire to exist among strangers on their own individual merits; others adhered to tradition, and depended in their struggle for existence on the support of the strong collective organization represented by the Community.

The Romans, who conquered the hellenistic world and inherited its civilization, also largely accepted the forms of cultural and social organization already in existence. The Greek 'poleis' were, of course, given the widest rights as friends of the Empire, and were treated as privileged citizens — more so than the Jews.

The Jewish communities were accepted within the empire as part of a single Jewish people who had acquired general religious and social privileges as Jews. This was a unique concession within the Roman Empire, dating back to Julius Caesar. Under it the Jews were permitted to live according to their Torah, which was recognized as part of the public law of the empire.

From the time of Augustus, the Jews were treated as simple subjects and bore the full weight of taxation. The Greeks were exempt from taxes and, as loyal and civilized citizens, took a full part in the institutions of local government.

The Jewish communities controlled the rights and status of their members and exercised judicial, fiscal and administrative duties according to the laws of the country rather than of Judea. There is no evidence of any profound difference between the observance of Judaism in the Diaspora and in Jerusalem, with the exception of laws governing questions of inheritance, judiciary, marriage rights or public policy, which followed local custom.

Palestine and the Diaspora

Religious life for the Jews was regulated from Jerusalem to a certain extent. It is difficult to be sure just how far or with how much authority. The relationship is indicated by letters from Jerusalem addressed to the Jews of Egypt, dated 143 and 124 B.C.E., inviting them to celebrate Hanukkah, the Feast of Lights. Over the years, the association took on a more elaborate form. Like the Jewish kings, the High Priests in Jerusalem regarded themselves as the spiritual guides and guardians of the Jews of the Diaspora, just as in the days of Hyrcanus II and Herod. The latter obtained important religio-ethnic privileges from the Roman rulers for them, in addition to political rights as imperial citizens. The Jews for a long time contributed their annual half-shekel to the Temple fund and large numbers took part in pilgrimages to Jerusalem.

Hellenic civilization was supranational and universal. Degraded hellenistic forms in Syria were mentioned in Chs. I and II, but these were not true of hellenism itself. At its best, Greek culture had a very strong attraction. It captivated and enthralled the oriental peoples who encountered it. As it spread through Greece, Egypt and Asia Minor, life was transformed and filled with new interests.

In the beginning of the Roman period, when some Diaspora Jews were attempting to penetrate the class of citizens, reserved for Romans and Greeks, one of the most effective means was education in a Greek school (the gymnasium). There, young Jews learned a deeper understanding of Greek culture. It could be assimilated side by side with their native customs and religion. Even Jews could maintain their cultural individuality and traditional dietary and cleanliness laws while adopting certain features of hellenic civilization. To Philo, a life of athletics and sport was an everyday phenomenon and there is ample evidence that in the theatres and ephebes the Jews had places reserved for them according to their stage of training.

Actors. Terracottas from Larnaca, Cyprus. Life in the Diaspora is suggested by the way of life of the Eastern Mediterranean.

Greek actress in a classic pose, antique bronze from Pompei.

One of the greatest achievements of hellenism was the new tradition of education. In every town, elementary schools were to be found. Great seats of learning, rather like mediaeval universities were founded at centers like Alexandria, Antioch, Tarsus, attracting students of all classes. The post-Maccabean Jews adopted the hellenic principle of individual perfection through liberal education and came to regard universal instruction as a basic necessity. Greek prevailed in the synagogue, in the official assemblies of the community, in their daily life.

THE SEPTUAGINT: THE GREEK BIBLE

One effect of this spread of Greek language, religion, philosophy and culture among the Jews was to create a demand for a translation of the Hebrew sacred writings into Greek. In the synagogues of the Diaspora, the language most used was Greek. Hebrew was not normally used and the Jews had to have their Scriptures provided in a language they actually spoke and in which they could propagandize. A Greek bible was clearly a necessity.

The most important center of the Diaspora was the Jewish community of Alexandria. In approaching the task of at least beginning a translation of the Hebrew Bible, they had the co-operation of King Ptolemy Philadelphus (285—247 B.C.E.) who made Alexandria the established center of hellenism and developed its world-famous Museum and Library.

The story runs, according to the Alexandrian "Letter of Aristeas", that Ptolemy invited— and paid — seventy-two elders from Palestine, who were quartered on the island of Pharos, off Alexandria, and produced in so many days a complete translation of the Pentateuch from Hebrew rolls brought from Jerusalem. From this story their work became known as the "Translation of the Seventy", or, in Greek, Septuagint.

The language they used was standard Greek, but they made a word for word translation, incorporating many Semitic and Hebrew expressions, which the Alexandrian Jews, who were used to hearing similar oral renderings of the Old Testament in their synagogues, could understand. The Septuagint became the cornerstone of the entire edifice of Jewish Alexandrian literature. Moreover, it acquired a supreme importance as the version used with the New Testament to make the bible of the Early Church.

The undertaking was unique. As Bickerman has pointed out, Greek translations of other oriental works were unknown in the world of antiquity. The translation benefitted Jews, proselytes and adherents. The translators were also inspired by a proselytizing zeal to convert the heathen world to a higher monotheistic religion. Philo says that the fame of the laws decreed by Moses penetrated all inhabited lands and spread abroad to the ends of the earth. In retrospect, he rationalizes the motives:

> "Some held it unfitting that the Laws were known only to a part of the human race and that a non-Hellenic part; the Greeks knowing nothing about it. Therefore they bestirred themselves about a translation of it. . . . . For this reason there is still held yearly a great festival in the land of Pharos (an island off Alexandria), in which not only Jews, but also many others take part in honour of the place where the translation originated, and to thank God for the old yet ever new deeds of good will." [Vita Moysi (Life of Moses) 2 : 136-137]

Moreover, perhaps in response to pressure from the cosmopolitan Jews of Alexandria, the translators included a number of books not regarded as part of the official canon by the Judean Jews, (see Apocrypha, Ch. III). Some scholars maintain that the translators also took the opportunity to provide for the more "modern" outlook of Diaspora Jewry and to tone down the candid anthropomorphic language of the Bible (referring to God as a physical personality), as in passages speaking of the deeds or the form of Yahweh and His relations to His people. The Old Testament Jew was not disturbed by references to "the arm of Yahweh" or discussions of His nature. Such Semitic forms were used freely in the traditions which Judaism inherited and were not taken literally. In the old days no one had been upset by, for instance, the prayer in Psalm 44 : "Awake, why sleepest thou, Yahweh." Indeed, in the hands of the prophets and wisdom writers, many such anthropomorphic metaphors had been handled in a more psychological, less physical sense. On the other hand, while they used some images as figures of speech, others are meant quite literally. Probably the translators had the same understanding. Accordingly, there is no consistent pattern of "toning down" or "anti-anthropomorphisms" in the Septuagint.

A CULTURAL RENAISSANCE

The growth of a varied Alexandrian Jewish literature, particularly before the beginning of the Roman period, was the natural response of its intelligentsia to the intellectual needs of educated people. The unprecedented translation of the bible was only a beginning. It laid the foundations for a Jewish literature in Greek. Alexandria became the most famous center for the meeting between these two cultures. Many of the most famous Greek philosophers and rhetoricians of the age made their home in the city which dominated the oriental-hellenistic world. A vivid intellectual life in which the Jews took an active part included public lectures, open discussions and a varied literature. It provided the forum for a meeting between Jewish and Greek thought at the highest levels. The Jews were eager to widen their interests and to make use of alien forms of thought and expression. That they did so is evident, not only from their literature, but also from echoes in Jewish learning in the oriental Diaspora and in Palestine. The impact of the discipline of Greek rhetoric on Hillel's dialectic principles has been noted (see Part I). This is one outstanding example of a wide range of effects produced by this encounter between civilizations. The literature which developed in Alexandria came, in the course of time, to include history, historical fiction, drama, learned works, philosophy and supplements to bibilical stories, as well as theological and religious works.

A pedlar. Terracotta from Alexandria.

Writers and Philosophers of the Diaspora

The long process of adaptation in the Diaspora did not create a uniform literature. Two major trends can be distinguished, illustrated by four of the best known Alexandrian works. Two, "Third Maccabees" and "The Wisdom of Solomon" belong to the class of folk literature while the "Letters of Aristeas" and the numerous writings of Philo Judaeus represent the philosophical and more worldly trend. Although the latter were extremely popular among the early Christians, the first two, while less interesting to their contemporaries, appealed more to the Jews of the Diaspora being closer to their own situation. In contrast to writings in Palestine of the same time (see Ch. III), the second group reflects pro-Greek aspirations and the spirit of compromise of its authors. For instance, the "Letters of Aristeas" encourages the Jews to abandon the "barbarous" features of their character. "Third Maccabees", written about 100 B.C.E. is more in the Palestinian tradition of Second Maccabees (quoted in Chs. I—III). Its theme is persecution at the beginning of the Roman period in Egypt during the days of Ptolemy Philopator, and it tells of a series of violent events, some true, some imaginary. The book ends on a note of deep satisfaction at the complete assimilation with the Greeks. Mixed marriages, business interests and the gay life of liberal Greek youth and wealthy classes are detailed as among the incentives to assimilation. They "wanted to be like the Greeks without being compelled to abandon Judaism. They strove after civic rights and the result was an unyielding refusal on the part of the Greeks to accept them into their society. The result was reciprocal hatred and grave clashes in the city streets." (V. Tcherikover).

The "Wisdom of Solomon" (the use of the name Solomon in the title is a literary prestige-symbol), dates from the middle of the 1st century B.C.E. and is a faithful example of the synthesis of Jewish and Greek ideas. It regards God as transcendental and apart from the world, a creative force fashioning the world out of formless matter, but working through an intermediary. This intermediary is Wisdom, personified as co-architect with God.

A Synthesis of Jewish and Greek Thought

To protect their countrymen from the influences of Greek philosophy and hellenist materialism, the Jews of the Diaspora, especially in Egypt, looked for a religious basis for everyday life. In their writings, miracles and acts of divine intervention are numerous. In addition, attempts were made to find a synthesis which would harmonize the basic principles of Jewish and Greek thought. Hence in the literature of the Diaspora there are divergences from the orthodox position of Palestinian Jewry on the idea of God and subjects such as immortality, and the pre-existence of the soul. The literature of the period is particularly important for the way in which it reflects the intellectual adaptation of the Jews and also the problems raised by Jewish traditions in contact with hellenic universal culture.

A Defence Against Anti-Semitism

The literature of the early Roman period was important for another reason. It played a part as religious propaganda and in defending the Jews against increasing anti-Semitic attacks. Outstanding among such works were the "Apologia for the Jews" by Philo (see below) and Josephus' "Contra Apionem" (Against Apion).

Apion was a well known anti-Semite who lived in the time of the Emperors Caligula and Claudius (see Ch. VI). His writings reproduced all the slanders current in gentile hellenistic circles, such as the cult of the ass in the Jerusalem Temple, the ritual blood libel, and the charge of lack of reverence and sacrilege towards the gods. The polytheist Greeks regarded the Jewish rejection of idols as a denial of God, which they called "atheism". Later, early Christians would be faced with the same charge of atheism (see Ch. XI).

In the face of such attacks, the Jews reacted. At the beginning of the Roman period, when anti-Jewish teaching reached its height, a defensive apologetic trend developed in Alexandrian and Diaspora literature. To the mockery and slanders of the Greeks, the Jews replied in philosophical terms that would be understood by their neighbours. If they stressed the "misanthropy" of the Jews, the latter threw open the doors of their synagogues and invited gentiles to come and worship the one God in their company. From this, the proselytizing movement described above was to grow.

PHILO JUDAEUS AND HELLENIC JUDAISM

The ideas voiced by Aristeas and the religious philosophy of the Wisdom of Solomon were repeated more than a century later (at the beginning of the Imperial Roman period) with especial emphasis and much profound and sophisticated argument by the great philosopher Philo Judaeus.

Living from the third or second decade B.C.E. to about 45 C.E. he was the supreme exponent of Alexandrian thought. His entire output represents a search for a compromise between Judaism as one lofty philosophy and Hellenism as another. Philo wanted to make Judaism an attractive universal religion, acceptable to the philosophically minded non-Jews of his day.

Philosophy

Philo's philosophy is an attempt at a synthesis between Hellenism and Judaism. The basis of his system is that there is a radical dualism between matter as a passive object and a completely spiritual deity who is active in creation.

Matter is perishable, transitory. Spirit is indestructible, immortal, conceived as a "breath" or radiation. The means of contact of the deity, or pure spirituality, with impure matter offers a major stumbling-block to the monotheist. Philo concludes that the link between absolute deity and the corporeal world is provided by intermediate causes or mediators who are themselves a combination of matter and spirit.

In biblical terms, these intermediaries are spoken of as "angels", Spirit, Wisdom, the Word, all of them treated as persons and as distinct from God Himself. Philo projects these aspects of "the word" into the philosophic terminology of his day. To him, the intermediaries or "active causes" are also "intelligent powers". They exist separately from the world and came before everything else that exists, although they are present in divine thought. They are the Logoi ("words") or, rather, components of divine intelligence. The Logos itself, the word of God ("Memra" in Hebrew) is the divine intelligence in a universal sense. This is well illustrated by the active cause in the Story of Creation: "And God said, 'Let there be . . . .' and there was . . . ." This contemporary expression is not abstract in itself, but a logical system of cause and effect can be derived from it. The Logos, therefore, becomes both the deity's creative power and the mechanism through which it works. Philo enlarged the concepts of Judaism, gave them a Platonic colouring and transformed an abstract Jewish notion into a philosophic proposition relating God and history in a "reasonable" manner acceptable to Greek philosophy.

Philo and Scriptures

Philo chose as a vehicle for his religious thought, not the new philosophic forms elaborated by his Alexandrian predecessors, but the Palestinian form of "midrash" upon a passage of Scripture. This could be compared outwardly to a short sermon on a scriptural text. It resulted in any number of interpretations for each verse or fact. Indeed the wildest fancy in allegory or deduction was allowed, even expected of the interpreter. "Everything in Scripture, from names, dates and numbers to the narration of historical events, or the prescription of rules for human conduct is to him subject to allegorical interpretation." (H. A. Wolfson). This discipline and Alexandrian Jewish philosophy had a profound influence on hellenist Jewry and on Paul (see Ch. XI).

Through such a method of interpretation, Philo combined Greek philosophy with the Bible and thus achieved a real interweaving of Jewish and Platonic concept.

He opposed the "intellectual" Alexandrian Jews who contented themselves with either concentrating on the ethical significance of the ceremonial laws, or else using a secret interpretation of the Scriptures to explain universal history and morality. Instead, Philo proposed a discipline whereby both the literal and figurative meanings of the Bible could be understood in a single process. Translated into Greek terminology, this made it possible to present the history of Israel in terms of the pursuit of virtue — the goal of Greek philosophy. Nevertheless, he makes his method subservient to pure Judaism. He preached the highest Jewish ethics based on the Torah and insisted on strict observance of the ceremonial laws.

Philo and Palestinian Judaism

Scholars have given a lot of attention to the extent to which adoption of the Greek language meant that Greek ideas penetrated into Judaism. The familiarity with Greek which the intellectual leaders of the time enjoyed, enriched their vocabulary of ideas as well as of words. It broadened their outlook and their intellectual discipline in the sense that they became more cosmopolitan, looking outwards to an international audience, non-Jewish as well as Jewish. At a certain point, however, the generally beneficial foreign influence seems to come to a stop.

Curiously enough, Philo's work remained unnoticed by the rabbis of Palestine. Even though he followed their method of interpretation, his system failed to gain their interest on either intellectual, theological or national grounds. Doubtless it was too cosmopolitan and Greek in spirit. Nevertheless, the fact remains that his works were mainly preserved through Christianity.

Christianity, indeed, borrowed many ideas from Philo, just as it did from sectarian eschatology and Pharisaic Judaism. His philosophy offered a compromise between Judaism and hellenism, between Israel and the pagan world. On the other hand, Jesus' approach was not allegorical, although, like the other Jews in Palestine, he must have been affected directly and indirectly by Greek thought and culture. The impact of Philonic philosphy on Paul is referred to in Ch. XI.

Decorative scene of the Nile. From a mosaic in Pompei's Casa del Fauno.

Columns VII to XI of the Qumran Manual of Discipline (The Rule of the Community). This is perhaps the most important of the Qumran writings from a theological point of view (see p. 184). *Line* 11 *of column IX (middle) contains a passage about the advent of the Prophet and of the Messiahs of Aaron and Israel.* (*see pp.* 197–8)

C. JEWISH SECTARIES AND CHRISTIAN ORIGINS

VIII

THE DEAD SEA SCROLLS AND THEIR RELATION TO EARLY CHRISTIANITY

PART I

SIGNIFICANCE OF THE SCROLLS

Some years ago, some manuscripts were discovered hidden in earthenware jars in a remote cave near the Dead Sea. They had lain there untouched for about two thousand years, and the language in which they were written is known to very few people today. Yet, instinctively, the world hailed their discovery as a major event. Why was this?

There can be little doubt that the reason is the natural interest of the western world in everything concerning the historical period which saw the birth of Christianity and to which the Scrolls belong.

The first problem about the Scrolls that had to be solved was who had written them. It was soon apparent that the answer would show some connection with the obscure contemporary sect of the Essenes.

The Essenes — Priestly Apocalyptists

The Essenes formed the third sect of Judaism, in addition to the Pharisees and Sadducees. We know of their activities and teachings mainly from the evidence of Josephus, Philo, Eusebius and Pliny the Elder (in his Natural History). All of these were admirers.

It seems that they were of an unworldly, isolationist character. They chose to live far from the tumult of cities in villages and communities of members — the "yahad". Their center, according to the old sources, seems to have been near Ein Gedi (south of Qumran and near the Dead Sea). In all they numbered about 4,000. Josephus and other ancient sources also relate that they were not a single isolated pocket within the Jewish community but that groups of them were to be found in different places throughout Palestine. Later evidence points to the existence of similar groups who practised a cult involving baptism in places from Samaria to Judea. All these sects cut themselves off physically from non-Essenes and from any contact with the world and dedicated their lives to moral perfection and ritual purity. To symbolize this emphasis on purity, they dressed in white and practised frequent lustrations (ceremonial washings).

All their possessions were shared and private property was apparently forbidden. They lived in communal houses owned by the community as a whole and the meals which they ate all together were, for them, an important religious ceremony. Their insistence on community of property was a departure from the social practice of the Pharisees.

There are many parallels between the thought of the Essenes and the Pharisees (see Ch. VII, 1) and they existed side by side. However the Essenes were far more strict about observing the Sabbath than the Pharisees, and were careful to abide by the most minute details of the Law. They encouraged long periods of silence and rose very early for their prayers. Josephus tells with amazement of their reverence for the sun.

Apparently they had a reputation for foretelling the future. Certain teachings which were looked upon as the sacred secrets of the colony, were never revealed to outsiders. Except for a few "marrying Essenes", the majority of them practised celibacy and refused to procreate. As a result, their membership was usually not very large, for it depended on attracting strangers to their peculiar way of life. Nevertheless, they made no attempts at propaganda for a new order of society. To become a member was no simple matter. A candidate had to undergo a rigorous probation and initiation ceremony, and to take an oath resembling that of the "haberuth" of the Pharisees. By this each initiate swore that he would conduct himself in accordance with the ethical principles of the group and would separate himself from "the community of the men of iniquity", their opponents.

Politically, the Essenes were, on the whole, on the side of the Pharisees. Amongst themselves they maintained absolute equality. Although extreme pacifists, they were willing to accept military discipline in times of national crisis. They are known to have fought heroically in the rebellion against the Romans, in which some of the commanders came from their ranks. Their apocalyptic beliefs demanded a life of self-denial and the discipline of a lofty moral code to prepare them for the coming of the End of Days. They clung to their belief that their discipline would hasten the "End" and would at the same time prepare them to live in the Kingdom of God. Their moral standards were "better" than those of the rest of their fellow-men, or so we gather from Josephus. They did not offer sacrifice in the Temple, "because they have more pure lustrations of their own."

Differences and Similarities between the Essenes and the Sectaries of Qumran

There are one or two differences between the accounts of the Essenes given in the ancient sources and the picture we have gained of the sectaries of Qumran. The old writers did not fully appreciate the theological motives of the Essenes in removing themselves from temptation and straining after perfection through a life of rigorous simplicity. Many uncertainties are apparently due to the fact that Josephus was concerned to explain the theology of the Essenes in terms which would be intelligible to the Greeks of the time. Qumran was not a "monastery", nor were the sectaries "monks" as those words have since come to be understood (see p. 207). Neither is it true to speak of their ritual separatism as a modern form of asceticism. It was rather, as F.M. Cross has termed it, "apocalyptic asceticism".

However, there are far more similarities between what we know of the sectaries of Qumran and the descriptions of the Essenes. They both went out into the wilderness for a time, as a preparation for re-birth into the New Israel, and to enter into the New Covenant of the Last Days. There, separated from the rest of Israel, they waited, as though on the threshold, for the Second Exodus — or Conquest. "Preparing the way of the Lord", disciplining themselves by the rules of the ancient "Wars of Yahweh", in anticipation of the final war and the dawning of the Kingdom of God. From what we know of them, it seems that both the Essenes and the sectaries were holy communities, seeking the Kingdom of God through different channels from those of contemporary secular and religious Jewish leaders in Jerusalem. Hankering after the ancient times, they patterned themselves upon the Mosaic camp of the wilderness, where sacrifice was offered. They were, therefore, priestly apocalyptists, not true ascetics.

THE DISCOVERY OF THE TEXTS OF QUMRAN

Until some ten years ago, the Essenes were known only from the reports of ancient authors. Then, suddenly, a vast store of information about them was revealed by the sensational discoveries of the Dead Sea Scrolls, or the texts of Qumran.

Most scholars recognize the close links between the two groups and many identify them completely, explaining certain discrepancies by the fact that the reports of Josephus and other historians were those of outsiders, while from Qumran we have the group's own account. Identification is accepted only as the best working hypothesis so far advanced. Alternatively, it may be that the divergences in their behaviour represent different stages of development of a single movement. The question arises again in connection with the Jewish-Christians in relation to Qumran, (see Part II, below).

The Scrolls and Manuscripts of Qumran

People everywhere were fascinated by the dramatic series of events by which, during the years since 1947, it has become possible to read, translate and publish what are now known as the Dead Sea Scrolls. They were found in three different groups of caves near the north-western shore of the Dead Sea. The most important of them is Qumran. The story of the findings need not be re-told here, but the effect of the discovery and its significance is worth considering.

Importance of the Discoveries

All previously known Hebrew biblical manuscripts were copies dated almost a thousand years later than the Dead Sea Scrolls. During that period a significant development had taken place. An official Hebrew Bible, known as the Masoretic text, was established and adopted as the standard text by the rabbis and the people. All earlier texts, such as those from which the Septuagint had been translated into Greek (see Ch. VII, II), were doomed to extinction.

This is one reason for the supreme importance of the Qumran Scrolls. The discovery of over one hundred ancient Biblical manuscripts — listed below — provided the earliest known material for the study of the text of the books of the Old Testament. Here were genuine products of the 2nd century B.C.E. to the 1st century C.E. Some of the non-biblical manuscripts — whether compiled by the sectaries at Qumran, or else brought there, refer by name to known historical figures, including personalities of the Hasmonean era. For instance, the sect commentary on the 2nd chapter of the Book of Nahum appears to refer to events which took place in 88 B.C.E. for they speak of "Demetrius, king of Javan", who may well have been the Seleucid Demetrius III.

They also throw light on sectarian thought among the Essenes — or among circles very close to that sect — during the early Christian period, namely the centuries between the book of Daniel (2nd cent. B.C.E.) and the 2nd century C.E., the period of maximum interest to the student of Christian origins. It has been observed that, through the Scrolls, we can for the first time feel ourselves contemporary with Jesus. It is this fact, perhaps, more than any other which has given the Scrolls their unique importance. They found an immediate response in the natural interest of the Christian world in the historical and cultural background from which both the Scrolls and the religion of Jesus emerged.

The possibility of connections between the two became apparent very early in the study of the new discoveries. The relation between the sectarian writings and other non-canonical Hebrew documents of the time called for a re-appraisal of contemporary Jewish literature and culture. The sect's writings reveal genuine Oriental cultural influences — from Iran

An earthenware jar, used for storing the Scrolls. Only two complete jars of this kind exist in the world. They were fitted with closely fitting lids and the Scrolls were stored inside, wrapped in several layers of cloth. Cedar oil and other resins may have been used in the process of storing the manuscripts to protect them from insects and rodents . . . "and anoint them with oil of cedar and put them away in earthen vessels." (The Apocryphal Assumption of Moses", see Ch. III). Evidence for this comes from fragments of ancient pottery and canvas cloth (see above), also found in the caves.

The entrance to Cave 1 *at Qumran by the Dead Sea, where a Beduin found a Scroll of Isaiah in* 1947. *The Sectarian Rule of the Community and the War Scroll were later found in the same cave.*

and other Near Eastern countries — as well as hellenistic influences which were affecting the whole intellectual climate of Palestine.

The parallels which exist between the Qumran writings and several New Testament books, such as the Gospels of Matthew and John, the letters of Paul and Hebrews, and certain Gnostic works, show that these all had a more Palestinian and oriental background than has often been thought. Above all, the existence of such a sect in the days of John the Baptizer and Jesus, raises all over again the question of their possible relation to the Essenic movement. It is possible that during the time he spent in "the wilderness", John did know the Dead Sea sectaries and their establishment and that he was influenced by their discipline. It is much less certain, in the light of what we know at this stage, that Jesus knew them, although, of course, he was a disciple of John's (see Part II below and Chs. IX, X).

At the time of the publication of the Scrolls, the controversy which arose on these sensitive points served to stimulate public interest in the Scrolls still further. It will take many years of careful study of the documents in relation to their background and the time at which they were written, for their historical and religious potential to be exhausted. We shall try to summarize the present state of knowledge briefly and, in Part II, will consider the relationship of sectarian Judaism to early Christianity.

The importance of the Scrolls is also supported by other evidence about the period during which they were written or deposited in the caves. From similarities in style of language or of writing, from carbon-14 process tests made on the cloth in which the Scrolls were wrapped, from coins and pieces of stonework in the caves, it has been possible to reach an exact conclusion about the dates of different levels of settlement by the community.

The More Important Documents

Among the more important of the documents to be discussed are the following, found in various caves near Qumran:

Two Scrolls of Isaiah (one complete) and fragments of all the books of the Hebrew canon (Old Testament), with the single exception of Esther. In addition, there are fragments of apocryphal works in Hebrew and Aramaic.

The items of greatest interest, however, are certain specific (non-biblical) sectarian writings, most of which became known for the first time and which provide the main source of information about the nature of the sect. These include the Sectarian Rule of the Community, and adjuncts; the Sectarian Thanksgiving Hymns; the War of the Children of Light against the Children of Darkness; the Damascus (Zadokite) Document which was also known since the beginning of this century; the Genesis Apocryphon; the Commentary on Habakkuk; the Commentary on Nahum; Works on Psalms, Hosea, Isaiah and Micah; Testimonia (Laws, liturgies, prayers, beatitudes, blessings, hymns and Wisdom of the Essenes); the "Description of the New Jerusalem"; an Exposition (Midrash) of the Book

View of Cave 4 at Qumran, one of the richest in manuscripts. Many thousands of fragments, belonging to about 330 *different original manuscripts, were found there. A small ravine separates the cave from the buildings of Qumran.*

of Moses; astronomical observations on Enoch and Jubilees, and other calendrical works mostly in fragments.

(A) THE CULTURAL CLIMATE OF QUMRAN

Since the sectarian writings listed above formed an integral part of the life and mission of the community, they provide the best guide to sectarian thought and to the inner meaning of their organization. We give a brief survey of the four most representative Scrolls.

1. *The Order of the "Yahad"*

The Scroll of the Rule of the Community, (in Hebrew: Serekh hayahad — the Order of the Community), is our main source of information about the sect. The community was made up of priests and laymen who had dedicated their lives to God and whose behaviour was ordered strictly according to the Divine rules embodied in the Law and Prophecy. According to this Scroll, the aim of the community was to attain to that standard of holiness and justice, equity and mercy, which the Scriptures showed to be the nature of God.

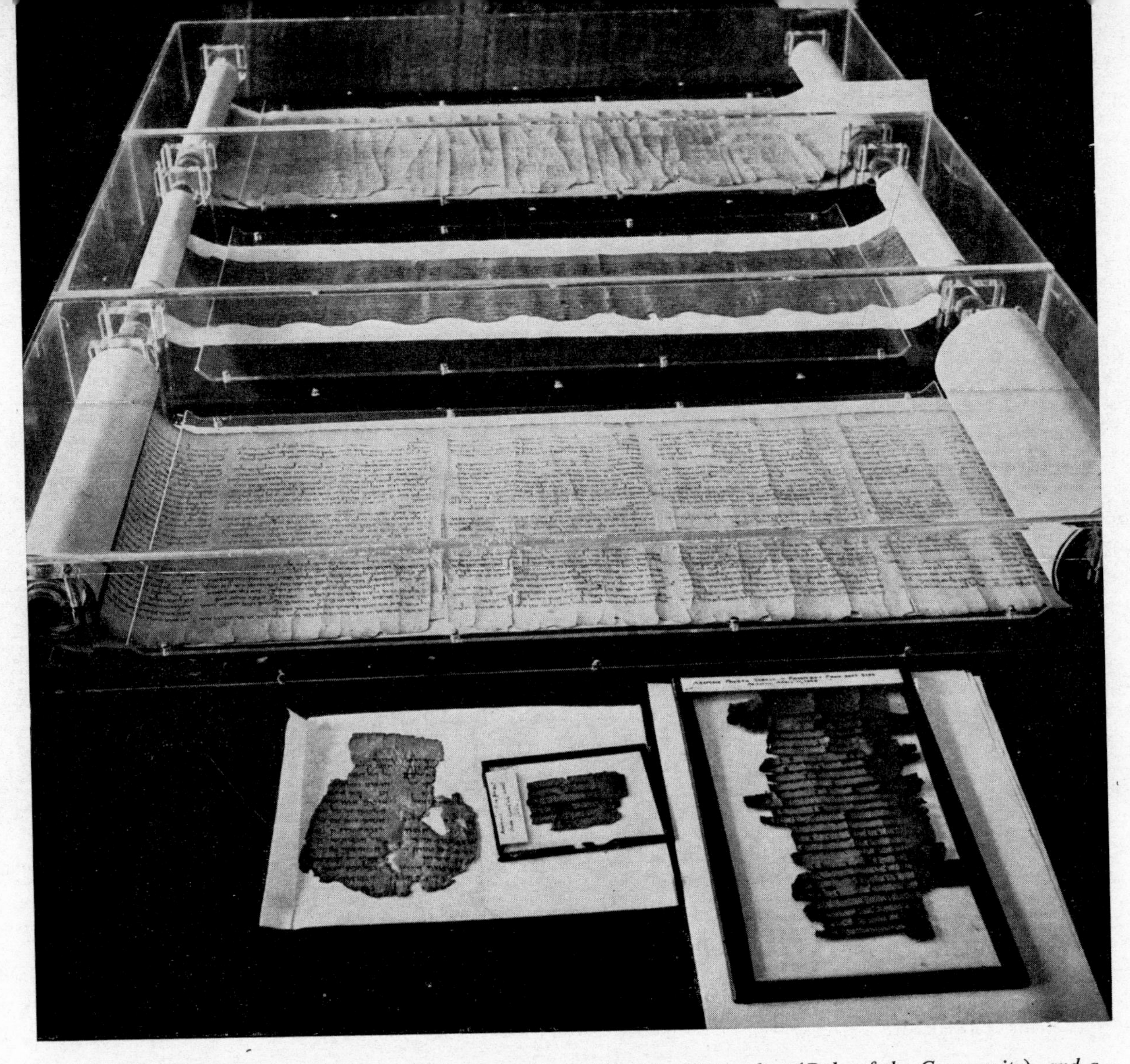

Four scrolls, including the Commentary on Habakkuk, the Manual of Discipline (Rule of the Community), and a section of the Scroll of Lemech. These are original writings of the sectaries, not copies of biblical works. They reflect the social organization and theology of the sectaries and are thus some of the most important of the Qumran texts.

The Scroll opens with a statement of the requirements for a candidate wishing to "enter into the Covenant", and this is followed by the form of the oath of initiation. This is the central ceremony of the sect, whether for a novice, "entering the Covenant" for the first time, or for a renewal of earlier vows. The Scroll concludes with the rules governing the organization of the community.

The members of the Community were strongly influenced by apocalyptic and eschatological considerations. They believed that they, the true Israel, were waiting for a literal establishment of Divine rule on earth. Until this should come about, the sect lived under the leadership of their elders and priests, engaged in constant bible study and extensive devotions.

The Sectaries and Sacrifice

The sectaries did not reject Temple sacrifice on principle. However, probably because they did not recognize the Jerusalem priesthood as being in the true line of succession from Zadok, they regarded the Sanctuary as defiled and the calendar in use unorthodox. "As the Qumran covenanters thought that the Temple was polluted, they could not take part in the Temple service of their time. Their inability to offer real sacrifices engendered an ambivalent attitude to their sacrificial rites." (D. Flusser). It is possible that they instituted a counter sacrificial cultus in their "camps". Considering themselves the "true" Israel, they organized a "legitimate" counter-priesthood.

They insisted that the prerequisite for valid sacrifice was that God's ethical and ritual laws be observed — a feeling they shared with many a prophet and priest of old Israel. The discovery of meticulous burials of animal bones around Qumran suggests that they

First column of the Rule of the Community.

made their own sacrifices, possibly on an altar made after the pattern of the Mosaic desert camp.

2. *The War of the Sons of Light and the Sons of Darkness*

This Scroll, one of the most outstanding of all the discoveries, and sometimes known as the Rule of War, is written in idealist and ritualistic terms. It contains a set of directions for a military operation by the "Sons of Light", i.e. the sectaries, Israel, or, in fact the tribes of Levi, Judah and Benjamin, against the "Sons of Darkness", the traditional enemies of the Jews: the Philistines, Idumeans, Moabites, Ammonites and Kittim, whom many scholars identify with the Greeks.

The camp of the Sons of Light is organized exactly according to the priestly arrangement made by Moses in the desert (Numbers 2:1–5:4). This choice of a precedent from the stay in the desert is typical. The larger portion of the Scroll is taken up with a description of an imminent conflict and then the directions for battle: deployment of forces and their description, trumpet calls, banners. The battle is an ideal one, a model for a messianic war.

The symbolism is carried further. For instance, during the "Holy War" all sexual activity is suspended and women are excluded from the camp. This requirement that warriors purify "their flesh" during a campaign is recorded in various places in the Old Testament, for instance the preparations for the covenant-making ceremony in Exodus 19:6 where the community imitates a "kingdom of priests" standing in the presence of God. It occurs in several stories about David. In 1 Samuel 21, David and his companions were unfit to eat of the bread of the offering (shewbread) unless they had kept themselves free from contact with women. The sectaries' attitude towards purity reflects the same ancient taboos about physical holiness and physical sin. Sexual acts contaminate a man and make him unfit to approach holy things or holy actions. Thus, in the camp of the "Holy War" in which God's spirit (or His angels, i.e., messengers) are present, purity must be complete. This disciplined code was a strong attraction for those devoted to an apocalyptic reading of history. When the trumpet should sound for God's final Holy War, the men of the "Yahad" would be drawn up in formation, rank on rank, ready to march side by side with the "holy ones", the angelic armies of God. This appears to have some affinity with the conceptions to be found in Second Maccabees and the messianism of the Enoch apocalypse (see Chs. II and III).

Such a military preoccupation seems difficult to reconcile with the pacifism of an apocalyptic sect whose members refused to endanger their purity by the violence of secular life or the pursuit of worldly gain. However, they were moved in this case by the desire to identify themselves with the ancient ideals of the desert and by their vision of the victory of God in the final war.

Opinions vary about the interpretation of this Scroll. Some find in it similarities with Roman military procedure. We do not know whether any real conflict was intended by the composers of the document, or whether they were thinking of an apocalyptic Armageddon, the ultimate conflict of mankind.

In either case, the sect seems to have been mobilized for the war of the Jews against Rome, which they may have interpreted as the beginning of the final holy war. Y. Yadin has assigned the Scroll to the Roman period and relates the weapons described to Roman weapons.

3. *A Genesis Apocryphon* (*a Post-Maccabean Scroll*)

This is an expanded version of some stories of Genesis, written in Aramaic and now edited by N. Avigad and Y. Yadin (Jerusalem). It forms an important addition to early apocryphal "midrashim", and has much in common with the rest of such literature (see Ch. III). The sections which have so far been deciphered contain a richly detailed story of the forefathers of mankind, beginning with a remarkable legend of the birth of Noah, related as if by Lemech himself.

The same story, including the biblical story of the Flood, is found in the Books of Jubilees and Enoch, connections which suggest that this Genesis Apocryphon comes from the same tradition and background as the Book of Enoch.

Another story deals with Abraham's descent into Egypt and lyrically tells of Sarah's great beauty and physical charms and her abduction into Pharaoh's harem.

In another section, there is an account of Abraham's vision and his erection of the altar of Bethel. The last section parallels another story, also told in the Bible and in Jubilees — Abraham's fight with the four Mesopotamian kings and his Covenant with God.

4. *The Zadokite Document*

In addition to their own writings, the sectaries paid great respect to the Zadokite Document, also called the Damascus Document, which contains a semi-historical account of the founding of a sect, possibly stemming from the early Hassidim or another non-conformist stream in Hasmonean times. Parts of several manuscripts of this work have been found in one of the caves near Qumran, indicating its popularity there.

The first fragments of the manuscript were found in 1910 in the Cairo Genizah (reliquary of old scrolls). It is now generally recognized that the document emanated from the Qumran sect as a protest against existing priestly religious leadership. It tells that they had withdrawn to "Damascus", under their own honoured teacher and leader, known as the "Star".

> "The repentant of Israel who went out from the land of Judah and sojourned in the land of Damascus."

Some scholars believe that "Damascus" is meant allegorically rather than literally, and that the sectaries retreated to an isolated locality east of the Jordan. The dissenters drew up their own "New Covenant", a series of laws which make up most of the document. The sect called itself the "Sons of Zadok", taking the name of the Old Testament ancestral High

Priest. They were organized as the party of the "New Covenant", and flourished under the inspiration of their leader, sometimes spoken of as the "Righteous Teacher".

> "All the men who entered into the New Covenant in the 'land of Damascus' but have again acted faithlessly and turned aside from the well of living water, shall not be reckoned in the council of the people, nor inscribed in their book, from the day the Teacher of the Community died until the Messiah of Aaron and of Israel arise." (Zadok. Doc. CDC. 8:21)

It was expected that the Messiah would come within forty years of the death of the Teacher of Righteousness.

The most important aspect of the Zadokite document is the detailed description it gives of the law of the sect, which was very similar to Pharisee law. It lays great stress on the idea of "election" of the members to be the chosen ones of God. When the Kingdom is established in Israel in the last days, the inner circle of the community — the circle of Twelve — will be "faithful witnesses in judgment, the Elect of God's favor to atone for the earth and to mete out punishment to the wicked." This concept is also central to early Christianity (see Part II, below).

The document is also of great interest for the construction which it puts on biblical history.

Other ancient non-biblical writings, many of which were found in Qumran, contain parallels to the Scrolls. The Book of Jubilees and the Testaments of the Twelve Patriarchs show the most striking resemblances (see relevant sections of Ch. III). Other books such as the Psalms of Solomon (apocryphal) also have important points of similarity.

(B) HISTORICAL BACKGROUND

It is generally accepted by the majority of scholars that the Scrolls of Qumran are the product of a historical period which began some time in the second century B.C.E. and lasted for three centuries until the collapse of the community about 70 C.E. Copies of Biblical manuscripts must have preceded the writing and copying of non-Biblical documents and these probably date from the second century B.C.E. This is supported by the Maccabean background which some scholars have urged for some of the documents. Among them, documents have been found which are older than the first use of Qumran as a settlement for the sect.

It appears that the Qumran sectaries were familiar with the whole of the Hebrew Canon of Scriptures (with the possible exception of Esther). The Torah and the Prophets were regarded as authorities on all questions of faith or practice. The Psalms, as well as being widely used in their devotions, served the sectaries as a model for the thanksgiving hymns they composed for themselves.

The way in which they used and interpreted the canon of Scripture and various other Biblical texts is of particular interest, for it differed from their contemporaries. For instance, from the frequency with which fragments of the books were discovered, it seems that they had a greater veneration for Isaiah and for the minor prophets, Nahum and Habakkuk, than for the writings of Jeremiah or Ezekiel. The prophecy of Nahum and Habakkuk, they believed, would be fulfilled in their own generation. Moreover they held unorthodox views on the calendar, more in line with those of the apocalyptic Jubilees (see Ch. III).

The Qumran library also included apocryphal works, including Enoch, Tobit, the Testament of Levi and Jubilees. This suggests that the sharp distinction between apocryphal and canonical writings which has become established in later centuries, was not known during the period between the Testaments, nor to the sectaries of Qumran.

It is possible that prophecy, especially any sections which could be interpreted in apocalyptic terms, was regarded, like the Torah, as the Word of God. Due respect was paid to other writings which had an immediate bearing on the covenantal nature and discipline of the sect. Similarly, the *original* compositions of the sectaries, such as the Rule of the Community, the Thanksgiving Hymns and the War Scroll, were obviously an integral part of the life and mission of the community. They may not, though, have been regarded as equal to the Scriptures in inspiration and authority.

HISTORY OF THE SECT

It is still early to attempt a coherent history of the community. It is believed that the original nucleus of the group was formed by a "haburah" of priests who withdrew to this isolated retreat in protest against what they regarded as the evil religious leadership of

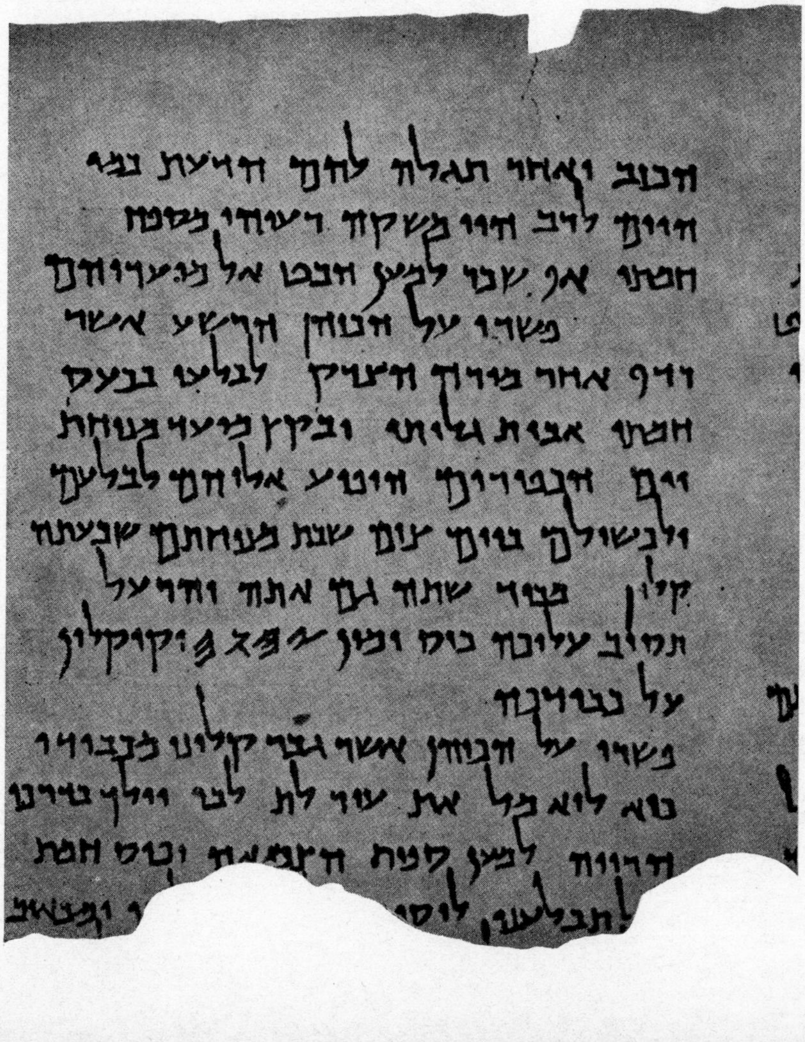

Column XI of the Commentary on Habakkuk. The biblical text is transcribed and then commented upon, verse by verse, the comment being introduced by a formula such as: "the explanation (pesher) of this is . . . . . ." In the sectarian commentary, the explanation is given in terms of the sect's own history.

Jerusalem during the Hasmonean period. A little before 100 B.C.E. an able leader appeared, the Teacher of Righteousness. He gave definite form to the life and organization of the sect and formulated its strict discipline.

Although in the majority view today, the general relationship of the Qumran sect to the Essenes is fairly obvious, a weighty minority view holds that the Essenes (and Qumranites) appear, in the light of the Scrolls, to have been a sub-group of Pharisees who were almost completely withdrawn from the Jewish community. Some scholars (among them Ch. Rabin) place the rise of the community of Qumran within the first century B.C.E. at the point where Pharisaism was succeeded by rabbinic Judaism. There was, in this view, a transition from the earlier stage of Pharisaism to a new stage where the rabbis became its official upholders. Even so Pharisaic institutions such as the "Haburah" continued to exist for some time, striving to preserve the ancient traditions of Pharisaism against the developing ideology of rabbinic Judaism. "The chief innovation of the second stage was that the Rabbis made an attempt to enforce the validity of the Law, as understood by the Pharisee schools, for the whole nation, not only for those who had made a vow to keep it (the haburoth) . . . the haburah must have fought against those relaxations of the Law which admitted hitherto despised outsiders into the fold, but then the fight easily spread to cover also any other relaxations of legal rigorousness." (Ch. Rabin). In either case, the sectarian spirit derived from the main stream of Jewish religious and prophetic thought. As will be seen, (p. 222), the sectaries have an even closer affinity with the cultural and religious background of the gospels and the sayings of Jesus than with rabbinic writings. Hence their vital importance for problems of the history and religious development of their time.

The Covenanters of Qumran represent a complex phenomenon which can be understood only in terms of the whole development of Jewish party life from the time of the Hassidim (see Ch. II). The main successors to the Hassidim were the Pharisees, but the Essenes, on one side and the Sadducees on the other, were offshoots from the same source. The covenanters of Qumran had their own doctrines and patterns of behaviour, but they shared with the other groups a general theological position, (see Ch. VII, I), indicating their derivation from a common source.

The Founder of the Qumran Sect

Because the community had a special relationship to the course of events that was to lead up to the end of the age, the members made their own interpretations of Scripture, under the guidance of the Righteous Teacher. To him, they believed, God had revealed the mysteries of prophecy and, provided they were faithful to him and his teaching, they would be numbered among the members of the Kingdom of God (Commentary on Habakkuk). Accordingly, the founder of the Qumran sect was regarded as having an even greater insight into divine intentions than the biblical prophets.

Nevertheless, the Righteous Teacher was never identified with any of the messianic figures described in the Scrolls. He was honoured as a legislator and interpreter of God and God's will, but not as a messianic figure — the new Moses whom God was to raise up. Redemption and atonement were not seen as flowing from his sufferings and death. In fact, as will be shown later (see pp. 197–198), two Messiahs may have been expected. At any rate, in the rules of precedence laid down for the common feast, a "Messiah of Aaron" is given first place, followed by the group of priests and only then is there any mention of the Messiah of Israel, who may be assumed to have been seen as a descendant of David.

It was the Righteous Teacher's main responsibility to give an explanation of the Torah and to interpret the mysteries of prophecy according to a revelation direct from God to him. Like the Pharisees, the sectaries sought support for Oral (unwritten) Law by linking this to their biblical interpretations. Obedience to God was not merely a question of observing ritual commands or keeping to the letter of the Law. They aimed at total submission to the will of God as this had been revealed in the past, as a first step towards their future sanctification. This exaggerated emphasis on the spiritual content of their religion was, of course, a matter of prime importance to them, for their very existence depended upon it. They lived only so that through diligent study of the Torah they might prepare for the coming of the Messiah and witness the advent of the messianic era. The mere existence and activity of the Righteous Teacher was their assurance that the age of the Messiah was at hand.

The Righteous Teacher and his Enemy

However, set up in opposition to the Righteous Teacher was the Wicked Priest. Originally a faithful servant of God, he had been corrupted by the influence of the material world

The "eagles" were sacred objects to Roman soldiers, who worshipped and made sacrifice to them. Independent evidence for this comes from Josephus' description of the Roman ensigns brought to the Temple after its destruction: "and set them over against its eastern gate and there they did offer sacrifices to them and there they did make Titus imperator with the greatest acclamations of joy." (*War, Bk. VI.* 6, 1)

that surrounded him. He had made himself rich in unlawful ways and persecuted the faithful community. Finally, he brought about the sudden end of the Righteous Teacher.

In retribution, the Scroll foretells, he and the "last priests of Jerusalem" would be handed over to his enemies, the Kittim. It is presumed that here the "Kittim" were the forces of Imperial Rome, whom the covenanters cast for the role of Divine agents of the Last Days.

One of the most important clues that suggest that by "Kittim" the sectaries did indeed mean the Roman army, is their statement that these soldiers made a practice of sacrificing to their standards and venerated their weapons.

There are still doubts about the identification of the Righteous Teacher and the Wicked Priest. The description in Habakkuk could apply to the situation at any time between the beginning of the Maccabean period (Chs. I and II) and the accession of Herod the Great (Ch. V) and his dynasty.

(C) ORGANIZATION AND CUSTOMS, AS REVEALED BY EXCAVATION

AN ESSENE COMMUNITY IN THE WILDERNESS

The shattered remnants of an Israelite fortress, deserted since the conquest of Judah by the Babylonians, had lain neglected since the sixth century B.C.E. Nearly five centuries later, Essene sectaries retiring into the wilderness built their settlement on the fortress' foundations. It was to be occupied in three separate periods, interrupted by two major disturbances. The first period of settlement, probably beginning in the reign of John Hyrcanus I, about 110 B.C.E. was brought to an end by an earthquake in 31 B.C.E. During the last years of Herod's reign, it appears that Qumran again lay abandoned. However, a second period of occupation followed from the beginning of the 1st century C.E. up to 68 C.E. Later on, it was taken over by Roman soldiers, then reoccupied by guerrilla fighters of the Second Jewish Revolt between 132 and 135. After that the site remained totally uninhabited, recovering something of its former importance only a few years ago.

During its occupation by the sectaries (110 B.C.E. — 68 C.E.) the site spread nearly two miles north and two to the south of the Qumran site, along the cliffs facing the Dead Sea. The people lived in caves and tents, operated a communal irrigation system (which they found on the spot), shared pottery made in a communal kiln, depended on common stores of food and water, read — and wrote — common biblical and sectarian Scrolls. The caves which held the manuscripts radiated to the north and south of a central building and contained the remnants of an enormous library. The settlement continued to thrive during the years of Jesus' ministry and the tensions of life under the Roman procurators until the dark days of the first Jewish revolt against Rome during which the buildings were destroyed.

From recent excavations, it appears that the principal community building was a square, approximately 37.5m (or 124 feet) on each side, with a huge defensive tower built on the north-west corner. This formed the nucleus for a complex group of structures. One large

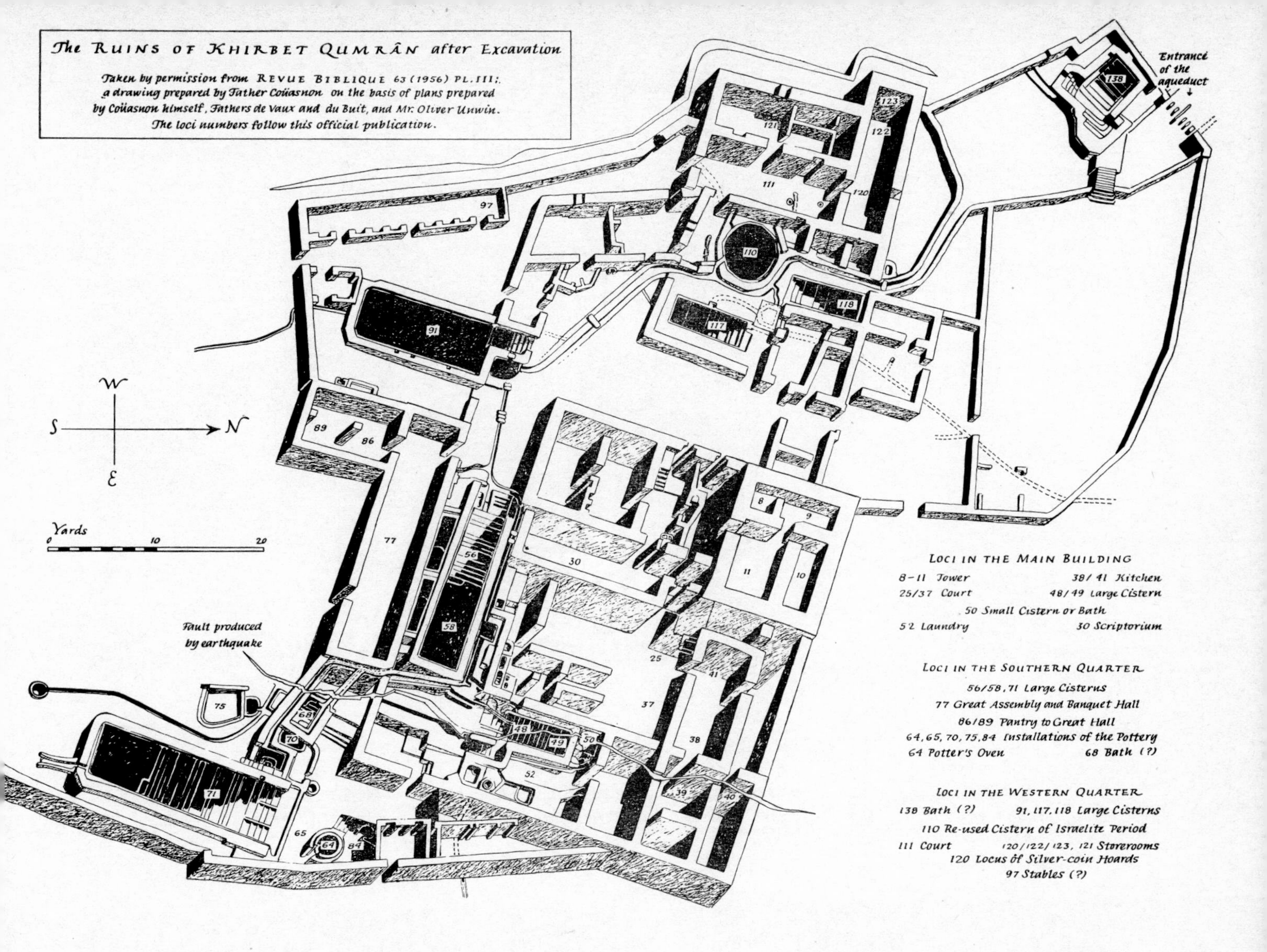

room to the south of the main building was apparently the main refectory. Next to it was the kitchen, which was found littered with a wide variety of earthenware vessels, drinking cups, decanters, wine flasks. A pantry was uncovered there containing over a thousand ceramic dishes, stacked in piles (which may suggest that Qumran catered at times to large numbers of pilgrims). An undamaged cylindrical jar of the same shape as those in which the manuscripts were stored in the caves, was also uncovered. There were also the remains of several fireplaces. Further to the south-west were four or five rooms which seem to have been assembly halls for the community, for the remains of plastered benches were still found against the wall, suggesting that the rooms were used for prayer, meditation or discussion.

THE COMMUNAL MODE OF LIFE

Excavation of one of the first-storey rooms in the main block uncovered the remains of a narrow plaster table 5 metres long (17 by 2 ft.) a plaster bench, a plaster hand basin with small depressions around the edge and finally two inkwells, one of brass, the other of

Hoard of 550 *silver coins, mostly Tyrian tetradrachmas and shekels, dated* 9 *B.C.E. to* 1 *C.E. Around are clay lamps, a pot, a jug and a plate.*

Remains of the furniture of the Scriptorium of Qumran. The benches and stools of brick and plaster served as seats and supports for the scribes (see p. 195).

Part of the aqueduct in the western quarter of the settlement (see top right corner of diagram of ruins on the previous page).

earthenware, still carrying traces of dried ink. These were built into the plaster floor of the room as permanent fixtures and constituted the original furniture of the "scriptorium" of the community. This was the center of literary activity and the place where at least some of the Qumran manuscripts were penned. The depressions in the plaster basin must have held water for use in the ritual purification of the hands necessary before copying sacred texts. This, incidentally, was a typical Pharisee innovation.

To the south-east of this building are the remains of the workshop of the brotherhood. Unfortunately, the only tools that had survived were implements for the smelting of iron ore and for baking earthenware.

For their water, the community had provided an elaborate system of channels and storage tanks which collected the water from the occasional winter rains. Within the settlement were seven major cisterns and six smaller pools or baths. These drew their water through a maze of sumps, settling basins and channels, from an aqueduct fed by a dam at the foot of the waterfall of Wadi Qumran.

Considering the community's demands for drinking water — and they did not immerse themselves in their drinking water — and the water required for their regular maintenance of ritual purity, it is possible that ceremonial baptisms were performed in the nearby spring of Ein Feshkhah, or in the living waters of the Jordan a few miles away.

The Qumran sectaries were one of several religious groups living in the Jordan valley and probably in Samaria and Galilee at the approach of the Christian era. The gospels refer to the gathering place of John the Baptizer near the Jordan and his extensive activity in Galilee (see Ch. IX).

THE COMMUNAL MEAL

The communal daily meal was the center of the community's life. Ritual baths preceded it. The members of the Yahad dressed in special garments and entered a private hall, barred to the uninitiated. Total silence was maintained while all took their seats and no food was touched until a priest had said a blessing. These meals were taken in "tohora" (purity) at midday and in the evening.

> "The novitiate shall not touch the banquet of the Many until the completion of a second year among the men of the Yahad." (Rule of the Community 1 QS 6:20–21)

After a first year within the Yahad, the novice was permitted to draw nearer to the communal life. Admission to the common meal was the final step, taken only after a full two-year term in the novitiate.

The communal meal had a messianic significance and was conducted as a ceremonial anticipation of the Messianic banquet — the celebration of the victory of the expected Messiah. The Rule of the Congregation gave precise instructions:

> "This is the order of the sessions of the 'Men of the Name' who are summoned to the Feast for the communal council when God sends the Messiah to be with them: The Priest shall enter at the head of all the congregation of Israel and all the fathers

of the Aaronids . . . and they shall sit before him each according to his rank. Next the Messiah of Israel shall enter, and the heads of the thousands of Israel shall sit before him each according to his rank. And. . . they shall sit before the (two of) them, each according to his rank. . ." (Adjunct to the Rule of the Community, 1 QS 1: 11–12)

In this, according to F. M. Cross, the "Messiah of Israel" is apparently intended as the Royal Messiah, whose coming the sectaries were awaiting. In the assembly of fully-fledged members of the community, the lay head and the priestly head of the community stood in the places of the Messiahs of Aaron and Israel. Apparently, there were two alternative conceptions of the actual event. A prophet would appear to announce either two messianic figures, the "anointed ones of Aaron and Israel" or, alternatively, "the Messiah of Aaron and Israel" in the singular.

Meals as Religious Rites in Judaism

There are similar parallels in apocryphal and rabbinic literature. The very nature of the occasion implies a sense of communion with the messianic figures of an older Jewish tradition. The Pharisees also had their religious meals in their "haburoth" (Ch. VII, 1). In any case, every meal in Judaism was, in some sense, a religious rite. From the time of the Old Testament, the meal had been the center and locus of Jewish religious expression. Up to the present day, a normal Sabbath meal begins with the washing of the hands and is accompanied by the blessing over the wine ("kiddush"). The head of the household raises his cup of wine at the meal table, or standing before two loaves of wheat bread, and pronounces one benediction over the bread and the wine, at the same time giving thanks to God for the Sabbath, a day of rest and joy. The meal is eaten to the accompaniment of the singing of hymns ("zemiroth"), or, as a duty, a discussion of religious subjects. At the end, a formal invitation is given to pronounce the blessing ("zimun"), precedence being given to priests. The blessing is pronounced either by them or, "by leave of the Cohen (priest)", by the head of the household. After the blessing, wine is drunk in salutation.

The cult meals of Qumran incorporated such traditional features, but added to them a messianic significance, making the communal meal a liturgical anticipation of the messianic banquet. It may have included ceremonies of remembrance, in the same way as the Passover. In addition, the sectaries looked forward to the future deliverance of Israel by the "Messiah of Aaron and Israel". These ideas may have been combined with the aspirations we find in the Qumran "Hymns of Thanksgiving" which include hymns for a deliverance from all the powers of evil and the enemies of Israel, (cf. p. 205).

Communal Living

All business transactions seem to have taken place at one point within the community structure itself, and not in the nearby caves where the manuscripts were hidden. This indicates the type of communal living mentioned in Acts and suggests a deliberate acceptance of the discipline of poverty: Acts 4: 32 ff.

On the other hand it has been pointed out that complete community of property which used to be attributed to the Essenes, might have applied only to the priests, who had no property, and not to the thousands of adherents.

The coins from the earliest to the latest level date from the time of John Hyrcanus (135-104 B.C.E) to the last of the Hasmoneans (40–37 B.C.E).

Burial Customs

Next to the Qumran settlement was its cemetery. This contains about twelve hundred tombs. Each one consists of a shaft sunk into the soft rock to an average depth of five feet, with a funerary chamber hollowed out under one of the long walls of the shaft. In this chamber the bodies were laid face upward, without first being placed in a coffin. The chamber was then sealed with rocks and brick and broken earthenware from the settlement and the trench filled in to complete the burial. This has been ordinary Jewish burial practice ever since (with the exception of the elaborate burial ossuaries, sarcophagi and mausoleums in the necropolis of Jerusalem.

Some of the graves were marked at the head and foot by a single block of undressed stone, but the majority were indicated by a simple mound of pebbles. The austerity practised by the sect is further indicated by the total absence of ornament on the graves or of funerary offerings. Contemporary Jewish graves elsewhere were also without funerary offerings but they were far more elaborate.

Most of the skeletal remains were of adults and were in a poor state of preservation. Some of the fragments indicated female skeletons but no remains of children's skeletons have been found.

(D) BELIEFS AND SACRAMENTS

The Messianic Era

The sectaries of Qumran believed that by acting out in their community life the way of the Kingdom of God and by anticipating its reality in their observances, they would thereby guarantee its existence and even assist its coming. In this sense, the messianic era could be hastened by human effort (see p. 212). Only after the "Kittim" (assumed to be the Greeks or Romans) of various countries had been eliminated could the triumph of faithful Israel be complete. It is the opinion of many scholars that the sectaries did not think of their kingdom of heaven in terms of a new heaven and a new earth, but rather as the continuation of human military success, achieved with God's approval. Like many people in the days of the prophets, they seem to have expected that all nations would then humbly flock to Jerusalem to pay their tribute to the serene and gracious victors. In this kingdom, worship would be controlled by the High Priests, similar in some ways to the situation of Ezekiel's vision.

The Present as the Prelude to the New Age: It must be remembered that the Community of the sectaries was at once the *future Congregation* of the Elect ("Men of the Name") and also a sect whose life in the present was seen as foreshadowing the dawning New Age. Their communal way of life was an essential element of their intense preoccupation with the life that would be realized in that New Age. That life would see:

Unity through the Spirit;

The end of the inequalities between the wicked rich and the oppressed poor; the sectaries saw themselves as a "Congregation of the Poor", which seems to anticipate Jesus' ". . . the poor shall inherit the Kingdom of God." The believers in Jesus gave themselves the name of the "poor" (ebionim) as found in the Psalms, a term which the first Jerusalem church used of itself (see p. 221).

The practice of a communal economy, as the prototype of the "economy of God": this same preoccupation can be seen among the members of the primitive Church.

The Sect had its Birth in Biblical Interpretation

Unceasing study of the Scriptures was the duty of all the sectaries. Certain portions of the day and night were allotted to the reading or interpretation of the Torah and Prophecy.

> "They shall eat together and worship together and take counsel together. In every place where there are ten men of the Council of the Community, there shall not fail from among them a priest. Each according to his appointed task, shall sit before him and in that order they shall be asked for their counsel with regard to every matter . . . Wherever the ten are there shall not cease to be a man who expounds the Law, day and night continually, at length, one to the other. Let the Many (the congregation) keep awake together a third of all the nights of the year to read in the Book, and to seek the right and worship together. . ." (1 QS VI, 2–8)

This intensive study developed an esoteric discipline of interpretation which, kept a closely guarded secret that was revealed only to the initiates of the community, gave them, they believed, the only true understanding of divine intentions. Things which today seem total abstractions were literal realities for the sectaries. They believed that the End of the World was to come within their own lifetimes. Out of this belief developed the apocalypticism of the sect and the concept of the New Covenant.

The New Covenant of Mercy and Repentance

> "When they are assembled for Community, everyone who comes to the Council of the Community shall enter into the Covenant of God in the sight of all the dedicated ones. And he shall impose it upon himself by a binding oath to return to the Law of Moses according to all that he commanded." (Rule of the Community, 1 QS V, 8ff)

The idea of a Covenant between God and man, which is central to the Rule of the Community and to the Zadokite document, is a direct descendant from the distant Hebrew past. In place of the old Covenant of Sinai, a new relationship, of divine initiative on the one side and the response of Israel on the other, has developed. The idea of the Covenant underwent a significant change among the prophets, beginning with Hosea, classically presented by Jeremiah (see ADAM TO DANIEL Ch. XXI) and referred to again in varying forms in Second Isaiah and Ezekiel, (VII, XV, XVIII, XIX).

Fundamentally, the new approach represented a reaction against the sterility of a formal ritual, calling instead for an inward spiritual response to a divine promise of mercy and forgiveness. This concept led into the vision of the creation of a new Israel out of the Remnant of the old Israel.

The New Covenant of the Zadokites and the Qumran sectaries put this Essene ideal on the same level as the great covenants of the past. Significantly, it is described in the literature as "berith hesed" (Covenant of divine mercy) and "berith teshubba" (Covenant of Repentance), which recalls the ideals of Jeremiah and Ezekiel.

Entry into the New Covenant took place at a solemn assembly of the sect, described in the Rule of the Community, which took place once a year at one of the Festivals. At the same ceremony, new members were admitted. Each year, the members were graded according to their records. New members had to undergo a period of probation and a searching examination. It is suggested by M. Black that "the main function of the Qumran 'monastery' was to provide a center for the convocation of the sect, no doubt also at other feasts, but primarily on the Pentecost festival" (the feast commemorating the giving of the Law), when new members were admitted.

THE MEANING OF ANCIENT BAPTISM

Daily priestly lustration rites seem to have been practised by the sectaries, in addition to baptism on admission to the New Covenant of the community. This formed one of the central "sacraments" of the Essenes and Qumran communities for, rooted as they were in older Judaism and, specifically, in the priestly laws of ritual purity ("tohorah"), they held that wickedness or sin pollutes the flesh of man in *the same way* as "unclean" objects pollute it. Hence no purity-rite of lustration (cleansing of pollution) could be effective *unless it were preceded by effective repentance* from within. This alone could atone for sins.

The Rule of the Community of Qumran sounds a warning against a candidate for membership being baptized without repentance:

> "Such a candidate shall not enter into the water (and as a result) to come into contact with the purity of the holy one, for they are not purified (thereby) except they repent from their wickedness." (Rule of the Community 1 QS 5:13–14)

Anyone undergoing the purity-rite, without repentance, even with "seas or rivers", is wrong in imagining it to be automatically effective. He remains an outsider, a man denied, likened figuratively by the Torah to a leper. But if he fulfills the condition of repentance, he will enter the Kingdom, for he is cleansed.

> "Then God in His faithfulness will purify all the works of man, and cleanse for himself the body man, in order to consume every wicked spirit from the midst of his flesh . . and to make him pure with a holy spirit from every wicked deed; and he will sprinkle on him a spirit of truth like water for impurity . . . so as to give the righteous understanding the knowledge of the Most High." (1 QS, 4:20–22)

Thus the gift of salvation is not to be achieved by purity of flesh alone. Instead, as both the sectaries *and* John the Baptizer insisted, it involves an act of inner purification and spiritual change, so as to bring salvation through the "spirit".

Josephus gives the same description of the concepts underlying the baptism of John the Baptizer. Salvation was conditional upon repentance. Repentance and atonement did not follow the purity-rite of baptism. It *preceded* it as a spiritual motive in its own right (see Ch. IX).

These practices stem, of course, from the mainstream of contemporary Jewish belief. Rabbi Jose the Galilean in an early tractate of the Talmud said:

> "Great is repentance, because it brings near redemption, as it is said: 'and a redeemer will come to Zion, and unto them that turn from transgression in Jacob' (Isaiah 59:20). Why will a redeemer come to Zion? Because of those that turn from transgression in Jacob." (Yoma 86 b)

Left: The great cistern of the Qumran settlement. The cisterns were cut out of the rock and lined with plaster. Right: This cistern had 14 *steps, giving access to the water at different levels. A crack running down the steps, across the floor of the cistern and into several rooms beyond was probably caused by the earthquake of* 31 *B.C.E. The upper portion of the steps in this and another pool were sub-divided into four separate sections, as though to regulate access to and from the pool itself. This may in the opinion of some scholars suggest periodic use of some of the cisterns as baptistries, since ceremonial lustrations played a prominent part in the observances of the community. Others maintain that baptism was primarily conducted where there was running (living) water, at Ein-Feshkhah or the Jordan, some distance away.*

The common room (Banqueting Hall) of the Qumran settlement, where the sectaries gathered for their most important ceremony. The building overlooked the Dead Sea, with the mountains of Moab in the background.

PART II

RELATIONSHIP BETWEEN SECTARIAN JUDAISM AND EARLY CHRISTIANITY

SIMILARITIES AND DIFFERENCES IN THE NEW TESTAMENT

One of the central problems in any discussion of the origins of Christianity is the question of its relationship to earlier sects within Judaism. In the foregoing description of the life and thought of the Qumran community, many theological and social comparisons may have been noted between this variation of Judaism and the teachings of the New Testament.

The sectaries practised baptism and held ceremonial, cultic meals; they lived in expectation of a Messiah; they upheld a doctrine of dual realms and spoke of a "New Covenant"; they saw themselves as a company of the "Elect", forming a new, spiritual temple. A brief examination of these key problems may make it possible to suggest how far this religious system on the periphery of Judaism acted as a preparation for the early church. In estimating the common features and differences in the practice and life of the two, modern scholars have tried to judge whether they can be traced to a distant, shared theological background.

(Later influences which were to emphasize certain differences between the sectaries and the apostolic church will be considered in the following chapters, IX – XII).

Organization and Liturgical Institutions of Qumran and the Early Church

The ruling assembly of Qumran and the Essenes, the "rabbim" or the "many", finds a parallel in the New Testament:

> "And all the assembly kept silence; and they listened to Barnabas and Paul as they related what signs and wonders God had done through them among the Gentiles." (Acts 15: 12)

From among the body of the "rabbim", twelve laymen and three priests made up a ruling Council. There is a striking parallel to the Twelve Apostles who governed the early Church in Jerusalem, not only with regard to the number twelve, which is firmly rooted in Old Testament tradition, going back to the twelve tribes of Israel, but also with regard to their function in the eschatological renewal of ancient Israel, e.g. Luke 22: 30:

> "that you may eat and drink at my table in my kingdom and sit on thrones judging the twelve tribes of Israel." (Luke 22: 30)

Equally important is the divergence in the composition of the councils of Qumran and Jerusalem Christianity; the former includes three priests representing the official orders of the house of Aaron, while the latter has no place for the priesthood here, or anywhere else in the supervisory apparatus.

The president of the sessions of the "rabbim" was the "mebaqqer" or "paqqid". He was the general director of the community, responsible for examining and training those who applied for membership in the haburah; he was also shepherd of the flock, and "father in God." The term is equivalent to the Greek "episkopos" (bishop), which is regularly used of officials in the early church with similar functions.

In conclusion, the question of direct influence from Qumran must remain open. Many of the parallels between Qumran and the early church can be explained in terms of their common foundation in the Old Testament, though there are detailed resemblances which suggest a more immediate common ancestor (i.e., Hassidim). Even if direct connections could be demonstrated, then the notable differences in principle and practice would show that the early Christians did not simply borrow earlier patterns, but adapted and altered them to suit their own circumstances.

As has been shown, the Qumran sect lived in a literal anticipation of the coming of the Kingdom of God. As a practical demonstration, all property was shared. Admission into the community meant giving up all private property:

> "And all who believed were together and had all things in common; and they sold their possessions and goods and distributed them to all, as any had need." (Acts 2: 44–45)

> "Now the company of those who believed were of one heart and soul, and no one said that any of the things which he possessed was his own, but they had everything in common." (Acts 4: 32)

This social pattern of sharing all things in common is a characteristic of many groups closely united by extreme opinions. The Jewish-Christian community maintained this form of life for many years before finally giving it up (see Ch. XI).

The Messianic Banquet and the Lord's Supper

"Partaking of the food in joy" by the faithful was the inspiration of the common meals which were held within the Church of Acts:

> "And day by day, attending the temple together and breaking bread in their homes, they partook of food with glad and generous hearts." (Acts 2: 46)

It is thought by many scholars that in the sacraments of the Lord's Supper and of baptism, the early Christian church was influenced mainly by contemporary oriental mystery religions. However, hellenistic elements had already been absorbed into Palestinian Judaism before New Testament times. There is no need to suppose that New Testament practice was borrowed directly from Greek sources.

This theory is revised by Ch. Rabin: "The communal meals of Qumran were influenced by the cult meals of contemporary religions. It may be observed in general that the whole system of organization of the sect of Qumran bears many resemblances to what we know of cult societies of the hellenistic world." It seems reasonable to believe, with many scholars, that, in the light of all that has been learned from the Qumran findings, the communal meal of the sectarian communities seems a more likely antecedent to the Christian rite. In fact it is now accepted in some quarters that the background to the Lord's Supper must be found in the Qumran communal meal:

> "I tell you, many will come from east and west and be reclined with Abraham, Isaac, and Jacob in the kingdom of heaven while the sons of the kingdom will be thrown into outer darkness; there men will weep and gnash their teeth." (Matthew 8: 11–12)

Glass drinking cup, decorated with applied glass threads. From Nazareth, dated between the 1st and 4th centuries C.E.

"And when the hour came, he reclined at table, and the apostles with him. And he said to them, 'I have earnestly desired to eat this passover with you before I suffer; for I tell you I shall not eat it until it is fulfilled in the Kingdom of God.' And he took a cup and when he had given thanks he said, 'Take this, and divide it among yourselves; for I tell you that from now on I shall not drink of the fruit of the vine until the kingdom of God comes.' And he took bread, and when he had given thanks he broke it and gave it to them, saying, 'This is my body.' " (Luke 22: 14–19)

Anticipation of the banquet of the Kingdom is an important element in all accounts of the Lord's supper, and the eschatological significance which it had from the beginning in the Palestinian church has been confirmed by the Qumran material.

The accounts in 1 Corinthians (11:20 seq.) refer to the communal meal (agape). It was presided over by the leader of the community and followed by a celebration of Holy Communion, in which the bread and wine were blessed by the celebrant. It seems that the prevailing spirit of joyful anticipation led to excesses among new gentile Christians, referred to in Jude 12 and 1 Corinthians 11. These necessitated reforms and led eventually to the separation of the Eucharist from regular meals.

Was the Passover the Background of the Lord's Supper?

Scholars have rightly differentiated between the earliest forms of the "Lord's Supper" and the later Eucharistic developments. Some maintain that in the Last Supper, Jesus was in fact celebrating the Passover with his disciples according to the age-old ritual:

"Now on the first day of Unleavened Bread, the disciples came to Jesus, saying, 'Where will you have us prepare for you to eat the passover?' He said, 'Go into the city to such a one, and say to him, "The Teacher says, 'My time is at hand; I will keep the passover at your house with my disciples.'" And the disciples did as Jesus had directed them, and they prepared the passover." (Matt. 26: 17–19)

However, the Passover is only one element in the background to the Lord's Supper. This is a Jewish memorial festival which in this period included eschatological elements. Thus it offers a pattern of the future action of God in redeeming his people from their existing bondage. Second Isaiah developed the theme of a return from Babylon as a second Exodus which would see the beginning of a new age. Similarly in the New Testament, the Exodus from Egypt provides the model for a new Exodus, with Jesus as its leader, like a second Moses. However, the Passover ceremony is not directly related to the regular "breaking of bread together" in the early Church. For a fuller background to the common meal described above in Acts 2:46, the Pharisaic and sectarian sacred meal provides, in the opinion of some scholars, the nearest suitable source. F. M. Cross adds: "This is not to suggest that the Church merely took over an Essene meal. Within the Lord's supper are notable original elements: the formulas which transform the old Passover into the feast of the New Covenant memorialize the sacrifice of the body and blood of the victim; the pledge of the Covenant. And there is no reason, I think, to suppose that the combination of the two elements, the memorial of the sacrifice and the anticipation of the Messianic banquet does not exist already in the most primitive traditions of the Jerusalem community."

Attitude to Marriage

Scholars have recognized that the Qumran sectaries had an ambiguous attitude to marriage both in practice and in their traditions on the subject. The accounts given by Philo and Josephus are also contradictory and confusing.

It appears, as we have seen, that the community regarded themselves as soldiers enlisted in God's Final War, who must keep their purity untainted so as to be ready at any moment, (see p. 188). Accordingly, their advice is that a man who wishes to live eternally before the throne of God should not marry. They did not reject marriage as an institution but marrying in the existing circumstances.

This advice, it has now become clear, was based on the asceticism that went with their concentration on the things of the "next world" and their belief that the present world would pass away at any moment. This attitude can perhaps explain Josephus' confusing statements and clarify the discrepancies between statements in the texts of Qumran compared to discoveries in their cemeteries, where a few skeletons of women were found. As explained (p. 181), it would not be correct to call Qumran a "monastery" nor the Jewish sectaries "monks". It is interesting, however, to note that "there seems to be a connection between Qumran and the early monastic development in eastern Christianity, not only the orthodox Christians but also the Gnostics of Egypt, who may have been ultimately descended from the Therapeutai. Naturally in the long history of monasticism, mediaeval and modern forms have diverged considerably from early Christian and Essene practice" (D. N. Freedman). See also Ch. IX, II, on the repercussions of John's movement.

Recent studies of the Qumran Scrolls have revealed previously unknown details about the sectaries which enlarge and explain the picture of them given by ancient historians or, for that matter, the concepts of modern scholars. These seem to point to the fact that celibacy was far from the universal rule and may have been an exception. Moreover, Qumran was only one of a number of Essenic communities. It is possible, therefore, that the settlement served as a central meeting-place for followers who actually lived elsewhere, while those in permanent residence were a kernel of the cult society. This would explain the comparative absence of women's and children's skeletons. Perhaps only the central directorate, or permanent population were celibate.

M. Jean Danielou suggests that all the sectaries, or their followers, were not ascetic to the same degree. Some were devout Essenes, devoted to the contemplative life and to celibacy, while others led a more normal life and were not so rigorously ascetic. The difference seems to reflect a more advanced mystic consciousness. The same discrepancy is found among the Jewish-Christians, where marriage was not condemned, but appeared to be looked down on. The attitude of the primitive Church seems to have sprung from similar theological considerations:

> "And Jesus said to them, 'The sons of this age marry and are given in marriage; but those who are accounted worthy to attain to that age and to the resurrection from the dead neither marry nor are given in marriage, for they cannot die any more, because they are equal to angels and are sons of God, being sons of the resurrection." (Luke 20: 34–36)

Like the sectaries, Jesus indicates that it is better not to marry in the present age. Paul speaks in a similar vein, expressing the hope that other Christians would follow his example and be celibate. At the same time, he agrees that under certain circumstances it is better to marry (cf. I Cor. 7, especially vss. 25–31).

PRE-HISTORY OF CHRISTIAN BAPTISM

To the sectaries of Qumran, baptism was not a "sacrament" in the modern Christian understanding of the word. It was a rite signifying repentance of sins upon entry into the eschatological community of God, (see Part I, above and Ch. IX). The theological concepts involved come so close to the way John the Baptizer thought that the Qumran texts are essential for a proper understanding of the original significance of the rite of baptism.

The Holy Spirit and the Community of the End of Days

The sectaries saw themselves as the called and chosen congregation of the End of Days. It is understandable that they believed that baptism on earth would cleanse them of ritual uncleanness, provided they repented first in the spirit, (see Part I, Baptism, 1 QS IV: 20–22). But, in "the end of days" baptism by the spirit would cleanse each of them of all the impurity that remained from his earthly existence and would make him absolutely righteous, fit for "understanding the knowledge of the most High." The same attitude was central to the teachings and movement of John the Baptizer, (see Ch. IX).

Similar theological language and emphasis on baptism as the gift of salvation by the spirit is apparent in the gospel of John:

> "Nicodemus said to him, 'How can a man be born when he is old? Can he enter a second time into his mother's womb and be born?' Jesus answered, 'Truly, truly, I say to you, unless one is born of water and the Spirit, he cannot enter the kingdom of God. That which is born of the flesh is flesh, and that which is born of the Spirit is spirit. Do not marvel that I said to you, "You must be born anew!" (John 3: 4–7)

POPULAR ATTITUDE TOWARDS PURIFICATION AND ATONEMENT AND PRIMITIVE CHRISTIANITY

The theological ideas of the uninitiated multitude, the amme-ha-aretz, may not have been as dogmatic as those of the Pharisee or Essene "haberim". Popular deviations were probably known. Josephus tells us, for instance, that the Essenes "would foretell things to come" and practised acts of purification of many kinds. The sectaries believed that the Holy Spirit inspired their leaders to predict the future, much in the manner of the prophets of earlier times, but it seemed to Josephus that they acquired this power by virtue of their ritual purity. This is a slight variation on the sectaries' own account of their views about the spirit and baptism. Some of them may have held the popular belief that baptism guaranteed remission of sins and the gift of the holy spirit, instead of the accepted sectarian view which insisted on repentance in spirit as the prerequisite for baptism.

Recent researches have thrown further light on this point. S. Lieberman, Ch. Rabin and others point out that the Pharisee "haburah" was equally concerned with ritual purity (see Ch. VII, I). Initiation was accompanied by a ritual bath (tebilah) and conferred the right of participation in the ritually pure meals. Priests immersed daily before eating the meal offerings and before certain sacrifices. Scribes immersed before writing such works as the book of Exodus. It is in the repetition of the purifying washings that the most striking parallel emerges between the Essene sectaries and certain branches of the early Church. As David Daube points out, baptism came to occupy a central place in rabbinic practice. He suggests that "tebilah" alone had become the central rite of initiation among leading Hillelites of the first century (Ch. VII). M. Black has concluded from this that "Pharisaic practices may have contributed to the Christian doctrine and observance of baptism as a single unrepeatable act. In the New Testament the establishment of "one" Baptism is no doubt to be set down to the influence of the Pharisee, Paul."

Later conceptions of baptism, such as those attributed to John the Evangelist, may have drawn on older popular ideas, as well as the inheritance of the "haburah". It is possible, therefore, that some at least of the roots of later Christian thought may lie in popular Jewish folk-theology.

Apart from the sectaries, the Essenes and the sect of John the Baptizer, there were other pious sects who held theological views which were similar. According to Pere J. Thomas' assessment of the patristic evidence, a baptist movement existed throughout Palestine and Transjordan, before 70 C.E., made up of different but inter-related groups who, in opposition to the Pharisees, substituted baptizing rites for observance of the Temple sacrifice.

Distinctions within Christian Baptism

Two of the elements of sectarian baptism: ritual purity and repentance as a condition of valid baptism, were present in the baptism of John the Baptizer. However, the second century Christian church faced a different problem. John had addressed Jews, but they were aiming mainly at gentiles. While the continuity is clear in the New Testament and, through it in the Church, there was also a change in emphasis which affected the basic ideas of repentance and purification connected with the rite. Christian writers continued to use the idiom of ritual purity as a kind of poetical imagery. The symbolism of adult immersion shows that it was understood that the old life of sin was washed away and a new life of purity begun. "A third element of sectarian baptism was developed and emphasized by Christianity: the notion that baptism brings remission of sins . . . The whole development leads from a baptism that could hardly be called sacramental to the entirely sacramental act of Christian baptism" (D. Flusser).

It is, of course, true that Christian baptism differed from the Essenes' rite in being a single unrepeatable act of initiation while the Essene rite of lustration was evidently frequently repeated. In the view of M. Black: "The most that it appears possible to say of the Qumran rite is that it prepared the way, at some considerable remove, for the full doctrine of Christian baptism. It may be a foreshadowing, but it is, in itself, a mere shadow of the full Christian rite."

The foregoing does not represent a full picture of the prehistory of Christian baptism. The question arises again in connection with the significance of John the Baptizer's rite. This will be considered in the next chapter, in the light of additional, new facts.

SECTARIAN MESSIAHS AND POPULAR JEWISH EXPECTATIONS

Any attempt at a reassessment of the ideas of redemption and redemptive history and the hopes of the Messianic age as they developed during the later period of the Second Jewish Commonwealth, must take into account the whole broad picture of Jewish life, and must include the riches of early Pharisaic and Tannaitic literature. These followed directly from the national revival of the Hasmoneans (Chs. II and VII) and reached the highest levels of ethical idealism and religious devotion.

Within the general development of the period, certain trends appeared at different — although not successive — stages. They were:

A. Nostalgic messianic expectations among wide circles influenced by the Pharisees and led by the Tannaitic rabbis before and after the destruction of the Second Temple, i.e. the first centuries before and after the beginning of the Christian era. Pharisaism provided an important link between the traditional heritage of Judaism and the Jewish-Christian community which claimed to be the New Israel. Students of Christian origins, tracing the historical continuity leading to Christianity from Tannaitic (Pharisaic) Judaism were thus sometimes led to regard Christianity as simply a derivative of this trend of Judaism, Jesus himself being called a renegade Pharisee.

B. The 1st century Community of the End of Days, identified with the sect of Qumran which, as explained, considered itself the "Elect", the chosen congregation of the End of Days.

Both these trends have a vital bearing on the circles from which came John the Baptizer, Jesus of Nazareth and the Jewish-Christian community. Both trends therefore should be considered in relation to their development during the two centuries. The first one (A) is not the whole picture and, by itself, it cannot explain the special nature of Jesus' eschatological and moral teaching.

A. *Popular Messianic Expectations*

Popular expectations concerned, first, the fulfillment of the political and material hopes of the oppressed Jewish masses. Mixed with these were religious concepts of national spiritual redemption. Thus the Messiah was a double figure: both king and redeemer, political and spiritual hero in one. Marvellous legends were woven around this figure and religious theories and ideas which hardly appear at all in the Old Testament became the accepted idiom of the times.

The idea of the Day of Judgment came to be identified with "the birth-pangs of the Messiah". The actual meaning of this phrase has nothing to do with the pain of bearing any one individual, but represents the suffering of the whole people during the age out of which the Messiah was to arise. Similarly, the "trumpet of the Messiah" was no actual trumpet, but the clarion-call of an era.

These beliefs go back to the 5th and 4th centuries B.C.E. and have their roots in the traditional expectations of a human king, belonging to the House of David, who should restore the political fortunes of the people. It must be remembered that in Hebrew "Messiah" means "anointed". The use of capital letters for the word in our translations has given it a much greater importance than it had for its original audience. Taken literally, the word merely refers to a time when the rightful line of Davidic kings would be restored. This Messiah would be righteous and holy and "pure from sin" in a human sense, unlike later concepts of Christianity. He would be an earthly king, but of subjects holy and sanctified, the "sons of their God."

In time, a belief in the speedy, supernatural coming of a supernatural person became associated with the older concept. The new idea had tremendous glamour. Apocalyptic imagery, fantasy and hyperbole worked on the common people to make them feel that they were taking part in great events. Evidence of this is the tremendous impression which John the Baptizer and Jesus of Nazareth made on the unsophisticated masses. In the weary oppression of rule by the Herodians and Roman procurators, the people turned for comfort to their hopes of a Messiah.

During the first century B.C.E. and later, these were expressed in the vivid descriptions of life after death found in the earlier and later Pseudepigrapha (Ch. III) and in the Qumran writings. There is an interesting early example of the style in the Psalms of Solomon, composed after Pompey had defiled the Temple (see Ch. IV). The trend was continuous. Hopes for the restoration of the Davidic dynasty were never completely abandoned. They gradually became part of a messianic expectation, rather than a political program.

One part of this whole range of messianic symbols was the vision of the war between "Gog and Magog" — the armies of the Kingdom of God and their enemies, who would be defeated. According to the New Testament apocalypse, the book of Revelation, the final conflict between the forces of good and evil would take place at Har-Mageddon (mountain of Megiddo, the scene of many historical battles). In the Greek transliteration of the name, it became Armageddon, a word which has since become an apocalyptic symbol for the whole of the western world.

The coming of the Messiah would be preceded by great disasters. But when he came he would set up a great and mighty kingdom with Jerusalem at its heart. He would end Roman oppression and "subject the nations to his yoke". Exiled Jews would be restored to their homeland, for gentiles would come from the ends of the earth to behold his glory, bringing exiled Jews to him as gifts. The same vision is inherent in the War Scroll of Qumran.

Mystic Messianic Expectations not Sanctioned by Rabbis

It may be noted that, in attempting to cheer their contemporaries, both the Pharisees of the earlier period (see Ch. VII) and the teachers of the Tannaitic period (i.e. the first two centuries of the Christian era), refer frequently to the glories of Israel and the certainty of ultimate fulfillment of the promises made to her.

But the popular idea of the "messianic" kingdom had no precise existence — sometimes it was eternal, sometimes of limited duration; sometimes of this world, sometimes not. Recurrent disappointments of popular hopes had moved wise rabbis, even though they believed in the coming of the Messiah, to treat apocalyptic aspects of messianism with reservations. They believed that Jewish expectations of the reign of righteousness, justice and peace, would not be brought nearer by such tempting short-cuts, nor by the actions of impatient humans.

Nevertheless, the people's emotions needed an outlet. Moderate tannaitic teachers "were not able to hold the nation back from its destruction at Roman hands, whether in successive riots or in the ultimate of war. It would perhaps be fair to say that that which tipped the balance against the forces of religious responsibility was the prevailing messianic ferment." (James Parkes). It is too simple to class the apocalyptists as activists. For the most part, they were not. They believed in direct divine intervention, just as did the Pharisees. But it is true that the apocalyptists forecast violence and a bloody end for the oppressor. Often militant patriots were stirred to action by these predictions of warfare and catastrophe. An unintentional alliance between apocalyptists and zealots ensued with the latter attempting to actualize in history the wide visions of the former.

This may explain why no messianic sayings were preserved in later Talmudic writings, although this is not a certain indication that none were uttered. L. Ginzberg has pointed out that there was a basic difference in outlook between the apocalyptists and the civic-minded (so-called "legalistic") Pharisees and that the latter views prevailed in the surviving rabbinical literature. Moreover, although "the Pharisees were strongly nationalistic . . . their nationalism was of a spiritual kind." They believed in the coming of a Messiah who may have been foreseen as fulfilling both a religious and a socio-political role, but they did not indulge in messianic expectations seeking to "speed up the epochs" or to "hasten the end". " 'Calculators of Epochs' is a fitting description indeed for the Qumran sect" (Ch. Rabin).

Neither did the rabbis give encouragement to the wild popular fanaticism which imagined divine sanction for every attack upon Roman authority. They looked for a Kingdom of Heaven that should be neither eschatological nor political, but the rule of God over his people. They feared the destruction of the last semblance of internal Jewish autonomy remaining in the days of the Herods and the procurators and opposed wild apocalyptic dreamings. Nevertheless, some scholars, including James Parkes, assume that "their silence in times of such general distress is most naturally interpreted as unwillingness to support the more spiritual conception of a messiah which was being put forward by the Judeo-Christians."

B. COMMON GROUND IN MESSIANISM

The most important point of contact between the Essene or Qumran circles and early Christianity is their common concern with the figure and work of the Messiah. In this, both of them show a developed apocalyptic messianism.

Messianic evidence recovered from Qumran consists of Old Testament quotations arranged in such a manner as to indicate that the brotherhood's expectations covered three distinct figures: the prophet promised in Deut 18:18 ff.; a priest, the Messiah of Aaron; and a consecrated layman, the Messiah of Israel who, as a Davidic Prince, would be the Saviour of Israel, a Warrior emerging at the end of the age to lead the armies of Israel in battle against their enemies, the "Kittim". They looked for the fulfillment of messianic prophecy in terms of three separate individuals:

> "and they shall not deviate from the whole counsel of the Torah to walk in any stubborness of their own heart but shall be judged by the first decisions (laws) by which the men of the Community commenced to be disciplined, until a Prophet comes and the Messiahs of Aaron and Israel." (Rule of the Community, 1 QS 9: 11)

> "and shall not be reckoned in the council of the people, nor inscribed in their book, from the day the Teacher of the Community died until the Messiah(s) of Aaron and of Israel arise. . ." (Zadokite Document, C.D.C. 19: 34)

So far as the Scrolls are concerned, the Rule of the Community speaks of a Messiah of Israel as the secular leader. In the War Scroll and the Benedictions, he sometimes takes a subordinate place to the High Priest. In the present state of our knowledge, it is difficult to decide whether the High Priest was also a messianic figure in the same sense but it is clear that he played a major role.

For the sectaries, the "Prophet like Moses" was evidently an important figure. At one time, the Teacher of Righteousness was identified with this prophetic figure and he may have had redemptive functions. The language used suggests a pre-Christian martyr-cult, recalling the rabbinical idea of the propitiatory power of the blood shed by heroes and saints of Israel. This idea lies deep in Jewish tradition and was noted in 1 Maccabees (see Ch. II).

It is doubtful whether the expectation of a Prophet like Moses was one of the liveliest popular beliefs in the Jewish messianism of the time, but it is agreed that it was an extraordinarily influential form of belief among Jews, Samaritans and Christians. This is clear from Josephus, the New Testament and the early Church Fathers. The Moses-Messiah theme lies behind far more of Matthew than just the Sermon on the Mount.

According to many authorities, the sectaries' expectations of an anointed priest and a Messiah concerned a partnership similar to those between Moses and Aaron or Joshua and Zerubbabel in the Restoration of the Temple (see "ADAM TO DANIEL" Ch. XX). This seems to add up to a triumvirate of deliverers, although it need not have been supposed that they would come at the same time. Probably, strictly speaking, only the secular Messiah of Aaron and Israel should be given the title "Messiah". It now seems clear that he was identified with the ideal Davidic prince of Ezekiel and other prophets. Added to him were the eschatological figures of the High Priest and the Prophet. For the establishment of the

Kingdom, they all had to be contemporary, but with the Prophet coming first to announce the beginning of the age, and the work to be accomplished through the Priest and King.

All three motifs — Prophet, Priest and King — are, of course, applied variously to Jesus in the New Testament. First as the Prophet like Moses, then successively as the King and the Priest. Moreover, the language and concepts of the early Jewish-Christian community including that of many sayings attributed to Jesus are full of the terminology of Jewish apocalyptic. The early Church saw itself precisely as an eschatological community. It is therefore, reasonable to suppose that its antecedents must be traced historically both to the sectarian communities in which apocalypticism flourished and to the popular Jewish expectations of a Davidic Messiah.

Distinctive Features of Christology

In the common tradition, in both the Qumran literature and the New Testament, the "Messiah" is described as appearing in the End of Days to receive an eternal kingdom. He comes bearing a sword and defeats the earthly and cosmic powers of wickedness. Thus both sources endow him with priestly, royal and prophetic elements.

The distinctions between the two come with the Christology of the New Testament, which speaks of a heavenly saviour, the "Son of Man", the Second Adam, terms which are absent in the Qumran doctrine. Students of apocalyptic have pointed out that the priestly apocalyptic of Qumran has no reference to this aspect, nor does its messianism reflect the influence of elements associated with a "heavenly man", a pre-existing Messiah. These scholars assume that a developed "transcendental" messianism belonged either to (a) a post-Essenic (or Qumran) stage in the development of apocalyptic; or, (b) to another parallel apocalyptic tradition within the Jewish-Christian milieu.

Christian messianic expectations interpreted all Old Testament prophecy dealing with the Messiah in terms of one unique figure who would be prophet, priest and king. The combination of the three titles as applied variously to Jesus represents a process which was not completed until after the New Testament, "in order to meet the questions and objections of critics that the full eschatological dramatis personae had not made their appearance." (D. N. Freedman)

"Moses said: 'The Lord God will raise up for you a prophet from your brethren as he raised me up. You shall listen to him in whatever he tells you.' " (Acts 3: 22)

"This is the Moses who said to the Israelites, 'God will raise up for you a prophet from your brethren as he raised me up.' " (Acts 7: 37)

This later view, however, does not alter the historical stages in early pre-Pauline Christianity, nor the messianic expectations of the people before Jesus. Besides developing Christianity out of a wider inheritance, the post-apostolic teachers of the second century and after, had gradually emancipated themselves from the language of messianic apocalyptic.

One of the best known features of sectarian doctrine, lies in the dualism which it saw between good and evil. This can best be illustrated by quotation:

"(God) created man to rule the world and He established two spirits by which (man) would walk until the time appointed for His Visitation (i.e. the Last Judgment); these are the spirits of Truth and Deceit (or Wickedness). In a source of light are the origins of (the Spirit of) Truth and from a well of darkness the origins of (the Spirit of) Error. The rule of the children of righteousness is in the hand of the Prince of Light (so that) they walk in ways of light; the rule of (all) children of error is in the hand of the Angel of Darkness (so that) they walk in ways of darkness; and when any of the children of righteousness err, it is through the Angel of Darkness . . . and all the spirits allotted to him (attempt to) make the children of light stumble, but the God of Israel and His Angel of Truth are a help to all sons of light." (1 QS 3: 17–23)

The First Epistle of John, in refuting the arguments of the Gnostics, put forward similar arguments with a different conclusion:

"Little children, let no one deceive you. He who does right is righteous, as he is righteous. He who commits sin is of the devil; for the devil has sinned from the beginning. The reason the Son of God appeared was to destroy the works of the devil. No one born of God commits sin; for God's nature abides in him, and he cannot sin because he is born of God. By this it may be seen who are the children of God, and who are the children of the devil; whoever does not do right is not of God ....." (1 John 3: 7–10)

There is an impressive amount of evidence for the wide use which the Jewish-Christians made of material which came from the Essenes. This can be seen not only in quotations but in influence. The Scrolls and also the earliest parts of the book of Enoch (2nd cent. B.C.E.) had a strong influence on several books of the New Testament, notably Revelation.

The Qumran sect believed that they were "the Elect of God". For, they believed,

"from the knowledge (comes) all that is and all shall be, and before their being He established all their designs, and when they become whatever they had been destined to become according to His glorious design, they fulfil their task and nothing can be changed." (Zadokite Document — C.D.C. III, 15, 6)

That is to say, according to the sect's doctrine of divine predestination, they constituted the "Lot of Light", while the rest of mankind were inescapably doomed to the "Lot of Darkness". This theme of the "Two Ways", or two spirits, which are represented in the War Scroll by the Sons of Light and the Sons of Darkness, is implied in the gospel of John. Quotations from this gospel, as well as from the Epistle to the Ephesians, show a common inheritance in their picture of a predestined struggle between God (or the spirit of Truth) and the devil (or the spirit of Deceit). In both, the children of light are possessed of a knowledge which enables them to distinguish between the two opponents. By the aid of the good spirit, the children of light are righteous; those dominated by the devil walk in darkness. In the Qumran writings, the "Prince of Light" acts as a helper to all children of Light. In John and the Johannine Epistles, the terms Counselor or "Paraclete" are used as additional names of the Spirit of Truth to "witness and intercede":

"And I will pray the Father, and he will give you another Counselor, to be with you for ever, even the Spirit of Truth, whom the world cannot receive, because it neither sees him nor knows him; you know him, for he dwells with you, and will be in you." (John 14: 16–17)

John's use of the word "truth" here is very reminiscent of the sectaries. Truth, moreover, is shown in actions as much as words:

"But he who does what is true comes to the light, that it may be clearly seen that his deeds have been wrought in God." (John 3: 21)

The common origin of this doctrine goes back to the Old Testament pictures of a heavenly court in which "the heavenly witness" or angel of the Lord stood opposed to Satan, the accuser. Clearly expressed in Zechariah and Job, these ancient ideas had become blurred by the time the elaborate angelology of Qumran developed. Partly under Iranian influence, the heavenly contestants have become the warring Prince of Darkness and Prince of Light. In the New Testament, through further development, the heavenly advocate has become a holy spirit testifying to truth in the hearts of those who "inherit" truth:

"Nevertheless I tell you the truth; it is to your advantage that I go away, for if I do not go away, the Counselor will not come to you; but if I go, I will send him to you. And when he comes, he will convince the world of sin and of righteousness and of judgment." (John 16: 7–8)

A New Emphasis in John

However, this dualism differently expressed in John and the role of Jesus, brings a new note of victory. The "Paraclete" — the spirit of truth — bears witness to Christ and the things that are to come.

Although Johannine literature has retained the ideas of the struggle and the final Armageddon yet to be fought, the coming of Jesus Christ has resolved the crisis. He has "overcome the world", i.e. the kingdom of the Prince of Darkness.

"Beloved, do not believe every spirit, but test the spirits to see whether they are of God; for many false prophets have gone out into the world. By this you know the Spirit of God; every spirit which confesses that Jesus Christ has come in the flesh is of God, and every spirit which does not confess Jesus is not of God. This is the spirit of antichrist, of which you heard that it was coming, and now it is in the world already. Little children, you are of God and have overcome them; for he who is in you is greater than he who is in the world. They are of the world therefore what they say is of the world and the world listens to them. We are of God. Whoever knows God listens to us, and he who is not of God does not listen to us. By this we know the spirit of truth and the spirit of error." (1 John 4: 1–6)

The same ethical dualism is to be found elsewhere in the New Testament, especially in Paul:

". . . following the course of this world, following the prince of the power of the air, the spirit that is now at work in the sons of disobedience." (Ephesians 2: 2)

Paul has a more militant attitude towards the struggle, but he is equally confident of the victory of Christ.

THE NEW COVENANT

The Qumran sectaries gave great emphasis to the idea of a "New Covenant". Exactly the same concept distinguishes Christianity from Judaism. (The New Covenant became in

Greek Kainos-diathēkē.. New Testament). Did both groups mean the same thing by this doctrine?

The Epistle to the Hebrews lays it down that whilst the generation of the wilderness were refused entry to the Promised Land because of their disobedience to God's commands, the new community is offered a *second* chance and all the blessings of a "new covenant". The old covenant had been redeemed when Christ appeared to the Elect:

> "Therefore his is the mediation of a new covenant, so that those who are called may receive the promised eternal inheritance, since a death has occurred which redeems them from the transgressions under the first covenant." (Epistle to the Hebrews 9: 15)

Until the time of Paul, Christian and sectarian ideas about the two covenants were very similar. For the sectaries, the new covenant defined social and ceremonial obligations as well as theological views. However, as Christianity developed, the theological aspect was emphasized at the expense of the other two. "The explanation of the situation lies in the eschatological interpretation of the new covenant in both Qumran and the New Testament. The renewal of the old covenant with prophetic emphasis on motivation as well as action is reflected in the practice of the two communities, and is based on repeated Old Testament precedent (Josh. 24, II Kings 22–23, Nehemiah 8–9). It is also an anticipation of the new covenant, based upon Jeremiah 31: 31–34, which would supersede the Sinai covenant, and transcend the law with its threats and sanctions against violators. On the contrary, the new covenant is written upon the heart, and its terms are fulfilled by the power of the Spirit, who ushers in the new age. In the New Testament, unlike Qumran, the new era is already present, while the old age is passing away; but the tension between them is never fully resolved, so that the early Christian lived 'between the times', already embarked upon the new life of the spirit, yet under the discipline of the old" (D. N. Freedman).

CONCLUSIONS

From the foregoing brief survey, some general conclusions may be drawn about the nature of sectarian beliefs, their links with parallel religious movements and with Primitive Christianity. These links can be considered under their historical or religious aspects.

A. *Historical*

WHY THE SECTARIES WERE ESTRANGED FROM THE COMMUNITY

The doctrine of the Two Ways which assured the sectaries that they had been divinely predestined to righteousness, provided them with a justification for their social and religious separation into a self-contained community or, as it were, a church.

Having cut themselves off from the services in the Temple, the sectaries developed a special attitude towards the ceremonies of their religion. First of all, they hoped that they would one day offer sacrifice according to their own rites, carried out by their own priests in a purified future Temple. On the other hand, they believed that their other rites, lustrations, and strict observance of the Law, could substitute for the actual Temple services. They speculated about this and, when they described their own sectarian rites, they borrowed the symbols of the Temple services. Finally, they arrived at the conclusion that their community in itself was a kind of spiritual Temple. There is good reason to believe that the Christian concept of the Church as a spiritual Temple came from the sectaries. Moreover, not only was such a church a union between men who were all especially holy but, as a spiritual Temple, it was superior to the physical building in Jerusalem. This development was to cast a long shadow over later events. In very much the same way that the sectaries' doctrine estranged them from their contemporaries, so did the same idea among the early Christians lead, eventually, to their separation from Judaism.

The Accusations of the Rabbis

In many ways the sectaries shared the religion of the rest of Jewry — only carrying its precepts to the extreme. Certain specific points, however, set the system apart. For instance, the idea that baptism plays any part in the forgiveness of sins is quite foreign to rabbinic Judaism. So also was the sectarian division of the world into the Sons of Light (themselves) and the sons of the Devil (the rest of humanity). The sectaries' doctrine of election "gives them the certainty that the separation is necessary and willed by God; their teaching, which compares their organization ('the community of holiness') to the Temple, frees them from dependence on the Jerusalem Temple service and severs all ritualistic links with the rest of Jewry." (D. Flusser)

The sect was well-known and influential. It had as long a life as the Pharisees. Possibly some of the sectaries hoped that the rest of Jewry might be won over to their doctrine in time. There may have been hopes among them that in the "last days" the totally wicked would be destroyed but that the majority would escape damnation at the last minute and enter into the New Covenant.

It is becoming apparent that the sectarian movement was a genuine attempt at internal reform within Judaism. Both in its obscure beginnings and in its developed forms of the Essenism of Qumran and early Christianity, it represents one of the most remarkable phenomena in the history of contemporary Judaism. Its principles of reform, withdrawal from the world, a return to strict obedience to the Law of Moses and genuine repentance can be traced not only to the Hassidim of the Maccabean period (see Ch. II) but beyond. They go back to the asceticism of ancient Hebrew Yahwism from which came the orders of the Rechabites or the Nazirites or holy men. According to rabbinical tradition, the earliest Hassidim were all Nazirites, (see Ch. III, Early Hassidim) who should not be confused with Nazarenes, one name given to the early Christians. It is assumed that apocalyptic asceticism was one development from the Hassidic movement, emphasizing their priestly character as well as their consecration as holy warriors. (see Ch. IX: The Nazirite Element in John).

JEWISH NONCONFORMIST MOVEMENTS

Additional facts have been revealed by a study of the Scrolls in connection with other related movements. A comparison of the works of the early fathers of the Christian Church (and also Gnostic works) with the Scrolls, has produced evidence for the existence of a widespread Jewish nonconformist movement in Palestine before the destruction of the Temple. This movement shared puritanical and ascetic tendencies and mode of life, practised a baptizing cult and held different views of the canon of Scriptures and different customs from the Pharisaic orthodoxy. On the basis of this evidence, the Essenes of Qumran may be considered as just one branch of that wider movement, which may have been much more important than appears at first. In spite of the differences within each of the splinter groups, the most impressive fact about this nonconformist element is its remarkable cultural and theological unity. At all the main points of belief and ritual, it presents a solid and unbroken front opposed to the established orthodoxy of the Jerusalem priesthood, while at the same time a common basis held them close to the more flexible Pharisees (cf. Ch. VII).

As a nonconformist movement, it could not, however, have as great or continuous an influence as the Pharisees. As Pharisaism developed into normative rabbinic Judaism, what was common to both Pharisees and the nonconformists survived, although some views may have been rejected as circumstances changed. The distinguishing marks of Essenism, for instance, made no lasting impression; these features died out of Judaism, leaving only traces. In the case of apocalyptic messianism, we conjecture that Jews generally, and not only Essenes and Pharisees, had strong convictions and fervent hopes in the two centuries leading up to the disastrous wars with the Romans; but that afterwards orthodox rabbinism abandoned the more radical views, along with much of the literature. Nevertheless, if the Qumran sect left no lasting impression on the mainstream of Judaism, the factors from which it grew must have affected primitive Christianity which developed out of the same religious climate of the first century C.E.

In view of this common background, therefore, it would probably be true to recognize that the movement which gave rise to both the Qumran sectaries and primitive Christianity eventually had its effect on the whole course of Western civilization.

B. *Religion*

The Dead Sea Scrolls have done more than merely illustrate Essene and early Christian development. The writings of the Qumran sectaries have greatly enriched New Testament scholarship by the convincing picture they have given of the cultural and religious milieu from which John the Baptizer, Jesus and the Jewish-Christians emerged.

It is reasonable to suppose that most of the teachings of Qumran were not original. Indeed we have seen in Chapter III (and IX) that the ideas involved had undergone a process of development through several groups and movements more or less influenced by earlier prophetic tendencies. The Qumran sect brought these ideas to fruition in the complete religious system which has been described. What was important in their teaching, including the broader apocalyptic trend from which it crystallized, became part of the Hebrew literary tradition and passed into Christianity, giving meaning to the theological terms which occur in the New Testament.

There is a sense in which it can be said that the primitive Church was a continuation of this whole body of ideas, including the more distant shared background and the common apocalyptic tradition. It was not merely by chance that much of the surviving eschatological literature was suppressed in rabbinical and academic Jewish circles and survived almost solely in a sectarian milieu.

The fact that the early Christian church continued the traditions of the Community of the End of Days can be seen not only in the static survivals of such material in Christian circles. It is also apparent, as O. Cullmann and F. M. Cross among others have argued, from the extent to which Qumran has provided evidence of the type of "esoteric" (non-conformist) Judaism within which the roots of primitive Christianity lie. Similarities in baptismal rites, communal way of living, the form of their organization and opposition to the Temple hierarchy and ceremonies, all go to make a strong case for some connection between the sectaries and the early Christians. The evidence for these resemblances is particularly striking in the early chapters of Acts. Here, and elsewhere in the New Testament, a certain stage in the development of this trend within Judaism can be observed. Its use there was different from its original function. The early Christians "used whatever they learned from the Qumran doctrine mainly to establish their own ideal of the Church as 'Civitas Dei' . . . . the theological structure of the sect was taken apart and the stones reused by early Christian thinkers to build a new and different house. Much other material also went into the construction of this new and larger edifice, both stones taken from other ancient houses (Greek and Jewish) and stones hewn out of truly original unprecedented Christian religious experience. . . . Therefore research on the Dead Sea Scrolls will never replace the study of Christian origins, but it will help us to understand some important aspects of early Christianity" (D. Flusser).

Another instance of survival is the significant manner in which the term "poor" — ebionim — was appropiated by different sectaries (cf. p. 200). It served as a proper name for the Jewish-Christian Ebionite movement (second cent. C.E.) which deviated from the primitive Church. These sectaries explained the prophetic writings in their own way; they faced Jerusalem in their prayers; and their manner of life was quite Jewish. They denied the virgin birth and the divinity of Jesus, used only Matthew's gospel, and would have nothing to do with Paul. It is no exaggeration to conclude that the Dead Sea documents have a definite bearing on the questions of Jesus' uniqueness as a prophet; the originality of his teachings; the origin of Christian sacraments; and the extent to which the beliefs of the Jewish-Christians were influenced by intertestamental Judaism, Essenes and sectaries.

In the opinion of M. Jean Danielou, who has made a penetrating study of the Dead Sea Scrolls and the origins of Christianity, "the domain in which Judeo-Christianity has had its deepest impact and where it survived longest in the Christian church was that of the organization of the cult. The Jewish origin of the general framework of Christian cult was usually contested half a century ago. . . . . It was customary to stress the influence of hellenistic mysteries on the form of the sacraments. The picture has changed completely, particularly since the discoveries of Qumran. The 'Sitz im leben' (setting in life) of the first Christian liturgy must be sought more among the cultic customs of Jewish Essenic communities. This is where analogies may be found in the modes of initiation by baptism, in the framework of the eucharistic institution, in the times set for prayer and in the ritual of festivals." This seems to have been the inheritance of the Jewish-Christians within the oriental environment of Judea, before its destruction. The changes that were to come to Jewish-Christian institutions when the scene shifted to a hellenistic environment will be considered in Ch. XI.

In general, in the present state of knowledge, with accepted facts still very few and the likelihood that much additional material has still to come to light, it is very difficult to reach firm conclusions. It is felt by many scholars that all the evidence still falls short of a completely convincing case for the derivation of Christian rites from this nonconformist side of Judaism. In addition to obvious similarities, there are many significant differences which must be taken into account. Due importance must also be given to their common background and inheritance in ancient Hebrew pre-Exilic prophetic vision and post-exilic apocalyptic thought.

On this point, the view held by Stanley B. Frost and other scholars is relevant: "Seeing that both Qumran and Christianity come from a common background only those phenomena where both diverge together from that inheritance can substantiate direct connection between the two movements. What has so far emerged is that Qumran and Christianity are parallel devolutions from Judaism, rather than movements in direct succession. e.g., 'The Two Ways' is found in the Manual of Discipline (Rule of the Community) and in the Fourth Gospel — but it is a staple in Old Testament thought in general." While this pattern is familiar from the Old Testament, especially in the wisdom literature but ultimately deriving from the promises and threats of the Sinai covenant, there are special features in the Qumran and Johannine literature which reflect a more recent development peculiar to the circumstances and attitudes of these groups. In these writings it is no longer a matter of confronting men with the ethical decision between good and evil, but rather the affirmation that an immutable divine decree has assigned to every man his lot in life and death, and has divided the whole world into opposing camps, the issue between them to be settled in a great eschatological war. This is no ordinary development from the doctrine of the "two ways" of the Old Testament books mentioned. Its distinctive features are found only in the Book of Daniel, which, however, belongs both to the period and the background of Hassidism, the immediate parent of the sectarian groups.

Historical relationships and Theological grounds of early Christianity

In examining the relationship between the Qumran community and the exponents of New Testament Christianity, some clarification of the real issues at stake is necessary.

In 1950, during the early days following the Qumran discoveries, W. F. Albright stated: "The new evidence with regard to the beliefs and practices of Jewish sectarians of the last two centuries B.C. bids fair to revolutionize our approach to the beginnings of Christianity .... and it is safe to say that nothing written on the sectarian movement ... can escape thorough revision in the light of the evidence now available ..." Subsequent study is constantly bringing new insights into this fascinating field. As a result, scholars are more and more coming to accept the view that the origins of Christianity lie in this nonconformist side of Judaism.

Students of history who have always assumed that Christianity was dependent on earlier Jewish institutions and teachings, did not find the implications of the Scrolls too startling, although some scholars were moved to make fundamental revisions in their interpretations of the New Testament. "... It is already being claimed that the books of the Essenes provide us with the closest approach that has yet been discovered to the Gospel of John and to Paul, at least in so far as conceptual background and language is concerned, and that the connecting link between the two was the work of John the Baptist." (G. Ernest Wright). In the view of Ch. Rabin: "The objective consideration of the relations between Qumran and Christianity has suffered from the exaggerations of some scholars, who denied all originality to Christianity, and in particular saw in the accounts of Jesus' life and ministry an imitation of the pattern set by the Teacher of Righteousness.

"The real question is: since it is generally agreed that Christianity drew largely from Judaism, from which type of Judaism did it derive? Here the answer appears now to be clear: in its organization, its oriental climate, and in many of its theological ideas from Paul onwards, it is much closer to Qumran Judaism than to Rabbinic Judaism as known from Tannaitic sources."

In evaluating the differences between Christianity and rabbinic Judaism, it is important to note the relative antiquity of the sources mentioned above; the Qumran literature, which is mostly pre-Christian and the Tannaitic sources which, at least in written form are much later, although they contain a good deal of older material. D. N. Freedman is inclined to believe that "the Pharisaism contemporary with Jesus was closer to both Christianity and Qumran than Rabbinism, and it would be generally fairer to say that Christianity emerged from the general Hassidic background, just as Essenism and Pharisaism did. Much of what

Christianity shared with Qumran it also shared with Pharisaism in this period. At the same time, the early Christians rejected much of what was distinctive of Qumran, e.g. the emphasis on the priesthood and the withdrawal from the common life, and also some of the special emphases of the Pharisees, particularly the authority of the oral law and its application to daily life. While they shared with the Pharisees a common messianic expectation, the early church had a much more developed sense of eschatological urgency, highly coloured by apocalyptic imagery. All three arose from a common source, specifically that form of Hassidism which accepted the authority of Moses, which was messianically inclined and believed in the resurrection of the dead and a final judgment, and which reflects both the theology and piety of a book like Daniel, which was accepted as inspired, by the rabbis as well as by the church and the Essenes."

Notable and Far-reaching Differences

To enquire into the relationship between the doctrines of the sectaries and those of the early Christians is not to ask whether, if, and to what extent, the latter would have to be changed or abandoned. Christianity has never denied the extent of its Jewish heritage. It follows that not everything usually regarded as distinctively Christian is necessarily a newcomer to the historical scene. It had its antecedents in sectarian and Jewish-Christian doctrine. To identify these Hebrew antecedents in no way invalidates the originality and authority of historical Christianity. Up to the present, no literary source — biblical, apocryphal or Essenic, has in any way altered the unique elements of Christianity, nor has any change in traditional Christian doctrine been made necessary. The impact of Jesus and Paul on later generations had itself produced variations in doctrine and in the significance of the different symbols.

From the following Chapters, it will be seen that after the death of Jesus of Nazareth, something more than a casual divergence of Christianity from a quasi-Essene or Qumran background appears to have taken place.

Whilst the writings of the Qumran sect exhibit certain points of contact with the documents produced by the apostolic circle, it is significant that the cardinal Christian doctrines of the incarnate diety, original sin, redemption through Calvary and the activity of the holy spirit, as an essential part of Christian experience, are nowhere to be found in the Dead Sea Scrolls.

Summing up the problem from a broader perspective, W. F. Albright, G. Ernest Wright, F. M. Cross and other scholars consider that the understanding of the common conceptions and features of life of the two Jewish "sectarian" communities, Qumran and the primitive Church (Jewish-Christians), has now entered a new phase in terms of a concrete and historic Jewish setting, which reveals important parallel aspects and common ground. They are derived from a common inheritance. Their eventual development in new, different directions must not obscure the significance of their common background. This, perhaps, is one of the most important lessons of the Scrolls.

Mosaic map of the 6th century church of Madeba in Moab. The place where John baptized Jesus is marked by a cross set in the Jordan. This is Bethabara, or, more correctly, Beth-araba, "ford town". It lies just north of the Hajla ford, close to the west bank of the river. A church was built on piles at the edge of the water, while a little further back stood the monastery of John the Baptizer.

IX

JOHN THE BAPTIZER

I. HISTORICAL

From the conclusions of the previous chapter, it is clear that in the historical context of the 1st century, John (Johanan), surnamed the Baptizer (ha-matbil in Hebrew), may be regarded as an outstanding personality belonging to Judaism and strongly influenced by sectarian theology, but not as an isolated strange figure. He became the leader of a Jewish sect and, historically, Jesus was one of his followers.

Until recent years, many aspects of John's background, beliefs and sayings remained a mystery. In the light of the Qumran scrolls, and their striking similarities in thought, ritual and belief, much of the mist surrounding him seems to have been dispelled. Many scholars find in him a link between certain groups of Judaism and Christianity and, more particularly, between Qumran and Jesus.

JOHN'S BACKGROUND AND EARLY LIFE

The forerunner of Jesus was born in the hill country of Judea, (exact location unknown) to Zechariah and Elizabeth (Elisheba), an elderly couple of priestly lineage. They brought up their son in the best traditions of Jewish piety, mixed with the less formalistic approach to theology which was typical of the provincial priesthood, in contrast to the more worldly Sadducees, who formed the priestly class of Jerusalem. As the son of a priest, John had a good knowledge of the scriptures. His message reflects deep and intensive thinking about the sterner aspects of the teachings of the Old Testament prophets.

On reaching manhood, he did not follow his father and take up active duties as a priest. Instead, he withdrew into "the wilderness".

Gospel tradition describes him dressed in a rough tunic made of camel-hair held at the waist by a leather belt. He fed on grasshoppers (they are still appreciated today, boiled or roasted, by the Beduins) and on wild honey. It is not likely that the life of a holy man was anything unusual in those days. Certainly not in country close to the Essenic settlements at Qumran, even if he had no direct connection with its inmates.

> "And the child grew and became strong in spirit, and he was in the wilderness till the day of his manifestation to Israel." (Luke 1: 80)

His austerity and the saintliness of his life, coupled with his passionate appeal for penitence, marked him early as a most popular preacher.

According to the gospel of Mark, John stayed in the "wilderness" living in solitude and meditation and, as Luke tells us, he seems to have been there until the time came for him to take up his ministry to Israel. At the end of the year 27 C.E. he appeared suddenly in the country round about the lower Jordan Valley, close to the fords leading to Perea, across Jordan, delivering his message:

> "John the baptizer appeared in the wilderness, preaching a baptism of repentance for the forgiveness of sins." (Mark 1: 4)

Beyond this we know practically nothing about him. We can judge his life mainly on the basis of the later evidence provided by the gospels: that his preaching laid emphasis on the Last Days and that it corresponded in many ways to Essene, rather than orthodox priestly teachings.

The Nazirite Element in John

As pointed out on p. 218, ancient Israelite asceticism was a strong current in sectarian life. Recent debate lays stress on the possible relationship of the movement of John with the pre-Christian sect of the "Nasareans" (not to be confused with the later Christian sect of the "Nazorenes" or Ebionites). The distinction is clearly made by the Church father Epiphanius in his "Panarion". The Nasareans show distant affinities with or descent from the ancient biblical order (or institution) of the life-long Nazirites. In biblical times and after, they were dwellers in the wilderness who abstained from wine, flesh and shaving the beard and apparently practised purificatory ritual baths. Epiphanius describes John the Baptizer as a dedicated Nazirite and tells us that James, brother of Jesus, was too (Ch. XI).

The possibility is very plausible in the case of John who had affinities with Elijah and the prophetic guilds which were similar to the Nazirite groups. There is reason to believe that there was some continuity between the ancient prophetic bands which had been active around the Jordan valley and later groups like John's or the Essenes.

An Authentic Career

In addition to the gospels and the Johannine writings, the facts and authenticity of John's short career as the great precursor or contemporary of Christ are best illustrated by the brief account in Josephus' Antiquities:

> "John who was called the Baptist, for Herod slew him who was a good man and had commanded the Jews that they should practise virtue both in respect of righteousness toward one another and piety toward God, so that they should come together in a baptism. For baptism would thus appear acceptable to him, not when they used it as a request for the forgiveness of certain sins, but as a purification of the body after the soul had been thoroughly cleansed by righteousness." (Antiq. Bk. XVIII 5:2)

The baptism of John, like that of the Essenes, was a well-known practice of the time, accepted as quite normal by Josephus. It was a symbol and central sacrament of the Essene community, for whom, as for John, it was a rite of repentance of sins and adoption of the life of the eschatological community of God (see Ch. VIII).

JOHN'S SURROUNDINGS

The Fourth gospel (John) provides information which helps to identify the area in which he was active as the country around the southern Jordan Valley. It describes him as baptizing in several places in this region. The gospel also says that John baptized east of the Jordan, in Perea (Jewish Transjordan), a region ruled by his political enemy, the tetrarch Herod Antipas, who later had John arrested and then executed.

Towards the end of his ministry, we find him baptizing in that area, in the Samaritan territory, at "Aenon near Salim, because there was much water there." (John 3:22). (see map in Ch. X). This was situated outside Antipas' jurisdiction, although the exact site of the town is uncertain. W. F. Albright has suggested a location south-east of Shechem, near the sources of Wadi Fariah, a busy meeting place connecting central Palestine and Transjordan. He believes this location to be close to the place where Jesus met the Samaritan

Aerial view of the Jordan valley, south of Tel-Damieh, near Wadi Fariah, assumed to be "Aenon near Salim" (*see p. 226*).

woman of Sychar, apparently Shechem, or a Graeco-Roman town in the same area as ancient Shechem.

Other sites are mentioned by name in the gospels, but they cannot be identified with certainty. In later centuries Christians built churches dedicated to him at Ein-Karem, near Jerusalem, where Christian tradition claims he was born. In a village south of Hebron, another church to him was built and, in the 4th century C. E., a basilica was erected at Sebaste-Samaria, the Graeco-Roman city. After his decapitation by order of Herod Antipas, the body of John the Baptizer was said to have been saved by his disciples and given due burial there (see John's death).

All this evidence may add up to the extension of John's activities among sectaries over an area covering the Jordan Valley, Samaria, Perea and perhaps northern Palestine, giving him a central place in Palestine and the world of the New Testament.

ARCHAEOLOGY AND JOHN THE BAPTIZER

Another gap in our knowledge of John's past is supplied from archaeology. There is one puzzling detail in the solemn formula with which Luke, alone among the Evangelists, places his ministry in world history:

> "In the fifteenth year of the reign of Tiberius Caesar, Pontius Pilate being governor of Judea, and Herod being tetrarch of Galilee, and his brother Philip tetrarch of the region of Ituraea and Trachonitis, and Lysanias tetrarch of Abilene, in the high-priesthood of Annas and Caiaphas, the word of God came to John, the son of Zechariah in the wilderness;" (Luke 3: 1–2)

Luke's statement stood alone until the discovery of an inscription on a steep rock-face near a tell which perpetuates the site of Abilene (see map Ch. X). It names Lysanias as governor of the region, at the time mentioned by Luke.

A Priests' Commission of Inquiry — John the Baptizer — Elijah

The prologue of the gospel of John relates John's encounter with the Levites and Pharisees, probably a delegation sent by the Sanhedrin. It took place at Bethany of Transjordan, shortly after John had baptized Jesus. This commission was apparently sent to find out John's claims to Messiahship. He answered all their questions in the negative. In fact he is represented in the gospel as a forerunner of some kind, though not one of the messianic figures.

> "And they asked him, 'What then? Are you Elijah?' He said, 'I am not.' 'Are you the prophet?' And he answered 'No.' "... he said: 'I am the voice of one crying in the wilderness: Prepare the way of the Lord, make his paths straight: as the prophet Isaiah said.' " "They asked him, 'Then why are you baptizing, if you are neither the Christ, nor Elijah, nor the prophet?' " (John 1: 21, 23, 25)

John and his successors seemed to turn for inspiration to the simpler time evoked by the legendary figure of Elijah. He spoke of wrath and fire, and of the axe laid to the root of the tree, all truly reminiscent of Elijah; also of one coming to judgment stronger than he.

John — a Prophet

The passage from Isaiah quoted by John is the biblical justification for the sectarian way of life, as explained previously. As the identical quotation is given in relation to John, he may have regarded himself in the same light.

How should this debate between the priests and the prophet-like figure be related to current beliefs? There is reason to believe that the forerunners of the Messianic age were expected to include both Elijah and a Moses-like prophet. These were some of the liveliest popular beliefs in pre-Christian Judaism. The terms were taken from ancient prophecy, (see p. 213). "The Prophet" reappears as a venerated figure in the above passage in the gospel of John.

This gospel emphasizes that the Baptizer rejected the titles of Elijah, the "prophet" or Christ. So a title is sought to fit his circumstances. He is called the "Voice crying in the Wilderness". He was a forerunner, of course, but, in the gospel tradition, the Baptizer was increasingly overshadowed by Jesus. There are grounds for believing that Jesus superseded John as the leader of the Johannine movement.

In all the sources we have, the underlying theme is that Jesus was the Messianic prophet but the official view which became permanent was that Jesus was the Davidic king and other views were adjusted to fit this picture. This fact, together with the specifically Palestinian setting of the gospel of John, suggests that this gospel was composed early.

In the view of C.T. Kleim, the gospel of John may have preserved the most primitive tradition of the story. To speak of Jesus as a second Moses repeating the miracle of the manna, was to borrow from the popular fund of expected 'prophets'.

The Stern Rebuke

As explained, the Qumran community's isolation and retreat into the desert was one aspect of their non-conformism. To "separate themselves from the abode of perverse men" followed from the sect's doctrine that humanity and Israel were divided into the two camps of the sons of Light and the sons of Darkness, (see Ch. VIII). This dualism and its complementary obligation of repentance is apparent from John's address to the masses:

"But when he saw many of the Pharisees and Sadducees coming for baptism, he said to them, 'You brood of vipers! Who warned you to flee from the wrath to come? Bear fruit that befits repentance, and do not presume to say to yourselves, "We have Abraham as our father"; for I tell you, God is able from these stones to raise up children to Abraham.'" (Matt. 3: 7–9)

This was a stern rebuke to the complacency of some who were "children of Abraham". Like the sectaries, John not only declared his belief in the Day of Judgment but also the view that mere descendance from Abraham is no guarantee of redemption. Their descendance does not prevent Israel from being "sons of vipers". The definition corresponds in its intention with the "sons of Darkness" of the Qumran sect. It is also placed by Matthew in the mouth of Jesus:

"You brood of vipers. How can you speak good, when you are evil? For out of the abundance of the heart the mouth speaks." (Matt. 12: 34)

JOHN AND JESUS

The gospels put considerable emphasis on the point of contact between John and Jesus. Early in 27 C.E. Jesus became conscious of his spiritual vocation. He left Nazareth amongst a crowd of people proceeding to the Jordan fords to be baptized by John, who was already active as an ascetic preacher, calling men to repentance, "Repent ye, for the Kingdom of God is at hand." He baptized those who came to him and confessed their sins and, through baptism, they received absolution.

Jesus' baptism at John's hands gave him his first impetus. The significance of the event shows the importance of John's influence on Jesus.

In the same year, after a first stay in Jerusalem, during which many people were attracted to him, Jesus went into the Jordan countryside "there he remained with them and baptized," (John 3: 22), after the manner of John. The Baptizer's disciples complained bitterly to their master who was then ministering at Aenon near Salim (see p. 226). John, as reported in the Fourth gospel, answered solemnly that his mission was to prepare the way for the Messiah and since he had appeared, John must vanish.

The motif throughout these encounters is the rite of baptism. Furthermore, it is a most important feature of Jewish-Christian theology, in which the baptism of Jesus figures more prominently than the nativity. Mark's and John's gospel open on the note of baptism and it is believed by some that this came first in the yearly liturgical recitals. That Christ's baptism was given such prominence in the Jewish-Christian milieu is also evidence for some contact between Essenes and John's movement. Immersion in live water as the visible sign of repentance and admission into the eschatological community, is the essential common element between Essenism and John's movement and all that it represented. The fact that Jesus was so baptized and that this was recognized as the beginning of his ministry makes it the more important as a link between the groups.

A TEACHING OF THE GREATEST SIMPLICITY:
"Repent for the Reign of God is at hand."

John announced that the great hope of Israel's religion was on the point of fulfillment. The reign of happiness so ardently desired was to be realized immediately. It was at hand. God was coming. The urgent call to sinners was to repent, for the Judge sat at their very doors.

Both John and, later, Jesus of Nazareth, came with the same message.

Their teaching was of the greatest simplicity. They were both prophets of a single oracle. It rang like the call of the "shophar"—like a trumpet note—down through the ages when Roman rule encircled the world. And they survived Rome. John and Jesus of Nazareth left the fulfillment of the heavenly end of history and the Reign of the Kingdom of Heaven to God. This was the essence of Hebraic prophetic faith, its zeal undiminished through the ages.

It may be argued in retrospect that there is a distinction between the prophets' faith that God's final intervention was at hand and what actually happened in history. But even if events did not work out as simply as had been predicted, it cannot be denied that something of tremendous importance for the world developed from the expectations and the tensions that accompanied them. The ancient faith in the sovereignty and triumph of God was shared by John and Jesus. If the words of Jeremiah, Isaiah or Ezekiel had some relation to what happened in history, this is no less true in the case of John and Jesus.

Jesus' Estimate of John

The status of John the Baptizer in his environment may be judged according to Jesus' assessment of his career — during the scenes at Jerusalem — as recorded in Mark and Matthew:

> "and they said to him, 'By what authority are you doing these things, or who gave you this authority to do them?' Jesus said to them, 'I will ask you a question; answer me, and I will tell you by what authority I do these things. Was the baptism of John from heaven or from men? Answer me.' And they argued with one another. 'If we say, "From heaven," he will say, "Why then did you not believe him?" But shall we say, "From men?" '— they were afraid of the people, for all held that John was a real prophet." (Mark 11: 28–32)

In effect, Jesus asked the scribes who wanted to know what school or teacher had trained him, whether the Baptizer needed any such qualifications, or whether he should not be recognized as a prophet as of old. John was a great independent preacher and teacher, a momentous figure in the apocalyptic and messianic movement of the day.

It has been argued that neither John nor Jesus was the founder of a school or a sect in Jewish life. They were not analytical or sophisticated scribes or Pharisaic doctors of law, and they did not pronounce 'halakhah' — the manner in which the actual precepts of Torah are to be carried out. But although the movements they founded did not have the elaborate organization of the Essenes or Pharisees, both John and Jesus provided their disciples with instruction, to be memorized and repeated. The teaching of the gospels belongs to this genre of instruction to be handed down to the followers and to act as the norm for the community. Because of the wide variety of groupings within Judaism, it was possible for such outstanding personalities to emerge and to be received according to their merits. We shall come back to the problem of the creative thought of Jesus in Ch. X.

AN HISTORIC ENMITY: HEROD ANTIPAS AND JOHN

It is likely that the second, illicit marriage of Herod Antipas coincided with the beginning of John's ministry. Josephus emphasizes the public character and popularity of John's mission and the baptizing that accompanied it. As Antipas learned of the large numbers of people that gathered around John from all over Palestine seeking spiritual guidance and leadership, he planned to capture him before he could initiate a serious movement among the restive "amme-ha-aretz". These, the "people of the land", included people of all classes, rich and poor, cultivators and artisans of varying shades of piety, but probably not Pharisees. John took good care not to be captured, staying outside Antipas' tetrarchy as far as possible, or on its margin.

It is difficult to ascertain what significance the preaching of John the Baptizer had within the inner Jewish messianic movement. It was undoubtedly part of the main stream of the movement's development, although Eisler's view in identifying him with the Essene "moreh-tzedek" (Ch. VIII) is an extremist view unsupported by existing sources.

Although John disclaimed messianic ambitions, it does not seem that he made any attempt to dampen the enthusiasm of the people who, under his influence, were "in expectation", nor did he do anything to quiet the fears of the authorities who were alarmed at his preaching on public affairs, particularly in the badlands of the Jordan Valley, an inviting area for plotting and warfare, or in the southern section of the valley bordering on Perea which was ruled by the tetrarch Herod Antipas. During the whole time that the Herodian family ruled Judea, Galilee and Perea, there were innumerable disturbances in Palestine, rebellious uprisings caused by messianic expectations and political tension. Some time after John began preaching, he publicly criticized the tetrarch for his adultery with his brother's wife, the Princess Herodias, for whom he had repudiated his first wife, the daughter of the Nabatean king, Aretas IV. Salome was the daughter of this second marriage and later, she, with her mother, were instrumental in having John beheaded. John had aroused deadly hatred at court and, eventually, the tetrarch had him locked up in a dungeon of the solitary fortress of Machaerus near the eastern shore of the Dead Sea.

John's Death

This was routine procedure for the time, but it left John at the mercy of the vengeful prince and princess. According to one tradition, attributed to Josephus, John was beheaded there. Another tradition (Mark) dramatized by countless writers and composers, places the beheading at the tetrarch's new palace in the capital he had built at Tiberias on the Lake of Galilee. According to this tradition, the Princess Salome, offered the granting of any favour by Herod on his birthday, was induced by her mother to demand the head of John, which was forthwith delivered on a platter. This tragic end appears to have enhanced John's prestige. Herod Antipas himself was finally defeated by Aretas of the Nabateans and shortly thereafter exiled to Spain. Josephus reports that the people looked on his defeat as retribution for his killing of John the Baptist.

The story of his death is told by Mark:

> "For Herod had sent and seized John and bound him in prison for the sake of Herodias, his brother Philip's wife; because he had married her. For John said to Herod, 'It is not lawful for you to have your brother's wife.' And Herodias had a grudge against him, and wanted to kill him. But she could not, for Herod feared John, knowing that he was a righteous and holy man, and kept him safe. When he heard him, he was much perplexed; and yet he heard him gladly. But an opportunity came when Herod on his birthday gave a banquet for his courtiers and officers and the leading men of Galilee. For when Herodias' daughter came in and danced, she pleased Herod and his guests; and the king said to the girl, 'Ask me for whatever you wish, and I will grant it.' And he vowed to her, 'Whatever you ask me, I will give you, even half of my kingdom,' And she went out, and said to her mother, 'What shall I ask?' And she said, 'The head of John the baptizer.' And she came in immediately with haste to the king, and asked, saying, 'I want you to give me at once the head of John the Baptist on a platter.' And the king was exceedingly sorry; but because of his oaths and his guests he did not want to break his word to her. And

The great fortress of Machaerus, east of the Dead Sea, where John was beheaded. It guarded the southern frontier of Perea with the Nabatean kingdom. Below is the Dead Sea and, in background, the hills of Judea.

Tiberias on the Lake of Galilee. Near the ruins, or underneath them, lay the palace built by Herod Antipas.

immediately the king sent a soldier of the guard and gave orders to bring his head. He went and beheaded him in the prison, and brought his head on a platter, and gave it to the girl; and the girl gave it to her mother. When his disciples heard of it, they came and took his body, and laid it in a tomb." (Mark 6: 17–29)

The narrative of the imprisonment and murder as told here and by the other gospels, yields incidental evidence of John's stature as a prophet. It is significant to compare it to Josephus' account, quoted above (p. 226).

It is necessary to weigh the statements in the gospels with considerable care since the real cause of the murder lay in Antipas' fear of political trouble. There is no glaring inconsistency between this account and the further assertion of the gospels that John roused the Tetrarch's anger, and, still more that of the Princess Herodias, by his stern rebuke. Allowance, however, must also be made for the folklore element present in the story as preserved.

II

SIGNIFICANCE OF THE MOVEMENT

THE HOLY SPIRIT AND JOHN'S BAPTISM

Sectarian, Jewish-Christian and Later Doctrines

According to the Rule of the Community of Qumran, quoted in Ch. VIII, baptism marks the point at which, through contact with the Spirit of Truth or the Holy Spirit, man repents and enters the new life of the kingdom. As practiced by the sect, baptism signified ritual purity and atonement.

If we examine the evidence of the gospels in the light of this new knowledge, we are bound to inquire whether the bestowal of the Holy Spirit on Jesus may be thought of in the same sense — as a desire for purity which can only be obtained by a previous "cleansing of the soul", the definition of John's baptism. The answer, maintains D. Flusser, is in the affirmative. The evidence of the three synoptic narratives and from the gospel of John all confirms this. As Jesus emerges from the Jordan where he has been immersed:

> "And when he came up out of the water, immediately he saw the heavens opened and the Spirit descending upon him like a dove; and a voice came from heaven, 'Thou art my beloved Son; with thee, I am well pleased.' The Spirit immediately drove him out into the wilderness." (Mark 1: 10–12)

> "And John bore witness, 'I saw the Spirit descend as a dove from heaven, and it remained on him, I myself did not know him; but he who sent me to baptize with water said to me, 'He on whom you see the Spirit descend and remain, this is he who baptizes with the Holy Spirit.' " (John 1: 32–33)

The God who "spoke" at the baptism is clearly believed to have conferred his holy spirit on his anointed. The original concept may have stemmed from the record of Isaiah:

> "Behold my servant, whom I uphold, my chosen, in whom my soul delights; I have put my spirit upon him, he will bring forth justice to the nations." (Isaiah 42: 1)

Later on, it was believed that the gift of the holy spirit was poured out on the early Church. Baptism of water and repentance were then seen as preliminary to the final baptism with the spirit which would come with the fulfillment of the kingdom in the plan of God. It was a question of the eschatological timetable. Paul discussed this in Acts:

> "And he said to them, 'Did you receive the Holy Spirit when you believed?' And they said, 'No. We have never even heard that there is a Holy Spirit.' And he said, 'Into what then were you baptized?' They said, 'Into John's baptism.' And Paul said, 'John baptized with the baptism of repentance, telling the people to believe in the one who was to come after him, that is, Jesus.' On hearing this, they were baptized in the name of the Lord Jesus. And when Paul had laid his hands upon them, the Holy Spirit came on them; and they spoke with tongues and prophesied. There were about twelve of them in all." (Acts 19: 2–7)

It is this contrast between the anticipation and the reality which Paul emphasized in connection with the disciples of John. What is meant is that they could have had no experience of the spirit in the full sense of the Kingdom as followers of John, because he came before. With Jesus all things had been fulfilled.

The ancient sectarian sub-stratum in Mark's record indicates that John would have shared the sectaries' belief that baptism was a rite symbolizing true repentance into the eschatological Kingdom of God, thus making it a spiritual baptism. Both among the sectaries and for John the Baptizer, repentance was linked with baptism. But he went further in not limiting the act of salvation to the few initiates, but in extending it to all ordinary people who appealed to him.

OVERALL SIGNIFICANCE OF JOHN'S POPULAR MOVEMENT

John the Baptizer and John the Evangelist

The prologue of John and its interpretation of the figure of the Baptizer, (How did John regard himself?) are proof of the similarity of his teachings and conceptions to those of the Qumran movement. There are links between their language and that of the work of the Baptizer. The link between the language of the Scrolls and John the Evangelist can probably be traced in some way to John the Baptizer. What connection had the Evangelist with the Baptizer? Conservative scholars think that the former was the unnamed disciple of the Baptizer (see Ch. XII). "Or is the explanation to be found in the assumption that the followers of John the Baptist took with them the language and vocabulary of the Baptist to Ephesus where the Evangelist became familiar with it and employed it in his writings?" (W. H. Brownlee).

In the past, scholars have sought to explain the Johannine dualism by reference to current hellenistic and especially later philosophies of varying types, but their critics have pointed out difficulties of one sort or another.

The surprising Qumran parallels to John the Evangelist have raised the whole question again. They place in high relief the opinion maintained by many other scholars that John is not the most hellenist of the gospels and that his strongest affinities were not with the Greek world and Alexandrian Judaism, but in a milieu where sectarian Jewish currents still ran strong and among traditions where Jewish Christianity was dominant. This puts him in the Hebrew, not the Greek tradition. The Fourth gospel may no longer be regarded as the latest of the gospels, but perhaps the most primitive, with its formative locus in John's teachings as well as in Jerusalem before its destruction, (see Ch. XII).

Evidently the earlier tradition of the Evangelist drew upon the religious concepts and terminology which were current in Palestine at the time. They were modified to suit later theological traditions.

It is quite possible that followers of the Baptizer founded loose congregations. Like the Essenes, the sectaries of Qumran or the early Christians, they regarded themselves as a community of the elect, baptized in repentance and in anticipation of the imminent New Age.

Is there any valid reason to believe, with some scholars, that John would have represented no more than one passing episode among many others in the history of marginal Judaism, had not Christ come under his impact at the beginning of his ministry?

A possible answer would draw us into what is, perhaps, the most obscure phase of early Christianity. No direct evidence has survived of the sect which he animated and which outlived him. John's influence was not ended with his death, although we do not know whether he did indeed become merely "a voice crying in the wilderness" as the Fourth gospel describes him. Scholars differ on the question of whether his followers remained for generations a well-defined and prominent sect, or whether they were absorbed into the main stream of Christianity.

Many prophets and false prophets lived in his time, but none exercised the impact which he made on history. This in itself would account for the repercussions of this movement in the circles out of which grew the primitive Christian community. But, unlike the disciples of Jesus, who did not remain within the framework of Judaism, the disciples of John, the "hundreds", who were baptized by him, were apparently not absorbed automatically into the Jewish-Christian stream. Their distant echoes are heard in obscure sects up to the non-Pauline gnostic stream of the late second century C.E. Sectarian influence is reflected in the activities of Simon Magus, the reputed father of early gnostic Simonism, who flourished in Samaria. Later legends make him a disciple of John the Baptizer. So was his partner and rival Dositheus, according to the popular tales which Luke retailed in Acts.

Repercussions

The influence of John was also felt throughout the Jewish Diaspora, for from the above quotation of Acts 19:2–7, we know of a group of his followers in Ephesus some twenty years later. His religious revival was productive of strange and varied developments throughout Palestine and beyond it. As with Christianity, which was accompanied and followed by strange sects who were often an embarrassment to the apostolic fathers, various sects had some affinity with John's movement from its earliest beginnings. B. Gartner connects the Nasarenes of Epiphanius with the Mandaean "Nasoraya", with the debated rabbinical "Notzrim" and the Qumran sectaries. Bearing in mind the Baptizer's influence on later Mandaeism, a gnostic sect of lower Mesopotamia (whose descendants exist to this day), it is suggested by M. Black that the Nasarenes may have been adherents of the baptism of John. Some ritual ablutions resembling the Essene ritual persisted amongst the "heretic" (gnostic) Palestinian sects in the second century Graeco-Roman non-Pauline Church, such as the Nasorenes and Ebionites. "Such rites may not have been fully shed till the Church's doctrinal position was fixed and accepted; when they survived after the second century, it was in heretical Jewish-Christian circles only." (M. Black)

Looking back historically, one can appreciate the continuity between the teachings of John and Jesus. This makes it more important to establish exactly what were the links between the two.

It is now an accepted fact that the "eschatological existence" of early Christianity, i.e., community life lived in anticipation of the coming of the Kingdom of God on earth, together with the forms which this life took, were not uniquely Christian in ideology, as many New Testament theologians had assumed until recently. Antecedents of these Christian forms and concepts are to be found in a non-conformist sectarian milieu and the movement of John the Baptizer (see Ch. VIII, I–II). As indicated, their thought is identical in many ways with that of the primitive church. R. Bultman, in evaluating these early trends concluded (writing before the Qumran evidence became available): "when regarded from the history of religions point of view, the earliest Church presents itself as an eschatological sect within Judaism, distinguished from other sects and trends, not only by the fact that it awaits the crucified Jesus of Nazareth as Son of Man, but especially by the fact that it is conscious of being already the called and chosen congregation of the end of days."

The ancient olive trees of Galilee have seen the march of history in a land immortalized by the holy men who lived in their shadow. This one is over a thousand years old.

Assuming, as most scholars believe, that the group headed by Jesus was not directly connected with the sectaries of Qumran, there remains the direct impact of John on Jesus, attested by the gospels. Further significant links with Christian origins are pointed out by E. Lohmeyer and M. Black: "The oldest roots of the Christian movement were certainly in Galilee and the North; and one of these may have sprung from a group of dedicated Nazirites. There would then be the closest of connections between John the Baptist and his baptizing movement and the Galilean movement; and a similar close tie with the priestly 'Nazirites' of Qumran." (M. Black).

John and the Qumran Community

A number of scholars have naturally been attracted to the theory that John was at one time associated with the priestly apocalyptists of Qumran. The little that we know of his message fits in very well with such a theory.

However, more recent knowledge gained from the literature of the Dead Sea Scrolls seems to suggest that it is an over-simplification to base any argument for such an association merely on John's life in isolation as well as in populated centers. The laconic and partisan references in the New Testament and the ambivalent attitude of the early Christians towards John prevent a detailed reconstruction of either the life of John or the teachings of the Baptist movement. Scholars disagree about whether John and his disciples constituted an Essene splinter group or a parallel apocalyptist movement and in the present state of our knowledge, it is impossible to pronounce judgment about the more attractive theory.

Nor can it be said, in the light of what we know of Qumran, that John's baptism was a new rite of repentance. The conceptual background of John's thinking and the language attributed to him are in some ways peculiarly Jewish. Consequently, the development of the original Johannine tradition must be sought where Essene influences persisted and where this phase of Jewish Christianity was dominant. Furthermore, the development and impact of the Johannine tradition can best be seen in historical perspective as outlined above.

CONCLUSION

The last chapter has shown that there has been a transformation in opinions held for years about the time and background of John and Jesus. "The Qumran sect was not a small ephemeral group. Its substantial community at Qumran persisted for some two centuries or more. Moreover, it was not restricted to Qumran, but, as we know from its documents, counted its camps and settlements in the villages of Judea. Its own sectarian literature is enormous and of profound and direct influence on Jewish and Christian movements of the first century A. D. and later." (F. M. Cross). In the opinion of this writer, "At best we can affirm that there are contacts between the preaching of John and the teaching of the Essenes of Palestine and those of Qumran." This conclusion accords with the end of Chap. VIII (II).

W. F. Albright states, "many books and fragments of the otherwise lost literature of the Essenes in the century or century and a half preceding the Crucifixion demonstrate the existence of religious circles which were the direct precursors of John the Baptist and Jesus. The Essenes were not 'pre-Christian Christians', as suggested in certain quarters, but Jewish forerunners of apostolic Christianity."

It is significant that John the Baptizer and the sectarian movement associated with him had particularly strong links with Galilee. Galilee had seen the origins of the messianic movement which was to grow up around Jesus and, according to E. Lohmeyer, the oldest roots of the primitive church were to be found in Galilee, in the wide sense of the "Galilee of the Nations" which included not only Galilee itself but the whole area of Northern and Central Palestine, including Perea and the Decapolis of Transjordan. Developments in Judea and Jerusalem could be traced to events in Galilee, (see map in Ch. X).

III

"GALILEE OF THE NATIONS" IN THE DAYS OF JOHN AND JESUS

By the end of the last century B.C.E., Galilee was predominantly Jewish although a number of gentiles lived in the northern section bordering Phoenicia, Coele-Syria and Syria. In early Hasmonean days, the area had still been known as the "Galilee of the Nations", or, rather, gentiles, but with the nationalistic policies of the Hasmonean princes, it had regained its Jewish character. This is evident from the background to the narratives about Jesus and his Galilean followers, and the trend is confirmed by Josephus. The gentiles remaining in Galilee were probably descendants of the Phoenicians (from the west coast of Galilee) and citizens of the remaining Greek "poleis" to the south and east. Imperial power was represented by Roman soldiers and occasional travellers from the surrounding territories.

The "amme-ha-aretz" who were in the majority, were simple folk — rough and ready mountaineers, land-workers, fishermen and herdsmen, artisans and traders. They were deeply religious, although without the refinements of the Pharisees (Ch. VII, I), and had a high standard of social behaviour, widows and orphans being well cared for. "Can anything good come out of Galilee?", was one Judean proverb (John 1: 40). The Talmud concedes that although quarrelsome — and who was not in the ancient Orient? — they possessed certain good qualities.

SOCIAL STRIFE

Galilee was one of the fertile districts of Palestine, but it was too densely populated for comfort. The lowest estimates of the number of its inhabitants range from half a million living in the rural districts and the few towns. A wealthy ruling class and priesthood gave an impression of prosperity, emphasized by the beautiful new capital which king Herod Antipas built for himself in the Roman style at Tiberias.

However, internal economic and social conditions were no better and may have been worse than the conditions described in the book of Enoch in the previous century (see Ch. III). The lower classes lived in dire poverty and there was constant strife between them and the tiny minority of wealthy people. The majority of poor people faced a constant struggle to keep themselves from starvation and meet the harsh demands of Roman or Herodian taxation. The distress of the lower levels of society can be strikingly illustrated from even a superficial consideration of the conditions of life of the Galilean group and the "multitude" that followed Jesus. The story of his feeding the multitude reflects conditions of dire poverty and points to the fact that people were hungry. The gospels emphasize that very aspect of life, although not in the modern phraseology of social conflict. More careful examination of the degree of poverty would reveal many undertones of social and political unrest. As so often in history, the two elements appear to be closely connected. The emphasis which Essenes, Zealots, and apocalyptic teachings place on social justice (the ideal kingdom)

None knew better than the Greeks how to depict the poverty and distress which were the common lot of the masses in antiquity. This Greek marble statue of an old market woman of the 2nd century B.C.E. was found in Rome.

reflect both the existing contrast between the two extremes of society and the state of agitation and discontent which it produced.

With a smaller population and fewer causes for social unrest, Galilee, or indeed all the Palestine of that time, could have been judged fairly prosperous by the standards of the day. The people's labours produced sufficient for the country, and the tax collectors — however it might be begrudged — got their share. To try and form an accurate mental picture of the country at the time it is necessary, first of all, to forget the canvas fantasies of Renaissance painters with their rich tapestries and classical architecture and also the arid, empty hills, clothed only in a "silence of eternity", which 19th century painters peopled with a few figures in contemporary Arab "fellaheen" dress — which was not what was worn two thousand years back.

A true picture must include the degree of wealth side by side with impoverished masses in a thickly populated province which was far from a backwater of the civilized world. It was the inevitable conflict arising out of this contrast that bred the continual riots and produced men prepared to use whatever violence might be needed to remove the evil of Roman and Herodian oppression. These men, termed "brigands" (terrorists) by the official authorities and also by Josephus (the historian who came two generations later), found their justification in ancient prophecies and the preaching of "popular prophets" who spoke in the veiled idiom of apocalypse.

ZEALOTS

The Mountains of Galilee were the cradle and permanent home of various groups of Zealots who carried on guerrilla warfare for many decades up to and after the destruction of the state. Among the Zealots, (see Ch. VI) economic and political stress produced the conviction that the enemy could be expelled and God's reign of peace and universal well-being ushered in only through an armed uprising by the humans most closely concerned — although with support from God.

The messianic aspect of the rebellion is indicated by an important passage from Josephus:

> "What most stirred them up to war was the ambiguous oracle that was found also in their sacred writings that about that time one from their country should become ruler of the world." (Josephus, War of the Jews, Bk. VI, 5:4)

This prophecy is attributed by some to Daniel. But it may have been one of many current at the time similar to Psalms of Solomon 17, quoted in chapter V. Moreover, many apocalyptic writings had their origin in circles outside Jerusalem and, other scholars suppose, in Galilee.

Like the Pharisees and other sects, the Zealots expected the New Kingdom to be established by God or his "anointed" (Messiah). This would be a leader chosen by God, endowed with divine grace and power, who would lead a revolt which, with God's help, would bring deliverance. Such a leader need not necessarily be superhuman.

It is possible that one of the differences between the messianic hopes of the Pharisees and the more simple attitude or "folk-messianism" of the Zealots, lay in the absence among the Zealots of mystic, eschatological, transcendental elements such as the resurrection from the dead and the heavenly Jerusalem. Instead of being content to wait patiently, like the Pharisees, the Zealots intended to hasten the divine hand by political revolt. Folk messianism was thoroughly social and political. How pervasive it became may be seen from the abortive attempts made during the revolt of 66 C. E. (Ch. XII) to establish a peasant commonwealth, as well as from the destruction of evidence of indebtedness and the massacre of the aristocrats (Sadducees).

Spokesmen of Revolt

It may be correct to attribute social and political unrest in Galilee to a combination of causes, rather than a single one. The most restless elements were not necessarily those under the influence of the heady infection of apocalyptic eschatology, although these were especially numerous in Galilee. They were the most articulate, but they depended for support and rationale on the prevailing social unrest.

From the time of the revolt over the census in 6. C. E. to the great rebellion in 66 C. E., there was a series of popular prophets and pretenders who instigated disturbances and had to be forcibly suppressed by the Romans or their Herodian agents. In addition to these political agitators, there were other messianic movements initiated by the preaching of John the Baptizer and the appearance of Jesus of Nazareth.

Though many scholars do not connect John the Baptizer or Jesus of Nazareth with the revolutionary movement, seeing in them more spiritual conceptions of the Messiah, the fact remains that Herod Antipas nurtured a deadly hatred born of fear towards John the Baptizer, whom he finally killed, and that he identified Jesus of Nazareth with the same movement. Accordingly he pursued this other spokesman of the disaffected classses. McCown and others stress the nationalist aspect of John's agitation and demonstrate consequently, that Antipas' suspicions of revolt were justified.

This meeting of the two spiritual giants — John and Jesus — during a period of unrest, catalyzed a sustained popular movement, fired by religious zeal and strengthened by the ruthless repression of the authorities. The fact that the echo of their words and deeds did not die, as had the other attempts at messianic rebellious movements, throws a new light on the inner nature of their own lives and those of their followers. They must be judged as active leaders as well as the originators of a new spiritual creativeness within the camps and settlements of the sectaries, in the villages of Galilee, Samaria and Judea.

Fishing boats on the Lake of Galilee, with the eastern shore in the background.

X

JESUS OF NAZARETH

Preamble

THE ISSUES IN A HISTORY OF JESUS

During the nineteenth and twentieth centuries, New Testament studies covered every aspect of the interpretation of Jesus and his message, ranging from theological interest in Jesus to a critical assessment of the historical and social setting to his life. One of the most controversial issues at the turn of the century was the question of the historical existence of Jesus and his own view of himself and his message.

The conservative critical school held that the gospels offer a solid record of the life of Jesus and the early Church. This approach suggested that the real historical Jesus should be sought from the material available.

The liberal school emphasized the Jesus of history as first and foremost a human, historical being, whose divine character can be appreciated only through a consideration of his own teachings, quite apart from the theology of the church, and who underwent a very human moral struggle. The opponents to the liberal view were the scholars of the Christ-myth school of radical criticism. They held that Jesus and the origins of Christianity were wholly mythical.

The best answer to this theory is that Jesus of Nazareth could not have been entirely invented. There must have been an individual Jesus, who once lived in Nazareth. The concensus of opinion supports his historical existence. In the light of all the available evidence, it should be possible for a modern historian to meet and understand the real, historical Jesus.

"Jesus was not a Christian, he was a Jew," said Wellhausen, the chief exponent of modern biblical criticism, in 1905. Now, in the light of all the knowledge we have gained of the non-conformist views that prevailed among the sectaries, the "amme-ha-aretz", John's following, the Zealots and, perhaps, the provincial Pharisees, it has become possible to draw a much more accurate picture of the spiritual climate in which Jesus grew up and in which he worked. This is of the utmost importance. Since we possess considerable written documentary evidence concerning Jesus dating from his own time, there is no reason to doubt the reliability of the materials attributed to him. The original Hebrew and Aramaic traditions in which his words were preserved have been lost but their exact wording, conveyed in the kind of translation Greek typical of the Septuagint, has preserved the semitic idiom of the oral tradition on which they were based.

THE SYNOPTIC GOSPELS

In evaluating John the Baptizer, we found that whereas he used to be considered an isolated figure, he and his movement can now be studied within a setting which gives an added significance to his teachings. To do this in the case of Jesus of Nazareth is much more difficult. We are still a long way from a full understanding of the texture of primitive Christianity.

In the opinion of modern critics of the New Testament, the gospels are not verbatim reports of a series of events, nor were they ever intended as history in the accepted sense of the word. Instead, they are a collection of different accounts, passed on by word of mouth and written down, first of all in Greek, two or three generations later. They contain a number of sermons about the extraordinary human personality, Jesus, who was regarded as divine only some time after his death.

There is a fundamental similarity between the four gospels which were formed during the seventy years that followed the crucifixion. Because of the similarities between the first three — Matthew, Mark and Luke, all of which tell substantially the same story and have much the same approach to the life and teachings of Jesus, these are known as the Synoptic

Gospels (from the Greek word for "to see together"). The gospel of John, although printed after the synoptics in modern Bibles, is in fact some 50 years older in parts.

The parallels between the synoptics may be illustrated by considering their treatment of some of the outstanding incidents in the life of Jesus: his baptism, temptation, Galilean ministry, journey to Jerusalem and Passion. For instance, compare:

Mark	*Matthew*	*Luke*
12: 36–37	22: 43–45	20: 42–44
6: 41–42	14: 19–20	9: 16–17

Opinions vary considerably about the dates of the gospels. According to some scholars, the earliest of the three was Mark, which was formed around 60 C.E. while the younger disciples of Jesus were still alive; and the gospels according to Matthew and Luke date from between 80 and 100 C.E. According to other scholars, there is nothing in the content of any of the gospels which calls for a date as late as 70 C.E. W. F. Albright believes that the whole New Testament was composed by 80 C.E. The original language behind the gospel of Matthew may have been Hebrew, while that of Mark and much of Luke seems to have been Greek. Later, they were written down and preserved in that language.

In general, it is agreed that the gospels contain a whole range of different elements — eschatological as well as social and ethical. Their special terminology often clouds their real meaning, but though they have a partisan attitude this does not make their testimony suspect. Thus in approaching the historical and social problem of Jesus, the historian must evaluate the testimony on its own merits and in the light of other information we have.

The literary-critical method restricted itself to these limited sources and did not pay sufficient attention to the life and thought of the early church and their effect upon the gospels. In contrast, the method of "form criticism" emphasized the actual conditions (the situation in life) in which the gospels took shape. M. Dibelus, R. Bultmann and others recognized the existence of legends, sayings, parables and dependent stories about Jesus, together known as "forms", among the traditions preserved by the early Christians and used in their services. Thus the "form" school of criticism has taken these elements in the New Testament and related them to the life and thought of the early Church (30–70 C.E.) and its use of the oral traditions before the formation of the present gospels. Their final shape reflects an artificial editing of the earlier traditions. To get back to the originals, the form critic must consider each "saying" or story in the light of its total "situation".

The original collector of evidence or "sayings" — or the evangelist of the first gospel — took the available traditions and tried to relate the actual life of Jesus of Nazareth to the expectations announced by the prophets.

According to the school of form criticism, the gospels should be treated as literature designed to inspire faith, or to meet situations arising in the life of the sub-apostolic church. This is in direct opposition to the traditional view that the gospels are original documents which existed before the sub-apostolic church. Rudolf Bultmann maintains that the original oral tradition was almost entirely made up of short simple sayings or stories. The references to time and place, he holds, were added by later editors when tradition became gospel. According to this school, many of the sayings ascribed to Jesus and some of the problems and tensions attributed to him had their origin later, in the development of the primitive Church. The gospels transferred to Jesus many situations which in fact belonged to a different period.

P. Carrington has tried to prove that the final reason for producing the gospels was for use as part of religious ceremonial. The importance of the practical role which the gospels played in the liturgy of the early Church is unquestioned. This was "a role which may well account in part for the survival of certain traditions at the expense of others." (W. F. Albright).

However, against the radical changes which are assumed by the form critics, it is argued by others that the gospels reflect the life of Jesus and the early church, and that their situations and problems were very similar. Of course, it is true that all the New Testament was composed in the light of the resurrection and reflects that tradition. The gospels offer countless instances of faithful transmission of ancient traditions even when they were an embarrassment to the church. This could not have been done to meet current needs nor for apologetic purposes. The controversies and discussion in the New Testament are chiefly over questions which were meaningful only in the period from 30 C.E. to the end of the 1st century. This is also true of the Pauline letters.

A Historian's Evaluation of the Gospels

To reach an understanding of the figure of Jesus and the various messianic and theological opinions of the New Testament, it is essential that they be considered objectively in the light of historical development. If we are to accept the gospels as trustworthy evidence of the traditions of early Christianity, we must apply to them the same critical judgment that is applied to the study of Old Testament religion in the context of the world of antiquity (see "ADAM TO DANIEL").

Consequently, the authentic Jesus and his authentic sayings must be seen in the context of the religious thinking of the generation or two that followed the crucifixion of Jesus. The changes that took place represent successive stages of development and expansion: First, there was the tension caused by the "event" of Jesus. Secondly there were the nonconformist religious views current among the Jewish-Christians. Thirdly, developments among the Jews of the Dispersion and among non-Jews in the days of the Apostles, have to be taken into account.

One danger to guard against in such a historical approach is the temptation to interpret Jesus' attitude to miracles, healings and the nature of God so as to suit modern tastes. Instead, the whole content and framework of the New Testament need to be evaluated in terms of the Hebrew-Oriental thought forms and traditions in which it was composed.

Thus a life of Jesus and a historical appreciation of his thought needs to be set against the background of the Jewish messianic idea and the way of thinking of the Qumran sectaries. As stated, the New Testament is a continuation of certain elements (eschatology, ethics, etc.) of the Old Testament, the bridge between them being provided by the writings of the Apocrypha and the literature from Qumran (Chs. III and VIII). The results of this application of modern techniques to the different strata of early Christian tradition is summarized in Part I of this chapter. Part II deals with differences of interpretation in the Jewish and Christian tradition.

CONTRIBUTION OF GEOGRAPHY AND ARCHAEOLOGY

It is impossible to produce a detailed and authentic map to show the movements of Jesus, still less to confirm the many popular shrines that commemorate his activities. It is not easy, either, to use the results of archaeological research in Palestine. The New Testament covers less than a century and the happenings with which it deals affected only a small group of private individuals, the Jewish-Christian sectaries. Nevertheless, archaeology does play a part in studying the times of Jesus and its importance is growing every year, as we shall see in this chapter and the next.

Travellers in modern Israel and Jordan are shown by their guides precisely where every major biblical event took place. For the most part these identifications, even when belonging to a venerable tradition, should be regarded with considerable caution. The places illustrated in the following two chapters are mainly of general historical or archaeological interest.

PART I

RECORD OF THE TIMES, LIFE AND HISTORY OF JESUS

THE BIRTHPLACE OF JESUS: BETHLEHEM OR NAZARETH?

"Jesus was born in Bethlehem of Judea in the days of Herod the King." (Matt. 2: 1)

The Gospel of Luke (2: 1, 4) adds that Jesus was born in Bethlehem because Joseph and Mary had to go there in order to be enrolled for taxation, and this would explain Joseph's journey from Nazareth to Bethlehem. This detail of the holding of a census in Palestine sets the story of Jesus' birth against the background of contemporary history.

However a discrepancy in time remains. While Quirinius was Roman governor of Syria (6–9 C.E.), a census was taken which resulted in a serious rebellion in Galilee and the creation of the sect of the Zealots. However, this is too late to coincide with the birth of Jesus which took place before Herod's death in 4 B.C.E. Various solutions for this problem have been put forward, one of them suggesting that the census mentioned in the gospels was an

The geography of the gospels needs to be approached with some caution. The life and ministry of Jesus are clearly reported there, but only a few of the places where he lived and worked are definitely named. Incidents or sayings do not necessarily belong to an actual place mentioned in an adjoining paragraph of the gospel story. Only fourteen or fifteen place names are given in the whole of Galilee. He visited other towns, but it is difficult to identify them. As a matter of sober historical fact, it is impossible to locate some of the sites mentioned in the New Testament with any accuracy.

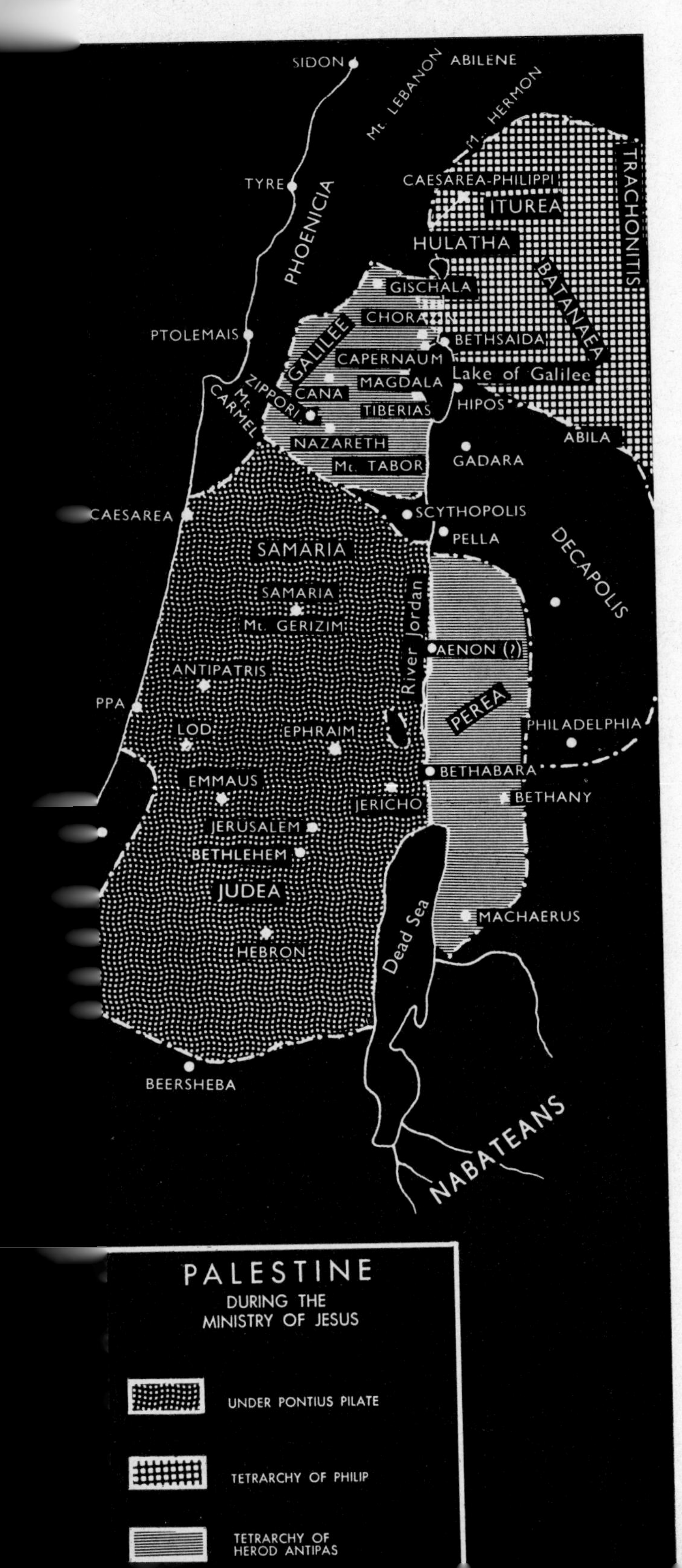

Jesus worked consistently in centers of Jewish life. His ministry was deliberately limited to the Jews. There is no trace of a planned effort to reach the non-Jews living in the hellenistic towns and villages which dotted the landscape of Palestine. Since the gospel narratives were intended, at least partly, to appeal to non-Jews, they would surely have reported it, had Jesus ministered freely to gentiles.

Many of the places in which he was active are known:

Nazareth was his home but when he was driven away by the people (*Luke* 4: 29) *he returned to Capernaum, the center of his Galilean ministry. He was active mainly north and west of the Sea of Galilee and he died in Jerusalem.*

Bethlehem is traditionally Jesus' birthplace.

Bethabara, (*p.* 224) *in the Jordan Valley, was where Jesus was baptized by John. From there, Jesus returned to Galilee. His preaching to the crowds and healing of the sick took place around the northern shore of the Lake of Galilee* (*Matt.* 11:20–24), *with Capernaum as the center.*

Magdala, the home of Mary Magdalene, one of many fishing villages.

Bethsaida the capital of Philip's Tetrarchy, included a settlement of fisherfolk whom Jesus wanted to visit (*Mark* 8: 22).

In Cana, Jesus first manifested his glory (*John* 2: 11).

Tiberias was founded by Herod Antipas (17–22 *C.E.*) *as his new residence. Like Zippori* (*Sepphoris*) *Herod's capital, it was an outstanding Jewish-hellenistic city. Jesus avoided them both.*

Tyre and Sidon were the twin ports of Phoenicia. Jesus visited their neighbourhood — "the parts" not the towns themselves — when Herod Antipas' men made Galilee unsafe for him (*Mark* 7: 24).

Caesarea Philippi, site of ancient Paneion, renamed in honour of Augustus Caesar, was famous for its hellenistic temples and culture. Jesus, again, only entered the outlying districts and villages (*Mark* 8: 27). *Near to Caesarea, Peter confessed his faith in Jesus as Messiah* (*Matt.* 10: 19).

The Decapolis, (*the ten cities*) *were important hellenistic centers. Jesus travelled through the region, but stayed outside their walls.*

Sychar (*Shechem*) *lay on Jesus' route southwards. There, at Jacob's well, he spoke to the woman of Samaria about the "living water" and the worship of God in*

Galilean landscape overlooking the northern end of the Lake of Galilee. Bethsaida stood on the eastern shore. In the background (left) Mount Hermon can be seen.

earlier phase of the same one. However, at that time Archelaus was king of Judea and it is not known that he planned a census. The solutions offered are all only suggestions. They may be weighed against the alternate theory, held by many scholars, that in fact Jesus was born in Nazareth and that the story of Joseph's and Mary's journey to Bethlehem and the birth of Jesus there was developed later, to justify a claim that he belonged to the House of David. Traditionally, the Messiah was foretold from the line of David, who came from Bethlehem. It is believed that the stories of the birth of Jesus may have been advanced by James, the brother of Jesus, as elements in an old family tradition. Jesus never made anything of either his birth in Bethlehem, nor his supposed descent from David. However, it seems reasonable to suppose that so far as they had records or traditions, these pointed to Davidic descent through Joseph for Jesus and James. It is difficult to evaluate how far these might bear on the question of the birth in Bethlehem. A hallowed tradition of the nativity in a cave to the east of Bethlehem has made the town celebrated throughout mankind but the story may have no solid historical foundation.

spirit and truth (John 4). He was careful to avoid the hellenistic city of Samaria, nearby.

Perea, across the Jordan, was visited by Jesus, although it was dangerous territory for him.

Aenon-near-Salim saw John's baptizing activities. In Machaerus, an isolated Hasmonean fortress on the southern border of Perea, the Baptizer was beheaded (Mark 6).

Ephraim, to which Jesus withdrew shortly before his death (John 11: 54).

Jericho, another hellenistic city, was visited by Jesus on his way to Jerusalem. He healed Barthemaeus there and was the guest of publican Zacchaeus (Mark 10; Luke 19).

Qumran lay south of Jericho, on the north-western shore of the Dead Sea. Jesus did not belong to the sect which lived there.

Jerusalem, the end of Jesus' journey.

On the road to Emmaus in Judea, Jesus appeared to the disciples and was known to the people in the breaking of the bread (Luke 24).

The human life of Jesus of Nazareth began simply enough. His home was in the small town of Nazareth, situated in the interior of Galilee, within a purely Jewish district which had been immune to the efforts of the Hellenizers.

Among the disciples of John, there was a group from this district and Jesus, then in his thirtieth year, was included among them (see Ch. IX). Baptism by John in the Jordan took place in an atmosphere of intense spiritual fervour. As Mark tells the story, the simple statement that Jesus was baptized indicates no more than a personal spiritual experience for Jesus. Later gospel accounts relate that the heavens opened and the spirit of God descended on Jesus like a dove while the voice of God was heard, saying, "Thou art my beloved son in whom I delight." This is typical of the language of visionary experience in which the apocalyptic movement expressed itself. Such a vision was well within the old Hebrew tradition and would have seemed natural to its original audience. The later gospels (Matthew and Luke) took the visionary experience of his baptism as the starting point for Jesus' ministry. The first disciples are said to have joined him at the same time.

For a time — exactly how long is uncertain, but it is assumed to be during the years 27 or 28 C.E. — Jesus remained in Judah in close touch with the Baptizer. It was a time of solitude and withdrawal, familiar to the sectaries of the Jordan Valley. The story of the Temptation, told with slight differences in Matthew (4: 1–11) and Luke (4: 1–12), is also attributed to this period. Tradition, and a commemorative monastery, have even selected a Mount of Temptation, halfway to the lonely fortress of Dokh, the place where Simon the Maccabee was murdered (see p. 49). There is also a vague tradition recalled in the gospels which represents Jesus as someone already known in Jerusalem at this time:

> "Now when he heard that John had been arrested, he withdrew into Galilee." (Matt. 4: 12)

With the imprisonment of the Baptizer in Machaerus, this indefinite period came to an end.

"The Kingdom of God is at Hand"

> "From that time Jesus began to preach, saying 'Repent, for the kingdom of heaven is at hand.' " (Matt. 4: 17)

The phrase "is at hand" must be interpreted in the sense of "near at hand" in time. What Jesus proclaimed was: "turn back to God and his Kingdom is all around you." It is not something new. It has always been there.

His message was, first of all, a continuation of the main teaching of the Baptizer. It must be considered in relation to the eschatological expectations current at the time which, as we have seen, were connected with the Jewish hope of deliverance from their present troubles through the coming of a new age.

Jesus in Galilee

Jesus began his campaign in Galilee in a general upsurge of emotion, and with the devout band of John's disciples, intent on carrying on the movement the Baptizer had begun.

The Galilee campaign seems to have started in 28 C.E. From the gospel traditions, it included the calling of his first five disciples, his teaching in the local synagogues and repeated acts of healing. During this time, his fame and popularity spread among the masses and his first controversies with the scribes in authority — if these are factual — took place (see Part II).

Ruins of the synagogue of Kfar-Nahum (Capernaum). This building dates from the late 2nd century and probably stands on the site of a more ancient synagogue. No trace remains of the town that Jesus knew.

The interior of a synagogue was very simple. The only indispensable piece of furniture was the "Ark" in which the holy Scrolls were kept. The stone relief at Capernaum (above) shows such a chest, on wheels. For the most part worshippers sat on the floor on mats, "Chief seats", facing the congregation, being provided for those entitled to special respect. The ruler of the synagogue sat in the "Seat of Moses" (lower right). In the Chorazin synagogue, part of an Aramaic inscription was found (lower left) naming Judan, son of Ishmael, as the builder of the synagogue.

The routes which Jesus followed or the location of the villages such as Bethsaida, Magdala, Chorazin (see map) which he visited, can only be traced in general. It seems clear, nevertheless, that he began his public career in and around Capernaum (Kfar Nahum) on the North-western shore of the Lake of Galilee (or Genesareth-Kinnereth). It stood in a small fertile plain, very hot in summer and swarming with flies and disease. The people who lived there were fishermen or farm-hands for a few landowners. Jesus appealed to the poor and the sick and he won fame as a healer, mainly of lepers and paralytics.

He was friendly with tax collectors (publicans) and outcasts such as the "sinner" Mary Magdalene. Some of the fishermen from this area, Simon Peter, Andrew, James (Jacob) and John, became his friends and devoted followers.

AMONG THE AMME-HA-ARETZ

From Capernaum, Jesus returned to his home in Nazareth. Here, naturally, he was regarded as merely the son of the local carpenter. He is said, however, to have seemed different to the people from what they had expected. To them, he appeared as merely an ambulant preacher with unorthodox views which he was eager to expound to the uninitiated villagers of Nazareth, the "amme-ha-aretz" — the mass of the population of all ranks — freedmen, slaves, artisans, lower civil servants such as the tax collectors, (the publicans). As a rule, people like these accepted the teaching and example of the orthodox Pharisees so far as they each felt disposed — and no further. The rather superior attitude which Rabbinic literature (the Mishnah and Talmud) adopted towards these "sheep without a shepherd" (Matt. 9 : 36) seems to indicate an admission by the Pharisee leadership that they could not compel the obedience of people who were outside their fellowship. "Synagogues of the amme-ha-aretz" are occasionally mentioned and these may have been places where the teaching was more congenial to the simpler folk, although it may not have been up to the high standards of the Pharisees.

Such teachings probably combined the ancient Hebrew traditions with relics of popular beliefs and folklore, familiar from Old Testament days. This formed part of the background of Judaism, of which Pharisaism was the most comprehensive form. It would be too sweeping a generalization to say that the people of Galilee who followed Jesus were neither Pharisee, Zealot nor sectaries. They may have included all these, even the sectaries. It is doubtful whether sharp lines of demarcation were drawn between them in the countryside. To classify Jesus himself in terms of the categories then in use, he was a well informed leader of the amme-ha-aretz. It is one of his outstanding characteristics that he associated with common people and did not despise "publicans and sinners".

However, although he was not an avowed Pharisee, there was a wide range of common ground between them. He has been described as a provincial Pharisee and J. Klausner and Ch. Rabin, who emphasize this common ground, go so far as to assert that their views were identical.

The gospel tells how one Sabbath, Jesus read at the service in the synagogue from the scroll of Isaiah, quoting the prophecy:

> "And he came to Nazareth where he had been brought up; and he went to the synagogue, as his custom was on the sabbath day. And he stood up to read: 'The Spirit of the Lord God is upon me, because the Lord has anointed me to bring good tidings to the afflicted; he has sent me to bind up the brokenhearted, to proclaim liberty to the captives and the opening of the prison to those who are bound.' " (Isaiah 61: 1) (Luke 4: 16–19)

This passage, with its emphasis on release and redemption, was understood eschatologically by both Jesus and his audience. It refers to the anointing of the prophet by the spirit and does not mean the royal messiah. Nevertheless, his listeners well knew that the word "anointed" meant the "Messiah", and it was incredible to them that this lowly young man from Nazareth, who was not of the line of David so far as they knew, could be the one chosen to lead the people against all their enemies. One of the fixed points of Pharisaic belief, accepted even in the provincial synagogues, was that the Messiah would

Fisherman pulling in his net. Roman mosaic of the 1*st century B.C.E.*

not come, nor would the Kingdom of God be established on earth, until the people had made themselves ready by repentance. R.T. Herford has well defined this attitude: "Those are the lines of a simple and severe belief which needed, for the maintenance of it under the suffering caused by Herod and Roman oppression, a rare degree of self-restraint and of heroic devotion to God in men who in this respect also meant sincerely to take on themselves the yoke of the kingdom."

The Pharisees and their followers rejected any attempt to bring the Kingdom by violence, which was what the Zealots were eager to do. Under cover of a religious appeal, the Zealot spirit found room to give expression to social and economic grievances and to work up enthusiasm for vengeance on the nation's enemies. It is possible that a fundamental disagreement between these two states of mind was to be found then in Nazareth, just as it was shortly thereafter in Jerusalem. In Nazareth, on that Sabbath, the people turned against Jesus, rejecting one, who, as the saying went, was no prophet in his own country. Jesus escaped and returned to Capernaum.

THE DISCIPLES

After that scene, Jesus withdrew with his disciples to the Sea of Galilee, where he used a boat for preaching and for travelling. He frequented the mountains; he met his followers in desert places. He built up an organization which he called, figuratively, his household or family. The record says that he chose twelve men from among his followers to be with him and to receive authority from him. They were the trusted servants of his house, he said metaphorically, and he sent them out to preach and heal.

Five of the disciples were selected before the others and they became senior to the rest of the twelve. They were Simon of Bethsaida, their leader, upon whom Jesus conferred the title of Kephas (or Peter, Petros in Greek) which means "the Rock". Next came James and John, called by Jesus, "the Sons of Thunder", or Boanerges; Andrew the brother of Simon, and Matthew who, unlike the other four, was not a fisherman but had been a tax gatherer (a publican) by the name of Levi. The Hebrew for Matthew is Matah-yah, which means Gift of God. Then came Simon the Zealot and Judas Iscariot (Ish-Karioth, or Man of Krioth, a village in Judah).

> "And he called to him the twelve, and began to send them out two by two, and gave them authority over the unclean spirits. He charged them to take nothing for their journey except a staff; no bread, no bag, no money in their belts; but to wear sandals and not put on two tunics. And he said to them, 'Where you enter a house, stay there until you leave the place. And if any place will not receive you and they refuse to hear you, when you leave, shake off the dust that is on your feet for a testimony against them.' So they went out and preached that men should repent. And they cast out many demons, and anointed with oil many that were sick and healed them." (Mark 6: 7–13)

INTENSIVE CAMPAIGN IN GALILEE

By this time, some six or seven months had passed since Jesus had been baptized by John. In the winter of 28 or 29, Jesus decided on militant — albeit peaceful — action.

In its devotion and mission, this campaign is reminiscent of contemporary patterns mentioned in previous chapters. Here were no warlike Zealots setting out on a revolutionary underground movement; nevertheless, in Matthew's account of their briefing, there is no compromise with a hostile world:

" 'Do not think that I have come to bring peace on earth; I have not come to bring peace, but a sword.' " (Matt: 10: 34)

"But if it is by the Spirit of God that I cast out demons, then the kingdom of God has come upon you." (Matt. 12: 38)

For this was to be the starting point of an organized campaign which, from a single leader and his few partisans would spread into a wide missionary movement that would, eventually, reach all mankind. Jesus' exhortation to them was to gird themselves for God's battle within the world, just as the sectaries did in their withdrawn solitude. Nevertheless, in its complete assurance of success the movement was aggressive and reckless: "The Kingdom of God has come upon you." How could they fail?

We would gladly know more of this campaign. All the gospels tell us are the carefully remembered instructions given by Jesus, the obligation to exorcise demons and heal the sick being particularly true to the idiom of his band of followers.

Very possibly, the Jewish and Roman authorities had not yet fully realized the possible consequences of Jesus' organization of twelve able leaders and their supporters throughout Galilee. But this time would soon come. Jesus may have felt that circumstances made the evangelization of Galilee a matter of great urgency and importance. At least, he called on his disciples to concentrate exclusively on that area, avoiding contact with Samaritan or gentile territory. Precise information about their progress is missing. What has remained are a few meaningful traditions which explain the unique nature of his impact.

THE SERMON ON THE MOUNT

At Passover time that year (29), there was a convocation of some five thousand of Jesus' followers "on the Mountain" (i.e. in Galilee) and we are told in one gospel that disciples of John were also present. This is hardly surprising since Jesus was the natural successor to John as leader of the popular movement which the Baptizer had initiated.

"Seeing the crowds, he went up on the mountain, and when he sat down his disciples came to him. And he opened his mouth and taught them, saying: 'Blessed are the poor in spirit, for theirs is the kingdom of heaven.' " (Matt. 5: 1–3)

The scene on the mountainside, with Jesus breaking bread among the multitude became indelibly printed on the disciples' minds as the high point of the crisis.

Jesus took the Old Testament literally. His attitude towards the Scriptures was essentially Jewish and orthodox. The key to this attitude and his approach to established authority is to be found in the introduction to the Sermon on the Mount:

"Think not that I have come to abolish the law and the prophets; I have come not to abolish them but to fulfil them. For truly, I say to you, till heaven and earth pass away, not an iota, not a jot, will pass from the law until all is accomplished.

Whoever then relaxes one of the least of these commandments and teaches men so, shall be called least in the kingdom of heaven; but he who does them and teaches them shall be called great in the kingdom of heaven. For I tell you, unless your righteousness exceeds that of the scribes and Pharisees, you will never enter the kingdom of heaven." (Matt. 5: 17–20)

The reference to the iota and the jot, is to the tiny tick on the "yod", the smallest letter in the Hebrew alphabet. In spite of his relation to Pharisaic teaching, Jesus was no Pharisee and did not sympathise with their position on Scripture. Basically, his attack was grounded in differences over the Oral Law (cf. Ch. VII, I). Jesus denied the Oral Law and questioned the motives of those who set great store by this discipline as a way of getting round the difficulties of the written Law. At the same time, he used Scripture to interpret the Law in an even more flexible way. Matthew, in chapter 6, may have put the question even more sharply than Jesus did elsewhere in the Sermon on the Mount, for, in the opening statement he had affirmed that the Law stood immovable, but had yet to be "fulfilled".

A Crucial Stage — Spirituality and Fulfillment of Jesus

One possible explanation that can reconcile the two traditions is that his declaration that he had come to fulfill the Law had, for Jesus a different meaning from the Rabbinic interpretation.

The Bible draws no distinction between ceremonial and moral law, for Law is equated with religion, and to the Jews both aspects were equally divine and eternal. However, in fulfilling the Law, Jesus placed most emphasis on the higher value of the ethical precepts as compared to ceremonial regulations. Thus to Jesus good works were more important than ceremonial cleansings; healing on the Sabbath, even of ailments which did not endanger life, was acceptable to the higher moral Law and in the relief of hunger it was permissible to pluck ears of corn on the Sabbath. In Jesus' view, only the spirit really counted. A man was good only so far as his spirit was pure; ritual purification could have no effect on spiritual evil. Hence his rejection of the idea that unclean things made men ritually unclean.

"But what comes out of the mouth proceeds from the heart, and this defiles a man. For out of the heart come evil thoughts. . . . These are what defile a man; but to eat with unwashed hands does not defile a man." (Matt. 15: 18–20)

Spiritual purity was immune to material contamination.

Another possible explanation is that Jesus at this crucial stage, in the second year of his public ministry, saw his coming as a fulfillment. In this light it may be possible to reconcile the ambivalent statements attributed to Matthew. It is also significant that the gospel of Mark opens on this note and quotes Jesus by association with the event of John's arrest. It seems to have marked a definite stage in the movement initiated by Jesus.

"Now after John was arrested, Jesus came into Galilee, preaching the gospel of God, and saying, 'The time is fulfilled, and the kingdom of God is at hand; repent, and believe in the gospel.' " (Mark 1: 14–15)

None of the various rival sites of "the mountain" appear to be more than early guesses. Any one of these Galilean ranges may have witnessed this phase of events.

Truly I say to you . . . . .

The closing verses of the Sermon on the Mount reveal Jesus aware of himself as a critic and an authority in his own right:

> "And when Jesus finished these sayings, the crowds were astonished at his teaching, for he taught them as one who had authority, and not as their scribes." (Matt. 7: 28–29)

> ". . . and they were astonished at his teaching, for his word was with authority." (Luke 4: 32)

Naturally, the official religious authorities — the scribes — emphasized fulfillment of the Law in terms of observance of the correct and midrashic interpretation of Scripture. But, reading his followers' definition correctly, Jesus was not restricted to precedent in his teaching as were the scribes but taught that in a conflict between regulations, one must choose the most important and accept the consequences. He spoke as one personally inspired, "Truly I say to you. . . ." with a note of inner and immediate certainty, protesting his independence. Whence came this certainty?

UNITY OF LIFE AND TEACHING

"When the people saw the sign which he had done, they said, 'This is indeed the prophet who is to come into the world.'" (John 6: 14)

In John's gospel, which retains the most primitive tradition of the story, Jesus reappears as someone much closer to John the Baptizer, who, as in the sectarian expectations, would be a prophet like Moses, a messianic and eschatological figure (see Ch. VIII), who must ultimately be the greatest of all, greater than king or priest, just as Moses is the greatest of all in the Old Testament. In other passages of Matthew, besides the Sermon on the Mount, this Moses-Messiah conception is even more evident. Jesus is an outstanding example of the great prophets and teachers who emphasized the ethical and spiritual content of religion.

HIS PERSONALITY AND SUPREME RELIGIOUS AUTHORITY

Above all, it is impossible to separate his teaching from his life. He was one in whom life and teaching were one. Much of his teaching was original not so much in each individual idea but in relation to everything that he was and was trying to do.

Jesus' impact on his deeply disturbed people and on succeeding generations cannot be decried. Even those who regard him from a purely human standpoint have done this aspect justice. Burning with prophetic zeal, dynamic, convincing, he could without apparent effort establish an immediate "rapport" with his audience whether rustic or urban.

The source of his "authority" — his power — lay in his own personality. People crowded to him, according to Mark, from Galilee, from Judah, from the Decapolis and from Tyre and Sidon and over all of them he exerted an extraordinary command. "His teachings and sayings welled up from great depths, as it were from the perception of his inmost being, affected very little by knowledge obtained from books ..... For Jesus, natural understanding took the place of the heaping up of information. He had an immediate intuitive insight into the heart of things .... Jesus was possessed of marked individuality and great self-confidence, believing in his own supreme authority and rebuking all who did not recognize his messiahship and his teaching." (J. Klausner).

For years, the mass of the people had clung desperately to their hopes of an imminent supernatural intervention as the solution for all their troubles. Jesus came to them as one already "called" or "chosen" for the "End of Days" — an attitude he shared with the Qumran sectaries, although he did not belong to such a community. He taught that "the Kingdom of God is in the midst of you" (Luke 17 : 21). It was a matter of personal decision whether or not each individual accepted its demands and became one of the Kingdom.

Jesus himself did not intend to create a new faith. It is commonly agreed among scholars that he lived and died a Jew and, during his lifetime, he did not openly claim any messianic role that could justify the charge of encouraging the worship of himself. Nevertheless, it is proper to say that if the gospels are accepted as trustworthy evidence — subject to their evaluation in the context of contemporary history and Jewish cultural patterns — then, "the central position he gave to his own person and the emphasis he placed upon loyalty to him personally, gave a radically new pattern to the old truths." (Stanley B. Frost)

What is important is that Jesus claimed full authority in Israel to speak for God. To discuss him from a purely human point of view would be dodging the issue. To the people to whom he spoke and among whom he worked, the issue — for man or for God — was quite plain and they responded vigorously for or against. The final clue to his character and authority was the same question he asked the religious leaders about John. Was it of men or of God? A leader could only be selected by God. Just as Moses and the prophets are spoken of in the Old Testament, so with Jesus and John. As Klausner points out, Jesus was fully conscious of his own supreme religious authority and this is at the basis of everything else.

THE REAL, HISTORICAL JESUS

To round up this part of the discussion, we could say that from a critical study of the gospels certain points had already been made clear at this stage — the second year — of his ministry.

First of all, the unique pattern of his whole personality and life which his disciples were to preserve as the true essence of Jesus. It is in this pattern that, in the opinion of a number of scholars, the true historical Jesus is revealed.

Such a coherent kernel of historical truth makes possible, in its turn, an evaluation of his interpretation of prophetic Jewish ethics. Clearly, in this respect, he was an extremist. God was his "Father in Heaven". The things of "this world" would "pass away". If he was interested in improving material conditions he did not think about them systematically.

He took an extreme stand on the interpretation of the Scriptures in relation to daily life which aroused the resentment of the Jewish leaders (who had equally been the targets of the prophets and had similarly resented them). From this conflict developed a tension which was to have unsuspected historical consequences — not only religious, but social and political.

It would be of supreme interest to be able to refer to Jesus' own interpretation of the scriptures but, unfortunately, the gospel record is too scanty. It is difficult to distinguish between what Jesus actually said and thought and what his biographers claim for him. However many of his sayings are clearly authentic. Their style and content are quite different from anything else in the New Testament — or in the rest of literature.

It is possible to extract the coherent story of Jesus and, from this, to explain how the events came about and how they were preserved in the memory of those who lived close to him. Much as there are parts of the gospel which are not plain history, the whole story cannot have been invented.

Developments which took place after his death (see Ch. XI) explain other aspects of the story embodied in the gospels. These aspects, many scholars believe, reflect not so much the actual career of Jesus as later disputes between Jewish-Christians and their social Jewish environment, and the defensive propaganda of proselytes of Jesus in the synagogues.

HEROD ANTIPAS PURSUES JESUS

"King Herod heard of it; for Jesus' name had become known. Some said, 'John the baptizer has been raised from the dead; that is why these powers are at work in him.' But others said, 'It is Elijah.' and others said, 'It is a prophet, like one of the prophets of old.' But when Herod heard of it he said, 'John, whom I beheaded, has been raised.' " (Mark 6: 14–16)

It might seem as though Herod had executed John because he had annoyed the royal court. Josephus, however, makes it clear that this was far from being the sole cause. It is reasonable to suppose that Herod feared John's potential political power. He was after a revolutionary movement, not a man.

"Herod said, 'John I beheaded; but who is this about whom I hear such things?' And he sought to see him." (Luke 9 : 9)

The relations between Herod Antipas and Jesus, obscure in the other gospels, are made clearest by Luke. Here it is quite plain. Herod had John beheaded, yet here was this Jesus apparently carrying on his work and continuing the movement begun by the Baptizer in Perea (Jewish Transjordan) within the territory of Antipas. From his point of view, the Baptizer-Jesus movement was all of a piece. It seems reasonable that, having rid himself of John, Herod would equally make some attempt to remove what must have seemed to him another, similar, enemy to his kingdom. (Whether this was actually so, we will consider later). Accordingly, the question arises why Jesus was apparently unhampered during the major portion of his mission in Galilee, whilst the work of one week in Jerusalem brought about his death?

The answer seems to be that the New Testament did have some memory of the responsibility of Antipas for the trial and execution of Jesus.

"for truly in this city there were gathered together against thy holy servant Jesus, whom thou didst anoint, both Herod and Pontius Pilate, with the Gentiles and the people of Israel . . . ." (Acts, 4 : 27)

"When Pilate heard this, he asked whether the man was a Galilean. And when he learned that he belonged to Herod's jurisdiction, he sent him over to Herod, who was himself in Jerusalem at that time. When Herod saw Jesus, he was very glad, for he had long desired to see him, because he had heard about him, and he was hoping to see some sign done by him. So he questioned him at some length; but he made no answer. The chief priests and the scribes stood by, vehemently accusing him. And Herod with his soldiers treated him with contempt and mocked him; then, arraying him in gorgeous apparel, he sent him back to Pilate. And Herod and Pilate became friends with each other that very day, for before this they had been at enmity with each other. Pilate then called together the chief priests and the rulers and the people, and said to them, 'You brought me this man as one who was perverting the people; and after examining him before you, behold, I did not find this man guilty of any of your charges against him; neither did Herod, for he sent him back to us. Behold, nothing deserving death has been done by him; I will therefore chastise him and release him.' " (Luke 23: 6–16)

Flight and Disappointment

It is apparent that Jesus was not satisfied with the result of his mission in Galilee. In Nazareth, Capernaum or neighbouring Khorazin, the crowds fell away after a time and he left Galilee to make one last attempt in Jerusalem. Before this, although Antipas had known of him, he had paid him little attention. Now this attitude changed.

According to the traditional view, Jesus' failure to arouse a great popular movement in Galilee and his realization of the opposition and dangers he faced, may have produced in him a "negative" attitude to the life of the present world. He saw it as valueless. Nothing was to be gained by resisting evil or fighting authority. Possessions were a hindrance to the spirit and should be given to the poor. Litigation was worthless; marriage of no significance. Nothing but the Kingdom of Heaven mattered and for this, home and family should be forsaken.

True, this interpretation makes the connection between Jesus' disappointment and the views he held before going to his death. However, it fails to take into consideration the fact that nothing is new in this attitude. Like John the Baptizer and his circle of followers, Jesus had started out on his spiritual career from the basis of the established pattern of contemporary nonconformist thought and behaviour (see Ch. VIII). His disappointment with the result of his efforts should just have confirmed his general disillusionment with human endeavour.

It is generally accepted that Jesus was challenging the religious authorities and — over their heads — the people to a new religious decision. Inevitably this would have political and social consequences, but they were not the main issue, any more than they had been in the utterances and challenges of the prophets.

For Antipas had realized that he was faced with the revival of a potentially dangerous movement and he made up his mind to arrest Jesus. M. Goguel says, "From that time forward, Jesus was obliged to flee from place to place and sometimes to conceal himself altogether." This also accounts for the fact that when he left Galilee, he had no host of supporters behind him. The case would have been different had he been accepted by the people as their eagerly awaited apocalyptic and messianic leader.

The threat which Antipas represented to Jesus and his disciples may be the motive for the saying reproduced in Mark 8 : 15, which has an authentic historic ring: "Beware of the leaven of the Pharisees and the leaven of Herod." This threat from Herod and the growing tension around him is the only satisfactory explanation for Jesus' withdrawal from Galilee to the tetrarchy of Philip, the land of the gentiles:

> "Immediately he made his disciples get into the boat and go before him to the other side, to Beth-saida, while he dismissed the crowd." (Mark 6: 45)

Mark also records an earlier argument (between Jesus and the upholders of the strict observance of the Sabbath) and follows it with a suggestion of an alliance between the Pharisees and the Herodians:

> "The Pharisees went out, and immediately held counsel with the Herodians against him, how to destroy him." (Mark 3: 6)

"The Herodians" were Antipas' agents and it is notable that this incident marks the end of his synagogue ministry and his withdrawal to the Sea of Galilee.

Mount of Olives, seen through the arcades of the Temple esplanade. The hillside boasts a variety of memorial churches. From left to right: the golden cupola of the Russian church of Gethsemane; the spires of the Russian monastery and church of the Ascension. Halfway up the hill stands the new sanctuary of Dominus Flevit.

At the end of his Galilee mission, however, the whole narrative gives an impression of flight and an attempt to escape attention. He is found now in Phoenicia, now in the Decapolis, now in Iturea, (see map). His disciples, although not mentioned in the confused account, were probably never very far away. In all, a variety of traditions exist to suggest that he became a fugitive from Antipas who was out for his life.

Scene at Caesarea Philippi

"And Jesus went on with his disciples, to the villages of Caesarea Philippi; and on the way he asked his disciples, 'Who do men say that I am ?' And they told him, 'John the Baptist; and others say, Elijah and others one of the prophets.' And he asked them, 'But who do you say that I am?' Peter answered him, 'You are the Christ.' And he charged them to tell no one about him." (Mark 8: 27–30)

This raises a complicated question. In spite of the great historical interest of this scene, its wording so clearly foreshadows what was to happen later that the gospel has obviously antedated a later phase of theology which was reached in the church only after a generation or two. The gospels used this incident to show that the disciples had a very immature view of messiahship. After the death of Jesus, there was no longer any need to discuss whether he had been one of the prophets, or John the Baptizer. Elsewhere in Mark and Luke, Jesus' own answer to the question is negative (Matthew reflects a later revision). The confession reported here implies that while Jesus had fully matured, the disciples had not.

From Caesarea Philippi, Jesus set out on a roundabout journey to Judah. He travelled through Perea (Jewish Transjordan) which was ruled by Antipas, but, even so, this was

safer than Samaria where he and his disciples had a hostile reception when they tried to cross it. However, an attempt to arrest him was made as they hurried through Perea.

> "At that very hour, some Pharisees came, and said to him, 'Get away from here, for Herod wants to kill you.' And he said to them, 'Go tell that fox, "Behold, I cast out demons and perform cures today and tomorrow, and the third day I finish my course. Nevertheless I must go on my way today and tomorrow and the day following; for it cannot be that a prophet should perish away from Jerusalem.' " (Luke 13: 37–33)

THE TRIAL OF JESUS

From the gospels we learn that Jesus finally came to Jerusalem to seek a hearing before his peers and to challenge them to believe in him. This is not the action of a mild personality, but that of a dedicated, determined man surrendering himself entirely to his sense of vocation. Henceforth, the decision rested with the Jewish people and their leaders. Failure would be theirs, not his.

Jesus had made up his mind that, for the sake of his own good conscience, he must stake his life against the enmity of officials and civil servants. He refused to save himself or to reassure his followers by flight. He went up openly to Jerusalem and made a messianic entry riding on an ass.

> "And Jesus found a young ass and sat upon it; as it is written: 'Fear not, daughter of Zion; behold thy king is coming, sitting on an ass's colt.' " (John 12: 14–15)

This was the day after Nissan 9, in the year 30 C.E. The Passover would begin on Nissan 15th.

If the story of the festive welcome staged by his followers is true, this could certainly be interpreted by those who wished as a messianic triumph. The mixed crowd who watched asked, "Who is this?" and were told, "This is the *prophet* Jesus from Nazareth." Chronologically, this was apparently Jesus' first appearance. Hence the crowd's question. Immediately he drew attention to himself by his claim to authority over the Temple courts. As a protest against the commercialization of the popular religion, he cleared the outer courts of the Temple of the tradesmen who crowded there. At the times of the great popular festivals, like the Passover celebrations, pilgrims thronged into Jerusalem from all over Palestine and from the Jewish settlements abroad.

The gospel of John puts this episode as much as two years earlier. We cannot be sure about the actual date for the evangelists were indifferent to the precise sequence of events. On his last visit to Jerusalem, Jesus openly resumed his daily teaching and preaching in the Temple precincts.

> "Jesus answered him, 'I have spoken openly to the world; I have always taught in synagogues and in the temple, where all Jews come together; I have said nothing secretly." (John 18: 20)

By now he had become a national figure. He could draw crowds from among the pilgrims in Jerusalem just as he had in Galilee. From the point of view of ecclesiastical and

From a 1st cent. Roman sarcophagus, this carved money changer suggests the men Jesus saw in the Temple courts.

political authority, this was an unforgivable sin. However, popular support for him was so strong that at first the authorities dared not interfere, although the tradition is that in his teachings he did not spare the rulers of the people. His attack on the organization of the Temple courts and the high-handed manner in which he carried it out earned him the enmity of the Sadducees, whose prestige depended upon the maintenance of the official religious system with the Temple at its center.

THE MILITANT JESUS

The End of Days at Hand

Jesus' own aims may have been far more pacific but, however hard he tried to give a purely spiritual meaning to the terms "Messiah" or "King of the Jews", in the Palestine of that time these were real, fighting slogans. The group among whom Jesus lived and moved was in any case filled with Zealot spirit. The gospels name a Simon the Zealot among his disciples, although he may have been an isolated case, deserving special mention. Peter himself, apparently, had similar inclinations.

When Jesus spoke of a kingdom in which there would be peace among all men, he aroused the passionate yearnings of the more pacific among his audience. His own aims can be understood in terms of the Essenes and Pharisees who prayed for the coming of the kingdom, but did not mean to arouse revolutionary action. Jesus refused to allow his followers to fight. Of course, some might be inspired by the proclamation of the kingdom to find in his words support for the militant nationalistic spirit of the Zealots, to whom the Kingdom of God was no mere metaphor. The phrase could have implied a real kingdom which could not co-exist with Caesar's realm. In this case the speedy coming of God's kingdom would require the immediate overthrow of Roman power and the disappearance of Herod Antipas from Galilee and Perea.

Jesus claimed divine authority according to a familiar traditional pattern. Substantially, his claims conformed to precedent but they differed in being associated, by his audience at least, with a particular set of social and political circumstances.

Roman Procurators had learned from experience with several other "messiahs" to expect trouble from such claims. Although it is unlikely that the Roman authorities were interested in what was preached, provided no official rules were broken, they could not stand quietly by and watch new enthusiasms be whipped up among the excitable Passover crowds in the capital. Encouraged by Herod Antipas and applauded by the Temple authorities (the Sadducees), the Procurator took precautionary action.

Both John and Jesus announced the forthcoming destruction of the rulers of the world. The authorities were not unreasonable in thinking such teachings dangerous. The point is important because it shows that the preaching careers of both John and Jesus were short. Even though the New Testament makes no clear statement to that effect, it seems likely that both were quickly suppressed. Under the circumstances in which they were active, it was inevitable that they should be condemned as subversive leaders and put to death. This seems to be the central truth of the events of their careers and the development of their movement. In both cases, their deaths caused a spiritual reaction among their disciples and the masses.

Even if Jesus was not a Zealot, and did not foment revolt, it was a foregone conclusion, as events proved, that many who listened to him would believe him to be the leader of the subversion for which he was condemned.

The Trial by the Sadducee Priests

From the point of view of public security, a man aggressive enough to empty the Temple of the traders who had long-standing privileges there, might suddenly embark on the "cleansing" of Jerusalem itself, freeing it from Roman policing. Such an affront to the Roman troops in Jerusalem and the governor resident in the praetorium nearby might be used as the pretext for severe repressive measures. Without waiting for such a development, the Sadducee Temple authorities seized Jesus. They, and the political interests connected with the High Priest, were not at that time concerned with his theology. They attacked him on the essentially political question of whether or not he claimed to be the Messiah. Thus it was as a political offender that they handed him over to Roman power for condemnation or imprisonment during the inflammable period of the Passover festival. According to the gospels, this happened on the night of Thursday, 13th Nissan, after Jesus had sat down for

The Garden of Gethsemane in the valley below the eastern wall of the Temple. Olive trees grow all over Judah and Galilee, living to very great age. These may be a thousand years old.

Banquet scene from a 3rd century B.C.E. carving on a Cypriote tombstone. Although this relief was carved in very different circumstances, the types shown, their expressions and gestures are far more suggestive to a historian of the period than the figures which appear in Renaissance portrayals of the Last Supper and other events of Jesus' life

the "Last Supper" — possibly the Passover celebration — with his disciples. After the meal, they went to the Garden of Gethsemane and there he was arrested by an armed band, his disciples scattering. It was also fear of persecution that made Peter deny Jesus as Messiah. The disciples were disappointed at Jesus' apparent failure. How much harder was it for them to accept their beloved leader's death as a political criminal.

Proceedings of the Sanhedrin

The gospels then tell a confused story of a trial by night by the Great Sanhedrin, on the charge of attempting to make himself king — claiming to be the Messiah. The trial as described shows many deviations from traditional Jewish practice and beliefs. The uncertainty about the actual course of events and about what Jesus claimed to be hangs over the narrative right until the end.

From the accounts in Matthew and Luke, it is clear that his inquisitors wanted him to admit to the claim that he was the Messiah—with all that that implied. The definition is yours, he said, not mine; and I do not admit your implications. Did Jesus deliberately hide his meaning? We can never be certain, but from his reported hesitation, his reluctance to commit himself about the implications of the symbols in which he spoke, a great deal of confusion resulted. By reading the record in the light of all that we know of the history of the times, it is possible to sense in this complicated balance of tensions one of the causes of his unwillingness to raise the banner of rebellion in Galilee — which caused his failure there — and also a remarkable lack of sophistication that made him play right into the hands of the craftier Sadducees. In itself, the claim to be the Messiah was not a religious offence. It could never have been sufficient for any Jewish tribunal to condemn him.

Mark's account of the trial suggests a reluctance to draw the obvious conclusion.

"And the inscription of the charge against him read, 'The King of the Jews.' " (Mark 15: 26)

If Jesus was arrested and executed as a revolutionary, he could not also have been accused and condemned on religious charges. True, the objections were made by certain religious authorities, but political charges were fabricated because they represented the most effective way of getting rid of an enemy.

What is clearly lacking from the gospel records are the political considerations that were mainly involved in the trial. By the time the gospels came to be written, there was a hallowed tradition that there had been a Jewish trial for some religious offence. By then there were no living witnesses to what had taken place behind the closed doors and the gospel narrative was allowed to go unchallenged.

Nevertheless, the gospel stories will not bear comparison with the established practices of Jewish and Roman law. Judicial procedure of the time is embodied in the Mishnah according to which the Sanhedrin was the supreme religious court of Jerusalem. Josephus refers to the Sanhedrin as only an advisory body, but in fact the court had both functions. It was bound by the rules of normal court procedure and met in the daytime — certainly not at night on the eve of Passover. Not only would such a trial have been completely illegal but the Mishnah makes it clear that none of the evidence produced at the trial of Jesus would have justified the death sentence. Added to this, the Mishnah agrees with the gospels in confirming that the death penalty had lapsed by that time:

"Pilate said to them, 'Take him yourselves and judge him by your own law.' The Jews said to him, 'It is not lawful for us to put any man to death.' " (John 18 :31)

Therefore Jesus cannot have been officially tried before the Sanhedrin at night.

The High Priest, we are told, turned Jesus over to the Roman authority because he had said:

"I will destroy this temple that is made with hands and in three days I will build another, not made with hands." (Mark 14: 58)

Despite Mark's denial, this eschatological vision with its apocalyptic phraseology, may well have been authentic. To seem to preach the destruction of the Temple could well have been taken as an unforgivable insult. Some thirty years later, we read in Josephus, another man was handed over to Roman justice for making just such a prophecy. The authorities were afraid that mystic messianic claims were merely camouflage for revolutionary intentions. To the Romans, the Jewish concept of a Messiah was unintelligible.

Legally, the statement about destroying the Temple and rebuilding it miraculously was — if true — more serious. Although perhaps an idle boast and not necessarily actionable, the Mishnah does provide for the punishment to be meted out to a false Messiah.

The court could decide on the death sentence, although in that case, the sentence had to be ratified by the Procurator.

The Council of the High Priest

Altogether, it appears on a closer analysis that the story would make better sense on the assumption, put forward by S. Zeitlin, that the court before which Jesus was arraigned was the inner council of the High Priest. The High Priest was a Roman appointee and he had the right to summon such friends and supporters as he chose to act as an advisory body on any occasion. This was thus a political body, not subject to any rules of judicial procedure.

Such a theory may not appear very convincing but it makes historical sense. It fits into the picture painted by Matthew and Mark of a meeting held at night, not in the chamber of the Sanhedrin, but privately, in the palace of the High Priest. It also explains the silence of the Pharisees. Although they were not friendly to Jesus, neither were they seriously opposed to him and they would certainly have raised objections to such harsh measures. It seems reasonable to assume that whatever happened between the late evening and the following mid-day was not known to them and they had no part in the arrest, trial or condemnation of Jesus. Neither Matthew, Mark nor Luke mentions them as being concerned. They drop out of the story at the beginning of the last week. Their likely attitude, had they been involved at this time, is suggested by the stand they took much later during the trials of Peter and Paul (see Ch. XI), when even Rabbi Gamaliel intervened to defend Paul. By then, the question of schism between the Jews and the early Christians had already arisen.

Paul Winter, in his analysis of the trial of Jesus, considers that many of the contradictory elements in the story may be regarded as later insertions which in any case are of secondary importance. These include: the investigation by Annas, the night session of the Sanhedrin, the mocking in the High Priest's house, the morning session without sentence (Luke), the scene with Herod Antipas, the Barabbas episode in its present form, Pilate's benevolence, and the scourging before death (John).

Left: Bronze coin dated 29–30 C.E. (Pontius Pilate's time), showing a vessel resembling a simpulum. The reverse has three ears of corn.
Right: Coin dated 31–32 C.E. inscribed Tiberius Caesar, the reverse decorated with a leaf pattern.

The gospel narratives tell us that Jesus expected his journey to Jerusalem would be a failure in worldly terms and would lead to his death. The historian asks, at whose hands and why? Here the gospels give us very little help.

One reason for the confusion in the story and the conflicting accounts given by the gospels is that evidence for what happened between the time Jesus disappeared with his guard into the doorway of the palace of the High Priest, until the moment he emerged from the praetorium of the Roman governor, is all hearsay. The doors were closed and none of his followers was actually present.

PONTIUS PILATE AND JESUS

The one portion of the gospel narratives of the Passion which does have historical value seems to be the procedure before Pilate. Indeed, modern scholars are tending more and more to agree that, contrary to Christian tradition, the authorities — that is Antipas and the Roman Procurator of Jerusalem, Pontius Pilate — took a much greater share in the arrest, trial and execution of Jesus than did the Jews.

The High Priest's inner council accused Jesus before Pilate of attempting to make himself king. Pilate, who enjoyed the prerogative of "ius gladii" in Judea, hesitated. The great festivals, with their excited crowds, had often produced similar problems. He listened to the priests, temporized with the mob, considered Tiberius — knowing that the Emperor would expect rebellions to be averted or — at least — immediately suppressed, and finally condemned Jesus to be crucified in the Roman manner. This painful and degrading method of execution was frequently used by the Romans against rebels in their provinces. In Pilate's view, the present case, with its threat of disturbances, called for similar forceful action.

Pilate had been appointed Procurator of Judea in about 27 C.E. He lasted longer than his predecessors and earned the reputation in Rome of a man who knew how to be firm with this unruly people. He regarded them as inferior, subject barbarians to be treated accordingly, with none of the rights and privileges due to Imperial citizens. In return, the Jews came to regard him as the embodiment of all evil, but his bad historical reputation is mainly the work of the Alexandrian, Philo, who accused him of arrogance, rapaciousness, and the ordering of executions without trial. Pilate learned, eventually, that the Roman practice of planting regimental standards carrying life-like effigies of the emperor was anathema to the pious Jews, but he never desisted. Nothing that he did ever earned their approval, not even the building of an aqueduct to bring water to Jerusalem from springs to the south-west of Bethlehem — although this was built with money taken from the public Temple Fund (see Ch. VII). The fact that he continued so long in office was partly due to the Emperor Tiberius' reluctance to make changes in his administrative officers and also, apparently, to his successful handling of insurrectionist movements.

His methods are a good indication of his character. Before Pilate's appointment the Roman police had used brutal methods in suppressing a movement of Galilean Zealots under Judas, whose family continued to lead the movement for sixty years. Both the New Testament and Josephus record two other police actions carried out by the Romans under Pilate. One was the massacre of eighteen Galileans during a punitive action in the village of Siloam, in the Kidron valley, below Jerusalem, a stone's-throw from Gethsemane:

> "There were some present at that very time who told him of the Galileans whose blood Pilate had mingled with their sacrifice. And he answered them, 'Do you think that those Galileans were worse sinners than all the other Galileans, because they suffered thus? I tell you, No; but unless you repent you will all likewise perish. Or those eighteen upon whom the tower in Siloam fell and killed them, do you think that they were worse offenders than all the others who dwelt in Jerusalem?' " (Luke 13 : 1–4)

In later ages Pilate's name became notorious for his part in the death of Jesus but, at the time, the event was of very little significance in Rome. Jesus acording to the Roman view, had died a "death of slaves" ("supplicium servile"—Tacitus, Hist. IV, 3, 11). Pilate was recalled only in 36 or 37 C.E., in response to a strongly worded protest from the Samaritans concerning his repression of religious observances at their shrine of Mount Gerizim.

THE GOSPELS AND ARCHAEOLOGY

Among the contradictory accounts of the trial in the different gospels, John 19 mentions a place which archaeological discoveries have proved to have existed.

> ' When Pilate heard these words, he brought Jesus out and sat down on the judgement seat at a place called The Pavement and in Hebrew, Gabbatha," (John 19 : 13)

The stone pavement, called Gabbatha, which means "raised land" stood on a rocky height at the foot of the Tower of Antonia. The striking fact that archaeology has confirmed the Greek and Hebrew names preserved in John cannot be accidental, claims W.F. Albright.

THE SCENE AT GOLGOTHA

The story of the crucifixion on Golgotha is shortly told. According to the tradition, there were women present who were later active in the Jewish-Christian church. In the evening, the body was laid in the tomb and the stone rolled into position to seal it (see illustr. p. 136). This completed a period of 24 hours from the beginning of the Last Supper. The burial of Jesus in the garden tomb of Joseph of Arimathea, outside the northern wall of Jerusalem, seems to have concluded the Passion narrative although this was always associated with the resurrection story.

WHERE IS THE TOMB OF CHRIST?

The traditional site of the crucifixion, continuously identified as such since the days of Emperor Constantine (approx 325 C.E.), is where the Church of the Holy Sepulchre stands within the walls of the Old City, Jerusalem. Its genuineness was authenticated by a vision of the Queen Mother, St. Helena, and Constantine accepted the tradition. But the original identification and selection of the site are suspect because they cannot be dated before the time of Constantine. A rival site, since the discovery by Edward Robinson in 1838 of a strongly built city wall, north of the Old City, is a hill called Gordon's Calvary. This debate has aroused tremendous "odium archaeologicum ac theologicum", as millions of Christians have found the deepest and holiest experience of their lives in a visit to the Church of the Sepulchre, while to others, for whom the monkish quarrels of the later Christian churches over ritualistic "mummeries" in that shrine have been anathema, Robinson's identification has been much more attractive. However, the problem has been put in an entirely new light by recent archaeological discoveries. Discussion of the site of the crucifixion required a study of the walls of Jerusalem in the first century (see map of Jerusalem in 30–70 C.E.). On the north and north-western side of ancient Jerusalem until its destruction, were three walls. The earliest ran eastward from the Palace of Herod to the Temple area. The second began at Gate Gennath, near the Towers of Hippicus and Phasael (see illus. in Ch. V), encircled the former wall and ended at the Antonia Tower. A third wall was begun by the Jewish king Agrippa I to protect northern exposed parts of Jerusalem. Before it reached the planned height, work was interrupted through the intervention of the Romans in 42 C.E. But it enclosed the large quarter on the hill Bethesda (Beth-Hasda) and other sections north of the second wall (and the site of the Holy Sepulchre shrine). This wall was completed hurriedly by the rebel government in 66–70.

In fact this wall was long thought identical in its course with the present north wall which passes the Damascus Gate. But Robinson found traces of it further north. Recently nearly 800 yards of it have been discovered. The rest of the course can be conjectured by noting land elevations and the ridges to the north-west. Old tradition favours the course of the second wall, but it is a queer line for a city wall as the middle section runs on lower ground. Walls were built for defence and military considerations would have dictated the inclusion of this low ground and the hillock of Golgotha within such a wall. No definite conclusion seems possible and the sites of the crucifixion and burial of Jesus are still uncertain.

WHAT FOLLOWED THE CRUCIFIXION?

For the events which followed the crucifixion of Jesus of Nazareth by Pontius Pilate, we have no historical evidence and no chronology. The story and its background are full of mystic phenomena which are treated as "gospel" in the New Testament.

Jesus' mission having apparently ended in the total calamity of the crucifixion, what was the reaction of the people who had looked to him for the fulfillment of their hopes of redemption and the restoration of the kingdom of Israel?

The first to be involved in this question were the first followers of Jesus, the early Jewish-Christians. They had still to establish the distinction between Jesus and the various

The Lithostroton pavement (above) in the Tower of Antonia, where Jesus may have been tried, was engraved for the "Game of the King" played by the Roman soldiers garrisoned there.

Left below: Excavated foundations of the Third Wall, lying several hundred feet beyond the present north wall of the Old City.

Right: Tomb attributed to Joseph of Arimathea.

pseudo-messiahs who had called for rebellion against the Romans. According to E.E. Jensen, "Much more than Mark, the later synoptics show many evidences of the desire to erase from the record of Jesus' life any suspicion that he had been a pretender king of

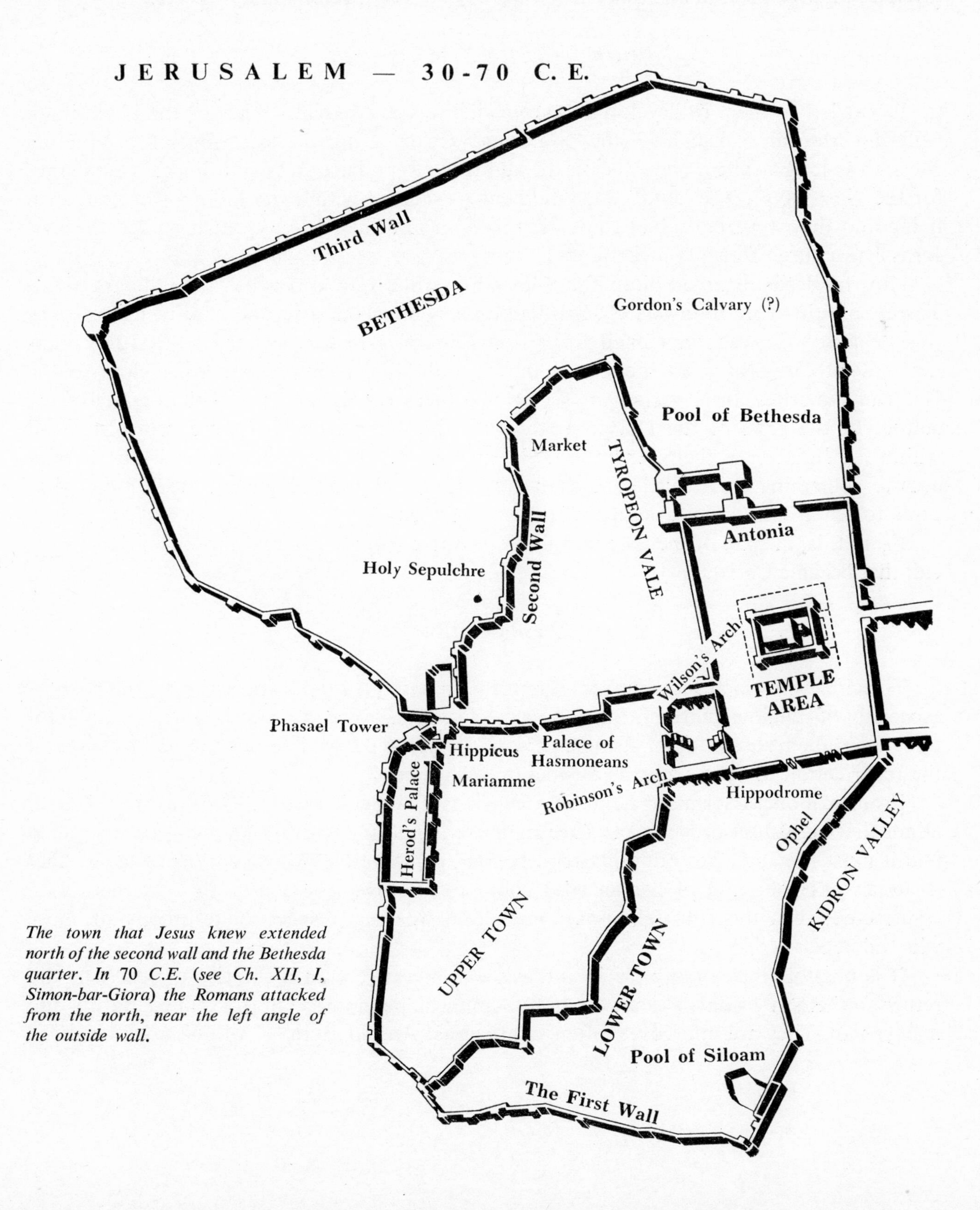

The town that Jesus knew extended north of the second wall and the Bethesda quarter. In 70 C.E. (see Ch. XII, I, Simon-bar-Giora) the Romans attacked from the north, near the left angle of the outside wall.

the revolutionary type common in his day." In spite of his enormous impact on his own and future generations, Jesus himself never showed the slightest desire to found a new religion or religious community. When he died, so far as we can judge from the record, he left his disciples no organization and no instructions beyond the special brand of his teaching.

Aftermath and a New Emphasis

It was left to them to develop a concept of Jesus as Messiah — but as the abused and suffering Messiah of Isaiah 53 (the "Suffering Servant"), not the victorious all-conquering Messiah so long awaited. Nevertheless, he had come to prepare an eschatological "remnant" for the "last days". The "end" was confidently expected within the lifetimes of men then living and they apparently had some organization and instructions which guided the first Jerusalem church from its inception.

How far Jesus regarded himself as Messiah is still disputed between the scholars. C. C. Torrey said that the "followers of Jesus had no new messianic doctrine, that which was new was the person". Except for a small group of his disciples, history has proved that Jesus was not understood in his own lifetime. Some of those who followed him were close to the Galilean Nazirites, or a variety of sectaries, others deeply infected with the hellenistic culture of the Jews of the Diaspora, together they represented a non-conformist trend within the Judaism of their generation. His martyrdom on the cross changed him in their eyes to something only a little less than God. Eventually, although not at the time, they came to see in him the incarnation of the Son of God.

From this, in spite of the absence of any directive from its object, developed the Christ-cult that became Christianity.

RESURRECTION

The circles in which Jesus moved were fully prepared for the resurrection of the dead — especially of religious martyrs. But their expectation of a general resurrection is a different thing from the resurrection of a single person. From the record it seems that the message of the resurrection of Jesus came as a shock to everyone.

From a modern scientific point of view, it is a difficult matter. The historian has to admit that he cannot prove or disprove it. There is nothing with which it can be compared and it must remain a profound mystery, beyond explanation. All we can do is to say that if Jesus was the kind of person who could inspire the conviction that he had been resurrected, then this, in itself, is a miracle and we must respect the testimony of those who did believe.

It is possible that among the haunts which were alive with memories of Jesus, he did return to them in visions. Visions are not uncommon phenomena in times of exaltation and martyrdom. They are, moreover, often contagious. An old myth — of unknown origin —

told that there were those who claimed to have seen Jesus rising after his death and ascending to heaven. This soon found hearers. The origin of the miracle story was attributed at first to Mary Magdalene and her women companions, widows who had unostentatiously followed him about and who tried to minister to his dead body in the cave tomb in the land of Joseph of Arimathea where he had been buried near the place of the crucifixion, the hill of Golgotha. Their audience interpreted the story to mean that those who experienced the vision had seen Jesus in the flesh. Afterwards Jesus appeared in a vision to Simon Kephas (Peter), Thomas and James.

Even Mark the first evangelist, or his editor, repeats the story of the women at the tomb without comment, closing his book with it (if in fact we possess the whole of his work — many believe that the original ending has been lost). He could not suspect that the story of the resurrection would quickly be judged unsatisfactory and be amended in the other gospels and repeated in Apostolic circles. To give confirmation of this material resurrection, it was necessary to indicate a tomb and to provide suitable conditions, as indicated (see "Where is the Tomb of Christ"). It is assumed that older, visionary recollections and folkloric material were buried in the later tradition which came from the repeated revisions of the gospel traditions. They became articles of faith and supplanted the original myth in the usage of the Primitive Church of the first century C.E.

The basis of the Christian faith was not the doctrine of resurrection, but acceptance of the resurrection of Jesus as an eschatological "event". With his death and its sequel, his followers believed, the New Age had dawned. On this belief Christianity was founded. Thus, while the "event" of resurrection and reincarnation belongs to a discussion of the phenomena of mysticism or to theology, it is fundamental to any understanding of the development of Christian doctrine.

Whereas the sectaries looked for their messiah in the future, the early Church believed that Jesus had been raised from the dead as Messiah. The "event" was in the past tense. F. M. Cross deduces "that the 'event' of Jesus as the Christ, his exaltation, his resurrection, the gift of the Spirit, distinguishes the two eschatological communities. . . . It is not faith that a messiah will come that gives Christianity its special character, but the assurance that Jesus rules as the messiah who has come and will come. . . ."

PART II

DIFFERENCES IN INTERPRETATION IN THE JEWISH AND CHRISTIAN TRADITIONS

This very brief survey has left aside a whole host of complicated, controversial problems. Different angles of approach offer a wide variety of interpretations and assessments of the different aspects of the story. Here, only the most outstanding questions can be touched on.

As noted in Ch. VII, modern Christian scholars take a more positive attitude to the sincerity of the Pharisees in their interpretation of the Law and their attitude to the problems of the day. This has done much to correct earlier misconceptions about irreconcilable differences between Jesus and the Pharisees and has made it much easier to reach a true understanding of the conflict that clearly underlies the gospels' theme. Though Jesus' interpretation of Law was unprofessional, his teachings were substantially only what he might have learned from any sensitive pious Rabbi in the synagogue. He attended the synagogue, at least for a time; he prayed in the Temple and he observed the feasts and laws; moreover, he was addressed as Rabbi. His sayings and the use of parables to illustrate his religious and moral teachings are Jewish and Pharisaic in both content and form.

What he criticized in Jewish piety was not the spirit but the form — the fasting, alms-giving and ostentatious prayer which did not involve the heart. This was a dispute inside Judaism. It could be very sharp and passionate without any ill effects. But when the quarrel was transferred and taken up by gentiles, after the New Testament had been completed, the results were disastrous. During the period of the New Testament, the Jewish Christians were a persecuted minority within Judaism (see Ch. XI). There was no friendship between Pharisees and Jewish Christians and it took a Rabbi Gamaliel to have the courage to speak in their defence, though he by no means encouraged them. Out of prejudice, the authors of the gospels obscured the connections between Jesus and the Pharisees and as the separation between Judaism and Christianity developed, so the anti-Pharisee bias was confirmed and strengthened (see p. 153–4).

On the other hand, where a clear difference between Jesus and the Pharisees did arise, "it may reasonably be explained by the assumption that the institutional responsibilities of the Pharisaic jurists made it impossible for them to adopt the radical attitude towards traditional law that was possible for a non-professional teacher of unlearned believers such as Jesus." (R. Marcus).

Whereas Jesus announced that not one jot or tittle of the Law should pass away and although he insisted that the instructions of the scribes should be followed, nevertheless, he demanded that his followers should go beyond them to standards of forgiveness, purity and love which no law could enforce. He aimed at a society transformed by his principles.

Where he did attack the Pharisees was on their misuse of their authority over the people, and this is apparent from the context. Moreover, the fact that he was eloquent and could move his hearers so deeply on just the subjects that earned the scribes their prestige may have been a major source of irritation to them. There is even evidence for this in the complaints of the "tannaitic" Rabbis that he scoffed at the teachings of the learned. Christians rightly believe that the creative quality of the thought of Jesus was most apparent in his original interpretations of the scriptures. Much of his teaching was probably on very different lines from the discipline of the schools. He spoke his mind bluntly, without respect for the authority of the Rabbis. He took no part in the academic debates and disputes of the scribes and neither he nor they, apparently, ever made any attempt to understand one another or to discuss their differing points of view quietly.

A proper understanding of Jesus' originality as a teacher shows that the Pharisees were no more his bitter opponents than they were "hypocrites" (see Ch. VII). The teaching and, to an extent, the practice of the two differed. Their fundamental faith in Judaism was identical.

The points of difference and, to some extent, their foundation, can be established as a matter of historical fact.

For instance, Jesus is widely quoted as saying that the Sabbath was made for man, not man for the Sabbath. This was accepted Pharisaic doctrine. A divergence appeared only when Jesus went further in the exemptions that might be permitted. A dozen passages can be cited showing that he criticized pious Pharisees for their excess of zeal in observing the minute details of the ritual laws while being far too careless in their humane duties towards the poor and the sick. Only two instances are given of Jesus directly challenging the current interpretation of Scriptures; once on the lawfulness of divorce and again on a man's right to forgive sin.

Many New Testament scholars still regard Jesus as a divergent Pharisee. Up to a point this is understandable. Pharisaism was the most important influence in the Jewish surroundings in which Christianity was conceived and from which came its life and conceptions. But this statement is qualified by the fact, (discussed in full in Ch. VIII) that Christianity was not the child of one single parent. Its ancestors must also be sought in the sectarian environment.

THE EXPECTATION OF A "MESSIAH" IN JEWISH AND CHRISTIAN THOUGHT

In the years leading up to 30 C.E. and for some time afterwards, as we have seen, expectation of a "Messiah" was part of the philosophical climate. It was expressed in the "expectation of deliverance" of the Essenes and in other writings of Qumran where it was given an even more dramatic form (see Ch. VIII). The faith behind it was rooted, as has been shown, in the eschatology of Old Testament traditions.

None of these "expectations" were very precise as to what the Messiah would actually be. For the pious recluse, the term probably meant some supernatural messenger (either one or more) sent from God. To him, as well as to a Pharisee, the national Messiah meant above all a righteous ruler of Davidic descent who would set the people of God free from heathen oppression. If Jesus cried that the Pharisees "shut the kingdom of heaven against men" (Matt. 23: 13) it perhaps suggests that at least they did not boast that they could open the door to the kingdom. When the Zealots thought of the Messiah it was as someone like a glorified Hasmonean prince; while for the Sadducees, the word apparently meant nothing at all or, at best, a phantom of prophetic or apocalyptic belief. The idea of a heavenly Messiah, it is believed, grew especially among apocalyptic circles in Galilee.

A personal Messiah was not essential to the messianic age as foretold in the classic tradition of the old prophets, nor as conceived by the apocalyptist. Even the book of Daniel which has a fully developed eschatological fulfillment does not refer to "a" Messiah. Even where such a being is mentioned, it is with one basic difference from the beliefs of a later generation of Christians. This difference is in the belief in the resurrection of the Messiah and in the doctrine of Incarnation. The idea is spoken of in one idiom in the Jewish literature of the time, and with a different ideology in the gospels.

The contemporaries of Jesus never spoke of a Messiah who would be rejected by his own people, or would depend for recognition on the personal surrender of each one of his followers.

According to the gospels, Jesus spoke of himself as the Son of Man — an impressive and mysterious title with a long apocalyptic and mystic history in Jewish tradition. If "Son of Man" was ever used by his contemporaries as the equivalent of the "Messiah", instances of that use have not survived. Although the Zealots who, on the whole represented apocalyptic trends, may have used the term to denote the Messiah, this practice was not adopted by the Pharisees.

Originally the word "messiah" was an adjective denoting the anointed priest, king or prophet. But in the late pre-Christian period, it always refers to a special messianic personality. In later Jewish thought, it developed into a concept used without reference to any specific person.

The main difference between Jewish belief and Christian doctrine is provided by Jesus in this role of "Son of Man". Jesus' views of himself are phrased in retrospect by the gospels in a manner wholly different from current Jewish concepts. They modified its meaning by combining it with the idea of the Suffering Servant of Isaiah 53, thereby merging humiliation and glory. It seems that Jesus understood it as applying not only to himself but to his followers, thus continuing the Old Testament collective interpretation of the Servant. He connected the Servant with the redemptive community and the anointed prophet — himself. There was no connection in his thought between himself and the Davidic king.

That combination was made by the early Church, as early as the gospels and the book of Acts. That he should appear on earth in poverty and humility to suffer and die, giving his life as a ransom for all mankind was a completely new idea. It culminated in the cross and "resurrection," bringing a new element into the drama and a new meaning to the messianic conception.

The early Church, just like the sectaries of Qumran, had a developed apocalyptic messianism with many similarities but also notable distinctions. The Qumran apocalyptic writings do not refer to the pre-existence of the Messiah, nor to the figure of "the Son of Man", nor do they include so many elements influenced by the concept of the "Heavenly

Man". They followed a trend contained in priestly traditions and relying more exclusively on the Torah (Pentateuch).

In contrast, Christian eschatology is much more directly an outcome of the Old Testament prophets.

Whereas in the Qumran literature and community, the Messiah(s) had not yet become a heavenly saviour and their founder, the Righteous Teacher was not expected to return as Messiah, the members of the early Church had moved forward to new ground. The "not yet fulfilled", the messiahship, had become the already fulfilled. The Messiah had come, had been raised and was enthroned.

Moreover Jesus claimed that the sure "signs" of the "New Age" were the healing of the sick, the blind seeing, the dead being raised and the dumb speaking. Whereas the Essenes rigidly excluded the unclean, the maimed, and the humble from the inner councils and cult of the community, Jesus extended a welcome to the unfortunate and the sinner. To Jesus, the "poor" were the humble outcasts. The "meek" who shall "inherit the earth" according to the beatitudes, referred to these "poor". The Essenes, on the contrary, used "poor" as symbolic of their community of recluses sharing their earthly possessions.

THE SON OF GOD AND THE KINGDOM OF HEAVEN

The liberal M.S. Enslin claims that although Jesus did not necessarily begin by identifying himself with the figure of the "Son of Man" described in Enoch or Daniel, he may at last have seen himself as this messianic figure. Vielhauer maintained that in the Synoptic tradition, sayings concerning the Son of Man are less important than those about the Kingdom of God. Does this help to answer the question: What did Jesus himself have in mind? To many it appears that he looked forward only to the Kingdom of God which was to be established almost immediately by God acting through him and his followers. He seems to have affirmed that he was the Messiah, although he denied being God, both at his trial before the High Priest Kaiaphas, and to a follower:

> "And Jesus said to him, 'Why do you call me good? No one is good but God alone.'" (Mark 10; 18)

Matthew who followed Mark, saw the contradiction between this denial and later Christian doctrine and edited the question and answer to read:

> " 'Master, what good things must I do, to have eternal life?' And he said to him, 'Why do you ask me about what is good? One there is who is good.' " (Matt. 19; 16—17)

Jesus would not tell his disciples the time of the coming of the Kingdom of Heaven. ("Heaven" is used in Hebrew in place of "God". In the Scrolls and other Hebrew writings the Kingdom-to-come is in a transfigured earth, not in "heaven"). Jesus did not claim to be omniscient. The Father and he are not equal in knowledge, but he did regard himself as possessing the authority committed to him by God, whom he called Father.

There is no mention of Jesus in the rich contemporary Hebrew literature. Is there any independent evidence about the gospel stories and the death of Jesus in the context of rabbinic literature, namely that of the "Tannaim" of the first two centuries C.E.? In the opinion of J. Klausner, "the Tannaim were, at the end of the first Christian century, far from regarding Jesus as anything more than 'a transgressor in Israel', and they were still accustomed to come into close religious contact with Christians." According to him and other scholars, vague Talmudic traditions know nothing of a death sentence passed by the Romans. Statements about Jesus which may be credited to contemporary writing include references to his illegitimacy, and his going down to Egypt where he learned magic. (This Egyptian story has some affinity with the gospel of Matthew, for what that may be worth historically). The various references have been dated by M. Goldstein and the clearest opinion they express seems to be that he "scoffed at the words of the wise and learned" (Gittin, 2; 57, 1),

The best known later reference in Baraitha reads:

> "It has been taught (in a Baraitha) — On the eve of Passover they hanged Yeshu (the Christian-censored Munich manuscript of the Talmud reads: Yeshu the Nazarene). And an announcer went out in front of him, for forty days, saying: 'He is going to be stoned, because he practised sorcery and enticed and led Israel astray. Anyone who knows anything in his favour, let him come and plead in his behalf.' But not having found anything in his favour, they hanged him on the eve of Passover." (Baraitha-B. Sanhedrin 43a)

There is no mention here of the charge which, according to the different versions in the gospels, led to his death — the charge of blasphemy, which Kaiaphas proclaimed had been committed by his claiming to be the Son of God and by assuming the name of the King of the Jews.

In place of a death sentence passed and carried out by the Romans, the Talmudic tradition substitutes death by stoning at Jewish hands, following a properly conducted trial on a charge of persuading Jews to idolatry, "deceiving Israel". The details are not accurate and, in some cases, may not have been meant literally.

There is a reference in Tosefta-Hullin II, 22, 23, to a Jacob (reproduced in the New Testament as James) of Kefar Soma who taught the "halakhot" of Yeshua or Yeshu ben Pandira and healed the sick in his name. Rabbi Eleazar ben Hyrcanus (95 or 109 C.E.) relates that he learned from Jacob of Kefar Sichnin, who taught in the name of Yeshu ben Pandira, an agreeable interpretation of Scripture, given in the manner of the Pharisees (reminiscent of the manner of Jesus' teaching). (Abodah Zarah 16 b. 17b. Tosefta — Hullin, 24).

A reference to the disciples in the Talmud Baraitha-B. Sanhedrin 43a, tells of a teaching succession in which Matthew is the leading name. Five disciples are named: Mattai (Matthew), Naqai (perhaps Luke), or short for Nicodemus (Nakdimon), Netzer (perhaps Andrew), Buni (perhaps John the son of Zebedee, one of the two disciples called

Boanerges), and Todah, (Thaddaeus). The only really recognizable names are Matthew and Thaddaeus and the fact that the gospels also speak of five disciples selected prior to the remainder of the twelve should be noted. Moreover, it looks as though Jesus was thought of as the head of a household or a teaching school like that of Johanan ben Zakkai, who was also allotted five principal disciples (see Ch. XII). This point receives some corroboration from a similar oral tradition in primitive Christianity.

In conclusion, there are references in the Talmudic literature to the "minim", heretics of various kinds who may have included Pauline Christians as well as Jewish nonconformists and Ebionites as well as (in the opinion of Ch. Rabin) Qumran sectaries.

The Cenacle or "High Chamber" of the Apostles (Acts 1: 13) has been identified with the scene of the Last Supper ever since the 5th century C.E. It is said to be close to the modern church of the Dormitians on Mt. Zion, right. The "high chamber" was restored by Franciscans in 1335. Two centuries later, they were expelled by Arabs, who alleged that the ground floor contained the Tomb of David. This has since been recognized by the State of Israel. Christians are admitted to the upper chamber.

XI

JESUS TO PAUL

AFTERMATH OF THE CRUCIFIXION

The account of the critical period that came immediately after the crucifixion of Jesus is not complete, although it is fairly coherent. Attempted reconstructions are hampered by the sparse and disconnected evidence which is given in the New Testament as explained below.

It seems possible that the Romans and the ecclesiastical authorities (the Sadducees) may have thought that, with its leader out of the way, the popular movement led by Jesus would collapse. There were several indications that this might be so. Even before the execution, Simon Peter had denied being Jesus' disciple and another member of the group, Judas Iscariot, had so completely lost faith in the movement that he had denied the validity of its leadership and had declared himself to the High Priest as ready to betray Jesus.

The record suggests that after the crucifixion, the disciples and a small band of followers returned to Galilee, while some stayed on in Jerusalem. The loose organization which had been formed in Galilee held together. In spite of his first denial, the needs of the moment called forth untapped powers of leadership in Simon Peter and he rallied the others.

SIMON KEPHAS — PETER

According to Acts (1:15), in the period immediately following the death of Jesus, Simon Kephas — Peter, also called Simon Bar-Jonah, the leader of the disciples, stood at the head of a company of about 120 people in Jerusalem. The death of Jesus had put an end to all political hopes and had made it dangerous even to speak of Jesus as the King Messiah. Quite obviously he had been crucified as a political figure. Also, Jesus may have held the old eschatological doctrine that Jewish Law would be cancelled by the advent of the Messiah and that "the Commandments will be voided in the world to come". In the messianic age, that is to say, there would be no need of punishment or restraint such as were necessary in the present age. Instead, everyone would be endowed by the Spirit with the desire and the capacity to do the moral will of God. Thus the Law, meaning sanctions, restraints and punishments, would be voided, but not the covenant and not morality.

The new movement apparently rested on a communal basis akin in many respects to an Essene "haburah". But more central to their theology was the resurrection of the Messiah and the gift of the Spirit. After the death of Jesus, his followers had to face the sober realities of life as an isolated group. They had no single picture of how the age of the Spirit was to displace the age of the Law. For many, the new age had only dawned and, until it was fulfilled, the Law had still to be obeyed and enforced. For others, not only had the new age dawned, the Spirit had been given. Therefore, the Law was upheld spontaneously in the heart of the believer and need no longer be enforced from outside.

In the first months and years of a movement founded upon belief in a supernatural Messiah, complete faith and unquestioned loyalty to an adored leader or "rabbi" were far more important than were the matters of organization associated with the later, developed form of Christianity. In this situation Simon Peter emerged as the outstanding personality. Impulsive, and given to visions, strong as a rock in his opinions (hence the "Kephas" — a rock) yet flexible and tactful, he was able to adapt the emergent movement to the varied pressures of the time and to weld into a group Jews from Galilee, Judah, the Eastern Diaspora and Asia Minor. Simon was a native of Bethsaida, a hellenistic town, (see Ch. IX) and therefore must have been familiar both with Greek and with the dialects of Galilee. A born leader, he was able to hold his uneven followers together and, later, to initiate the missionary zeal of the apostolic age. He was at the head of the Jewish Christian sectaries during the first critical years of the organization until about 44 C.E. Associated with him in the first phase of the organization were John and James, the sons of Zebedee.

The "good news" (Kerygma in Greek) which the Apostles brought, was no proclamation of the Messiah's enthronement. They expected Jesus to make a second appearance, robed in the splendour of a Messiah, prepared to bring the present age to an end. Originally, the apostles thought that this would happen soon. In the meantime, their aim apparently was to answer the "ignorance of foolish men" and silence the denunciations of Jesus as a revolutionary agitator.

In doing this, the Twelve Apostles and the early Jewish-Christian community emphasized the parallel aspect of Jesus' message — his ethical teachings.

> " 'Moses said, "The Lord God will raise up for you a prophet from your brethren as he raised me up. You shall listen to him in whatever he tells you." ' " (Acts 3: 22)

By identifying Jesus with the prophet promised by Moses, Peter here uses a symbol common to the sectaries, which was to leave many traces in the earliest church's interpretation of the work of Jesus. Significantly, a later sect who also revered Jesus without recognizing him as divine, the Ebionites, also identified Jesus with the "true prophet". There has been an attempt to identify Simon Peter with the Simon Zealotes who was the founder of the Ebionite Sect, but this is a minority view.

The Pentecost Piligrims in the Year 30

The Feast of Weeks — Pentecost — comes seven weeks after the time of the crucifixion and the gospels tell us that during this period the Galileans — who spoke Hebrew or Aramaic — were joined by Jewish pilgrims who had come to Jerusalem for the Passover and remained for the Feast of Weeks. They were full of the elation and tensions of their pilgrimage to the holy places and a great event awaited them.

Fragment of a statuette of a woman, from Dura on the Euphrates, Mesopotamia.

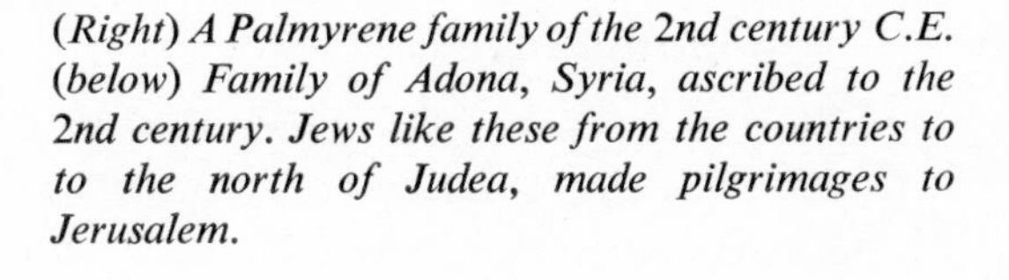

(Right) A Palmyrene family of the 2nd century C.E. (below) Family of Adona, Syria, ascribed to the 2nd century. Jews like these from the countries to to the north of Judea, made pilgrimages to Jerusalem.

The disciples met in a "high chamber" (Cenaculum), fixed by tradition on Mount Zion, and the newcomers came to them there. Luke (Acts 2) describes them vividly, listing the different geographic regions represented, an area stretching from Italy through the Eastern Mediterranean as far as Parthia, east of Mesopotamia.

> "And at this sound the multitude came together, and they were bewildered, because each one heard them speaking in his own language. And they were amazed and wondered saying, 'Are not all these who are speaking Galileans? And how is it that we hear, each of us in his own native language?... we hear them telling in our own tongues the mighty works of God.' And all were amazed and perplexed, saying to one another, 'What does this mean?' But others mocking said, 'They are filled with new wine.' " (Acts 2: 6–8, 11–13)

It would probably be sounder history to interpret "speaking in other tongues" as the actions of an excited cosmopolitan gathering rather than of people in a trance. To them, Simon Peter spoke of the marvel of God and the miracle of resurrection. His words were effective though the figure of 3,000 for those converted is a round number.

"Among the 'converts' were also hellenistic Jews of the diaspora. These Jews it was who provided the basis for Christianity as a religion. If it had not been for them,Christianity would have remained a Jewish sect like the Essenes." (J. Klausner)

From Acts, it is clear that the early disciples joined other Jews in prayers in the Temple and Synagogue. There is a reference to Peter and John going up to the Temple at the hour of prayer (Acts, 3: 1) and at the Gate Beautiful they healed the man who had been lame from birth (3: 7–8). When the group wished to establish themselves as a community, they met either in the outer court of the Temple or in the homes of their more well-to-do members. These homes provided the centers for specifically Jewish-Christian religious activities, particularly the common meals, (Acts 2: 46).

Jewish-Christians and a New Interpretation of Scriptures

One of the group's most important activities was their careful search in the Old Testament for writings that could be interpreted as referring to, or foretelling, the recent events on which the sect was founded. The Jewish Christians were certain that ancient events and teachings had a contemporary significance. This was precisely the attitude of traditional apocalypticism. That it was shared by the Qumran sectaries is clear from the discovery of the lists they made of appropriate texts of scripture, including messianic passages and other sections which they believed referred to the Messiah. Scholars have for a long time believed that the author of Matthew must have had such a list, because of the way in which he shows at every point how the events of Jesus' life were fulfillments of scriptural expectations. Nevertheless, on two cardinal points the Jewish-Christians' interpretation differed from the traditional:

a. in relating the message of Jesus as Messiah to Mosaic Law; and
b. in their attitude towards the traditional Jewish view of themselves as the only ones who would benefit from the Kingdom of God, under the terms of the covenant he had made with Israel (which was the whole basis for their religion).

XXVII. Western shore of the Lake of Galilee. Here and on the eastern shore in the background, Jesus lived and worked (see p. 255).

XXVIII. Sunrise on the Lake of Galilee, near the site of Magdala.

XXIX. Church of the Holy Sepulchre. The courtyard dates from the time of the Crusaders. The staircase on the right leads up to Calvary (see p. 273).

XXX. The women who mourned Jesus (see p. 277) may have looked like these mourning women dancing to the rhythm of a funeral dirge (from a Roman fresco).

Jesus had never taught that the Jewish Covenant Law might be voided but that it would be implemented through the power of the Spirit rather than from fear of the sanctions of the Law. Until then, he had only claimed the right to a practical interpretation of God's will which sometimes differed from the Pharisees. While the faith of the Jews had taught them to expect a Messiah who would show them the way to share in his own righteousness, it had said nothing about his changing either its ritual or its moral laws. The worship of the Jewish-Christians remained "a form of Hebrew structure and worship, their Bible is the Hebrew Bible; their theology is a Hebrew theology; their ancestors are the Hebrew Patriarchs; they are the true descendants of the ancient Israel. . . the old-fashioned Jewish piety flowed right on into Christianity without a break. It was the historical basis of the existence of Christianity in the world." (P. Carrington)

THE DISCIPLES IN CONTROL

The apostles proclaimed Jesus as the Messiah foretold by the ancient prophets. The formula they used was careful to avoid the word "king", for by his resurrection he had been shown to be even greater than David. If Jesus' movement was to survive his execution, it had somehow to be made clear that he had been far more than just another in the contemporary series of pretended messiahs. Any political hopes that his followers may have had were destroyed. But they were profoundly convinced that they had met the risen Lord and they testified that he had indeed come back from the dead.

On this basis the outlook of the small community was transformed. From the insignificant followers of an unsuccessful revolutionary, they became the carriers of a message of hope to all men. God had allowed his Messiah to be degraded by crucifixion, only so that he might be the more exalted. At his trial, Jesus had not denied being the Messiah. Indeed, he had said:

> "And Jesus said, 'I am; and you will see the Son of man sitting at the right hand of Power, and coming with the cloud of heaven.' " (Mark 14: 62)

With his coming, all men would be restored — flesh, blood and spirit. This craving for the preservation of the personality in spite of human death, was very general among the Jews of the first century — orthodox believers and Jewish Christians alike. Paul, an ardent Pharisee, shared these feelings. He carried over into Christian thought messianic and apocalyptic views held by the Pharisees. Jesus was regarded as the "Son of Man" or the heavenly man. In Jewish and pre-Christian terms, he was the Messiah, born of man and woman. This is evident from I and II Thessalonians and 1 Corinthians which reflect the speculations which Paul used to elucidate the importance of the work of Jesus and to account for this extraordinary matter of the resurrection.

Bible critics and theologians have argued about the conflict which must have existed between the idea that the Kingdom had been fulfilled in the person of Christ, or that fulfillment would come through the primitive Church. "It is doubtless universally conceded that after the death of Jesus, in primitive Christianity and after Paul, this tension between present and future, promise and fulfillment, really exists" (O. Cullman). According to the gospel, Jesus believed that he personally represented the long-awaited fulfillment. The primitive Church, however, saw this fulfillment in itself and its apostles.

EARLY CHRISTIANITY AND THE QUMRAN SECTARIES

Chapter VIII (conclusion) referred to the common features of the "life of the two Jewish sectarian communities, Qumran and the primitive Church" (M. Black), and the common ground between them in philosophical background and language. In both, we find the same confusion between present and future, promise and fulfillment.

Both were communities who lived in a state of tense expectation; the second awaited the second coming of the Messiah, the "Parousia", who would put an end to all contrasts between the present world and the world to come. In preparation for this event, both communities banished private property and established a total community of goods.

> "And all who believed were together and had all things in common; and they sold their possessions and goods and distributed them to all, as any had need." (Acts 2: 44–45)

However the Jewish Christians faced additional problems. Their common fund, casually administered by the Twelve, was not only intended for the community's own needs but for the maintenance of a number of widows.

Moreover, their communal ideals had also to survive recognition of the fact that the "end of days" was not something that might be expected at any moment. As the apocalypses in the gospels show, the end was expected in connection with the fall of the Temple and, on the Old Testament pattern, a generation was allowed for this consummation. (The expected period was thus 30–70 C.E.) It is a historic fact that the disappointment of their immediate hopes led, eventually, to the abandonment of their communal form of life. It is possible that leadership by the Twelve was formally established at this critical moment. The group was not a Church in a technical sense but its new organization suggests a compromise, bringing it more into line with contemporary Jewish life. Thus while it may be assumed that the community started out with an economic pattern similar to that of the Qumran sectaries, changing circumstances which the New Testament suggests, brought about a change in its mode of life and, consequently, in its theological outlook. The first apostles have to be seen against some such real-life setting.

The Jewish-Christians and the Sectarian Milieu

In general, the way of life of these Jewish Christians was very little different from that of the orthodox Jewish majority. They observed circumcision, the precepts of the Torah, the Sabbath and the fixed Festivals. In fact, the early Jewish-Christians considered themselves members of the Synagogue, not only until Paul but for many generations after him, and they were not expelled from the Synagogue. The gospel record shows them to have been far more regular worshippers in the Temple or Synagogue than the dissident Essenes or Qumranites. But their belief in a risen Messiah and their celebration of the messianic banquet in anticipation of his "return in glory" set them apart not only as nonconformists but as a new sect, until a great gulf came to separate them from other Jews.

Many of their religious and social practices seem to reflect the influence of the Qumran community of the "End of Days" (see Ch. VIII). Nevertheless the Jewish-Christians were not isolated recluses and they allowed "worldly" considerations an important place in their religious thought. However, the emphasis on individual spiritual purity among both the sectaries and the Jewish-Christians gave them a more spiritual conception of the Messiah. Both communities held passionately to their belief in the resurrection of the dead.

The school of "form criticism" of the Bible denies that Jesus ever thought in terms of an organized community within Judaism, or that he had any such idea when he chose the Twelve. When Jesus sent his disciples out to preach his message, this had nothing to do with the organizational structure of the early Church as described in Acts. In other words, although Jesus chose disciples, he did not choose apostles. According to this school of thought, the Twelve became the leaders of the Church only during the period after the death of Jesus when the establishment of the group began to take on a new meaning. Naturally, the men concerned needed to show that their authority was fully sanctioned according to the customs and ideas of Jewish sectarian theology of the day.

The establishment of such a group implied the founding of a fellowship of specially "chosen" men who were to prepare the way for the Kingdom of God. The choice of the number — twelve, the number of the tribes of Israel — shows the clear connections here between this stage of Jewish Christianity, the Qumran sectaries and traditional Jewish eschatological thought. The number twelve was a potent symbol. Since there were only eleven of the Galilean disciples left (Judas Iscariot having died an unnatural death), it was imperative to add a new name to bring the group to full strength.

By using the parallel of the life and thought of the Qumran sectaries (Ch. VIII) the New Testament record can yield much evidence about the beginnings of the Primitive Church and its organization. The community of Qumran was a priestly body, non-egalitarian and with a strictly defined hierarchy. Its "unity" (or "yahad") depended on its "ruling class" of the "twelve" in the "Council of the Community" (Qumran). "It is valuable from a historical point of view to find here a partial analogy to the twelve apostles of the Church. In the primitive Christian community, the Twelve constituted just such a Council." (B. Reicke). Moreover, an inner group within that Council was formed by three "priests", so called as a mark of special honour.

Just as in Qumran, the members of the group called themselves "companions" (haberim) or "brethren," or "believers". The two also shared an intense concern for the inner purity of the group; saw their new life as "the way" and their new congregation as "the many" ('rabbim').

The group also shared another tradition of the sectaries, which saw itself as a spiritual Temple in which spiritual sacrifices were made — namely prayer.

This particular aspect of Jewish-Christianity has left its mark on most of the literature of the New Testament. Considering the pattern of the Church's primitive catechisms in the Pauline Epistles, and in Hebrews and the Epistle of James, E.G. Selwyn considered that "the evidence points to a conception of the Church as a 'neo-Levitical' or priestly community; . . . it is particularly noticeable in the first Epistle of Peter 2: 1–10."

> "..and like living stones be yourselves built into a spiritual house, to be a holy priesthood, to offer spiritual sacrifices acceptable to God through Jesus Christ.... But you are a chosen race, a royal priesthood, a holy nation, God's own people, that you may declare the wonderful deeds of him who called you out of darkness into his marvelous light. Once you were no people but now you are God's people; once you had not received mercy but now you have received mercy." (1 Peter 2: 5, 9–10)

The Second Epistle of Peter, with its concern for brotherly love, the true way, light in the midst of darkness, true and false teachers and the final destruction of the world by fire is strongly reminiscent of the writings in the possession of the sectaries of Qumran. The discovery of those writings made it clear that, in spite of earlier opinions to the contrary, such early Christian teachings belonged to a strictly Palestinian milieu, closely related to the thought of the Essenes and similar sects flourishing in the 1st century C.E. While II Peter is generally regarded as the latest of the New Testament documents, its affinities with Qumran imply a much earlier date. This may also be true of the whole New Testament.

Jewish Christians and the Temple Ritual

Whether it is a fact of great significance, or merely a coincidence, the Book of Acts makes it clear that the primitive Church found its cradle not in any synagogue, but in the Temple itself. Nevertheless, they came into sharp theological conflict with the Temple officials, whether Sadducee or Pharisee, and with aspects of official Temple rites. In this the Jewish Christians reflected all other nonconformist movements of the day, but they were much more specific in their desire for a spiritualization of Temple worship, and the rejection of animal sacrifice. Some of the "Nazarenes" (one name given to the Jewish-Christians), like the Essenes, refused to take part in the Temple sacrifices, but there is no evidence that any large number of their contemporaries found this particular ritual inconsistent with their essentially spiritual religion.

> "Thus says the Lord: 'Heaven is my throne and the earth is my footstool; what is the house which you would build for me, and what is the place of my rest?' " (Isaiah 66: 1)

This trend is the theme of the story of Stephen, told in Acts VI and VII. It is notable that the mouthpiece for this line of thought should have been a Jew with a hellenistic name, probably a Greek-speaking native of the Diaspora. It seems that some of the Jews of the

Diaspora were opposed to animal sacrifices at the Temple for no other reason than that they were ineffectual. Moreover, there were hellenistic Jews who claimed, for parochial or political reasons, that they had no need of the Temple in Jerusalem. Possibly as a reaction to the superior attitude of the Palestinians, who gloried in the Temple, these Diaspora Jews maintained that they could remain loyal Jews without making the Temple the center of their faith. The Jewish-Christians as a whole "differed from other sectarians, both Hebrew and Hellenists, because neither Jesus himself nor his followers made the Temple the center of continuous and consistent attack" (James Parkes), so Stephen may merely have been voicing an extremist view held by a minority of Jews.

On the whole the Pharisees and the doctors of law treated such deviations tolerantly. There was no custom of excommunication within Jewry at that time. At most, heretics or nonconformists earned the title of "posh'e Israel", (sinners in Israel). The point at which the authorities drew the line may have been where an attack seemed likely to undermine respect for the Temple and its ritual among Jerusalem Jewry in general. "For the basic fact was that the Temple and the Synagogue possessed considerable disciplinary powers, that Jewish officials were prepared to use these powers; and there is no reason for assuming that they did not believe that they had adequate means for keeping within bounds this new sect" (James Parkes). There is also reference to Paul being punished severely by the synagogue authorities in various places.

THE MARTYRDOM OF STEPHEN

As the number of Jewish-Hellenist adherents of the new faith increased, some quite deep-seated conflicts developed between them and the "Hebrew" disciples. This is apparent, among other things, from the situation which first brings Stephen's name into the record. The disciples from hellenist lands appear to have felt discriminated against by the longer-standing Palestinian sectaries. There was a quarrel about the right to "serve tables" (i.e. to administer the communal meals), for the Hebrews apparently questioned the ritual cleanliness of the hellenist Jews. Moreover, the hellenist widows, complained their compatriots, were neglected in the "daily distribution". Probably there were additional differences about matters of doctrine. To settle the immediate questions, however, a fellowship of seven was appointed: "men of good repute, full of the Spirit and of wisdom", to deal with lay matters, leaving the Twelve free to concentrate on preaching.

The first of the seven to be named was Stephen, "a man full of faith and of the Holy Spirit". All the rest have Greek names and one is specifically described as "a proselyte of Antioch". "The complaining party were Jews — Jews of the diaspora who, though they were not few in Jerusalem and in the church of Jerusalem, were overshadowed by the Palestinian Party, to which the Twelve as Galileans naturally belonged. The Committee of Seven chosen, as the sequel tells us, to remedy the difficulty, all bear Greek names. It is natural to suppose that all the Seven were 'Hellenists' and that Stephen's opponents were of the same class." (H. J. Cadbury). (The hellenists were mainly Jews from Syria and Asia Minor — not Greece or Rome).

STEPHEN AND THE SYNAGOGUE OF OPHEL

The martyrdom of Stephen is considered to have taken place about 32–33 C.E. and there is archaeological evidence for, at least, the site of the opening moves.

> "Then some of those who belonged to the synagogue of the Freedmen (as it was called), and of the Cyrenians, and of the Alexandrians, and of those from Cilicia and Asia, arose and disputed with Stephen. But they could not withstand the wisdom and the Spirit with which he spoke. Then they secretly instigated men, who said, 'We have heard him speak blasphemous words against Moses and God.' And they stirred up the people and the elders and the scribes, and they came upon him and seized him and brought him before the council, and set up false witnesses who said, 'This man never ceases to speak words against this holy place and the law; for we have heard him say that this Jesus of Nazareth will destroy this place, and will change the customs which Moses delivered to us.' " (Acts 6: 9–14)

This synagogue of the "freed-men", ex-slaves from North Africa, Italy, Egypt and Asia Minor, is the only one from the period before 70 C.E. of which anything remains. In that year Romans had completely destroyed all synagogues. In Ophel, the oldest section of the lower city of Jerusalem, however, a Greek inscription was found naming Theodotus as founder of the synagogue of the freedmen. It is thought that he belonged to the Jewish Roman family of the Vettenus, which seems to indicate that he or his ancestor was a Jewish freedman from Italy.

In the charges brought against Stephen, there is a clear similarity to the authorities' case against Jesus. The same accusations of disrespect towards the Temple and the Laws of Moses are made against both. Jesus, of course, had been condemned on political issues but there have been other interpretations of his trial. The similarities in the accounts as given, however, end with the charges. Stephen is not silent before his accusers. Instead he argues passionately and with brilliance, showing how all prophets had been rejected by the people at one time or another:

> "Which of the prophets did not your fathers persecute? And they killed those who announced beforehand the coming of the Righteous One, whom you have now betrayed and murdered, you who received the law as delivered by angels and did not keep it." (Acts 7: 52–53)

Greek inscription in the "Synagogue of the Freedmen". It reads: "Theodotus, son of Vettenus, priest and synagogue-president, has built the synagogue for the reading of the Law and the teaching of the Commandments, and (he has built) the hostelry and the chambers for those from abroad who need them. . . . (the synagogue) which his fathers and the elders and Simonides had founded."

This was hardly a conciliatory defence and the people "were enraged against him". Stephen concluded with his vision of God standing in the heavens: "I see the heavens opened and the Son of man standing at the right hand of God." At this defiance, although Stephen had not been found guilty and no sentence appears to have been pronounced, he was dragged out by the crowd and stoned to death.

The possible similarities between his trial and that of Jesus are perhaps less significant than the fact that Stephen seemed not only to side with sectaries, but to express more advanced views than theirs, while the reference to the Righteous One links the movement to the Essene type of sectaries, (see — the Righteous Teacher, Ch. VIII).

Who were the "Hebrews" of Acts?

One of the earliest names of the first Jewish-Christians seems to have been "Ebraiou". They were apparently made up of the Twelve and similar Jewish-Christians who were much more conservative in their attitude to Jewish tradition than the hellenists. Later Jewish-Christian sects called the Church under James "the Church of the Hebrews in Jerusalem" and this usage is found in the "Homilies" of Clement. It is claimed by O. Cullman, Y. Yadin and others that the title of the Epistle to the Hebrews and the apocryphal "Gospel to the Hebrews" are both late echoes of this usage. The synagogue of the "Hebrews" was apparently composed of Jews who hankered after the "classic origins" of their religion, the almost mythical time of the prophets.

There are references in the Book of Acts which point to the existence of different tendencies within the primitive Church, besides the Galilean group of Peter and his disciples. It is suggested by W. Grundmann and O. Cullman that "Peter and the Twelve as a whole appear to have taken a mediating position between the Judaizers and the Hellenists" (O. Cullman) and to have held the different elements together.

The Community and the Authorities

We learn from the record that all these groups exulted in their hopes of the imminent fulfillment of all things which "God hath spoken by the mouth of his holy prophets." To understand the implications of this we must, as we have seen, take into consideration the whole picture of the apocalyptic, social and political factors then operative. These tended to produce precisely that revolutionary upheaval which Herod Antipas, Pontius Pilate and, later, King Agrippa I, together with the materialistic Sadducee aristocracy, were bent on avoiding.

Among the authorities, only the more intellectual Pharisees recognized the fundamental loyalty of the apostles and their associates and refused to use violence to suppress them. In fact, for a few years, the different groups of lofty idealists, living more or less secluded although growing in numbers, did little to make themselves felt either within Palestine or in the diaspora. Indications of conflict between the Jewish-Christians and the authorities are very rare during the first few years.

PREACHING TO THE SAMARITANS AND THE "GOD-FEARERS"

However, Stephen's death made an understandably deep impression on the rank and file of the Jewish-Christians. The first repercussions of this upsurge of persecution were felt among the "hellenistic" disciples who fled from Jerusalem and dispersed into the towns of Judea and Samaria. They felt that not only the Sadducees, but the people as a whole, found them a convenient target for feelings of religious prejudice. Nevertheless, Peter and his group stayed in Jerusalem as the focus which held together the ill-assorted band.

One of the hellenists who had earlier been chosen among the "Seven" was Philip. He disregarded Jesus' admonition to "go not into any way of the Gentiles and enter not into any city of the Samaritans", and boldly went "to a city of Samaria" and preached his gospel.

Among his converts was another leading sectarian, Simon Magus. His action brought to a head the opposition of the Jerusalem group to any attempts at conversion among the Samaritans. They were considered only half-Jews (see ADAM TO DANIEL, Ch. XX) and the first Jewish-Christians fully believed that only genuine Jews (in the ethnic sense of the word) were to be received into the fold.

As a counterweight to Philip, Peter himself and John the son of Zebedee were sent to Samaria by James who, as the brother of Jesus held a position of particular influence as 'mebaqqer' of the early church in Jerusalem, not as a member of the Twelve, but administering the community with them. They were thoroughly dissatisfied with their encounter with Simon Magus but by approving the converts made in Samaria, they confirmed the change in the original view that Jesus had come only "to the lost sheep of the house of Israel."

Philip continued to proselytize in the towns of Judea, Philistia and in Caesarea. His converts included a number of gentile God-fearers (see Ch. VII, II). They were called upon to accept the ritual ablution, and a mild observance of Jewish ceremonial laws, in addition to their central affirmation of belief in the coming of Jesus and the significance of baptism.

Peter himself converted Cornelius, a Centurion of Caesarea. Called to account by the "circumcision party", Peter put his case to the apostles and brethren who were in Judea and silenced his opponents.

> "And they glorified God saying, 'Then to the Gentiles also God has granted repentance unto life.'" (Acts 11: 18).

In other words, the sectarian Church no longer felt itself strictly confined to Jews. From Jerusalem, it spread out into Judea, Samaria and the Coastal plain where Joppa, Lydda and, especially Caesarea became centers remembered in Christian tradition.

"But Philip was found at Azotus, and passing on he preached the gospel to all the towns till he came to Caesarea." (Acts 8: 40)

Hellenist Jews driven from Jerusalem after the death of Stephen founded other churches, evidently at first exclusively among Jews.

"Now those who were scattered because of the persecution that arose over Stephen travelled as far as Phoeniciaand Cyprus and Antioch, speaking the word to none except Jews." (Acts 11: 91)

The conversion of non-Jews had so far been on a very small scale and did not, at that stage, raise any question of an open breach in Judaism.

THE TRIAL OF PETER

Nevertheless, the Sadducee authorities in the Temple resented the story of the resurrection of the "curse of God that was hanged", especially coming from people who, disregarding the ceremonial laws, openly proclaimed their dedication to the precepts of the dead Messiah. As a warning, they arrested the leaders of the sect, Peter and John the son of Zebedee, and gave them a strict injunction to cease their teachings. However, for lack of any serious charge they were released.

The authorities intended the gesture as notice that they regarded the sect as a dangerous nuisance. Instead, it aroused public interest in the new ideas and increased their popularity and the number of conversions:

"But many of those who heard the word believed; and the number of the men came to about five thousand." (Acts 4: 4)

At this, they were rearrested and brought before the Sanhedrin to face the full anger of the Sadducees, To their defence came one of the leading Pharisees, a man named Gamaliel, "held in honour by all the people" and of a patient and reasonable cast of mind. He pointed out that many previous messianic claimants had arisen in the past, among them Theudas and Judas the Galilean. But they and their movements had vanished, leaving no trace. Rather than take the risk of shedding innocent blood, it was better to let this new movement collapse of its own weakness:

"So in the present case I tell you, keep away from these men and let them alone; for if this plan or this undertaking is of men, it will fail; but if it is of God, you will not be able to overthrow them. You might even be found opposing God!" (Acts 5: 38–39)

The council took his advice and contented themselves with having the apostles flogged and then set free.

Peter was arrested again in 44 C.E. by the Jewish King Agrippa I. This time he miraculously escaped from prison. After this, he seems to have been active until about 50 C.E.

in the missionary work outside Jerusalem that was carrying the movement throughout Syria and eastern Asia Minor.

KING AGRIPPA I, THE LAST KING OF JUDEA

The trial of Peter was an exception to the generally peaceful relations between the Pharisees and the Jewish-Christians, which were encouraged by the policy of Agrippa I, grandson of Herod and, like him, King of Palestine. He was a favourite with the Emperor Caligula, who released him in 37 from political exile in Rome, and appointed him king of both the former tetrarchy of Philip, and Abilene. This made Herod Antipas jealous (see Ch. IX) for he was only a Tetrarch and longed to be king. He went to Rome to plead his cause, but there he became involved in charges of conspiracy againt the Emperor, was deposed and banished to Gaul. His territory of Galilee and Perea were then, by grace of the Roman Emperor, added to Agrippa's northern realm. The territory of Judea and Samaria were later (41) also added by the Emperor Claudius. This made Agrippa king of all Palestine, like his grandfather.

According to Philo, Josephus and the Talmud, after all the humiliations suffered in his checkered career at the hands of Romans and Greeks, he showed signs of a reformed character. He became devoted to the teachings of the Pharisees and enhanced the sanctity of the Temple. He behaved, in short, as a native Jewish King, thoroughly loyal to his people. He built the Third Wall of Jerusalem (see end of Ch. X) and, during his three years' reign, he proved an asset to the general welfare, in contrast to his hated grandfather.

Agrippa and the Jewish Christians

Modern historians are divided in their estimate of Agrippa and some may be prejudiced against him for his persecution of the Jewish-Christians. His attitude to the Jewish-Christian sectaries did not derive from any hatred of messianists, but rather from his views on Temple worship. As king, he regarded its ceremonial requirements as the law of the State, a matter of politico-religious policy. He considered the rights of the state to override all other individual human rights and felt entitled to use the disciplinary powers entrusted to him to enforce them. These may have been involved in the case of Stephen. Following certain incidents which remain obscure, James, the son of Zebedee, was executed and other leaders molested, among them Peter, who was arrested but escaped. This sudden persecution apparently took place in 44, towards the end of the reign of Agrippa I. Thereafter the sectaries were left undisturbed for about twenty years, until about 62.

The year 44 saw an important political development. After the death of Agrippa, all the former tetrarchies of Palestine, formerly entrusted to Jewish princes, were annexed to the large Syrian province administered by Roman Procurators under the Roman Legate (governor) residing at Antioch.

Coin of Agrippa 1, *dated between* 42/43–46 *C.E. Left: insignia of canopy and tassles. Right, reverse, three sheaves and two leaves.*

THE FIRST CHURCH IN JERUSALEM UNDER JAMES

Teaching and proselytizing in Jerusalem and the rest of the country increased very greatly following the institution of the Twelve. After some time James, the brother of Jesus, was an unexpected addition to the leadership of the Twelve. This took place, apparently, at the time when the "new Israel", i.e. the Church, became an organized institution with leaders belonging to the dominant group.

From the evidence of patristic fathers, it seems that Peter, James and John deliberately renounced their own positions after a few years, in order to make James, the brother of Jesus, Bishop of Jerusalem and sole leader of the Church. However, among modern scholars, there are those who believe that James held this position from the very foundation of the Jerusalem church, while Peter devoted himself to missionary work. The Pseudo-Clementine gnostic writings, which were friendly to Peter, nevertheless clearly subordinate him to James. Clement calls James the "Bishop of bishops", "leader of the holy church of the Hebrews". For so long as the church in Jerusalem held the leading position, even among the churches founded by Paul, James was at the head of the whole Jewish-Christian movement.

James was a life-long Nazirite, a survival from the Old Testament institution (see Chs. VIII, IX). Because of these beliefs and his orthodox behaviour, James escaped the Sadducee attacks. He was, in any case, a familiar figure in the Temple. According to Josephus he wore the long white garment of the priests and, as a Nazirite, he lived a strictly ascetic life, rather like John the Baptist, for which he was widely honoured:

> "Holy was he from the womb of his mother,
> Wine and strong drink he drank not,
> Nor ate animal food (flesh, meat)
> The razor went not upon his head;
> With oil he anointed not nor used the bath-house.
> For him alone it was lawful to enter the holy places;
> Nor did he wear wool, but linens;
> And he entered alone into the sanctuary,
> And was found kneeling upon his knees,
> And asking forgiveness for the sins of his people,
> Till his knees were hardened like the knees of a camel."
> (Hegesippus, quoted in Eusebius, E.H.II. 23, 5–7)

Hegesippus also tells us that, after his death, James was succeeded by his "cousin", Simon bar-Clopas, who was executed for being a member of the House of David. Eusebius records fifteen members of Jesus' family who held the position of "bishop" of Jerusalem — the "Caliphate of James" was the term which Stauffer used to describe this succession.

James' most substantial claim to the devotion of the Jewish people was the widely held belief that he, like Jesus, was a descendant of David. It seems that the Jewish-Christians boasted two lines of succession. One was the "royal" succession from the family of David which had been claimed in Jerusalem, if not in Galilee, by or on behalf of Jesus. The other was the apostolic succession from Peter to the Twelve. The text of Acts never states openly whether Peter or James held the foremost position. By inference, it seems that James had more influence, especially in the expanding oriental field. His title of the "Righteous One" was bestowed at the time of Jesus but as Paul rises to ascendancy within the leadership, James is allowed to fade out of the picture. This can be explained by the special nature of the Book of Acts, as explained below.

The Epistle of James may be said to represent the standpoint of the Jewish-Christians at this time before they were influenced by Paul's ideas or doctrine.

Up to about 70 C.E., the Church of Jerusalem was under the authority of a leader supported by "prophets" or "teachers" who, equal or subordinate to him, had a voice in all important decisions.

> "So the church throughout all Judea and Galilee and Samaria had peace and was built up; and walking in the fear of the Lord and in the comfort of the Holy Spirit it was multiplied." (Acts 9: 31)

A PRE-PAULINE PHASE

The early following of Jesus was made up of his Galilean supporters plus the first Jerusalem community of Jewish-Christians. Later other sectarian groups joined them — the Nasoreans (Notzrim in Hebrew), (see Ch. IX), the Ebionites with their antecedents in the Nazirite movement, the Therapeutes of Egypt and other sects in Samaria, Eastern Palestine, Galilee, Syria and Asia Minor.

The followers of Jesus, scattered in Jerusalem, Galilee, and beyond the borders of Palestine, found a rallying point in the belief that God had acknowledged Jesus of Nazareth as Messiah. More than this, nothing is certain. The conflicts that developed between a variety of opposing views apart from this central belief had already engendered new sectarian trends. Ultimately, the ideas developed by Paul gained the upper hand. But this was not made clear from the first due to the special nature of the Book of Acts.

THE BOOK OF ACTS

Readers of the New Testament may or may not be ready to interpret it in the light suggested by the methods of "form criticism", as outlined. But that sectarian thought (as illustrated in their writings, (see Ch. VIII, I, II), should force a reappraisal of the New Testament, is a foregone conclusion. Old Testament discoveries had already accustomed scholars to making major adjustments in their thinking. But New Testament scholarship is now in the initial stage of reappraisal based on these new outstandingly important documents.

The main single source for the history of the first few years of the early Church is the Book of Acts and it is generally agreed that the book was written at least thirty years after the events recorded in its opening chapter.

It is assumed that the book was written by Luke, the author of the third gospel, about 62 C.E.

"... a narrative of the things which have been accomplished among us, just as they were delivered to us by those who from the beginning were eyewitnesses and ministers of the word, it seemed good to me also, having followed all things closely for some time past, to write an orderly account for you, most excellent Theophilus." (Luke 1 :2–3)

If Luke did indeed write Acts, he did so after the period he spent with Paul, probably a generation after the beginnings of the Jewish-Christian movement in Galilee and Jerusalem. By that time many things had changed. What had been originally a sectarian movement within Judaism was becoming a predominantly gentile Christian community. Luke was writing with this audience in mind and his approach was consequently different from the spirit of the first generation Jewish-Christians.

His record need not be rejected as unreliable, but it must be remembered that he was writing at the end of a period of controversy, when Pauline views had triumphed. Accordingly, while Peter is the principal character of the first half of Acts (Chs. 1–15), and other apostles, such as John the son of Zebedee, Philip, Stephen, James the brother of Jesus, Barnabas and others are given an important role, the author's real concern is with everything connected with Paulism. He compresses the early phase of Jewish-Christianity, which is of paramount importance historically, and obscures many things in his desire to direct attention away from the initial inner conflicts and towards the later Pauline stream. The latter half of Acts (Chs. 15–28) deals with events which the author probably knew at first hand, and here he keeps more faithfully to the course of events in which Paul is the central personality.

Modern scholars have attempted to fill in the gaps and to find new insight into the existing record by means of "form criticism" as well as from a study of contemporary patterns in sectarian literature.

PAUL

Paul was a native of the city of Tarsus, a Roman town with a long-established Jewish community, mainly traditionally minded. He grew up speaking Aramaic and Greek and trained as a Pharisee. As a young man anxious to learn from the Palestinian rabbis, he attached himself to the school of Gamaliel. Their teaching combined with his natural inclinations to make him a fanatical devotee of the ancient traditions of Judaism.

This brought him into conflict with the nonconformist trends and, in spite — or perhaps because of his closeness to them, he seemed particularly bitter against the hellenist Jews. At the outset of his career he was involved — although not as an active participant — in the controversy and death of Stephen. From then on he joined in the persecution of the Jewish-Christians out of a sincere belief, as he explained, that they represented a threat to the true worship of God. Eusebius was later to observe that before he became a Christian apostle Paul was a Jewish apostle. In all his career he was activated by a passionate and sincere devotion to the service of God.

> "I myself was convinced that I ought to do many things in opposing the name of Jesus of Nazareth. And I did so in Jerusalem; I not only shut up many of the saints in prison, by authority from the chief priests, but when they were put to death I cast my vote against them. And I punished them often in the synagogues and tried to make them blaspheme; and in raging fury against them, I persecuted them even to foreign cities." (Acts 26: 9–11)

To help him in this work of purification, Paul obtained letters from the High Priest recommending him to the synagogues of various groups in Damascus:

> "But Saul, still breathing threats and murder against the disciples of the Lord, went to the high priest and asked him for letters to the synagogues at Damascus, so that if he found any belonging to the Way, men or women, he might bring them bound to Jerusalem." (Acts 9: 1–2)

Damascus had provided a refuge for dissident groups from Palestine for many decades previously. Paul was afraid that their more tolerant views would make this important oriental Jewish community particularly vulnerable to the growing influence of the Jewish-Christians, many of whom had fled to Damascus after the death of Stephen. As a counter-measure, he asked for power to arrest any members of the sect and bring them back to Jerusalem to face the disciplinary authority of the Sadducees.

The legal basis for such action rested in the right of the central council of the metropolitan Jewish religious authority — the Sanhedrin — to full control over all Palestinians in relation to religious law. The unquestioned authority of the Sanhedrin was illustrated later by Paul's own experience. Although a Roman citizen he was frequently called to account by the Jewish Palestinian authorities and he never appealed against the legality of their actions.

By profession Paul was either a weaver or a dealer in woven materials. His trade took him to most centers of Palestine, Syria and Asia Minor. This fact explains the enormous scope of his travels and missionary activities, which he financed from his own resources.

PAUL'S CONVERSION

Armed with his introductions, Paul set out to Damascus. On the way he experienced the event that revolutionized his whole life. He referred to it repeatedly ever after:

> "And in the synagogues immediately he proclaimed Jesus, saying, 'He is the Son of God.' And all who heard him were amazed and said, 'Is not this the man who made havoc in Jerusalem of those who called on this name? And he has come here for

this purpose, to bring them bound before the chief priests.' But Saul increased all the more in strength, and confounded the Jews who lived in Damascus by proving that Jesus was the Christ." (Acts 9: 20–22)

'Wherefore, O King Agrippa, I was not disobedient to the heavenly vision," (Acts 26: 19)

In the history of the development of Christianity, Paul's conversion was also the major event. But treated purely as history, it raises a number of questions. What events led up to that fateful moment? What actually took place? How far were his earlier beliefs and training influential in his conversion?

A Supernatural Experience

The traditional Christian approach is that nothing led up to it and that it was an instantaneous supernatural conversion. It is arguable that its supernatural character has to be upheld. But this need not mean that the event cannot also be examined. This unusual psychological phenomenon, which need not be rejected as a fabrication, can very well be looked at in the light of all the influences that might have contributed to it. As an experience it is by no means unique among visionaries. Paul himself, although he must have given it so much thought — for he refers to it frequently right through his epistles — was never able to make it clear, even to himself, whether he had had a purely subjective, personal vision; or whether it had been a real external event.

Could his disturbed emotions have been caused by guilt? Were they influenced by the memory of his part in the death of Stephen? Did remorse for the many people his fanatical zeal had sent to persecution and martyrdom suddenly overwhelm him? Had he, in fact, come to regard the image of Jesus not as "the accursed of God", but as the first of the martyrs — a finger of accusation pointed at him?

"And when we had all fallen to the ground, I heard a voice saying to me in the Hebrew language, Saul, Saul, why do you persecute me? It hurts you to kick against the goads." (Acts 26: 14)

"And he fell to the ground and heard a voice saying to him, 'Saul, Saul, why do you persecute me?' And he said, 'Who are you, Lord?' And he said, 'I am Jesus, whom you are persecuting; but rise and enter the city, and you will be told what you are to do.' The men who were travelling with him stood speechless, hearing the voice but seeing no one. Saul arose from the ground, and when his eyes were opened, he could see nothing, so they led him by the hand and brought him into Damascus." (Acts 9: 4–8)

Other Influences

Another angle of approach is to consider the human influences involved. It is known that the sectaries who filled Paul's mind lived not only in Damascus but also in the surrounding region. In connection with the Covenanters of Qumran (see Ch. VIII), there is a difference of opinion between scholars on the subject of the locality of the "Sons of Zadok" known as the "Covenanters of Damascus". It is not certain whether these sectaries did actually live in Damascus or whether they used the word as a symbol for some remote place in Transjordan. In either case, other groups of sectaries, for instance members of the sect of the Nasoreans, certainly lived there. Eusebius records that in the village of Hoba, "there are Hebrews who believe in Messiah, called Ebionites". A later Roman prefect of the 3rd century relates that after Herod's massacre of the children in Bethlehem, the family of Jesus escaped to Kochba. Epiphanius also says that Ebionites lived in Kochba and Panias (west of Damascus, near Caesarea Philippi, see Ch. X). According to a Talmudic source, Dosithean sectaries (a group who had escaped from the Samaritans) also lived there.

The theory recently advanced by Z. Lurie that Paul came across such sectaries on his way to Damascus cannot be ruled out. There is a written tradition dating from the time of the Crusades that Paul came to Kochba on his journey there. Could encounters with members of Essene sects living in that town and other places south of Damascus have had a profound effect on a conscience-stricken Paul?

Such a theory in no way contradicts Paul's account and it would be in keeping with the emotional crisis which may very well have been touched off by the natural remorse of a sensitive personality. The second question of how far Paul's own beliefs and earlier training were involved can best be answered in the light of the succeeding events, described below.

PAUL THE CONVERT

One of Paul's first teachers of Jewish-Christian beliefs was Ananias:

> "So Ananias departed and entered the house. And laying his hands on him he said, 'Brother Saul, the Lord Jesus who appeared to you on the road by which you came, has sent me that you may regain your sight and be filled with the Holy Spirit.' And immediately something like scales fell from his eyes and he regained his sight. Then he rose and was baptized." (Acts 9: 17–18)

Paul retired for a short time to the hinterland of Syria and Transjordan for the familiar period of self-communion and preparation, then he returned to Damascus where he spent some three years. There, to the amazement of the Jews and proselytes, the erstwhile persecutor of the sectaries preached the new gospel. The governor of Damascus was a Nabatean, appointed by King Aretas IV and, as Paul's fame spread, he attempted to arrest him. Paul escaped with the help of his friends who, one night, let him down over the wall of the city in a large basket. In the opinion of most scholars today, this happened in 37–38 C.E. (not 33 as was thought according to an earlier chronology). Paul proceeded to Jerusalem where he became acquainted with the leading teachers and prophets of the sect:

> "And when he had come to Jerusalem he attempted to join the disciples; and they were all afraid of him, for they did not believe that he was a disciple. But Barnabas took him, and brought him to the apostles, and declared to them how on the road he had seen the Lord, who spoke to him, and how at Damascus he had preached boldly in the name of Jesus. So he went in and out among them at Jerusalem." (Acts 9: 26–28)

Barnabas was a "hellenist", a native of Cyprus and a Jew with strong Greek sympathies. He was less rigid in his opinions than Peter or James and more worldly-minded than his

XXXI–XXXII. Two types of Oriental women in the early Christian period (see end Ch. XIII). The 3rd century C.E. sculpture on the left shows a stylized beauty from Palmyra in Syria. The face of the Egyptian lady on the right suggests intelligence as well as charm (Fayoum, 2nd century C.E.)

XXXIII. These early Christian Oriental patricians were painted on the wall of a 2nd century C.E. tomb at Marwa in the Decapolis, east of Jordan (see end Ch. XIII)

XXXIV. The desolate canyon of Nahal Hever in the Judean Wilderness, last refuge of Bar-Kosba's partisans (see Ch. XIII). The southern end of the Dead Sea and the mountains of Edom can be seen in the background.

rabbinically trained Pharisee convert. Probably Barnabas was closer to the hellenist Philip, the liberal missionary-evangelist. The role of this group of hellenists in bridging the gap between the Palestinian Jewish-Christians and the gentiles has only recently come to be recognized. Barnabas stood midway between the theory and practice of the primitive Palestinian Church and the later, distinctive gospel of Paul.

Paul probably remained for some time in Jerusalem. From there he returned to his native city of Tarsus, where he remained for some nine or ten years. This period of Paul's life (38–48) remains very obscure. No doubt it was a time of preparation on his part. It seems that during the period he was influential in the founding of the churches in Cilicia, which included gentile members. Towards the end of the time, Barnabas brought him to Antioch to help in proselytizing there. This was a most important Jewish missionary center and one in which the Jewish Christian leaders in Jerusalem took a great interest.

CONFLICTING VIEWS ON PROSELYTIZING

During the years Paul spent in Cilicia, significant changes were taking place in the young movement in Palestine. On the question of proselytizing among the gentiles, two different views were slowly crystallizing. The traditional Jewish approach to non-Jews was to be polite but not to make any attempts to bring them closer. As a result, in Antioch and Asia Minor there were groups of gentile Godfearers at different stages of conversion to Judaism. This was the position which Paul found at the outset of his journeys and which faced the first hellenistic refugees from Jerusalem after the martyrdom of Stephen. Despite their efforts, and those of Barnabas to spread the new gospel, little progress was made in the face of a generally unfavourable attitude from Jerusalem.

There are factual reasons for this, of which evidence remains.

The church of Jerusalem was controlled by the family of Jesus, who were in the position of a royal family waiting for the return of the king, the "Son of David". They and the other disciples referred to as "pillars" had high office in the church and vied with one another for some kind of reflected or delegated authority. In fact they made it very difficult for a newcomer who had not "witnessed" the death of Jesus to gain any kind of authority in the church. "There was something of a struggle for power which attempted to keep Paul within bounds on the basis that he was not an apostle of Jesus during Jesus' lifetime." (J.B. Tyson) The controversies that arose within the Church over this issue are very revealing of the situation that existed there at the time. They confirm the view held by V. Tyler, S.G.F. Brandon and others that the Jerusalem church had no particular ambitions to embark upon a mission to the gentiles. "What does Messiahship mean to gentiles? Jesus is to be the new king of Judah and this will have an indirect bearing on the gentile world. Basically the messiahship of Jesus is meaningful only for the Jewish people. Therefore, there seems also to be no question in the Jerusalem church about the abandonment of long-established Jewish practices." (J. B. Tyson).

S.W. corner of the ancient wall of Damascus. Houses built on the remains of the Arab ramparts can still be seen, suggesting the house from which Paul was lowered in a basket to escape from the city when all the gates were being closely watched.

The Apostles in Jerusalem considered that Godfearers and gentile converts should come to the synagogue. They were proud of their religious heritage and had no intention of denying it. The Jewish-Christians demanded circumcision and obedience to the food laws of their proselytes. The question was not a new one. The great Pharisee Hillel had taken a fairly opportunist position with regard to proselytes (see Ch. VII) and Rabbi Joshua ben Hananiah thought that a proselyte who "performed the prescribed ablution, but had not been circumcized, behold he is a proper proselyte." Eliezer ben Hyrcanus and other sages thought differently. The old controversy continued undecided, the majority taking the view that Judaism was indivisible. If they wished to, proselytes could understand and adopt the traditional way of thinking of Judaism and become full Jews. If not, they could observe the more universal "seven rules of the Sons of Noah" (see p. 308) and stay on the fringe of Judaism. Eliezer ben Hyrcanus said that all gentiles would become "self-made proselytes in the time to come."

However, amongst the hellenistic Jews of the Diaspora, a feeling developed that regarded this proud detachment as out of keeping with the new zeal. Further, they believed that they knew their gentile neighbours better than the authorities in Jerusalem and could speak to them in more convincing terms.

It was against this background that the controversy developed between Antioch and Jerusalem at the time of Barnabas and Paul's apprenticeship. They saw the Pharisaic Jews preaching Judaism to the gentiles and bringing proselytes to their synagogues. Why should not the disciples of Jesus do likewise? It was at about this time that the Greek followers of Jesus, who had never known him, began to call him the "saviour" ('soter' in Greek). From this, the Antiochians called them by a new name: "Christians" because they called Jesus the Messiah, which in Greek is Christos. In Palestine, his adherents were still called Nasoreans. This term for Christians has been preserved in Hebrew (Notzrim) and Arabic (Nassarah) to this day.

THE CHURCH OF ANTIOCH

The Church of Antioch was a mixed group, in which both Jews and gentiles joined in worship and fellowship. They had their meals in common and it appears that they did not observe the laws of forbidden foods carefully. Peter was lenient in this matter but James, the strict Nazirite, could not reconcile himself to such practices. He sent emissaries to Antioch to demand that gentiles who believed in the Messiah should be circumcized and should pay strict attention to the ceremonial laws. Otherwise they must be separated from the Jews. Peter and Barnabas acquiesced, although they had worked in Antioch and had not insisted on these observances.

To Paul, it seemed that the very existence of the fellowship in Antioch and the whole of his work there was threatened. His gentile followers were not accustomed to observance of the Jewish ceremonial laws and could not face such a stringent requirement as circumcision at a mature age.

Can Gentiles be Christians?

The controversy came to a head over the churches of Galatia (Antioch in Galatia, Iconium, Lystra, Derbe) some of which Paul had founded during his early journeys. It forms the subject of Paul's Epistle to the Galatians. He was harrassed by the traditional Jews and challenged by the Palestine leaders of the church who found his teaching unorthodox and excessively liberal. Among the Palestinian Jewish-Christians, it was fundamental that the only true believers in Christ were those who had been Jews from the beginning. This in fact was in line with Jesus' own instructions:

> "These twelve Jesus sent out, charging them, 'Go nowhere among the Gentiles, and enter no town of the Samaritans, but go rather to the lost sheep of the house of Israel." (Matthew 10: 5–6)

But times had changed. The views of Paul and Mark were in line with historical development. While Paul was content to be a Jew to the Jews, he was absolutely opposed to the suggestion that a gentile must become a statutory Jew in order to be accepted as a true believer in Christ.

In order to maintain unity within the expanding church, Paul agreed to refer the issue to Jerusalem. He arrived there in the famine year 49 and submitted his missionary work to the judgment of the "chiefest apostles", James, Peter and John. He also undertook to enlist aid on his journeys from the brethren for the "saints in Jerusalem" who were in dire straits after the famine.

The "Apostolic council", even James, adopted a compromise agreement which made concessions in matters of circumcision and forbidden foods to the gentiles who had confessed Jesus as Messiah but did not extend it to the Nasorean Jews. James declared:

> "therefore my judgement is that we should not trouble those of the Gentiles who turn to God, but should write to them to abstain from the pollutions of idols and from unchastity and from that which is strangled and from blood. For from early generations Moses has had in every city those who preach him, for he is read every sabbath in the synagogues." (Acts 15: 19–21)

This left gentile believers free of the stricter traditional laws but bound to observe the "Seven commandments for the Descendants of Noah" (i.e. all mankind) which include abstinence from things offered to idols; from things strangled (instead of slaughtered kosher fasion), from murder and from adultery and the sexual licence common in pagan hellenistic society.

The agreement of Jerusalem provided much greater leeway in approaching the gentiles. Paul and Barnabas were sent back to Antioch with two "prophets", Judas and Silas, and with instructions restraining the "Judaizers" (probably the sectarian "Hebrews") from interfering with their mission. It was agreed that Paul was authorized to preach to the "sons of the uncircumcized".

This decree still made certain ceremonial demands on the gentiles and immediately after the Council, Paul began waiving even these. He also preached, of course, "to the sons of the circumcized" but had little success among them. In any case, the center of gravity in the church was shifting from Palestine to the diaspora so that any remaining limitations were becoming impossible. The agreement at Jerusalem had not answered the crucial question of the churches of the diaspora, nor settled which faction — Jewish or gentile — in mixed churches, was to have the say. Paul had solved the problem, implicitly, in the gentile-Christian sense. This event is the climax of the first part of Acts which presents it as an event of outstanding importance — as it was. It played an important part in determining the form which historical Christianity was to take.

PAUL'S TRAVELS

The detailed story of Paul's missionary journeys (see map of the Pauline world) need not be taken further. It is, perhaps, more useful to consider some of the perplexing problems posed by the radical change in Christian theology which marks the second stage of Paul's life and work. In any case "Paul did not initiate missionary work to the gentiles; even without him, Christianity would have extended around the Mediterranean; but he gave the religion of Jesus the form in which it was capable of conquering the world, without receiving damage to its own soul . . . no source depicts Paul as a missionary seeking to win unconverted Jews, or pure pagans. His letters were addressed to churches already in existence, and they assumed that the truths essential to Paul's theology were already known to those churches." (H. Lietzmann).

It is, therefore, valuable to consider the statements which indicate his peculiar teachings and beliefs and put them into historical perspective.

EMERGENCE OF THE NEW PAULINE THEOLOGY

The earliest members of the Church did not break at once with the Temple, nor did an inevitable break with Judaism follow automatically on the death of Jesus, or immediately after Paul is said to have denounced the Law. The new movement needed time to establish its proper form. This followed from its essential nature and the interaction of the factors involved, Jews and gentiles, the Jerusalem church and Paul's mission and doctrine.

The second part of Acts (Chs. 16–28) and the epistles of Paul deal with the progress of this interaction and with the resulting expansion of Christianity through western Asia and Southern Europe. The Epistles of Paul, however, have to be read with the conditions that caused them to be written well in mind. They were written at times of great religious agitation. Paul was defending his position against those whose opinion, equally passionately held, was different from his own. He states his case earnestly. Alongside his arguments are references which suggest the adaptation of his principles to the practical realities of the day. From it all, there emerges a picture of a complex personality, full of contradictions. It also becomes clear that the creation of a major religion, with a new theology and a new church, involved a great deal of mundane detail and many practical problems as well as sublime considerations of theology and ethics.

SON OF GOD — NOT SON OF DAVID

It is possible that to Paul and Mark, the Messiah was less a "Son of David" than a "Son of God". E. Lohmeyer suggests that basically the Jerusalem Church held the first view, and the Galilean church the second. Following Paul, Mark is also in the Galilean tradition. But he extends that tradition by glorifying this Messiah after his apparently degrading death by crucifixion. After that political defeat, it had become essential that Jesus should transcend the national limitations of a Messiah of David. It therefore became accepted doctrine that Jesus was not the Messiah who would "restore the kingdom to Israel" but was a spiritual Messiah only, the "servant of the Lord", the suffering messiah in the classic vision of Isaiah 53. This doctrine removed any suggestion of political rebellion from the disciples as much as from Jesus himself, and also made Jesus something much greater than a nationalistic Messiah to the Jews alone.

Whether consciously or unconsciously, Paul — a Jew of the Diaspora — ignored the nationalist, political side of messiahship and concentrated on the universal aspects common to apocalyptic Judaism. His main objective was to explain Jesus' "Sonship", rather than his physical life. He wanted to show him as the eternal and pre-existent instrument of divine revelation. On this basis, emphasis on his universal significance avoids both the hierarchical organization of the relatives and close friends of Jesus, and the numerous ceremonial laws to which their religious observances were subject.

There was a further consideration. Proclamation of a new faith in Jesus had met with little success among the Jews. In order to win gentiles to the faith, it was advisable not to demand more than the Pharisees required of Godfearers — devotion to a new faith, without ritual requirements.

Paul was the ideal spokesman for this more liberal approach. He was much more in tune with the diaspora way of thought and, later, with that of the gentiles. Probably, between the time of his first conversion in Palestine and the beginning of his mission some

Stage coaches like this carried travellers over the paved Roman roads used by Paul on his journeys through Syria and Asia Minor or Greece.

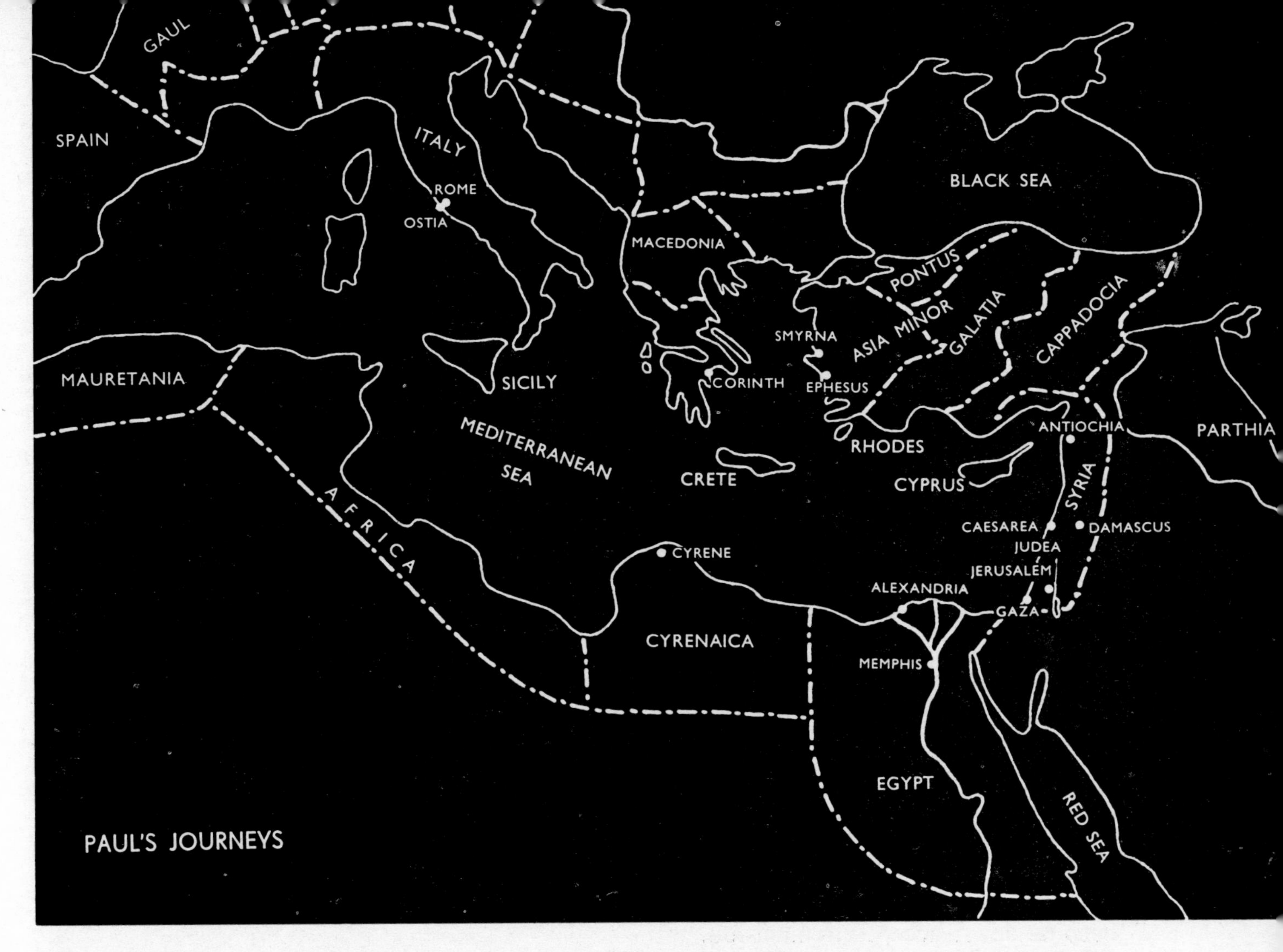

Paul's first missionary journey, made in 45 C.E. was to Cyprus and some cities in Cilicia, Asia Minor (identified as Pisidia and Lycaonia). The second journey took him again to Asia Minor, then to Philippi, Thessalonika and Corinth in Greece. On the third he went to Asia Minor, first to the existing churches in the south, then to the upper, inland areas. From there, he went to Ephesus (near the present-day Smyrna) where he spent a long time. His later work (up to 59 C.E.) was in the region of the Aegean Islands. During this time his headquarters were Ephesus in Asia Minor and Corinth in Greece.

Inscription on the white marble doorway of the "Synagogue of the Hebrews" at Corinth.

fifteen or more years later, many of the stricter principles of the sectaries became modified. Paul's trade made him a part of the prevailing economic system and it is not likely that ideas of the communal sharing of goods and life came easily to him.

Paul's Alternative Doctrine

The agreement of Jerusalem produced a momentary lull in the controversy but this did not last long.

It is a matter of sober fact that after 50 C.E. Paul faced the opposition not only of Jews who disbelieved in Jesus but also, because of his personal interpretation of Christ, the old guard of the Jerusalem church. They continued to insist on circumcision, the keeping of the Sabbath and feasts and avoidance of all non-kosher food. The whole of the Epistle to the Galatians and portions of the Epistles to the Romans, the Corinthians and the Colossians are devoted to these questions.

> "But even if we, or an angel from heaven, should preach to you a gospel contrary to that which we preached to you, let him be accursed. As we have said before, so now I say again, If any one is preaching a gospel contrary to that which you received, let him be accursed. " (Galatians 1: 8–9)

After fourteen or fifteen years of experience, some scholars hold, Paul had realized the difficulties that lay in the way of observance of the laws of Judaism outside Palestine. It was not practical to demand of slaves and hired workers that they observe the Sabbath and the feasts, or keep within the dietary laws. Many Diaspora Jews were unable to adhere strictly to the rigid laws of the Tannaitic rabbis. Nor could Godfearers, sincerely wishing to become Jews, accept circumcision.

Instead of the Law and the Torah — Faith

Paul found a formula that would cover most of these Jews and proselytes. So long as they believed in the spiritual tenets of Judaism they could be counted true Jews. Ritual laws covering all aspects of personal and community life had been sacred and necessary. But the "Messiah who had already come" nullified all this. Faith had now taken the place of the law.

> "Let it be known to you therefore, brethren, that through this man forgiveness of sins is proclaimed to you, and by him every one that believes is freed from everything from which you could not be freed by the law of Moses." (Acts 13: 38–39)

Other scholars have pointed out that Paul did not see the question as a practical one. He himself, like many others, was a strict diaspora Jew and he was not looking for a way of making things easy. He was concerned with an important point of theology and his letters are full of the argument.

Salvation had come to Israel not through obedience to the law, but through the promise given to Abraham. In the same way, this promise was now given to the gentiles. Obedience to the Law was not a condition of salvation, but its consequence. Now, the gentiles had been saved by the electing grace of God made plain in Jesus Christ, as the Jews had been saved earlier by descent from Abraham. Under the circumstances, there was no point in imposing the Law of the Jews on gentiles, who were saved not as Jews, but as gentiles. It was only necessary for them to be obedient to God who, through his spirit, would both reveal what they should do and give them the power to do so.

Using prophetic and Philonic terms (see Ch. VII, II) Paul proclaimed that circumcision of the heart had been substituted for circumcision of the flesh. The physical national Israel of the covenant made with Abraham, had been replaced by an Israel of the spirit, knowing no national boundaries.

A man, Paul declared, "is justified by faith apart from the works of the Law" and observance of the Torah. Mere obedience to the Law was no longer sufficient as a means to salvation and divine grace. The essential requirement was faith in Christ.

Christ, the spiritual son of God, was without sin. Yet he had suffered and been crucified. Because he was sinless his sufferings and his death were in atonement for the sins of mankind. Ever since Adam, the first man, had committed the first sin, mankind had died of the weight of their transgressions. But Jesus had been sacrificed to atone for them. As a sign of their salvation he had risen from the dead. Because he had been punished, although without sin, his sufferings and resurrection ensured redemption from mankind's heritage of sin, his "original sin", and from death alike.

Thus faith took the place of the Law. The Torah of Israel with all its multiple regulations was declared null and void.

To Paul, the Torah must be replaced by faith in the Messiah who had redeemed mankind from sin and death. By grace of this Messiah who had been crucified and had risen from the dead, all mankind had been made equal. Gentiles need feel no barrier to their approach to this faith and to the new religion. Since Jesus had been crucified to achieve this redemption of the whole world and of all humanity, it could henceforth be said:

> "There is neither Jew nor Greek, there is neither slave nor free, there is neither male nor female; for you are all one in Christ Jesus. And if you are Christ's then you are Abraham's offspring, heirs according to promise." (Galatians 3: 28–29)

By virtue of this redemption, on the Day of Judgment, when Jesus would appear "at the right hand of Power" to sit in judgment on the nations and the world, he will save those who believe in him. Because of him they shall be saved from death — and for this they had no need of the Torah.

The first Christians were waiting for this appearance — the "Parousia" of Jesus. Their slogan was "Marana-tha" — "Our Lord Come". It is not "Maran-atha" — "Our Lord has come", as has been mistakenly believed.

Nevertheless, although Paul minimized traditional Judaism, and substituted Christ for the Torah, L. Knox emphasizes that he expressed his arguments in "a form of thought with which the Jews were entirely familiar."

Paul's denunciation of Judaism and its traditional symbol, the Law, had little effect within Palestine and in centers of strong Jewish sentiment. Turning his back on the traditionalists among the Jews, he was driven to the hellenistic Jews and gentiles. This meant equal acceptance of the hellenistic and Roman view of life.

However, in his organizational work, Paul relied on the Jewish communities of the diaspora, with their closely-knit ties, spiritual basis and political semi-nationalist features. The new movement which Paul proclaimed was a Jewish movement. It appealed to the pagans by declaring that they could become disciples of a new anointed king of heaven, who had walked the earth in physical reality.

There was some justification for the Romans' suspicions of conspiratorial, political aims behind the Christian movement. In one sense they were indeed bent on world conquest. The distinction was that their kingdom was of the spirit alone.

CHRISTIANS PROTECTED BY THE JEWS' LEGAL SAFEGUARDS

Paul's aim of drawing gentiles as well as Jews into the Church, and considering them equal, was supported by the laws of the Roman empire. Ever since Julius Caesar, the Jews' right to practise their own religion had been recognized, and the Romans were tolerant of Jewish proselytizing. Adoption of Judaism was not a crime, neither was conversion to Christianity, provided it included Jews by birth and faith. Paul was claiming the same privilege for gentile converts. However, with the sole exception of the Jews, other Roman citizens throughout the Empire were required to fulfill public, imperial religious obligations. To refuse or neglect these observances publicly could be counted social atheism. However, if a gentile wished to embrace Judaism, in whole or in part, as a new Christian, Roman law allowed him to do so. On this basis, the Christians could and did enjoy the protection that was given to Judaism, even after the destruction of Jerusalem in 70 C.E.

Once the Christians became known as separate from the Jewish community among whom they worshipped, they lost this immunity. They were not declared illegal but became "unlicensed". This made them fearful of committing "atheism" in case they attracted the unfavourable attention of Roman officials. This predicament may have faced them when, in 64, Nero found it convenient to turn the fury of the mob against them after the fire of Rome.

NEW SACRAMENTS IN PLACE OF THE TORAH

Paul wanted "freedom in Christ". To him, the substance of religion was not the ceremonial regulations and restrictions. But apparently there were some to whom these were the heart of Judaism. In their place, Paul strengthened two ritual sacraments of the Jewish-Christian church although, as he says, he was simply transmitting what others had passed on to him.

The first, baptism, was the distinctive feature of their ritual (see Chs. VIII, IX) and had been immortalized by John the Baptist. When Paul was at Ephesus, he found an Alexandrian Jew, named Apollos, baptizing in the name of John.

> "He had been instructed in the way of the Lord; and being fervent in spirit, he spoke and taught accurately the things concerning Jesus, though he knew only the baptism of John." (Acts 18: 25)

After his "conversion" by friends of Paul's, Aquilla and Priscilla, Apollos played an important part in the Christian missionary work. Paul was three years in Ephesus, up to the year 60.

The significance of baptism was to develop from its original sectarian meaning (see Ch. VIII). But it is clear that Paul and his disciples came to regard their new form of baptism as a fundamental rite, as important and as holy as faith in Christ.

> "One Lord, one faith, one baptism." (Ephesians 4: 5)

The other sacrament was the ritual of the Eucharist (see Ch. VIII, II), even though Paul had nothing to do with its institution. Modern research has made much clearer the connection between the Eucharist and the communal meal of the sectaries. "It is certain however that the original structure of the Eucharist, the grace, blessing of the bread, then of the wine, are related to the Jewish 'berakhot' (blessings). It will be noted in Matthew and Mark that the two blessings precede the meal, as in the community of Qumran." (Jean Danielou, S. J.). The early church took over existing institutions and ordained their use in the Christian community.

By emphasizing the combination of Last Supper, Crucifixion and Resurrection, the early Christians — and later generations — overcame the problem originally posed by their founder's agonizing and humiliating death. In addition they kept alive the tradition of the concrete facts of the birth, death and resurrection of Jesus.

A MIXTURE OF JUDAISM AND HELLENISM

In many ways, Paul comes close to the thought of the "Wisdom of Solomon" (see Ch. VII, II). "The whole body of teaching in hellenistic Judaism, even what we know to have been derived from Greek philosophers, was somehow read into the words of Scripture. This basic trend manifests itself in various ways." (R.H. Pfeiffer). In the view of this eminent interpreter, Paul followed this trend by "joining confusedly traditional Jewish notions to echoes of Hellenistic thought. . . . "

Paul was able to place the historic personality of Jesus in a realm beyond time and space. To do this he used especially the Philonic Jewish-hellenistic doctrine of the logos (see Ch. VII, II). This enabled Paul to present his case in Greek philosophical terms, acceptable to his more sophisticated hellenistic audiences. They listened to him attentively. But that Christ had risen from the dead was more than they could swallow. The theory that the

Messiah had already come implied an unacceptable finality. The hellenistic theory of the "logos" applied to Christ in a formula expounded in the Epistle to the Colossians, removed the personality of the Messiah still further into the realm of timelessness.

Extravagant Apocalypticism

The change in approach within the church's missionary work from Jews to gentiles presented many problems to Paul. It is not surprising that his teachings aroused such resentment among the Jews, whether Christians or not, for he seemed to go out of his way to outrage their feelings in the way he spoke to the Graeco-Roman gentiles. He would, for instance, lay stress upon the "uncircumcision which is by nature". This was language that a hellenist understood, but it was anathema to the Jews. Altogether, his epistles to the gentiles seem to go to extremes in over-simplification of theological issues. When some of his converts in Thessalonia seemed to have lost faith in the "Coming" (Parousia) because of the long delay, he consoled them in language familiar from apocalyptic imagery:

> "For the Lord himself will descend from heaven with a cry of command, with the archangel's call, and with the sound of the trumpet of God. And the dead in Christ will rise first; then we who are alive, who are left, shall be caught up together with them in the clouds to meet the Lord in the air; and so we shall always be with the Lord." (1 Thessalonians 4: 16–17)

Jean Danielou connects this theme in Paul with old Jewish apocalyptic beliefs in the millenium (see Ch. III) when the Messiah would appear and all the saints be resurrected. Paul integrated these beliefs into his usual theme of the Parousia, the reign of Christ. "The Epistles to the Thessalonians indicate that this was the belief of the Christians in Greece as St. Paul emphasizes outstanding features, on the assumption that his correspondents were awaiting an earthly reign of Christ. This doctrine rests on a foundation that was later developed in the Johannine apocalypse. Its main tenet is that of an intermediate stage where the resurrected saints are still on earth and had not yet reached their final state. Nothing is said of the nature or duration of this stage. This is one of the aspects of the mystery of the End of Days." (Jean Danielou, S.J.).

THE PERSONALITY OF PAUL

It is clear that the practical organizer and leader of men was also by nature a visionary. He was totally incapable of resisting the mysticism of the time, either within Judaism or abroad. Many pagans with deep religious feelings could thus be drawn into Christianity. These were devout people who, when dissatisfied with their own religions turned to the mystery religions of the Egyptian Isis, the Asiatic Mithras and others. Paul's version of Christianity appealed in the same way as these pagan mystery cults.

Klausner believes that "there was in Paul a dualism amounting to polarity. On the one hand, he was a dreamer and ecstatic, seeing visions, 'speaking with tongues', given to mysticism; but, on the other hand, he was a man of action and a master of logic, an excellent leader and a talented agitator, a wonderful administrator and a diplomat who knew the time for everything. Naturally it was impossible for a man like this to live only for the dream of the Parousia. The practical man in him was aroused — one might almost say — the practical Jew in him . . . . . It must be said immediately that without adaptation and compromise Paul could not have succeeded as well as he actually did during his own lifetime . . . . Jesus was able to produce but a few disciples. Only complex personalities like Paul, in whom are combined delusion and rationality, mysticism and practicality, can create . . . . a church, that is to say a religion existing in the world of practical affairs." (J. Klausner)

THE DEATH OF JAMES AS "TRANSGRESSOR"

"By means of the exaggerated words of adoration which Paul applied to 'Christ Jesus', this Christ became more and more a supernatural figure, and after a little an actual son of God." (J. Klausner). This author believes that Paul finally swayed the Jewish-Christians away from their Jewish conservatism and to his side. This is the explanation he gives for the death of James, the brother of Jesus. He had spent a lifetime of devotion in the Temple and had never been molested. Then, suddenly, in 61 or 63, the High Priest Hanan brought him before the Sanhedrin as a "transgressor". He was martyred with other Jewish-Christians. At the time, another Rechabite (the biblical name for a Nazirite) tried to intervene and prevent the martyrdom. Josephus relates this fate sympathetically:

> "Festus was now dead, and Albinus was but upon the road; so he (Hanan) assembled the Sanhedrin of judges, and brought before them the brother of Jesus whose name was James, and some others, and when he had formed an accusation against them as breakers of the law, he delivered them to be stoned: but as for those who seemed the most equitable of the citizens, and such as were the most uneasy at the breach of the laws, they disliked what was done . . ." (Antiq. Bk. XX, 9: 1)

But in quoting him, Hegesippus, a patristic writer of the 2nd century, "re-wrote" him and by setting the remark in the wrong context, gave rise to the illusion that Josephus himself had blamed the subsequent fall of Jerusalem on this miscarriage of justice by the Sadducees. This became one of the clichés of patristic literature which was distinguished by a resurgent anti-Jewish spirit.

In fact there is no connection whatever between the persecution of James in Jerusalem in 62 and Nero's persecution of the Christians in Rome two years later. In his account of Nero's brutality, Tacitus reveals a strong anti-Christian bias, which was not shared by the Jews of Rome. There have been attempts—the most recent by P. Carrington, to prove that the persecutions in Rome were connected with the Jewish repudiation of the new Christians. However this reflects an attitude which developed among the patristic writers half a century later. The sober fact is that at the time (62–64 C.E.) the Jews of Rome actually showed a complete indifference to Paul and his journey to Rome or his disputes with the Jews of Jerusalem. This is demonstrated by the verses which come nearly at the end of Acts:

"And they said to him, 'We have received no letters from Judea about you, and none of the brethren coming here has reported or spoken any evil about you. But we desire to hear from you what your views are; for with regard to this sect we know that everywhere it is spoken against.' " (Acts 28: 21–22)

However, the separation of Christianity from Judaism was coming closer in the west. In its later phase of expansion, the church had developed a mixed membership in place of its earlier exclusively Jewish character. This half-Christian, half-Jewish organization had spread throughout Syria, Asia Minor, Macedonia, Achaia and Crete and had established itself in Italy. Rome had become an important center, on a par with Jerusalem, Antioch, Ephesus and Corinth.

THE CHURCH IN ROME AT THE END OF THE FIRST CENTURY

H. Lietzmann and other scholars have called attention to the Jewish-style formula that the Roman Christians used in public worship at the end of the first century. "This church was not born of the Pauline tradition, but had only a remote and outer contact with it. It grew directly out of the Greek-speaking synagogue, and represented a conception of Christianity such as we must assume was held in those circles of proselytes who were converted by the Christian preachers from Antioch . . . . its religion was that of the Hellenistic proselytes, who, on their Jewish side had adopted the specific ethic of Judaism, while spiritualizing its ritual by allegory" (see Ch. VII, II). "This conception did not hinder them in Antioch or in Rome in taking over cult-forms and liturgical prayers from the synagogue." (H. Lietzmann).

Emperor Claudius. During his reign, Peter seems to have come to Rome.

Emperor Nero (54–68 C.E.) who persecuted the Christians.

Paul's Last Years in Rome

On his last visit to Palestine in 61, after his third great journey, Paul was arrested. He was travelling with a Greek gentile from Ephesus and took him into the Temple. This was an act of defilement which, according to Jewish law, might be punished by death. This was announced by a Greek inscription on the gate of the Temple, which has survived.

Paul had visited the Temple to fulfill a Nazirite vow as a demonstration of his continued reverence of Jewish law. However, among the pilgrims and people of Jerusalem were many enemies. They started a riot which brought Roman guards hotfoot from the Antonia Tower (see Ch. X). They arrested Paul and as they hurried him back into custody, keeping the crowd back from him, he turned and addressed the people from the steps leading to the Tower.

Paul was kept in custody in Caesarea for two years. Then, having appealed to the Procurator Festus, he was granted the right of all Roman citizens to be heard by Caesar. In Rome it is possible that he was freed by Nero in 62 and immediately set out on a fourth journey. This may be a legend. But if he had been released that time, it is certain that he was again arrested in Asia Minor and sent to Rome during the time of Nero's persecution of the Christians. There, in 67 C.E. while the whole of Palestine was in armed rebellion against Rome, he was beheaded by a sword and buried at a place three miles out, on the road to Ostia.

Recent excavations in Ostia, which acted as the sea-port for Rome, have proved that a Jewish community existed there from as long ago as the first or second century B.C.E.

The size and workmanship of a synagogue discovered there suggests that the colony was a large and prosperous one. The synagogue's major decoration was a bas-relief on marble representing the golden seven-branched candelabrum of the Temple of Solomon.

WHERE WAS PETER BURIED?

After his arrest in Jerusalem in 44, Peter apparently went to Rome to preach the gospel. According to Suetonius, the emperor Claudius expelled all — or many — of the Jews from Rome in 49, after rioting in their quarter caused by an "impulsore Chresto", apparently a propaganda drive for Christ. The Jewish community was soon restored. The Christian movement must by then have included a number of pagan converts.

A gentile Christian church had been founded in Rome, not by Paul, but possibly by men connected with the church at Antioch. H. Lietzmann believes Peter was instrumental in this progress and that from Corinth "quite probably, he had gone thence to Rome and had persuaded the church to the way he preferred," that is, in opposition to Paul's influence. Historians disagree on the time and weight of Peter's Roman mission and whether he returned to Rome in 64. There seems to be a larger degree of agreement on a date in 67 C.E. for his death during Nero's persecution. He was crucified and buried on a hillside at the place where the Vatican was later built. A story dating from the end of the second century runs that his grave was a humble ditch roofed with brick tiles. The whole area had earlier been covered by a royal park or a pagan cemetery. In the second century, a Roman priest, Gaius, claimed that a "trophy" or tombstone had been discovered which identified the tomb for the worship of the faithful. But on this point complete certainty seems to elude us.

In the third century, Constantine's architects enclosed the trophy in a marble casing and, later on, the whole area, including the surrounding pagan cemetery, was covered by a basilica to the memory of St. Peter. In 1939, the ancient tombs were dug up and provided a fruitful subject for discussion.

The debate may be summed up in the words of O. Cullman: "The archaeological investigations do not permit us to answer in either a negative or an affirmative way the question as to the stay of Peter in Rome. The grave of Peter cannot be identified. The real proofs for the martyrdom of Peter in Rome must still be derived from the indirect literary witnesses, and from them we have reached the conclusion that probably Peter actually was in Rome and suffered martyrdom under Nero. The excavations speak in favour of the report that the execution of Peter took place in the Vatican district."

The realistic bas-reliefs of the triumphal Arch of Titus are of the greatest interest for the history of the siege and fall of Jerusalem. Laurel-crowned Romans are shown carrying the seven-branched candlestick, made of pure gold; the silver trumpets and the golden table of the shewbread (see p. 334).

D. THE GREAT WAR AND ITS AFTERMATH

XII

BREAKDOWN AND RECONSTRUCTION

THE LAST PROCURATORS

The list of the seven Roman officials who governed Judea after 44 C.E. would be of no greater importance to us than similar lists in other provinces, did it not contain the names of Procurators whose deeds precipitated the course of events (just as Pontius Pilate stands out in the list of seven previous officials from 6–41 C.E., before the reign of the last Jewish king, Agrippa I; see Ch. XI).

Left: Coin of Nero's reign, the time of the last Procurators, Felix to Florus (58–59 *C.E.*), *Right: Contemporary coin inscribed with palm branch.*

The disturbances which had accompanied the life of Jesus continued except for a short interval of tranquillity during the three years of Agrippa's reign. However, after his sudden death, the Emperor Claudius again made the greater part of Judea a Roman province, ruled from Caesarea by a Procurator. A series of appointments to this position followed, some of them most unfortunate. The list runs:

Cuspius Fadus (44–46)
Tiberius Alexander (46–48)
Ventidius Cumanus (48–52)
Antonius Felix (52–60)
Porcius Festus (60–62)
Albinus (62–64)
Gessius Florus (64–66)

The first two Procurators (44–48) knew how to handle the Jewish community and their mandate was a relatively peaceful one, except for continual incidents involving the Zealots. These were a mixed band, some of them, like Ptolemy and his followers, little more than the "brigands" the authorities thought them all. Leaders like Theudas were true patriots, carrying a messianic message to the people — the *"amme-haaretz"*, who acclaimed all alike. Theudas was a messianic miracle-worker, who promised to part the Jordan at the head of his followers and to cross it on dry land. Instead, his followers were easily dispersed by Roman troops and the false messiah's head brought to Jerusalem.

Fadus, as Procurator, also faced trouble over the old question of who should have custody of the High Priest's holy vestment. This was assumed to be a responsibility of the government, but when a delegation from the Jews appealed to the emperor in Rome, it was laid down that its guardianship was a matter for the priesthood.

There was continued Zealot activity while Tiberius Alexander was Procurator (46–48) and he had the sons of Judas the Galilean, the great Zealot leader, crucified. During his rule the famine occurred which is mentioned in Acts (11 : 27–30). Some relief was brought by Queen Helen, of Adiabene in Mesopotamia, who had been baptized and converted to Judaism. She purchased grain in Egypt and dried figs in Cyprus and came to Jerusalem to distribute them among the people (see p. 166).

A Deteriorating Situation

With the appointment of Ventidius Cumanus, the situation began to deteriorate. Serious riots occurred, largely the result of the brutality of Roman legionnaries on police duty. Then the Samaritans set upon a band of Galilean pilgrims crossing Samaria on their way to Jerusalem. The pilgrims were murdered and the resulting inter-racial riots were quelled by Cumanus at the expense of the Jews. However, when the news reached Rome, Cumanus was deposed and the Samaritans brutally punished.

One of the delegation sent to Rome to explain the cause of the riots was Jonathan, a son of the High Priest Ananias. Later on, after Jonathan became High Priest, he requested the Emperor Claudius to appoint as the next Procurator, one of his favourites, a freedman named Antonius Felix. His rule was capricious and tyrannical and, coupled with a worsening economic situation, widespread discontent favoured a very serious increase in Zealot partisan activity. This included an extreme terrorist group of *sicarii*, distinguished by the short daggers which they wore hidden under their cloaks and then used to spread death through the land. The Zealots were active against the authorities, the rich and the high Sadducean priesthood. Felix harrassed the people and their priests, even hiring sicarii to terrorise and remove enemies. He even connived at the murder of the High Priest, Jonathan, who was stabbed to death in the Temple. A new messianic movement, half-religious, half-political, gained wide support as yet another false messiah, who came from Egypt, gathered disciples and threatened the Temple.

AGRIPPA II

Felix ruled for eight years (until 60) but in 57, the young Herodian prince, Agrippa II, achieved his political ambition and became "king" of the north-eastern districts of Palestine which his father had governed before him. He was even granted the right to oversee affairs at the Temple and to appoint the High Priest. Because of powerful support in Rome he was able to outlast the Great War, during which he co-operated with the Romans, even helping to subdue Galilee.

In the summer of 60, Porcius Festus succeeded Felix as Procurator. He was welcomed at Caesarea by Agrippa and his sister Berenice, the thrice-married beauty. The ancient sources (Josephus, Juvenal) are careful to record the gossip about her alleged incest with her brother. Nor were they kind to her beautiful sister, Drusilla, whose last husband was Antonius Felix. When Festus came to Caesarea, Paul was imprisoned there awaiting trial (Acts 25). The presence of Agrippa, a Jewish prince familiar with Jewish beliefs and customs, seemed to Festus a good opportunity to get to the bottom of the disputes surrounding his prisoner. At a solemn session of the tribunal, with Agrippa and Berenice present, Paul delivered a spirited defence of himself which, according to Acts, made a favourable impression.

The strain and increasing tensions of a life becoming ever more difficult, moved the gentile inhabitants of Caesarea to turn against the Jews, refusing them equal civic rights in their own city. Caesarea, they claimed, had formerly been a Greek "polis", even if it had been founded by Herod, and Jews could not claim equality. Caught between two fires in the riots that followed, Antonius Felix referred his troubles to Rome and was recalled by Nero. In his place, came the honest and conciliating magistrate, Porcius Festus. He made real attempts at pacification which were interrupted by his death two years later. This was a real misfortune for Palestine.

THE PLUNDERING PROCURATORS

It left the country at the mercy of two Procurators, one more disastrous than the other. Josephus describes the one who came next — Albinus — as a man who plundered everybody. He even turned the growing insurgent activity to advantage. Totally corrupt, he would empty the prisons of partisans caught by his police and sell their freedom for a high price. The "sicarii" were able to liberate their friends by mulcting peaceful people for funds to pay ransoms to Albinus. Such behaviour in the governor was a pattern for the rest of society. Even the High Priest exacted forced payments from the peasantry and the brothers of Agrippa II became highway robbers. In the streets of Jerusalem pitched battles were fought between two contending priests and their followers. It was apparently at this time that the Sadducees and the High Priest took justice into their own hands and martyred James the brother of Jesus and his followers (see Ch. XI).

However, compared with the misdeeds of his successor, Gessius Florus (64–66 C.E.), Albinus seemed a benefactor. Florus made no attempt to check the mounting disorder and instead he became involved in lawless acts of every sort, shamelessly enriching himself at the expense of the people. Finally, with the whole of government and social organization at breaking point, Florus realised that he must expect to be dismissed and called to account. While he was looking around for an excuse to cover up his own tyranny and mismanagement, Nero played into the governor's hands by finally announcing his decision concerning the Jews' civil rights in Caesarea. The decision was that the Jews had no case and no claim to any legal status or protection. Fearing attack, they fled to shelter outside the city. At the same time, Florus seized the Temple treasure. It was the last straw.

Years of oppression and Zealot propaganda had worked on the people of Jerusalem to bring them to the state of the early Maccabees who had faced the whole might of Antiochus.

THE REBELLION BREAKS OUT

"... the soldiers did not only plunder the place they were sent to, but forcing themselves into every house, they slew its inhabitants; so the citizens fled along the narrow lanes, and the soldiers slew those that they caught, and no method of plunder was omitted; they also caught many of the quiet people, and brought them before Florus, whom he first chastised with stripes, and then crucified. Accordingly, the whole number of those that were destroyed that day, with their wives and children (for they did not spare even the infants themselves) was about three thousand and six hundred." (Josephus; War of the Jews, Bk. II, 14, 9)

With the situation slipping entirely out of his hands, and the extremists in control of the masses, Florus made ineffectual attempts at reprisals. Ignoring the appeals of Agrippa II, Berenice, the High Priest and other notables to restrain his troops, Florus sent soldiers into the upper quarters of Jerusalem to terrorise and pillage.

Fresh Roman troops were brought into the city in a hopeless effort to regain control, but the crowd attacked them, the revolutionaries in the lead, even keeping the soldiers from reaching their garrison in the Antonia Tower. Agrippa called his people together and tried to persuade them to submit to Rome, on the promise that Florus would be replaced. It was no good. The king was sent packing out of Jerusalem and the two factions within the town began their preparations.

At the head of the revolutionaries and the majority of the people was the Zealot leader, Eleazar ben Hananiah, son of a former high priest. He and his Zealots took possession of the Temple area and surrounding streets in eastern Jerusalem, while the High Priest and his party controlled the higher part of the city west of the Temple area. This was where the palace and fortress of Herod stood.

Eleazar and his party were eager to fight. As a proclamation of defiance, tantamount to a declaration of war, he announced that the daily Temple sacrifice in honour of Caesar which had been the symbol of Rome's sovereignty, would be discontinued. The remaining Roman soldiers in Jerusalem were massacred, the High Priest assassinated and the Herodian Palaces burned.

The rebellion was the signal for a wave of violence throughout the eastern world. In towns of mixed population, inter-racial riots and pitched battles between Jews and gentiles followed. According to Josephus, 20,000 Jews were massacred in Caesarea, 10,000 in Damascus and 50,000 in Alexandria. The Jews retaliated by occupying the gentile towns of the Decapolis, as well as Ptolemais, Anthedon, Gaza and Samaria.

With the breakdown of local Roman rule, the governor of Syria, Cestius Gallus, marched into Palestine in the fall of 66 C.E. with an army of 30,000. After trying without success to restore order in Galilee, he laid siege to Jerusalem. The insurgents put up a fierce defence and Gallus prepared to retreat to Caesarea. At Beth-horon, his army was encircled, defeated and routed. One of the Roman eagles was captured. Gallus himself abandoned his troops and their equipment and fled to Antioch.

Coins of the Jewish War: From left to right: Libation chalice with archaic Hebrew inscription "Shekel of Israel, Second Year"; Second: reverse, showing a spray of three pomegranates, inscribed "Jerusalem the Holy"; Third: Vine leaf inscribed "Deliverance of Zion"; Fourth, reverse, chalice, inscribed "Year Two."

This victory intoxicated the insurgents, but there could be no more fighting until the spring. Before then, they must make their plans to be ready for all eventualities.

This time, the Sadduceans and the priests were determined not to let the revolutionaries get full control of the people. They intended to keep matters in their own hands. A great assembly of all the people, rebels and aristocracy included, was called at the Temple. In the face of open war with the Roman Empire, national unity was essential. The assembly elected governors of the various districts, to be in charge of military operations. The defence of Jerusalem was entrusted to Joseph-ben-Gorion and the ex-High Priest Hanan. Idumea was placed under Joshua ben Zaffa and the Zealot, Eleazar ben Hananiah. Galilee was put in the hands of Joseph ben Mattathias, also scion of a priestly family. This is the future historian who, under the name of Flavius Josephus and writing in Greek, was to record the struggle in his books, "Antiquities of the Jews" and "The War of the Jews". He found himself in a most difficult position. He had to fortify the main towns of the district which must expect to bear the brunt of the first enemy assault and prepare to hold them with troops, brave enough, but totally untrained. He relates in detail how he raised an army of tens of thousands (he says 100,000 — certainly an exaggeration) and proceeded with defence works. He had opponents on his own side in Galilee. Johanan of Gischala (Gush-Halab) and Justus of Tiberias maintained that he was not sufficiently whole-hearted about the program. These Zealot chiefs in Galilee and Simon bar Giora in Judea kept up a continual campaign of terror and it became apparent that they were aiming at leading a holy war against both Rome and their own people.

Meantime the defences of Jerusalem had been strengthened and all possible preparations seemed to have been made for the spring of 67, when the Roman counter-attack was expected.

THE INTERNATIONAL SCENE

At this fateful moment, the international position of the Jews was in fact by no means promising. We learn from Josephus however, that the Palestinian Jews thought otherwise. They believed that conditions in the Empire would favour their fight for independence:

> "Now at the time when this great concussion of affairs happened, the affairs of the Romans themselves were in great disorder. Those Jews also who were for innovations, then arose when the times were disturbed; they were also in a flourishing condition for strength and riches, insomuch that the affairs of the east were then exceedingly tumultuous, while some hoped for gain, and others were afraid of loss in such troubles; for the Jews hoped that all of their nation which were beyond Euphrates would have raised an insurrection together with them." (War of the Jews, Preface, 2)

This suggests that the Jews expected only those co-religionists who lived in the non-Roman diaspora to side with them. In the hellenistic (Roman) Diaspora, many reasons would prevent Jews from co-operating with a "rebel" Palestine: Roman policy towards Jews was not the same throughout the Empire. Palestine proper, Rome regarded as a restless, disaffected province which needed watching closely. Consequently within the country it favoured the gentile minorities in the Decapolis and other towns, which had always been its allies (see Ch. VI), against the Jewish majority. Nowhere was the old maxim of "divide and rule" more applicable as a means of dominating a country than in Palestine. However, outside Palestine, Roman policy towards the Jews was almost reversed. Ever since Julius Caesar, the Jews of Egypt, Syria and Asia-Minor had enjoyed tacit Roman protection against local Jew-baiting. Though they might be emotionally stirred by their brethren's attempt at independence, they were too well aware of the political and military might of Rome to have any hopes of success for a rebellion in Judea.

Outside Palestine, it would have been hard to find a single optimist who would not agree that this rash action was going to be crushed swiftly and ruthlessly. It was one thing to send a tithe for the central sanctuary in Jerusalem, or to participate in a pilgrimage to that holy place. It was a very different matter to talk of open rebellion against Rome — the very protection for the Jews of the Empire against the animosity of other gentiles. To flout it would result in a serious threat to their own safety. So much was this the case that not even the moderates in Palestine expected their help.

However, in the non-Roman Diaspora, the Jews could join the struggle only if permitted to do so by their rulers. Such permission was unlikely to be forthcoming. When the Great War broke out in 66, none of the Jews' potential allies were prepared. Parthia, Rome's greatest enemy, who might have been counted on for help, instead adhered to the peace treaty concluded with Rome two years previously. The king even congratulated Titus on his victory. It seems that the Jews of Palestine embarked upon decisive military action against Rome with divided counsels. Matters had gone so far that moderation was outweighed.

There were a few upheavals set off by Palestinian refugees in Egypt and Cyrenaica in North Africa, but they occurred after the rebellion in Palestine had been cruelly suppressed. It has also been suggested that the Palestinian Jews had made a plan with the merchants of Jaffa to organise a blockade of the sea routes that carried food to Rome. If this is so, the plan miscarried and Jaffa was destroyed by Vespasian.

Bust of Emperor Vespasian, acclaimed emperor by his legions in 69 C.E., while the Judean war was in progress.

I. THE GREAT WAR

The revolt in Jerusalem came at a crucial moment in Roman history. Nero was just then working on grandiose plans for world conquest. When news came that the Roman legions had been defeated in Palestine, Nero sent one of his most distinguished generals, Titus Flavius Vespasianus, to avenge them. A brilliant tactician, Vespasian was a man of considerable experience. He had taken part in the subjugation of Britain in the time of Claudius, and he knew that the Jewish people faced him divided among themselves — however united they might seem at first.

Vespasian arrived in Antioch in the winter of 66 and began to gather his army. To the locally available Roman forces, he added contingents supplied by Rome's allies and even sent his son, Titus, to Alexandria to bring the XVth legion Appollinaris. When the whole army finally assembled at Ptolemais (Acre) in the spring of 67 it was 60,000 strong and led by Rome's ablest military commander.

War in Galilee

The campaign opened with a reverse for the Jews in Galilee. The inhabitants of Zeppori, an important town, frightened by the Roman advance, and ready to negotiate a truce, capitulated and begged for an occupying garrison to protect them from Zealot reprisals. The Jewish troops disbanded, other Jews fled to the fortified towns, while Josephus took refuge in Tiberias. From there he sent news of developments to Jerusalem and then entrenched himself in the fortress of Jotapata, which was surrounded by deep ravines on three sides. Vespasian occupied and burned the open towns to the south, then laid siege to Jotapata. Inside the fortress Josephus led a fierce defence for forty-seven days. Even though the Romans brought up siege engines, they could not break through. This raised morale in other towns and villages which were inspired to heroic resistance. The village of Yaffa, near Nazareth, fought back against the Xth Legion, commanded by Trajan. When it fell,

The village of Eilabun in Galilee lies to the east of the hills of Jotapata, which Josephus defended at the beginning of the Revolt.

5,000 people had been killed and 2,000 more were sold into slavery. In Shechem the Samaritans rebelled and 11,000 died in their defeat.

Finally, in July, exhaustion and treason defeated Jotapata. Let secretly into the town by a traitor, the Romans massacred the inhabitants and 40,000 died. Thousands of the insurgents threw themselves from the city walls rather than surrender. Josephus hid in a cistern with some companions. They finally stabbed themselves to death but Josephus, who had intended to kill himself with his friends, lost his nerve at the last moment and surrendered. Vespasian, perhaps sensing his moderate opinions, kept him at his headquarters. Josephus claimed that he had prophetic insight and opportunely foretold that Vespasian and his son Titus would rise to rule over the Roman Empire.

Tiberias surrendered. Other Galilean towns which came within the domain of Agrippa II were besieged and captured. In subduing the district, the Romans had the full cooperation of Agrippa. Several thousand people were summarily drafted for penal labour groups in Greece and another 30,000 sold into slavery. In October, Gischala, the last Galilean stronghold, fell and the campaign in Galilee was over. Vespasian sent his troops to winter quarters to rest, the Vth and XVth legions in Caesarea and the Xth in Beth-shean (Scythopolis).

Did the Essenes Fight?

It was at about this time that the settlement of the Essenes in Qumran was destroyed and, later on, used as a Roman outpost. It seems likely that at least some of the sectaries there put up resistance. The war against Rome may have seemed to them like the beginning of the final Holy War they had so long expected. "Certainly in other circles of Judaism, apocalyptic fanaticism activated the suicidal revolt," (F. M. Cross). Josephus underlines Roman persecution and torture of the Essenes committed during the revolt and records that a certain John the Essene was appointed general of Jewish forces in north-west Judea in the early stages of the war.

The War in Perea and Judea

With the collapse of Jewish resistance in Galilee, Johanan of Gischala fled to Jerusalem. Once there, he began rallying support and undermining the authority of the Sanhedrin and Sadducee leaders. He even roused the people of the town to attack them in their stronghold of the walled Temple esplanade. The Zealots had strong backing in southern Palestine and, with the help of 20,000 friendly Edomites from the Negev, they established informal rule throughout the countryside, terrorising the towns and setting up revolutionary tribunals that sent aristocratic leaders to their deaths. Any influence the moderates may have had was ended.

It seems that around 68 the peaceful group of Jewish-Christians left Jerusalem and migrated to Pella, east of the Lake of Galilee.

The inscription reads "Quarter silver shekel" with three palms or sheaves. Reverse: right, has the letter "daleth" (69–70 *C.E.*) *encircled with laurels and palms.*

In the early spring of that year (68) Vespasian set out on his campaign to reduce Judea. Striking south from Caesarea he first cut it off from the sea by occupying the coastal towns. Then he led his troops through Shechem to Jericho in the Jordan valley. At the same time, a detachment under Trajan had captured Perea, thus cutting Judea off from Transjordan. Most of the population fled before the invader, leaving Vespasian at least nominally in control of the wide circle of countryside around the capital, from Samaria in the north, through Hebron to the Negev in the south. However, just as he prepared to begin the assault on Jerusalem, the campaign was interrupted by the news of the death of Nero.

In Italy, rival factions and pretenders jostled around the empty throne. Vespasian, more wisely, stood apart and waited. Finally in July 69 he triumphed. Proclaimed emperor by the legions in Egypt, Palestine and Syria, he took ship for Italy, leaving his son Titus in command of the Palestine campaign.

SIMON-BAR-GIORA

However the respite brought no advantage to the Jews. Internal dissensions meant that the moment the fighting against the Romans stopped, civil war flared up among three rival factions within Judea.

The Romans were only technically in control of the country. Although Roman legions policed the area and occupied the main towns, the army preferred to spend most of its time in its own comfortable camps and life for the people of the countryside continued unaltered. Within Jerusalem, Johanan of Gischala's reign of terror had lost the support of much of the population and when a new, daring zealot leader, Simon-bar-Giora appeared, the people of the countryside and the capital together turned to him as their deliverer. Simon had trained an army of several thousand in preparation for the assault on Jerusalem. He aimed at freeing it from Johanan of Gischala, then leading the defence of the city against the Romans. His first attack gained him control of the upper city and drove the Zealots under Johanan back to the area around the approaches to the Temple. Within the inner stronghold of the Temple, however, a third faction led by Eleazar ben-Shimon had been fighting a savage struggle against Johanan and his followers, continuing the Temple ritual uninterrupted, even while soldiers fell dead around them. Between the three zones ferocious civil war continued.

Above: Reconstruction of siege engine with battering ram and bridgeheads for scaling walls. The huts on the right protected the besiegers from attack from above as they approached the walls. Below: Reconstruction of a ballistic engine described by Josephus, shown in position for firing darts.

Meanwhile, during the winter of 69–70, Titus had been reorganising his army, adding another legion and enrolling auxiliary troops. Finally, in March 70, a huge army, including 4 Roman legions, was split into a number of columns, all converging on Jerusalem. At the same time Passover pilgrims in their thousands streamed unmolested to the Holy City. Titus appeared before the walls of Jerusalem on the eve of the holiday and established his headquarters on Mt. Scopus, to the northeast of the town. His army encamped before the Third Wall which Agrippa I had built only a few years earlier.

Titus brought up his siege train and began to batter the walls and towers of the north-western defences with his catapaults. We have Josephus' description:

> "The engines, that all the legions had ready prepared for them, were admirably contrived; but still more extraordinary ones belonged to the tenth legion: those that threw darts and those that threw stones, were more forcible and larger than the rest, by which they not only repelled the excursions of the Jews, but drove those away that were upon the walls also. Now, the stones that were cast were of the weight of a talent, and were carried two furlongs and farther" (Wars. Bk. V, 6 3.)

With the beginning of the Roman assault early in May, the rival parties inside Jerusalem agreed to pool their forces for a united defence. Simon and his followers manned the north-western section of the ramparts and Johanan controlled the eastern, near the Temple walls. A series of Roman assaults, and Jewish counter-assaults followed. After fifteen days of grim and bloody fighting, the Romans breached the third Wall of Jerusalem and entered Bethesda, the lower northern quarter (see diagram p. 275).

From this point, the desperate battle was continued over each line of fortifications. As the second wall was attacked, the city's population, swollen as it was with the mob of holiday pilgrims, retreated further within the walls of the lower and then the higher city, protected by the Towers of Antonia and the Forts of Herod. At the foot of the towers, Titus had four "aggeres" or earthworks built for his great siege engines. Through Josephus, he offered the defenders a truce but, suffering though they were from famine and sickness, the insurgents rejected every peaceful move. Crowded within their dwindling stronghold they held on. This was partly out of fear of their tyrannical leaders but, mainly, from a passionate determination never to surrender. Titus then blockaded the city by sealing it within a stone wall, some 7,200 metres long, reinforced with bastions. There was no longer the slightest chance of getting food into the city. Sorties against the Romans were blocked and any deserter who attempted to escape was caught by the Romans, and mutilated or crucified in sight of the town. Ravaged by famine, strange and inhuman crimes were committed by some of the besieged.

THE DESTRUCTION OF THE TEMPLE

Finally, after over a month of increasing privation, Titus built bastions facing the Antonia Tower and led the final assault against the town. A savage defence was led with the utmost tenacity and ingenuity by Johanan of Gischala, but it was hopeless. On a day in

Titus who succeeded his father Vespasian as emperor.

July 70 C.E., the Antonia Tower was taken and totally destroyed. On the same day, says Josephus, the daily sacrifice in the Temple ceased. For the final battle for Jerusalem was fought around the precincts of the Temple itself. The remaining insurgents had taken refuge there and withstood the last dark week of the siege with the Romans battering — literally — at the inner Temple Gate. After it all, the Gate still stood unshaken. The Romans could force their way through only by setting fire to it and, although — as Josephus claims — Titus tried to avoid that final calamity, the fire spread to the Temple, the flames fanned by extra firebrands thrown by the Roman soldiers in defiance of their commander's orders. Finally, on the 10th of the month of Ab (August, 70), after fierce fighting, the Temple of Herod crumbled in flames. Titus was acclaimed Imperator, (or Victor), in the smouldering courts and the Romans placed their eagles before the Eastern gate and offered sacrifices to them (see p. 193).

Josephus insists that Titus intended to spare the Temple, but G. Allon has denied this attempt at a defence of Titus. Some historians, following Josephus, believe that the destruction of the Temple shows that at the decisive moment Titus lost control of his troops.

However, it must be remembered that Jewish resistance had aroused strong feelings among the Romans who, from experience since the days of Pompey, realised that the Temple was the symbol for all Jewish exclusiveness and intransigence. It was not only the sanctuary to which every male Jew made regular pilgrimage but, above all, a symbol of national unity and strength. Its destruction ought therefore, in Roman eyes, to mean the collapse of the nation's resistance. Some such reasoning may explain the brutality the Romans showed the gallant defenders of Jerusalem. Titus ordered the rebels to surrender and be spared. When they refused, he ordered the whole town burned. Then he pursued Johanan and his Zealots who had fled to the upper town and besieged the towers in which they had taken refuge. For another week they fought on, refusing a surrender that would not guarantee them liberty. Then the end came. After five months of bitter siege and fighting, Jerusalem lay a city of charred ruins and, on the 8th September 70 with the Romans in full control Titus celebrated his victory. Simon and Johanan had gone into hiding underground. When they were finally taken prisoner, they were not executed. Titus kept them for his triumphal procession in Rome the next year.

Detail from the Arch of Titus (see p. 321) erected by a proud Rome to commemorate the successful war against the Jews. The arch stands near the Colosseum which Titus completed in 80 C.E. These two monuments, the Colosseum and the Arch, combine the most famous symbol of Roman majesty with the tragedy of a defeated enemy.

Right: Coin issued by Vespasian to commemorate his victory, showing a Jew and Jewess mourning under a palm tree and inscribed "Judea Capta". Left: Processional chariot; below the letters S.C. short for Senatus Consultor.

TRAGIC SEQUEL

The loss of life through the siege and the fighting was enormous. Josephus gives a figure of 1,100,000 which, although exaggerated, is an indication. The sequel to the defeat was as horrible as anything during the siege. The old and weak and anyone identified with the rebels were slaughtered. Able-bodied men were sent to the Egyptian mines or to feed the wild beasts of the theatres and circuses of Rome and the provinces. All under 18 were sold as slaves. Josephus estimates that 97,000 were sold into slavery. In fact, over the whole of Palestine, a much larger number met a bitter fate.

Jerusalem had been entirely wiped out. Only three Towers of Herod and a part of the Western wall were preserved, partly as a memorial to the town and also to serve as a garrison for the occupying force. In the words of Josephus this had been:

> "the greatest (war) not only of the wars of our time, but, so far as accounts have reached us, well nigh of all that ever broke out between cities or nations." (War, Preface).

Josephus was writing for a Graeco-Roman audience and, apparently, had no fear that his claim might be ridiculed.

What the Jewish warriors and their followers had lacked in military training or equipment they had made up in religious, patriotic fanaticism. In spite of their much larger forces, infinitely better equipment and much higher standards of training and methods of warfare, the Romans had the greatest difficulty in reducing the country. In the end, with a few intervals, the war lasted seven years, for the Romans had to embark on a series of long sieges with periods of rest for the soldiers in between. The Roman historian, Tacitus, who was an avowed enemy of Jews and Christians, confirms this fact and, in doing so, pays grudging tribute to the Jews. So did Vespasian and Titus who issued coins with the legend "Judea Capta" (captive) or "Devicta" (defeated).

The Agony

Palestine was reorganized as the imperial province of Judea, with a Roman governor installed once more in Caesarea. Although the war was over, the rebellion of the Zealots led by the Galilean Eleazar ben-Jair continued in the sparsely populated eastern and southern districts. They held out in three main centers of resistance: the fortresses of Herodium near

Bethlehem, Machaerus in Perea and Masada at the southern end of the Dead Sea. Soon after Jerusalem fell, Herodium was taken. Machaerus held out for a long time, finally surrendering only when its defenders were permitted to leave in safety.

MASADA

Masada held out for three years. Flavius Silva who succeeded Bassus as governor had to carry on the siege which was begun in 72.

The Romans managed to bring their siege engines up to the top of the mountain in 73. By then the defenders had built a second wall within the ancient outside ramparts. As these first defences crumbled, they retired within the second, only to have this wall set on fire by the Romans. The end was in sight. Rather than fall into Roman hands, the Zealots retired into Herod's palace. Cried their leader, Eleazar:

The fortress of Masada perched on a mountain top, facing the Dead Sea. The dike constructed by the Romans to reach the fortress is still indicated by the white incline at the left. Traces of their camp at the foot of the mountain can be seen to the left.

Payment of tribute to Rome. Stone bas-relief of the 1st century C.E.

"Since we, long ago, my generous friends, resolved never to be servants to the Romans, nor to any other than to God himself, who alone is the true and just Lord of mankind, the time is now come that obliges us to make the resolution true in practice. And let us not at this time bring a reproach upon ourselves for self-contradiction, while we formerly would not undergo slavery, though it were then without danger, but must now, together with slavery, choose such punishments also as are intolerable; I mean this, upon the supposition that the Romans once reduce us under their power while we are alive. We were the very first that revolted from them, and we are the last that fight against them; and I cannot but esteem it as a favour that God hath granted us, that it is still in our power to die bravely, and in a state of freedom, which has not been the case of others, who were conquered unexpectedly. It is very plain that we shall be taken within a day's time; but it is still an eligible thing to die after a glorious manner, together with our dearest friends .... for that fire which was driven upon our enemies did not, of its own accord, turn back upon the wall which we had built; this was the effect of God's anger against us for our manifold sins, which we have been guilty of in a most insolent and extravagant manner with regard to our own countrymen. ..... Let our wives die before they are abused, and our children before they have tasted slavery; and after we have slain them let us bestow that glorious benefit upon one another mutually, and preserve ourselves in freedom, as an excellent funeral monument for us." (War, Bk. VII, Ch. 8, 6)

Beginning with their women and children, the defenders killed themselves. When the Romans entered the place the next day they found the fortress which had defied them for so long manned only by corpses. One woman survived, states Josephus, and it was she who related the last days of Masada!

VESPASIAN'S DECREES IN PALESTINE

As peace came to the country, several towns which had been destroyed were colonized with pagans. Shechem was renamed Neapolis (present-day Nablus). Veterans were settled in Colonia and Emmaus in Judea. Roman control over the country's economy was tightened. To this end, all land was declared the domain of the Emperor and was farmed out to prominent citizens who leased it to other tenant-farmers. The ground land-owners had to pay a higher "rent" than what they had previously paid in taxes.

Vespasian laid no plans to interfere with or curtail Jewish civil rights. However, he did inpose a new discriminatory tax — the "fiscus judaicus" — of half a shekel upon them. In place of the self-imposed levy which every Jew had paid to the Temple in Jerusalem, the "fiscus judaicus" must henceforth be paid to the Temple of Jupiter on the Capitol in Rome. In itself, it was no new burden on the Jews of the Empire, but it did violate the principle of equality. For the first time, the Jews as a group became a special source of revenue. They alone must pay a tax because they were identified with their rebellious people. In time this was to create a new attitude towards them until eventually the Jews became regarded as an alien element within the Roman empire and Christendom.

If Vespasian did not set out with this intention, he, and those who succeeded him, were determined to crush any resistance of the Jews of Palestine and had learned how this might arise. He ordered the hunting out and execution of all who claimed Davidic descent or might encourage messianic hopes. The policy was followed by the emperors of the Flavian dynasty (see p. 330): Vespasian (60–74); Titus, his son 74–81; Domitian, brother of Titus (81—96).

II. ISRAEL RISING FROM THE ASHES

THE MECHANICS OF SURVIVAL

The war that had destroyed hundreds of settlements and cost hundreds of thousands of lives had also wiped out or dispossessed the leaders and ruling class of the country, especially in Judea. Those who remained faced a humiliating discrimination from officials and pro-Roman agents. The aristocracy which had been the people's representatives were now equally despised by the Romans and by a disillusioned population.

The Pacifists Take the Lead

From Josephus, we learn that many towns of the coastal plain to the west of Judea, the whole district north of Jerusalem, and a number of towns in Galilee which had not been actively involved in the fighting, were treated leniently. Their inhabitants were given special privileges, in contrast to those districts which were declared the domain of the victor by right of conquest. Chief among the more favoured towns was Jabneh (Jamniah) and its port. It retained its civic rights and comparative prosperity and became a center for the more pacific elements of Palestine's leaders who were seeking a secular substitute for the destroyed capital.

JOHANAN BEN ZAKKAI

While the war was still raging, certain elements among the Pharisees within the doomed city had realized that arms were not going to save the Jews, nor advance Judaism. *But they were convinced that the Jewish religion, properly organized, could tide the people over the difficult period of the 'evil Kingdom' even without formal autonomy.*

On this basis they had pleaded for moderation, uselessly. During the internal quarrels among the leadership inside Jerusalem, Johanan ben Zakkai, spiritual heir to rabbis Hillel and Gamaliel, had himself smuggled out of the blockaded city in a coffin and made his way to the Roman camp and Vespasian. The Roman general respected the rabbi and listened to his request for permission to

> "preserve Jabneh and its scholars, to save the house of Gamaliel (the First) and to secure doctors to treat Rabbi Zadok (who had been fasting for 40 years to obtain respite for Jerusalem)". (Babylonian Talmud, Gittin, 56, 2)

The Romans believed in encouraging peaceful elements within the districts they ruled and they granted these modest requests. On such a slight foundation Johanan dreamed of building a *program of survival* based on a reorientation of life within the country.

Prisoners being brought before the Emperor; officers holding eagles and standards. Bas-relief of the Arch of Constantine (1st cent. C.E.)

Need for Reorientation

The mass of the Jews were stunned by the disaster which had overtaken them. Peaceful and moderate men, however, were not so surprised. For years they had been living in fear of national collapse. Now, therefore, they were prepared. Instead of dwelling on the calamity and adding to the general mourning and distress, they looked for spiritual lifebuoys that could ward off the people's despair and could help towards re-establishing a normal life. Resignation was better than despair, but it demanded self-discipline and reorientation towards a new national program. The teachers who worked towards this end were helped by the sobering effect which disaster had had upon the masses. The wild dreams of Israel's supremacy and messianic visions had been dispelled by a grim reality. Any hope of comfort or guidance must now come from the pacific, Tannaitic teachers.

Two things above all were needed. First, the formation of a new center and institution to be endowed with all the authority formerly exercised by the Sanhedrin and the Patriarchal family of Gamaliel which was momentarily in eclipse; secondly the enactment of new but essential laws to confirm the authority of the new center. Both these were achieved.

Consolidation

Jabneh was declared the seat of the High Court, the place from which all major decisions would be issued. These included, for instance, the regulation of the calendar, a most important problem: (to assure that the festivals were properly observed). A series of "takanot", (enactments) were at once proclaimed to emphasize that Jabneh, in everything but sacrificial offerings, was to have all the powers and rights of Jerusalem. ". . . . Thus Jabneh, the city of Philistine origin, became the vineyard for scholars who love the Torah. Here as occasion arose takanot were issued. Here valuable traditions were collected and redacted, particularly those related to the Temple ceremonies, for the purely intellectual interest in this field was accompanied by the hope that soon again the Temple might be rebuilt and the restoration of its worship depended upon authentic record of its ritual. Here, too, teaching and research were zealously conducted." (L. Finkelstein)

In addition to this academy, Johanan established another in Brur-Chail in the south, which is further evidence that life was slowly returning to normal in various parts of the country.

Realistic Idealism in Religion and Public Life

With the national sanctuary destroyed and desecrated, sacrifices could no longer be offered. The priestly cultus became superfluous. The destruction of the Temple thus marks the end of the Sadducee sect within Judea. The Pharisees had a long history of opposition to the Sadducees because of their insistence on tradition and privilege and because of the corruption that had spread through the Temple organization.

Now, the gap left by the loss of the Temple had to be filled. Many of its ceremonies and religious observances were transferred to the synagogue in a manner that had long since been adopted by the Jews of the diaspora and, to some extent, in Judea itself. "For a long time, it had been customary in Palestine and even more so in the diaspora, to have ceremonies and prayers at the times when the Temple sacrifices were performed, the idea being that thereby everyone took part in the national cult. These ceremonies now painlessly superseded the sacrifices themselves." (Ch. Rabin).

Above all, Johanan and his followers saw it as their major duty to restore peace to the country. To do this, they needed a means of focussing "life on those factors of proved stability, which for ages past had been the source of their great capacity for survival." (S. Baron) The synagogue and the new seats of learning became the centers of the people's life. Leadership and guidance were provided by the Sanhedrin of Jabneh. Their leadership is generally acknowledged to have been the salvation of Pharisaic-rabbinic (normative) Judaism. Israel's inheritance was salvaged. Not only had Johanan ben Zakkai found the formula for the preservation of Israel as a nation. His life's work served to define anew its historic function.

A New Spiritual Patriarchate

The academy of Jabneh established a new type of leadership, that of the scholarly Tannaitic rabbis, (see Ch. VII, 1). Although they were not immediately acknowledged by the new Roman authorities, who were not friendly towards the Jews of Judea, their influence among the people assured their position. In this they were also probably helped by the favourable material conditions in the maritime plain. The Sanhedrin of Jabneh was made up of 72 "ancients" — Tannaitic doctors of law, with no political orientation. At their head was the "Nasi", or Patriarch. As time went on, their prestige increased and the Diaspora acknowledged their decisions. (The Romans were not concerned about internal rulings and judgments of Jewish courts).

GAMALIEL II

Before his death, Johanan ben Zakkai was succeeded by a brilliant descendant of Hillel, Gamaliel the Second. He belonged to the spiritual aristocracy which Johanan had sought to preserve and, at the same time, was a patrician, owning considerable estates in the district. He was a contemporary of Emperor Domitian, who succeeded Titus in 81 C.E. (see p. 338). It was under this emperor that the first general persecution of the Christians took place, affecting the Christians in Rome no less than those elsewhere. The Jewish Christians in Jerusalem fell under the suspicion of harbouring political dreams of Davidic messianism. However when Domitian realized the peaceful nature of their faith, they were released and the persecution of the church halted for the moment.

Domitian ruled with a severity that hardly encouraged recovery in the stricken country. Taxes were imposed and exacted without mercy and, later, his government was to issue the edict banning circumcision (see below).

Gamaliel tried to relieve the pressure on the Jews wherever he could. He enacted *takanot* aimed at improving relations between Jew and gentiles. He regularized the liturgy and insisted on its adoption. He put through economic reforms. As a practical leader, he tried to obtain a unified code of laws by ruling that Hillelite interpretations of Biblical law, where they differed from those of the school of Shammai or other schools, were to be the only valid ones. Alternatively, all teachers had to submit to the decisions of the high court at Jabneh. Gamaliel wanted to prevent disunity and the familiar sectarian quarrels, but the other scholars of his day rebelled against such excessive authority. In the end, the old academic freedom of discussion was restored. It is reflected in the Talmudic controversies and their great contribution to Jewish learning.

The Patriarchate

Through their efforts to bring peace and stability to the country, the Jabneh Sanhedrin gradually won Roman recognition and cooperation, giving a firm basis to the Palestinian Patriarchate which was to guide the destinies of the Jewish nation for many generations.

The government of Caesarea accepted the Patriarchate as the supreme authority for the whole Jewish community in Palestine and within the Empire. Thus it replaced the Temple ceremonial as the focal point for Jewry. The Patriarchate continued the theocratic conception of the Jewish nation and the close connection between religious faith and political survival. As a political as well as a religious leader, the Patriarch was able to retain a large measure of internal autonomy for his people. In addition, the respect with which outsiders regarded him was an added protection for the whole of Jewry.

Judea at this time was very far from a community of exclusively pious people. It had naturally its synagogues and schools, but also an expanding economic life, and a class conflict between rich landowners and numerous tenant-farmers. It is clear from the incidents referred to in the Talmud that ties with the diaspora were strengthened and foreign influence continued. The Talmud includes anecdotes on disputes between rabbis and wealthy men, or instances of unorthodox thinking, which are hardly surprising under the circumstances.

Gamaliel's Faith

Before Gamaliel, Johanan ben Zakkai had already repeated the classic self-accusation of the ancient prophets, that all Israel's troubles were brought upon herself by her sins.

Gamaliel once answered a grief-stricken disciple who feared that Israel's future sins would go unpardoned, now that there was no Temple from which to beg forgiveness:

> "My son do not weep; we have a means of atonement as effective as this. And what is it? It is deeds of loving kindness; as the prophet (Hosea) has put it, 'for I desire mercy and not sacrifice.' "

He and his followers did not lay the blame for Israel's downfall on their enemies, but on the people. The Jews' greatest sin, said Gamaliel, was that "they were deficient in the study of the Torah" and statutory commandments.

Doubters and Visionaries

Disillusionment was stronger among sections of the population who were too far from Jabneh, or out of tune with its teachings. This is reflected in a poetic and apocalyptic form in the late apocryphal writing known as Ezra IV (Ezra II). He tried in his own way to counter the pessimism and lack of faith of his generation by postulating that the world in which we live is imperfect and passing. It is evil and man is unfortunate in being born into it. Israel, who must carry God's message to the world, has suffered as a sign that the world will be reborn and that the new world will be without evil. Unlike his predecessors, this apocalyptist shortens the classical millenium for the time of this rebirth to a period of four hundred years. There is a similar note in some of the contemporary teachers quoted in the Talmud (as in Erubin 13, 2).

During this period a group of Nazirites appeared in the Kidron Valley of Jerusalem and near Hebron; another community of sectaries devoted themselves to a life in expectation of the end of days. Their message is reflected in the apocalyptic "Second Baruch".

It seems doubtful whether the Tannaitic rabbis actually issued a forthright denial of the messianic vision. Apparently, their teachings did have some connections with the hopes and ideals of the apocalyptists and even the political aspirations of the Zealots. Johanan ben Zakkai was not an avowed enemy of the Zealots. What the rabbis taught was that the future of the world should be left to God. Man's immediate concern must be with the world as he knew it. In the forefront of his mind must be the dictates of the Torah as they applied to everyday life, not visions of an undefined "End of days".

This more positive doctrine probably helped the people to accept the new leadership of the rabbis.

A Confusing Period

The actual course of events during the first and second centuries C.E., especially developments within the conflicting spiritual trends, is difficult to establish with any certainty. Reliable data for the period are scarce. Josephus' history did not go beyond the reign of Vespasian. The only other sources are patristic or talmudic writings and these are very scanty and must be approached with some caution. All the authors, rabbinical or patristic were involved in and affected by the separation which developed between Jews and new Christians (see conclusion below). Each saw his own point of view and ignored any other interpretation. A better understanding of many of the problems connected with this crucial period has been reached only recently, by means of a critical study of what material exists, carried out by modern methods of scholarship.

THE NEED FOR A POSITIVE EVALUATION

Any attempt at an objective evaluation raises queries of whether earlier historians and scholars, Jewish or non-Jewish, have really given sufficient weight, objectively, to the other side of the picture. This question is especially appropriate in relation to the key-problem of the real importance of Israel's history — its *raison-d'etre*. Having followed the whole course of that history, we may at least lay to rest one widely-held non-Jewish intellectual misconception, that Israel's history ended with the destruction of its Jerusalem sanctuary. (The corollary to this, that it did so in order to give way to Christianity, is a view that is definitely beyond the realm of objective history.)

Far from this, it is true that, extraordinary though it may seem, neither Israel nor its way of life had been destroyed. The people remained in the land. Although its independence was lost, the Jewish community rose from its ashes, like a "brand plucked from the fire" (Zechariah, 3, 2). In spiritual life and cultural values some of Israel's greatest achievements lay before it. Looking back over its whole history, one can mark a continuous line of development. The prophetic era gave way to the messianic period and this, in turn, diverged into a variety of sectarian trends, including Jewish-Christianity. All of these formed part of a single historical tension which did not reach its climax at the Crucifixion and then come to a sudden end. The original flood of inspiration did not peter out into a merely political explosion in the rebellion of 66–70 C.E. The messianic tensions which underlay the rebellion carried on into the future. Idealistic, other-worldly, scorned by Roman historians and mistrusted by many Tannaitic teachers, they nevertheless contained the seeds of a future flowering that could stand side by side with Christianity. It must be admitted that this side of the Jewish revival has not been given its due importance in any historical evaluation of the period. In fact, the Jewish people, clinging to a messianic hope which lent itself equally to secular and spiritual interpretation, emphasized sometimes the one and sometimes the other aspect.

DID MESSIANISM DECLINE?

Luckily for the Jewish people, weariness and self-control produced a period of peaceful reconstruction for the next forty years. The normal rhythm of life was restored not only in the maritime plain, but also in Judea, around Jerusalem, in Galilee and Transjordan. Did this mean that the tensions of messianism faded? To regard this as even a remote possibility would be to ignore the evidence. The Romans liked to think it might be so, whether they considered Jewish visions or the dream of the new Christians. However they overlooked the fact that for the Jews, the defeat of 70 C.E. was much more than a purely political episode. It had its place in the Jewish picture of a world approaching the final and crucial point in its history.

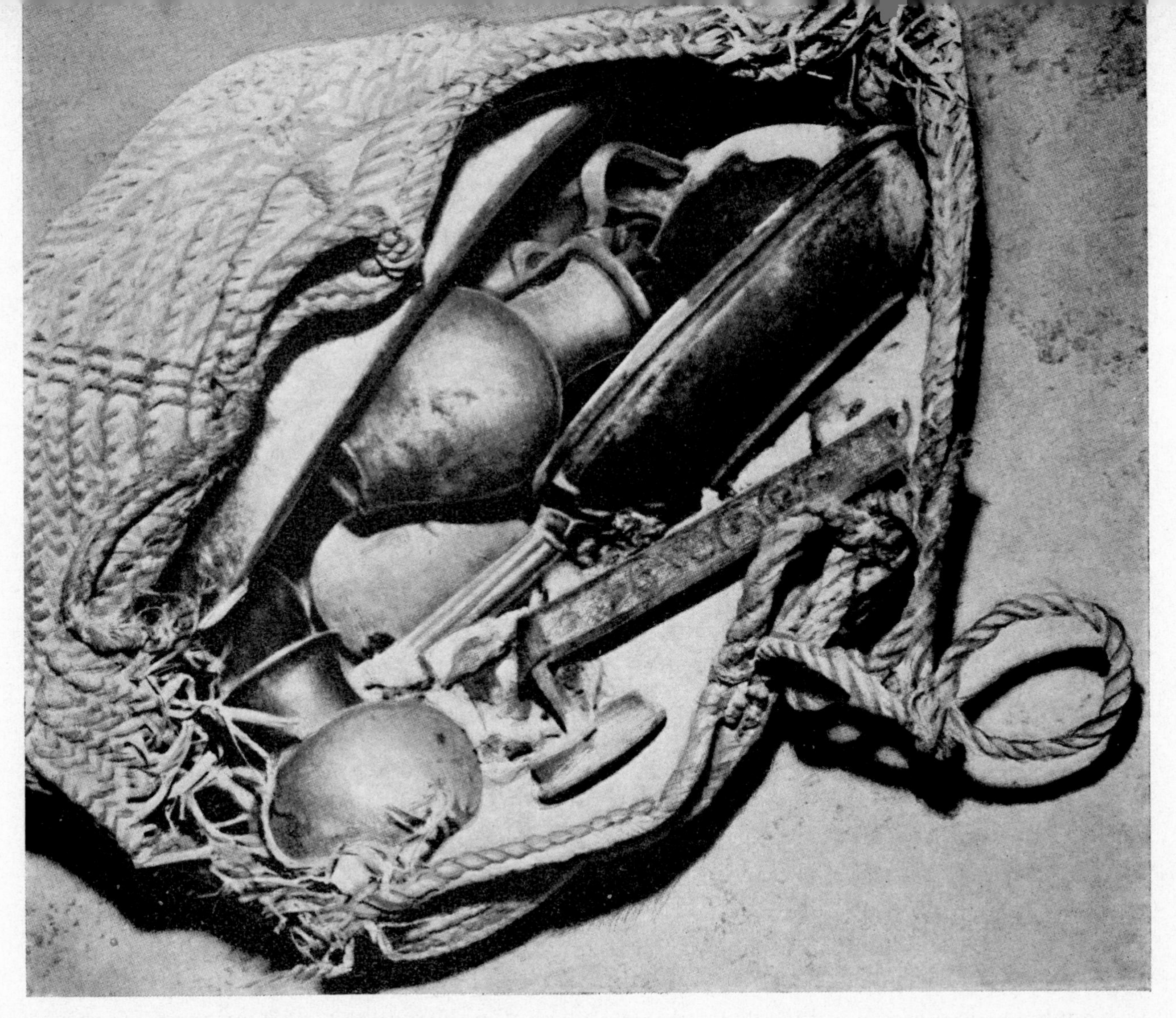

A basket containing metal vases, cultic objects, bowls and a large key was found in one of the caves of the Nahal Hever canyon, where Bar-Kosba's partisans hid from the pursuing Romans, (*see p. 355 seq*).

XIII

BAR-KOSBA PRINCE OF ISRAEL

I. NEW WAVES OF MESSIANISM UNDER TRAJAN AND HADRIAN

That the messianic tension had not weakened became clear forty years later in 115 when a wave of rebellion swept through the whole of the eastern diaspora, from Egypt, Cyrene and Cyprus to Mesopotamia. This coincided with the campaign of the Emperor Trajan (98–117 C.E.) against the Parthians and with an earthquake which destroyed Antioch and a number of towns in Asia Minor in the same year.

The Parthians were hereditary enemies of Rome and Trajan set out to settle accounts with them once and for all. At the same time, he wanted to secure control over the increasingly important trade routes to India and the Far East. Just at this moment, a revolt of the Jews in Cyrenaica then in Egypt threatened to cut his armies off from their main Italian base. A naval commander, Marcius Turbo, was detailed to pacify the disturbed Mediterranean regions. To prevent the spread of rebellion throughout the empire, Trajan assigned an outstanding general Lucius Quietus, the task of suppressing Mesopotamian Jewry.

The King-Messiah of Cyrene

Led by a Cyrenian King-Messiah, Lukuas-Andreas, the first attacks of the Jews were directed against their gentile neighbours. In Cyrenaica, before the Romans could intervene, they captured and destroyed the capital, Cyrene. But the messianic background to the uprising was also anti-Roman. At first Palestine, Syria and Asia Minor, in spite of their substantial Jewish populations, stood aside. Then Lukuas and his followers aimed at invading Judea with the declared aim of liberating it from Roman domination. Instead, according to a report preserved only by a 13th Century Syriac writer — Bar-Hebraeus, — the Romans inflicted a heavy defeat on Lukuas and executed him. To celebrate his victory, General Lucius Quietus, now the governor of Palestine, erected a statue of Trajan over the site of the Temple in Jerusalem.

In Egypt, the struggle was fiercer. Inflamed by Zealot refugees from Palestine, the Egyptian Jews set out to settle old scores with their Greek neighbours. In reprisal, there was a wholesale massacre of the Jews of Alexandria. On the evidence of facts briefly recorded in Egyptian papyri chronicles, V. Tcherikover points out that, in despair, the Jews turned to the inflammatory visions of a pseudo-messiah and were thus drawn into a hopeless two-front war against the Greeks and Rome.

The campaign in Cyprus also began with a Jewish victory that they were given no chance to enjoy. In a united attack, the Jews destroyed the capital, Salamis, and, according to an ancient source, massacred no less than 240,000 (!) pagans in the island. However, this obvious threat to control over the sea route to Italy brought the full weight of Roman anger against the rebels. Fresh from Trajan's great victory over Parthia, they wreaked a bloody vengeance. Finally, it was decreed that no Jew might ever settle on the island again. If any Jew were found by a Cypriot, even after a shipwreck, he was liable to immediate execution.

ALLIES AGAINST ROME

F. M. Heichelheim maintains that the Jewish uprising against Trajan was of great international importance and was probably encouraged in western Mesopotamia by one

This marble relief from Bethshean, commemorating the Fretensis Legion, shows the Emperor Hadrian with a figure of Neptune of Victories.

of the other Palestine commanders opposing Rome. "The King of Adiabene, scion of a family with well-known Jewish contacts, knew, in order to save his throne and line, how to use Jewish discontent and Messianic hopes effectively to menace Trajan's supply lines." Twenty years later, in the time of Bar-Kosba, Rabbi Simon-bar-Yohai, another messianic opponent of Rome, prophesied lyrically,

> "when you see a Parthian horse tied to the graveyards of Palestine, watch for the approaching steps of the Messiah."

HADRIAN'S EDICTS

The violence of Trajan's repression naturally aroused further bitterness and this came to a head under his successor, Hadrian.

Hadrian had played a prominent part in Trajan's Eastern campaigns and had had plenty of opportunity to assess the unbroken defiance of the Jewish people and the weakness of the Roman position. He decided to give up the newly conquered provinces and, instead, to conclude peace with Parthia and then consolidate the rest of the vast imperial possessions.

Hadrian had been educated in Athens and was deeply imbued with Greek culture. As emperor he dreamed, as so many emperors had before him, of achieving greater cultural homogeneity throughout the "Imperium". Because they had not been deeply involved in the latest unrest, he thought the Palestinian Jews would be tractable. When he visited the country in 130 and 131, he spoke appreciatively of the stand they had taken and even held out vague promises of rebuilding the Holy City or, possibly, reconstructing the Temple. How seriously his intention should have been taken is a moot point. What is certain is that the non-Jewish inhabitants of Caesarea, the Decapolis and the towns which had been settled by Roman veterans after the Great War, were strongly opposed to any encouragement which might raise Jewish standards and hopes. On the contrary, those hopes were dashed as it became clear that Hadrian's plans for Jerusalem concerned a cosmopolitan Greek-style "polis" in which the Jews would be encouraged to adopt the prevailing standards of the Graeco-Roman world and abandon "barbarous" practices such as circumcision. The Romans completely misunderstood the nature of circumcision, equating it with castration. Hadrian determined to stamp out the practice by strict application of a new edict against circumcision which he published in 127 C.E. He then proclaimed that Jerusalem would henceforth be known as Colonia Aelia Capitolina, and began rebuilding it with a temple dedicated to 'Jupiter of the Capitol' erected on the ruins of Herod's Temple.

According to the historian Dion Cassius, whose writings are our main source for these years,

> "Hadrianus built a new city over the ruins of Jerusalem and called it Aelia Capitolina. In lieu of the Temple of God he dedicated a Temple to Jupiter. This brought on a bitter and long war as the Jews could not abide strangers living in their city and foreign temples erected there."

Hadrian's action was more than the Jews could accept. Their shock at his duplicity did not destroy their messianic hopes. When their grandiose dreams of a rebuilt Temple were shattered, men swarmed into Jerusalem from every side, bolstering up each other's courage and vowing to use force to fulfill their dream. The personality of Simeon bar-Kosba served as a focus for all their hopes. When he appeared on the scene men turned to him, acclaiming him as the long-awaited Messiah. Sixty years after the destruction of the Temple, the Jews were up in arms once more against their Roman overlords.

THE FIRST YEAR OF THE WAR OF BAR-KOSBA

Dion Cassius records that the Jewish underground had been quietly reorganizing ever since Hadrian's imposition of the edict against circumcision. They had recruited guerrillas, prepared secret hide-outs and underground passages and begun to lay their plans.

From the scattered and sometimes obscure references in the Talmud and the Roman chronicles of Dion Cassius, Eusebius and Spartianus, a story of magnificent courage and heroism on the part of leader and people emerges. Following the discovery of dozens of papyri in Wadi Muraba'at (1952) and in Nahal Hever in Israel in 1960–61 we know a great deal more about the war and its protagonists than we did. From these contemporary documents the drama and tragedy of the few crowded years of Bar-Kosba's leadership can be seen against the details of their military and material background.

Emperor Hadrian, who built a Roman city and camp over the ruins of Jerusalem.

Simeon Bar-Kosba was a man of giant stature and reckless courage. He was also a good organizer and an astute commander. Under his leadership, guerrilla warfare was begun early in 131. His forces in southern Judea, reinforced by additional partisans from Galilee were able to hold the Roman garrisons in check and then gradually to gain control over a large part of the country. Bar-Kosba knew his own strength. He was careful to avoid open combat with the superior Roman forces and instead used guerrilla tactics, harrying them incessantly, giving them no chance to rest or to come to grips in a decisive battle.

Within a few months the first objective of the rebellion was gained. Jerusalem was practically freed and a Jewish army was once more in control. In the year 131 the insurgents proclaimed the dawn of a new era, striking coins which they dated in Hebrew, 1st Nisan (Spring) and the 1st Tishri (New Year) in the 1st and 2nd years of the Era of Liberty.

ISRAEL: A NEW COMMONWEALTH

For two years Bar-Kosba remained in control. He revived ancient traditions and established a new commonwealth as a theocratic state which had the support of the whole country. Sacrifices were renewed, the High Priest Eleazar officiating under the shadow of the giant commander and prince of Israel. More importantly, he worked in close cooperation with Rabbi Akiba, the outstanding scholar of his day. Akiba was a saintly man, who, for all his gentleness, was a successful popular leader.

This brief period of Jewish independence rekindled the flame of messianism and the people, with Rabbi Akiba in the lead, acclaimed Bar-Kosba as the King-Messiah. His original name they changed to Bar-Kochba, the son of the star of Jacob, adapting a classical biblical phrase:

> "A star shall come forth out of Jacob,
> and a scepter shall rise out of Israel." (Numbers 24: 17)

Y. Yadin, who led the discoveries of the papyri in the caves of the wilderness of Judea, has pointed out that in none of the documents found in Muraba'at or in Nahal Hever does the name Bar-Kochba ever appear. Whether in formal documents or private letters, he always signed himself Bar-Kosba, his real name, and he is always referred to by this name. Yadin believes that the "Bar-Kochba" was an unofficial nickname given him by his followers and admirers and that he objected to its use. Invariably his letters are addressed democratically to his "brethren" and worded: "From Shimon ben Kosba .... ending, Shalom." Seldom did he use his title, "Prince of Israel".

However Bar-Kosba's patriotism and religious fervour may be assessed, he seems to have been an unusually statesmanlike rebel leader. He maintained the existing efficient Roman administrative machinery, adapting it to new conditions. In place of the emperor as titular owner of the whole land of Palestine, he substituted himself as head of the state of "Israel", leasing estates to tenant-farmers to cultivate. From the papyri found in the caves, it is clear that in many cases these estates were sub-let and the transactions legally recorded and protected. Bar-Kosba seems to have tried to distribute the nation's land among the largest possible number of cultivators and to have done everything possible to ensure an adequate food supply for an emergency. Attempts at profiteering or slacking were heavily punished. One of the coins which he issued is shown on page 133.

Jerusalem was still exposed to Roman attack and there is no evidence that he attempted any rebuilding of the sanctuary. He grouped his forces in strategic fortified positions from which they would make repeated sallies to keep the Romans at bay. The Roman legate, Tineius Rufus, had long since taken refuge in the fortified garrison and sent to his colleague

Roman blockhouse in southern Judea.

Publius Marcellus of Syria for reinforcements. The garrison remained in Jerusalem on the defensive, but in an ever weaker position.

By February 133, a reorganized national army had undisputed control of the southern coastal plain and the area of Judea. Bar Kosba established his capital and headquarters in Herodium, in the palace Herod had built several miles south-east of Jerusalem. Only a few traces of this town remain. While it acted as Israel's strategic center the place must have been full of soldiers; its warehouses serving as the state's ordinance stores and granaries.

Roman Regrouping

It is still not clear what importance the rebellion had internationally, nor what were its repercussions in the diaspora. According to Dion Cassius, help of every sort came from the Jews outside Palestine, who attacked the Romans, sometimes through their own underground, sometimes in open clashes.

The Roman empire was then at the peak of its power and prosperity and commanded a tremendous military potential. His local governors having failed, Hadrian recalled his ablest general, Julius Severus, from Britain, equipped him with four legions, several auxiliaries and a large fleet and despatched him to crush the upstart commonwealth in Palestine.

Realizing the difficulties of dealing with partisans who could launch surprise attacks from hidden strongholds, the Romans in Palestine began to build roads from the ports to the centers of rebellion. Meanwhile, the Jewish forces rebuilt the defences of Jerusalem, adding a fourth wall north-west of the town at the place where Titus had mounted his successful attack. Traces of this wall have been found in recent years.

The new Roman army arrived in the country and began its assault in Galilee, which was quickly reduced. Then, in spite of a desperate defence, the Roman troops devastated the rolling countryside of Beth-Govrin (Eleutheropolis) and destroyed the settlements at "the royal mountain", the coastal plain of Shephela in the south-west. Their intention was to subdue one position after another and make sure that it could not fall back into Jewish hands.

Bar-Kosba's Mountain Strongholds

The fall of Beth-Govrin, late in 133, was followed by the winter rains and a respite of several months until the spring of 134. The Romans were pushing through the road to Hebron and clearly threatening Herodium. Bar-Kosba decided to regroup his forces in the restricted territory of the highlands of south-east Judea. This was a poor area, thinly populated and with a few poverty-stricken villages which sixty years earlier, after the fall of Jerusalem, had served as a stronghold for the Zealots.

This barren area was the traditional haven of political refugees, separatist groups, ascetics and dreamers. Its inaccessibility and special geological formation of steep cliffs and gullies, with numerous caves hidden in the sides of deep canyons (see illustrations), made

Boat sailing across the Dead Sea, from the 6th Century Madeba mosaic map.

it ideal for guerrilla warfare. Thousands of partisans with their families, flocks and a few possessions poured into the area and there lived precariously awaiting the inevitable assault.

The papyri reflect the rising tensions as food in the area grew shorter and everyone, combatants, cultivators and artisans had to tighten their belts. There are also many references to the difficulties of transport from outlying areas. The oases of Eingedi on the Dead Sea shore served as supply bases and Bar-Kosba's ships sailed across the Dead Sea bringing in supplies from Jews still living under Roman rule in the Nabatean "Province Arabia". From his headquarters, Bar-Kosba and his staff supervised the distribution of land and food, intervening without hesitation to punish anyone responsible for increasing tension. One case was of a man named Ben-Aflul. Bar-Kosba made an example of him as a warning to others.

Meanwhile, the farmers carried on with their normal activities, sending provisions to the partisans in Herodium and the other rebel strongholds. The fact that trade continued normally is shown from the dozens of contracts that were drawn up between the rebels and the farmers.

THE PAPYRI FROM THE CAVES OF THE WILDERNESS OF JUDEA

Extensive commercial and military correspondence of the time of Bar-Kosba was found in two localities in the Judean wilderness. One, the caves of Wadi-Muraba'at, discovered in 1952, south of Qumran yielded material which has been deciphered mostly by J. T. Milik and colleagues. The other, the cave of letters in Nahal Hever in Israeli territory, was found in the most dramatic and dangerous circumstances in 1960–61 and was widely reported in the press of the world. The significance of these letters has been demonstrated by Y. Yadin.

> These papyrus documents, about sixty in number, have given us a new unexpected insight into the history of Judea during the sixty years between the first war (66—73) and Bar Kosba's commonwealth.
> One group, written in the Nabatean language, dating from the middle of the lst century to the beginning of the second, deals with family and legal business of people living in Zoar (southern Dead Sea, near the site of the legendary Sodom), at the time the Nabatean Kingdom was changed into the Roman "Province Arabia" (106 C.E.). A second group, written in Greek, concerns the business affairs of a widow, Babta, who lived near Zoar (106—132 C.E.).
> The third group of papyri, written mostly in Hebrew and some in Aramaic, deal with the administrative matters handled by Bar-Kosba's secretariat. This group includes letters written by Bar-Kosba himself and are of the greatest interest for the history of the period.

THE FALL OF BEITAR

However, with the spring of 134, the Romans took up their campaign again. Jerusalem was besieged and destroyed, but no details of its fall are known. Slowly Roman legions closed in around the perimeter of the Jewish refuge, cutting off all possible communication with the rest of the country. Bar-Kosba and the priest Eleazar withdrew to the fortress of

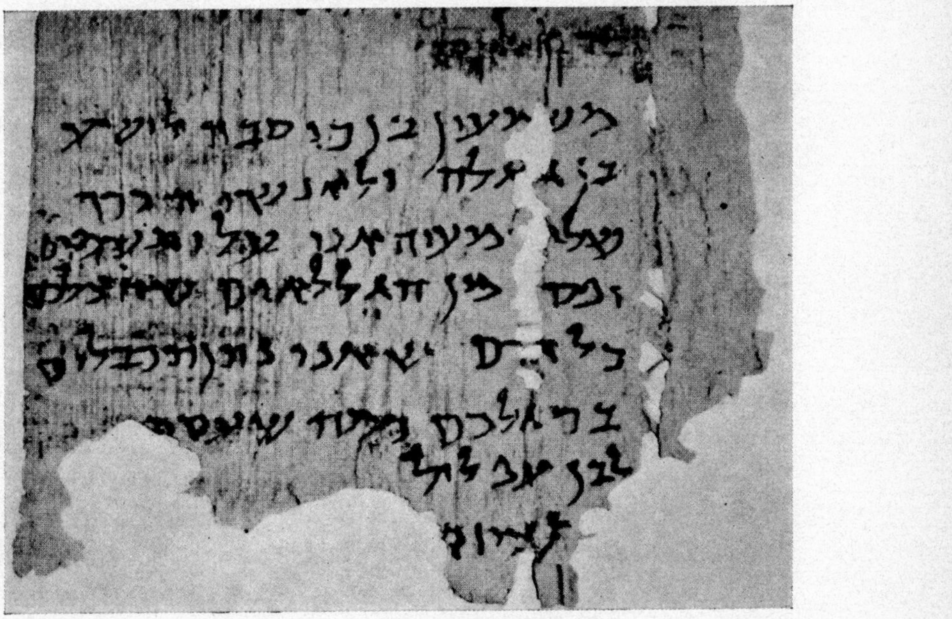

Letter written by Bar-Kosba to Joshua ben Galgola, in command of the rebels in the wilderness, (found at Muraba'at).

Beitar, leaving his lieutenant Bar-Daroma the desperate task of holding off the Roman forces by a last stand at Herodium. The defence of Beitar faced tremendous difficulties. The fort was without water, for its supply down in the valley had been cut off. There was a section among the defendants who opposed the leader and demanded surrender. A Talmudic source suggests that this dissension was led by Eleazar who was killed by Bar-Kosba.

In any case the Jewish forces held out against their attackers until, in August 135, a final assault from the Romans captured the town and Bar-Kosba was killed. Thus ended the messianic dream. The dead at Beitar were left where they fell and not buried until 3 years later. Some five hundred Jewish strongholds were destroyed and 985 villages razed. Dion Cassius records that 580,000 warriors had met their deaths. This was not all. The Romans took terrible reprisals at the end of which Judea lay almost completely in ruins and tens of thousands of Jews, men and women, of all walks of life, were sold in the slave-markets of Hebron and Gaza, as cheap cattle. Another Talmudic source recalls that "No bird was seen flying in Palestine for fifty years." Decades later, passers-by still rent their clothes in mourning as they passed the sites of the ruined settlements.

TRAGEDY OF THE HIDE-OUT AT NAHAL HEVER

Once Beitar had fallen, Yeshua ben Galgolah removed "camp" to an inaccessible cave of Wadi Muraba'at. He took the files of his administration and he and his companions brought what personal archives they had. There, in the cave, the letters reproduced here were found.

Yonathan and Massabala and other insurgents, fleeing from Masada and Eingedi near the Dead Sea, pushed on further north, the enemy in pursuit.

The Gruesome Tale of the Skeletons

It appears that the Romans were not prepared to consider their victory complete until every little pocket of resistance had been wiped out. They intended to make sure that no active group of partisans was left to start rousing the villages and towns of the area in the future. The fleeing companies of rebels were pursued into the most inaccessible canyons and there the Romans set about starving them out. The rebels, with their families, hid in caves high up in the canyons of Nahal Hever. They had with them sacred books, a few papers, family souvenirs, meagre provisions, a few clothes and pieces of cloth and, for the women, some yarn and ornaments. The legionnaires built two camps on top of the plateau on either side of the bed of the canyon, lying 400 metres below. From there, they could watch every movement the insurgents made, so that they were literally immured in their hide-outs. Provisions in the caves could have been sufficient for only a few months but it is impossible to say whether the hunted rebels perished from thirst and hunger. They may have died fighting in last desperate sorties from the caves or, like the defenders of Masada

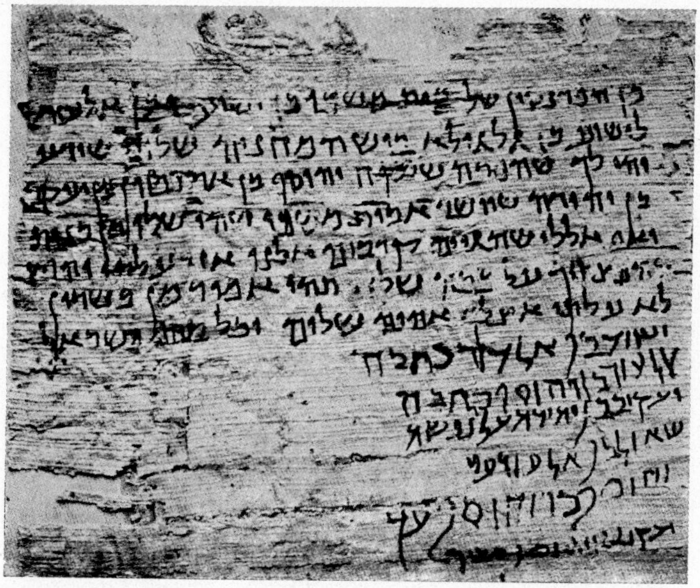

Letter written to Joshua ben Galgola by the two headmen of the village of Beth-Masheku, warning him of the approach of Roman troops, (found in Muraba'at).

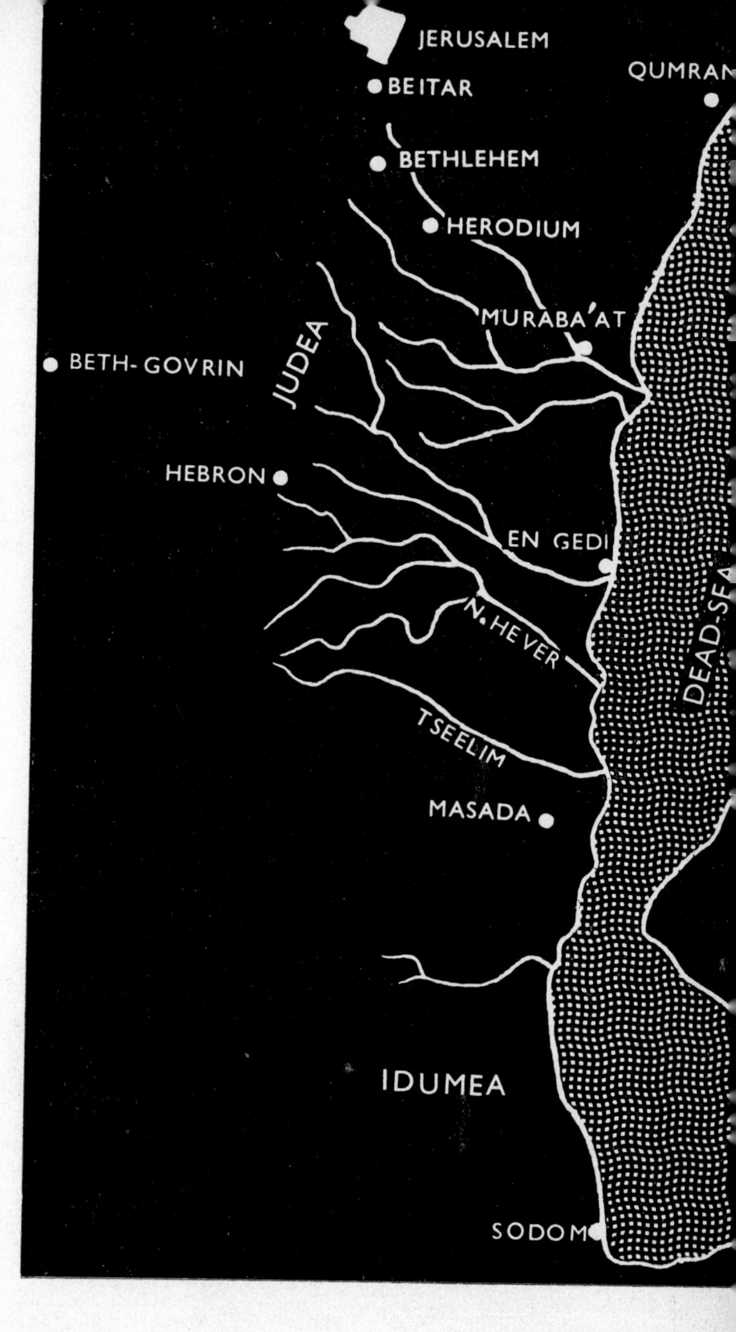

The Bar-Kosba war was fought over the hill country of Judea and finished in the wilderness near the Dead Sea, in the canyons of Nahal Hever and Muraba'at.

under Eliezer ben-Yair sixty years earlier, may have slaughtered themselves rather than be captured (Ch. XII, I).

Through the centuries, in this totally uninhabited region, the caves preserved evidence of their slow death. The first to die were wrapped in shrouds by the survivors and their bodies buried. Dozens of skulls, including those of women and children, were found in baskets covered with mats, while groups of headless skeletons lay nearby. The reality of this gruesome memorial defies imagination. These skeletons, bleached during 1825 years, mutely cry out the anguish of the last few dozen insurgents. The papyri, family papers, contracts, fragments of religious scrolls and other belongings nearby bespeak the human desire to cling to a few possessions even as their owners retreated to a last, hopeless, refuge.

The Romans built two camps to overlook the entrance to the caves in the face of the canyon. From them, the besiegers could observe every move of the zealots. One camp, (below), was perched on the northern edge of the cliff of Nahal Hever. Below it, were the entrances to several caves which penetrated deep into the mountain. One of them, indicated by the arrow on the left, was nicknamed the Cave of Papyri by the expedition. The other Roman camp, (right) stood on top of the southern edge of Nahal Hever. Far below, in the shaded area on the cliff face, was the cave where skeletons, shrouds and baskets of skulls were found in the furthest recesses. On some of the skulls the remains of hair could still be seen and some of the bones still had skin on them. These macabre remains earned the place the name, "Cave of Horror" from the expedition led by Y. Aharoni and Y. Yadin. Below right: a man died of starvation and thirst, his head resting on a crumpled shroud.

The Cave of Horror: Like the defenders of Masada, these fighters chose death rather than surrender. The small number of male skeletons is not accidental. It is assumed that most of the men were killed in battle outside the cave, in desperate efforts to bring food and water to the besieged women and children. A story in the Talmud tells of the son who ate the flesh of his slain father in the last desperate stand of the fighters and their families: ". . . Those Jews who were hidden (in the caves) devoured the flesh of their slain brethren. Every day one of them ventured forth and brought the corpses to them which they ate . . . Then the Holy Spirit cried out, for these things I weep."

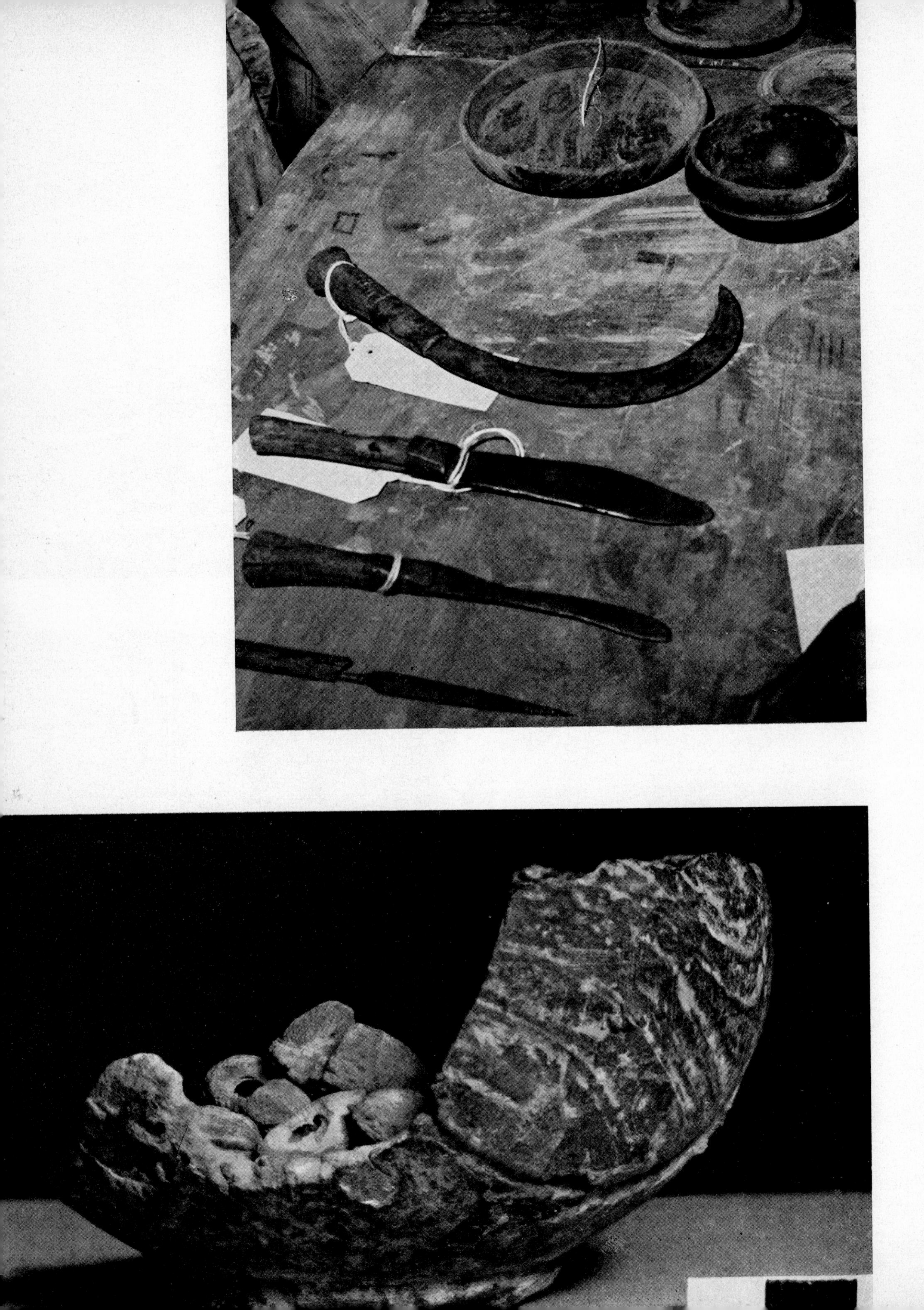

Top left: These weapons and wooden bowls were in a basket found deep within the cave on the northern cliff face; Bottom left: Olive stones in a wooden bowl; Above: Rolls of papyri, including letters from Bar-Kosba; Right: This child's shoe was found, almost untouched by time, in the northern cave.

A PAGAN JERUSALEM

With Roman arms victorious and the country at his feet, Hadrian continued his rebuilding of Jerusalem as a pagan city, "Colonia Aelia Capitolina". He colonized it with a mixture of Levantine veterans or traders of different kinds from the Syrian coast and Egypt. Above the site of the Temple stood an equestrian statue of the emperor. Jews and Jewish-Christians alike were forbidden to enter the town on pain of death. It is probably at this time that the province lost the name of Judea, and, to satisfy the non-Jews of the country, became Syria-Palestina, after the southern coastal plain of Philistia. Shortened to Palestine, this remained the name of the country for another eighteen centuries.

This period marks the lowest ebb in Jewish life. As part of the persecutions, Rabbi Akiba and Rabbi Hanina ben Teradion were martyred for teaching the Law and all Jewish observances were banned.

The overthrow of Bar-Kosba's brave defiance sounded the death-knell of Jewish nationalism in Judea. From an overall historical perspective, this interlude was not a rebellion of Jewry against the whole might of Rome but, rather, a local war fought against Roman legions in the minor province of "Syria-Palestina". All had shared in the uprising and suffered in its aftermath, although noncombatants and rabbis who had not sided with Bar-Kosba may have been spared death. But, after the collapse of the Jews' brave defiance, when Roman rule was reestablished, Simeon, the son of Gamaliel II, gathered the stricken remnant around him and obtained permission to resume his duties as Patriarch of the academy which he moved from Jabneh to Usha in Galilee.

During the Great War (66–73) and the War of Bar-Kosba, the Zealots had been almost completely wiped out. Leadership of the Jewish community was left in the hands of the moderate party led by the Patriarchs of the house of Hillel who, while preserving the traditional values of Judaism, guided the people along a path of self-restraint. They found the way to a modus vivendi with the government and the external world which it represented. Thus the Patriarchate held the people together and made possible the continuance of normative Judaism among them.

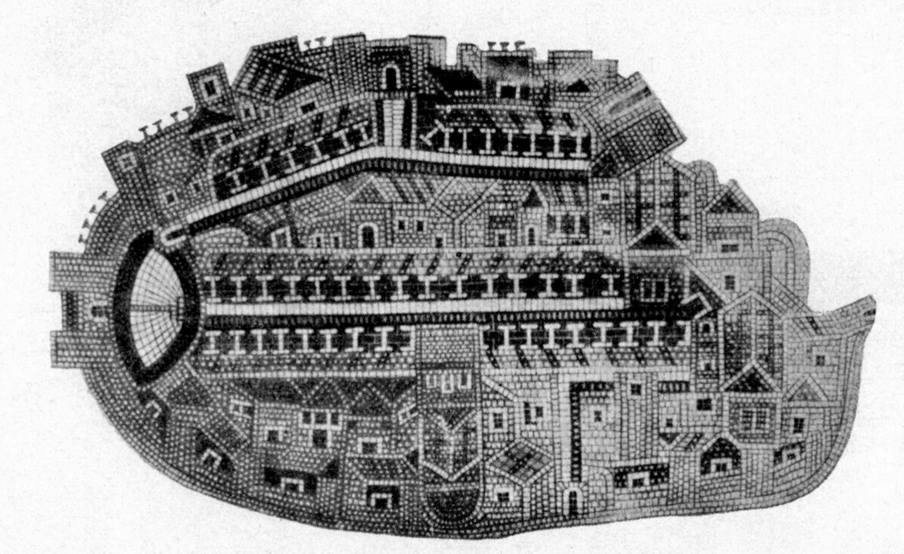

Aelia Capitolina, (Jerusalem) as shown in the Madeba mosaic map.

II. JEWS AND JEWISH-CHRISTIANS, 130—140 C.E.

Looking back, it is possible to distinguish a number of parallel trends which developed within the country:

Chapters VIII, X and XI gave some account of the development of the principal trends: the sectaries of Qumran, the Jewish-Christians and their proselytes. Among the broad masses, messianic and nationalist creeds had continued to flourish. The dissenting movements, which were of such vital significance for the future, all began among apparently quite unimportant peripheral groups. The impact which they each had on events during the second century C.E. can be assessed according to their importance for future history.

A Time of Stress for the Nascent Church

The darkest hour for Judaism after Bar-Kosba was also a time of stress for early Christianity. Hadrian's repression, like those of the emperors who had preceded him, affected Jews and Jewish-Christians alike. After the flight of the Jewish-Christians from Jerusalem to Pella in 68–70, Simeon, the cousin of Jesus, brought part of the community of the faithful back to Jerusalem. There, the church was organized under the leadership of a single bishop who still kept the authority of the family of Jesus, advised by a council of presbyters. Eusebius lists thirteen "bishops of the circumcision" who officiated in Jerusalem before the disasters of 131–5. He may have been referring to the bishops and twelve presbyter-elders in the same tradition. The churches of Caesarea and Alexandria at a rather later date had similar traditions regarding the early episcopate.

Hadrian's policy of destroying every vestige of Jewish prestige and keeping the Jews away from their holy places, was applied to the Christian sectaries as well. "Just as stone images, odious to monotheists, stood over the ruins of the Temple . . . idols consecrated to Adonis were erected at Golgotha and the grotto of Bethlehem, which the faithful in the land venerated as the birth-place of Jesus, was planted with a pagan sacred wood . . . ," (Vincent and Abel). Even earlier, in 110 C.E., Bishop Ignatius of Antioch was martyred under Trajan.

A few Christians, presided over by Bishop Mark, lived on for some twenty years in the new Aelia Capitolina. The Jews knew them as "Notzrim". Though they had taken no part in Bar-Kosba's rebellion from which they dissociated themselves and denied the messianic fervour surrounding him, (and, according to his contemporary Justin, had been made to suffer for their omission), the numbers of the Christians had been reduced by the events and by the proscription of circumcision. From fear of arousing the suspicion of the authorities, they had no connections with gentile members of the faith. It seems that they did keep in touch with the Jewish-Christians of Pella and other sectaries scattered in northern Trans-jordan (see Ch. XI). However they had no ties with the apostolic order of the west (where a system of plural bishops had developed), nor with the gentile Pauline churches of hellenists in Asia Minor and the west. All these sects constituted separate groups on the margin of the nascent church. For the moment, the church was content for its authority to be dispersed among various local episcopal groups, scattered throughout the ancient world. Unity was a matter of local loyalties.

Menorah and Cross in the Synagogue

Jewish law was not binding on the gentile churches, but there was no objection to its continuance within the Jewish-Christian synagogues. Of course, where Jews and Jewish-Christians co-existed in a single community, problems arose. Certain controversies between Jews and Christians are reported by the church fathers in the middle of the second century. There were apparently a series of ruptures, though conditions varied from place to place and time to time. They were the forerunners of a schism between the synagogue and the church which was still, at this period, many years away (and outside the scope of this book). This was a time of transition from the synagogue tradition, during which converts to Christianity among the Jews were not yet completely separated from Judaism. The churches of Corinth and Rome were at this stage.

The Bishops of Rome in the first centuries were usually Greek and the language they spoke was Greek. Curiously enough, the inscriptions reflecting the new faith in the west and the east, were accompanied by the sign of the menorah — the seven-branched candelabra. This symbol of Judaism was also added to a tombstone in the third century basilica of Abdath in the Negeb, as illustrated below.

The churches of Syria and Asia may have completed the transition sooner. It seems that they were already provided with an apostolic literature which was more complete than the Roman. The church in Jerusalem, so the ancient reports tell us, had a gospel called the Gospel according to the Hebrews. For the time being the currents of Christianity flowed

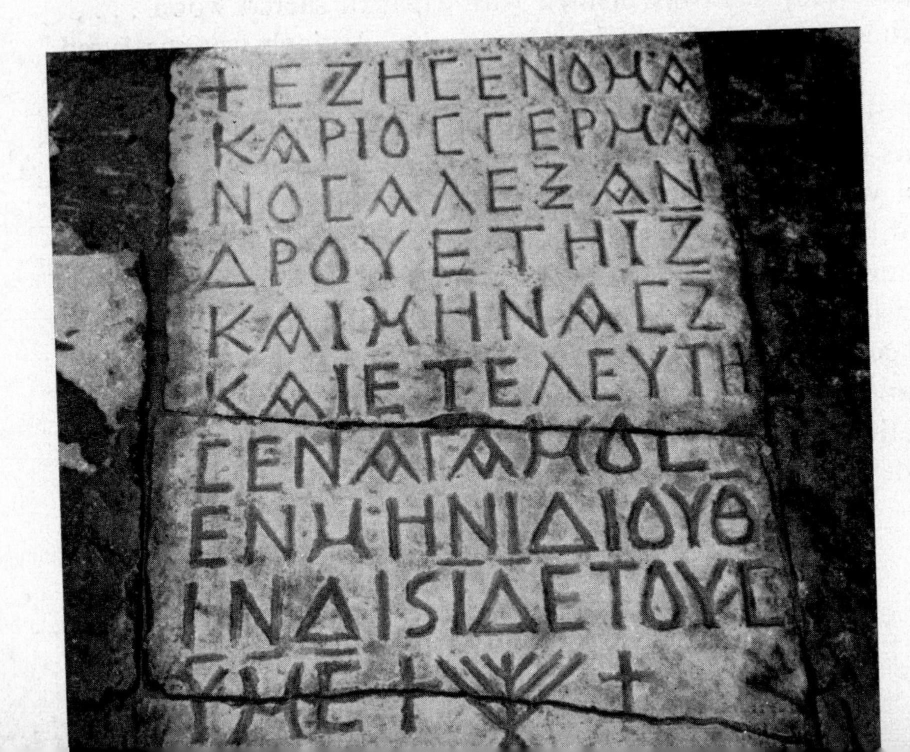

Marble tombstone in the 4th century basilica of Abdath showing a seven branched candelabra, flanked by two crosses.

east to west rather than west to east and it would be many generations before the early Christian movement in the east felt the impact of the western early Church and Rome.

FIRST STEPS TOWARDS A SEPARATION

The rare, generally inaccurate Talmudic references to the personality and work of Jesus (see Ch. X), are one indication that the teachers and rabbis of the first century were not particularly concerned with the new sectarian deviation on the fringe of the synagogue, although they were passively aware of its existence. Another explanation is that the sages living in Palestine during the second century, if and when quoted by the compilers of the Mishna and Gemara, were not interested in such things. For a long time, the Jewish-Christian group served as a mediating force between the two faiths, so closely linked through their common heritage. Until the time of Bar-Kosba, they had equally shared a common destiny. However, he had found the pacifist Jewish-Christians an undesirable element in a time of national emergency. It is evident that from this time, the sect lived in increasing isolation.

Internal Consolidation

Simultaneously (at the beginning of the second century) the leaders of the Jewish people were seeking every possible means to revive and strengthen the national spirit in their defeated land. One instrument in this was to encourage the greatest possible religious unity as part of a whole program of internal consolidation. This unity had no place for deviations like the Christian sectaries. The common links between them and the rest of Jewry accordingly began to disintegrate. The trend was hastened by an increasing bitterness which developed towards the end of the century. The Christian apologists began to argue that the political impotence of the Jews in Palestine was a sign that the new separatist faith represented the "true Israel".

Another cause of dissension were attempts made by Christian missionaries, like Theophilus and Ignatius in Antioch in the second century, to persuade the pagans they wished to convert that the ancient prophets had lived in conformity with Jesus' teachings, rather than the contrary. Not only did they claim Davidic descent for Jesus, but also began to date the beginning of Christianity back to Moses, or Abraham, even to Abel. While Christians generally appropriated the whole of the Old Testament and interpreted the persons and events in it along typically Jewish lines, they considered some of the people admirable and some reprehensible. They thought of them as Christians and Jews in the sense that the good ones were of the people of God and the bad ones were not. James Parkes contends that this point was pressed further, to the prejudice of the Jews: "Christians, alas, *never* absorbed into Christian history any reprehensible character of the Old Testament (Cain). Those characters were Jewish; the Christians were only the virtuous ones!" This scholar believes that "the very taproot of historic antisemitism lies in the division of the

Old Testament into two stories, one of virtue — the pre-Incarnation Christians, and one of incorrigible viciousness, that of the Jews." (James Parkes).

The "birkath ha-minim"

The rabbis did not take any immediate notice of the Christian challenge, but, some years later, according to Eusebius (in his "Historia Ecclesiastica", IV, 18, 6), the rabbinic authorities of Palestine sent letters to the synagogues of the diaspora formally rejecting the messianic claims made on behalf of Jesus and calling for Jews who believed in them to be excluded from the general religious community. It seems that "the letter to the synagogues was but the reaction to a situation already created by the Christians" (James Parkes). This author dates the action before the end of the first century, among other reforms introduced after 70 C.E. He estimates that the process of separation between Jews and Christians took place between 90 C.E. and its completion in 135 when a different Messiah was accepted (Bar-Kosba). However, this seems a rather short period, even for that crowded age.

The Malediction Against the "Minim"

It is still not certain whether this new clause did have the desired effect of keeping the "minim" (the sectaries) out of the synagogue or whether it merely gave official recognition to the split between the Christian and other schismatics and the national body of Jewry.

It is possible that the malediction against the "minim" as a whole may have been inserted into the liturgy by the Patriarch Gamaliel II as part of his drive to establish a single accepted norm in place of the variety of rulings and practices followed by different Jewish sects scattered through the empire, including the hellenistic diaspora (see Ch. VII, II). Gamaliel probably used the term "minim" for all the different heresies and sectaries that flourished at the time, not only the Jewish Christians, and he was probably unaware that his action would result in a break between the mother-church of Judaism and its dissenting offspring. The final severance of Christianity from Judaism was also partly a late response to the sectarian trend which created evident tension between the Qumran sectaries (Ch. VIII) and other Jews.

The final break did not come immediately. There was probably more than a century of gradual division leading up to it. It is doubtful whether the Jewish community consciously wished to eject the "minim", while Jewish-Christians worshipping in the synagogue had no reason to refuse the protection which membership gave them according to Roman Law (see Ch. XI). However, in the course of time, the malediction did produce a clash of interests. It is argued by some scholars that it excluded gentile proselytes from being accepted into a mixed Jewish-Gentile synagogue, though this does not seem to be in keeping with the customs of the times. In any case, formal schism did not take place until the third century and is beyond the scope of this book.

What is perhaps more pertinent to this period and place, is that the members of both faiths — though they were unaware of it — were passing through a series of crises into a new phase of their history. One or two generations had yet to pass before the Jewish community in Palestine would regain its impetus and, through sheer determination, begin to flourish once more. Its pattern had been set by the new course laid down after 70 C.E. by leaders like Johanan ben Zakkai and Gamaliel II. The Sanhedrin over which they had presided continued to produce intellectual leaders of their calibre whose influence and teachings were to rescue the "genius of Israel" and lay the foundation for a new normative Judaism which would survive political disaster.

As a result of the war of 131–135, the centers of Jewish population shifted from the south to the north, to Galilee, for most of the destruction of life and property had been in Judea, which was left desolate. When Antoninus Pius revoked or modified the Hadrianic decrees, the scattered scholars reconstituted a new Sanhedrin in Usha of Galilee. The effective center of Jewish thought was moved to Tiberias, which had been spared in the wars.

PALESTINE IN CHRISTENDOM

During the second century, the Jewish Christians expanded faster in the less-Jewish districts of the country and in Syria. This is reflected in Acts which mentions new proselytes in hellenistic towns and rural areas. This was apparently the case during the actual life-times of the apostles, and even more, it reflects a situation which existed a generation or two later at the time Acts was being written.

At the same time, the Christian church in Palestine was losing prestige compared to the expanding gentile church in countries far from its birthplace. Part of the reason for this is the depression of Jewish life within Palestine, which affected the Christian section as much as the rest of Jewry. Although the whole of Christianity rested on the foundation of the early church of Jerusalem, its birthplace could no longer influence its development. Evolution of Pauline and gentile Christianity had passed out of the hands of the sub-apostolic church. In Palestine and the East, the churches appeared to follow a disunited sectarian pattern. In time they came under the strong influence of Jewish sects such as the Nasorenes or Elkasites. In patristic literature, some of them are referred to as "Ebionites", "the poor", the term for the early Christians in the New Testament, (see Ch. VIII, II). These churches of Palestine and its borders remained self-contained, drawing their strength from within. They never contested the authority of the bishops of Antioch, Alexandria or Rome. They were content to remain isolated, withdrawn, making a richly varied contribution to gnostic literature.

During the third century C.E. the original church of Palestine would sink below the horizon of gentile Christianity, intent on establishing itself throughout the world, giving

Above: Detail from a mosaic in the Beth-Alfa synagogue (3rd century C.E.) showing the Ark of the Law flanked by seven branched candelabra. Below: Entrance to synagogue of Bar'am in Northern Galilee (3rd century C.E.).

first place to the dominant church catholic of Rome. The latter ignored the decease of her elder sister. Fortunately for future studies of the primitive church, its memory and its gnostic theology were preserved, mainly through patristic writings from Justin and Iranaeus to Epiphanius and Jerome. This exotic literature is now receiving more attention as a supplement to archaeological evidence in the study of the origins of Christianity.

With the center of Christianity transferred from Jerusalem, Palestine kept its unchallenged pre-eminence as a center of pilgrimage, something which has continued until the present day. Meanwhile, the generations of Christians who had remained in Aelia Capitolina (Jerusalem) were content to submit to Roman authority and to wait patiently until a Christian emperor, Constantine, would rule in Rome and, in 324 C.E., establish religious peace. Then their holy places would be cleared of the structures and idols which Hadrian had decreed two centuries before and the building of the numerous Christian shrines in Palestine could begin. This development was contemporaneous with a tremendous expansion in the building of synagogues and Jewish memorial monuments throughout Palestine.

THE SYNAGOGUES OF PALESTINE

After the fall of Jerusalem, numbers of synagogues were built for worship alone, in place of the "beth-midrash" of the Pharisees, known before 70 C.E. Recent excavations have uncovered a good deal of information about the actual buildings, although none that have been discovered can be dated with certainty before 70 C. E.

The synagogues of the 2nd and 3rd centuries were built in the current Graeco-Roman style and were freely ornamented with plants, animals and even human figures. Some of the signs of the Zodiac occur sometimes. They were all built so that the worshippers faced Jerusalem.

A synagogue was governed by a council, or sanhedrin of elders, modelled after the Sanhedrin of Jerusalem. In a large town there would be many elders, but a small community might have less than seven. The New Testament, incidentally, is a better source for information about synagogue services and organization in the early period than Jewish sources, which are all very much later. The Jewish-Christians first of all worshipped in the general synagogue and, later on, followed its ritual very closely in their own separate synagogues or churches.

INDEX

Names, Subjects, Authors, Illustrations(ill) and Maps in ADAM TO DANIEL,"I" and DANIEL TO PAUL,"II".

ACKNOWLEDGMENTS FOR ILLUSTRATIONS

(identified by page numbers)

Photo Alinari, Florence: Frontispiece, 15 b, 29, 94, 98, 105, 109, 127, 167 le, 178, 264, 310, 318, 327, 331 t. & b, 337, 339.

Photo Anderson, Rome: 114, 193, 319, 333, 334.

Archaeological Museum, Venice: 143.

Archives Photographiques, Paris: 3, 15 b.le., 22, 23 b. & r, 67, 82, 152, 156, 157, 158 t. & cent., 171, 174, 254, 347.

Ely Avivi, Achzib: 43.

Photo A. Berger, Tel Aviv: 125 t. & b, 249, 251, 252 t, 283, 284.

Bibliotheque Nationale, Cabinet des Medailles, Paris: 133.

British Museum, London: 4 le. & cent., 20, 52, 55, 78, 119, 140, 162, 270, 299, 322, 325, 330, 335.

Prof. F. M. Cross, Harvard University and Prof. J. T. Milik, Paris: 183 b.r., 195, 196 b.r., 202, 353, 355. Abbé J. Starcky, Paris: 120, 185, 203.

Photo Giraudon, Paris: 31 t.r., 60, 75 t. & b., 131, 236, 252 b.r.

Rafael Giveon, Mishmar Ha'emeq (courtesy Haifa Museum): 10.

Prof. Nelson Glueck, Hebrew Union College, Cincinnati: 227.

Photo D. Harris – W. Braun, Jerusalem: 122, 336, 356, 357 b., 358, 359 t.

Hebrew University, Jerusalem: 187, 191.

Israel Department of Antiquities, Jerusalem: 357 t., 358 b., 359 b.

Israel Exploration Society, Jerusalem: 224, 352, 360.

Israel Government Press Division, Tel Aviv: 121 t. le., b.r., 124, 179, 186, 237, 243, 252 t.le., 258, 328, 362, 366 t.

Matson Photo Service, Los Angeles: 46, 121, 130, 274 t.

Prof. C. C. McCown, Pacific School of Religion: 13 b.r. & le.

Metropolitan Museum of Art, New York: 4 le., 15 t.r., 30, 31 t.le., 73, 85, 90, 99 le., 108, 146, 151 le. & b., 165, 168, 240, 268, 287.

Photo J. Mualim, Tel Aviv: 366 b.

Ny Carlsberg Glyptotek, Copenhagen: 99 r.

The Oriental Institute, University of Chicago: 183 t.r.

Palestine Exploration Fund, London: 1, 26, 47, 48, 49, 59, 88, 126, 150, 252 b., 306, 350.

Stewart Perowne, Kyrenia, Cyprus: 132 b., 232.

Photo Prior, Tel Aviv: 11.

Prof. J. B. Pritchard, Church Divinity School of the Pacific, Berkeley, Cal: 83.

Photo Roget-Viollet, Paris: 56, 100.

Prof. James F. Ross, Drew University, Madison, Wis: 15 t.r.

Prof. O. R. Sellers, Santa Fe, New Mexico: 37 b.

Photo Soeurs de Notre Dame de Sion, Jerusalem: 274 t.

Sopritendenza alle Antichita della Campanie, Napoli: 74, 145, 153, 169, 172, 349.

Foto Terra Santa, Jerusalem: 35 b., 110, 132, 133 b., 167 r., 263, 274 b.r.

Merritt ("Corinth"): 312 b. Penna ("Maccabei"): 37 t. J. B. Segal, London ("New Mosaics from Edessa"): 287 t.

COLOUR PLATES

I	facing p.	16, Réalités, Paris
II	"	16, Metropolitan Museum of Art, New York
III	"	17, Soc. Scala, Firenze
IV	"	17, Réalités, Paris
V	"	32, Metropolitan Museum of Art, New York
VI	"	32, A. Guillot, Paris
VII	"	33, Réalités, Paris
VIII	"	33, Prof. F. M. Cross, Harvard University
IX-XI	"	96, The Oriental Institute, Chicago
XII	"	97, Réalités, Paris
XIII	"	97, Soc. Scala, Firenze
XIV	"	112, Photo A. Berger, Tel Aviv
XV	"	112, British Museum, London
XVI	"	113
XVII	"	113, The Oriental Institute, Chicago
XVIII	"	128, C. Lo Bianco, Rome
XIX	facing p.	128, Soc. Scala, Firenze
XX, XXI	"	129, C. Lo Bianco, Rome
XXII	"	" " "
XXIII	"	144, Metropolitan Museum of Art, New York
XXIV	"	144, Soc. Scala, Firenze
XXV	"	145
XXVI	"	145, Courtesy, Ruth Michaelson
XXVII	"	288, Photo A. Berger, Tel Aviv
XXVIII	"	288, Courtesy, Ruth Michaelson
XXIX	"	289
XXX	"	289, C. Lo Bianco, Firenze
XXXI	"	304, Ny Carlsberg Glyptotek, Copenhagen
XXXII	"	304, Soc. Scala, Firenze
XXXIII	"	305, Prof. C. C. McCown, Pacific School of Religion
XXXIV	"	305, Photo D. Harris — W. Braun, Jerusalem